THE CHRISTMAS COLLECTION

TITLE PAGE

Previously ISBN 0-88704-232-5

7777 West Bluemound Road P.O. Box 13819 Milwaukee, WI 53213

A-CAROLING WE GO

TRUMPET
BRIGHT 'N' BRASSY
Medium Fast WALTZ

Words and Music by
JOHNNY MARKS

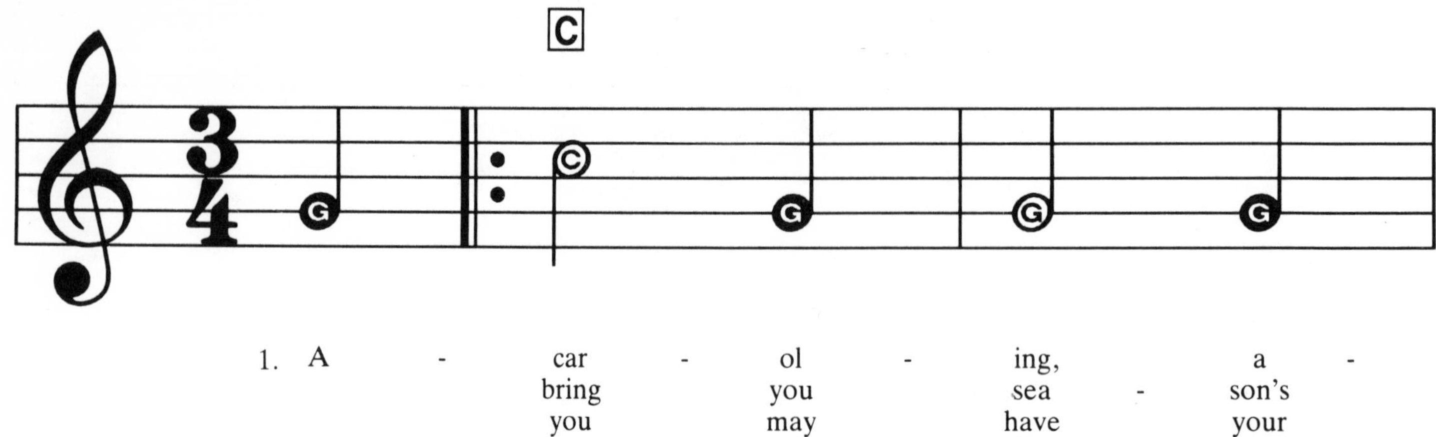
C
G
C
G
G
G
1. A - car - ol - ing, a -
bring you sea - son's
you may have your
car - ol - ing, a -

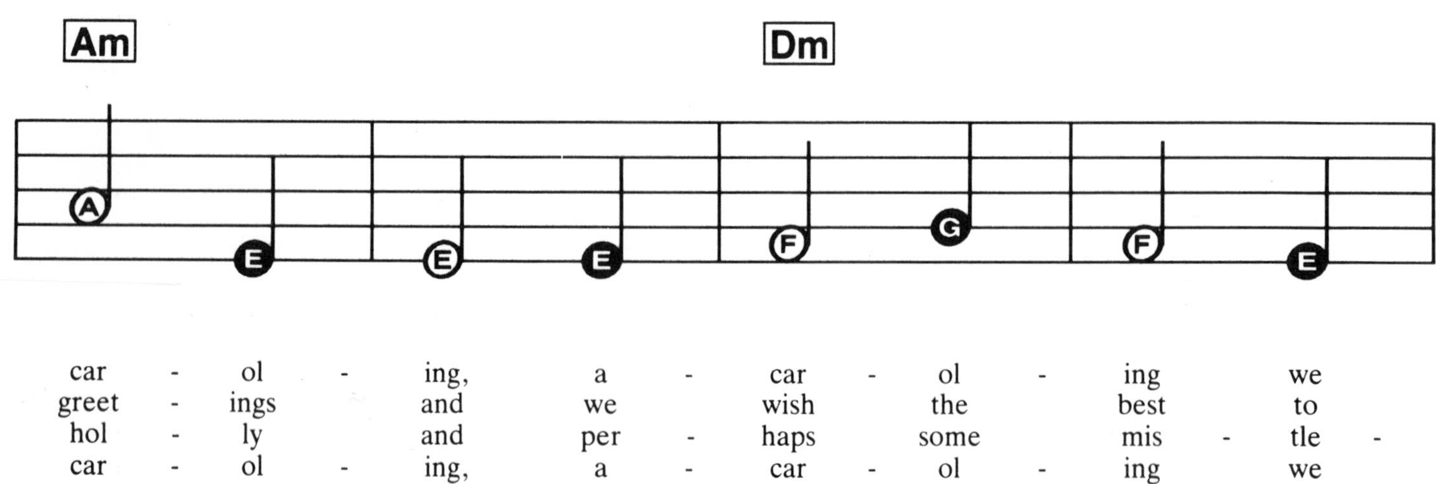
Am
Dm
A
E
E
E
F
G
F
E
car - ol - ing, a - car - ol - ing we
greet - ings and we wish the best to
hol - ly and per - haps some mis - tle -
car - ol - ing, a - car - ol - ing we

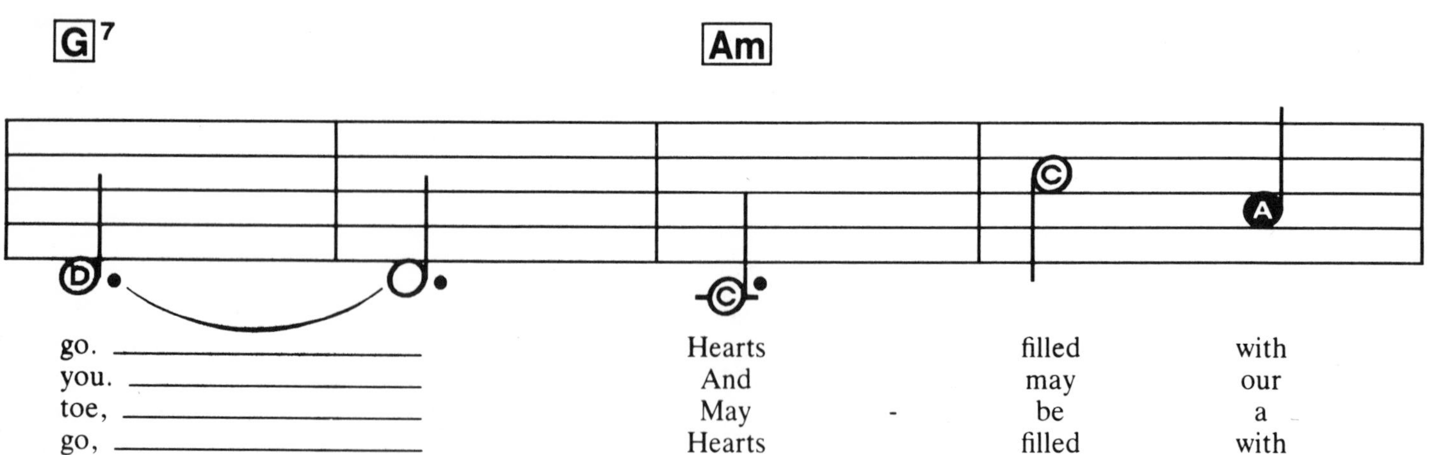
G7
Am
D
C
C
A
go. Hearts filled with
you. And may our
toe, May - be a
go, Hearts filled with

Em Am7 D7
mu - sic and cheeks a -
wish last the whole year
fir tree and may - be
mu - sic and cheeks a -
Dm7 G7 C
glow. From house to house we
through. Come join us if you
snow. But would - n't it be
glow. From house to house we
Am Dm7 G7
bring the mes - sage of the King a - gain,
will as we are sing - ing once a - gain,
won - der - ful if we could have a - gain,
bring the mes - sage of the King a - gain,
Am Em Am
Peace on earth, good

F
E
Am
will
to
men,
Peace
Em
Am
1.2.3.
F
G7
on
earth,
good
will
to
C
F
G7
C
men.
Instr.
2.
F
G7
C
2. We
3. Now
4. A
will
to
men.

ANGELS FROM THE REALMS OF GLORY

ORGAN
FULL 'N' BRILLIANT
Medium SWING

C

An - gels from the realms of glo - ry,
Shep - herds, in the fields a - bid - ing,
Sa - ges, leave your con - tem - pla - tions

F G7 C

Wing your flight o'er all the earth; Ye who sang cre -
Watch - ing o'er your flocks by night, God with man is
Bright - er vis - ions beam a - far. Seek the great de -

E D7 G7

a - tion's sto - ry, Now pro - claim Mes - si - ah's birth.
now re - sid - ing, Yon - der shines the ___ heav'n - ly light.
sire of na - tions, Ye have seen this ___ na - tal star.

C Dm

Come and wor - ship, Come and wor - ship, Wor - ship Christ, the

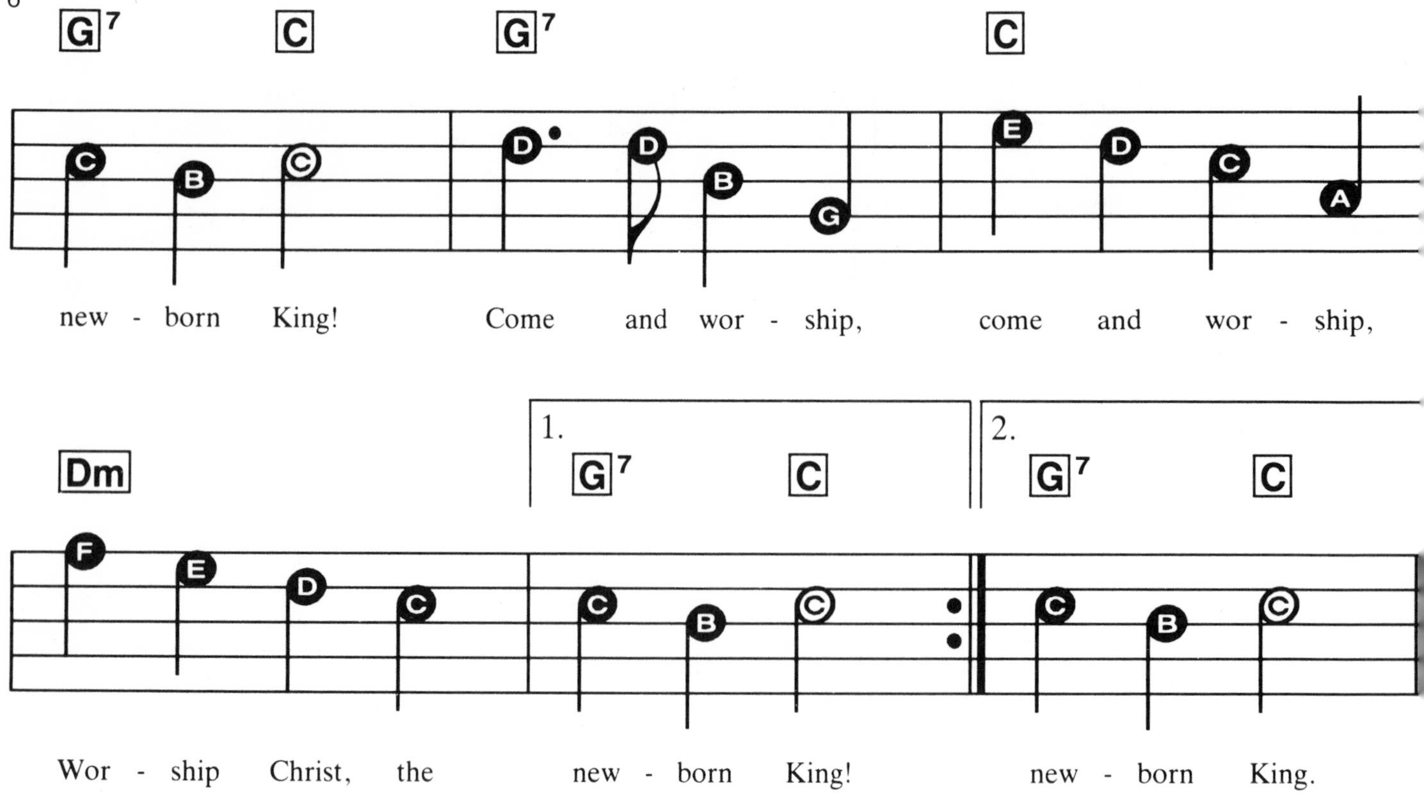
G7
C
G7
C
new - born King! Come and wor - ship, come and wor - ship,
Dm
1.
G7
C
2.
G7
C
Wor - ship Christ, the new - born King! new - born King.

ANGELS WE HAVE HEARD ON HIGH

ORGAN
CLASSICAL
Medium SWING

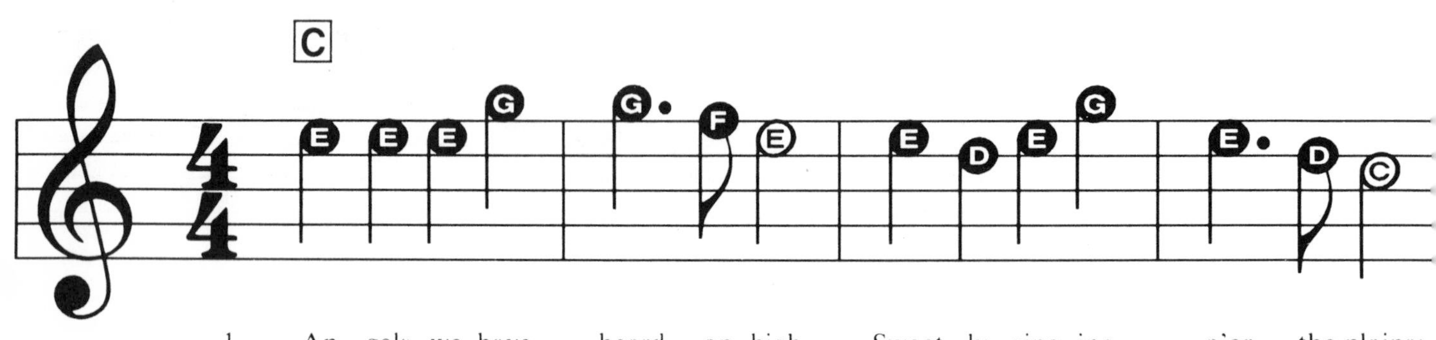
C
1. An - gels we have heard on high, Sweet - ly sing - ing o'er the plains;
2. Shep-herds, why this ju - bi - lee? Why your joy - ous songs pro-long?

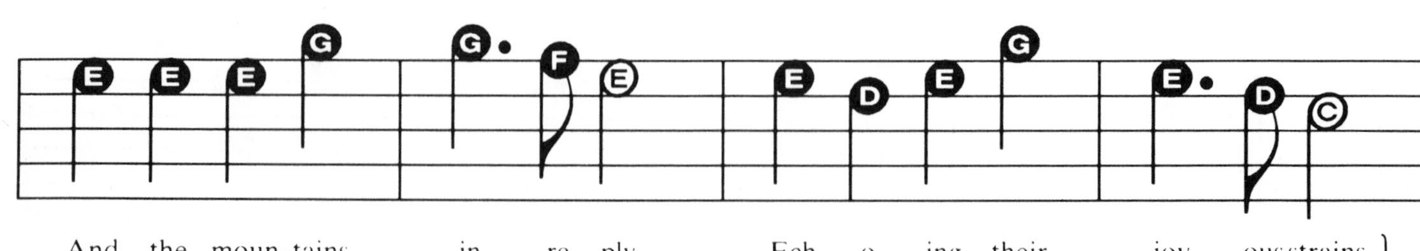
And the moun-tains in re - ply Ech - o - ing their joy - ous strains.
What the glad - some tid - ings be Which in - spire your heav'n - ly song?

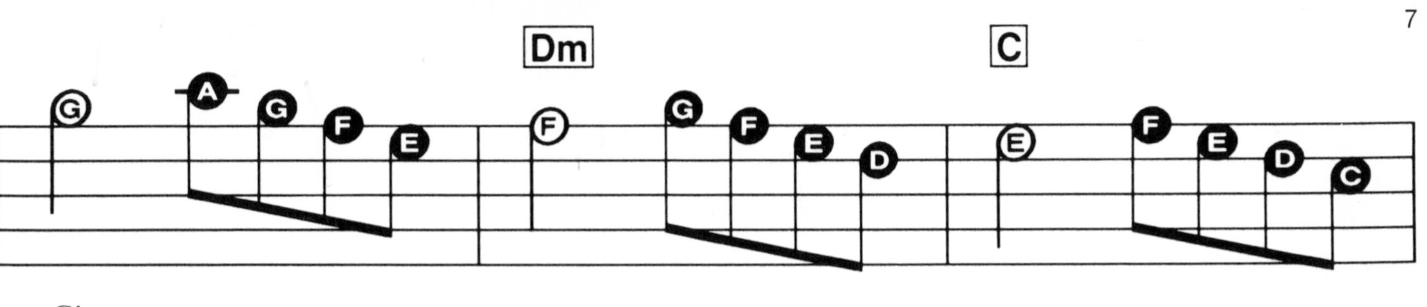
Dm
C
Glo - - -

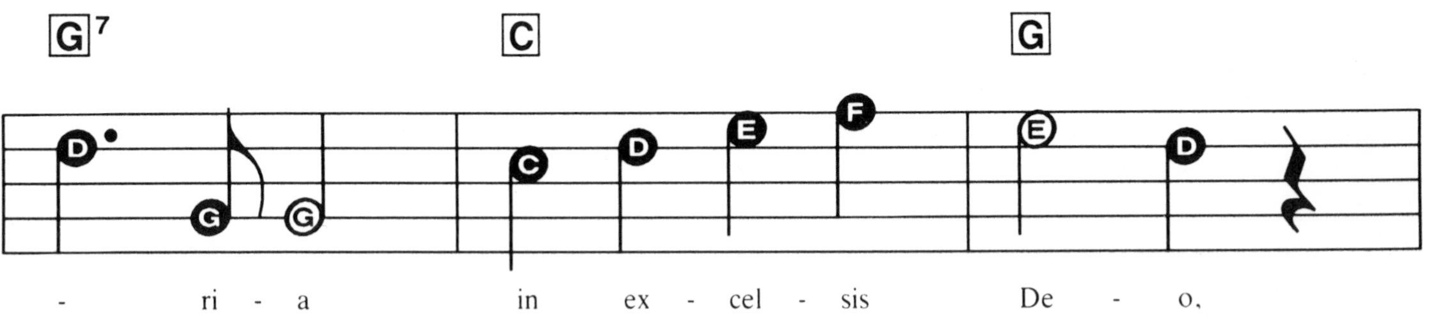
G7
C
G
- ri - a in ex - cel - sis De - o,

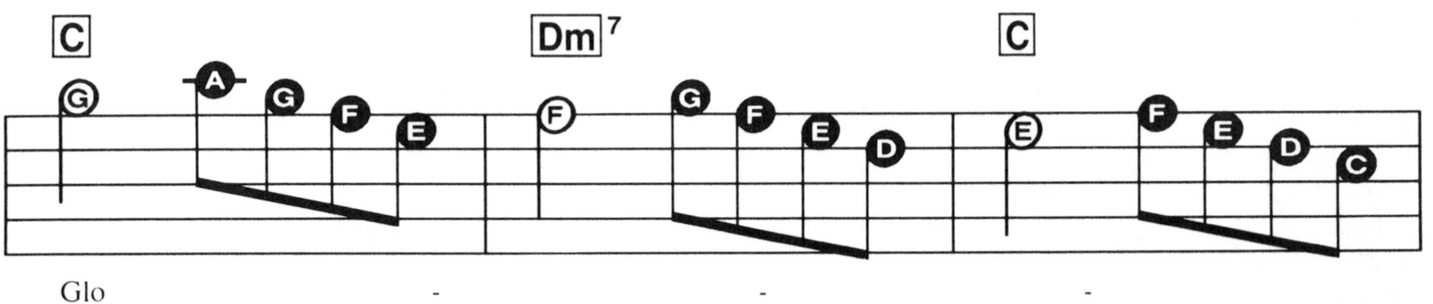
C
Dm7
C
Glo - - -

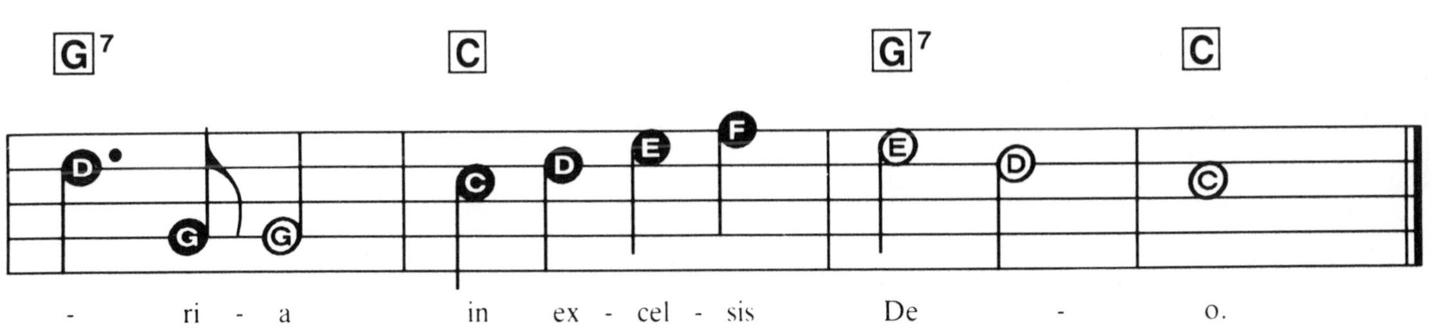
G7
C
G7
C
- ri - a in ex - cel - sis De - o.

AULD LANG SYNE

CLARINET
FULL 'N' BRILLIANT
Medium SWING

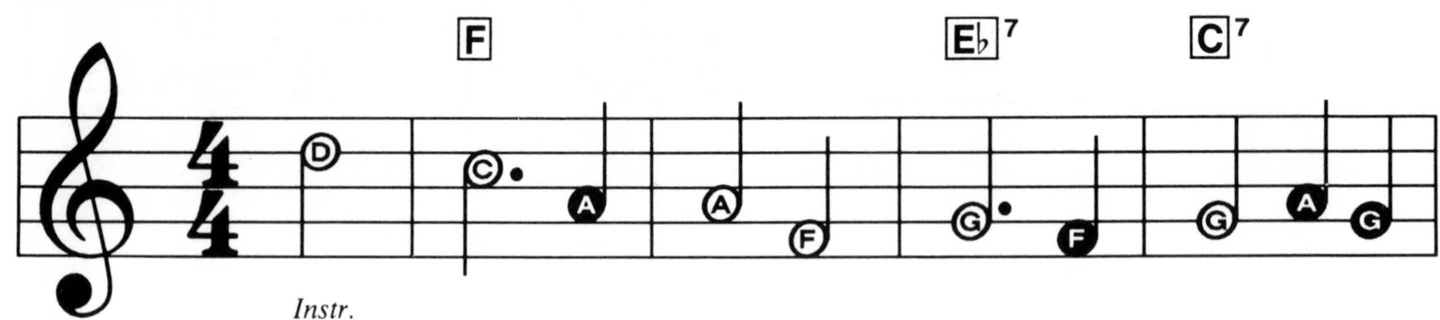
F
E♭7
C7
D
C
A
A
F
G
F
G
A
G
Instr.

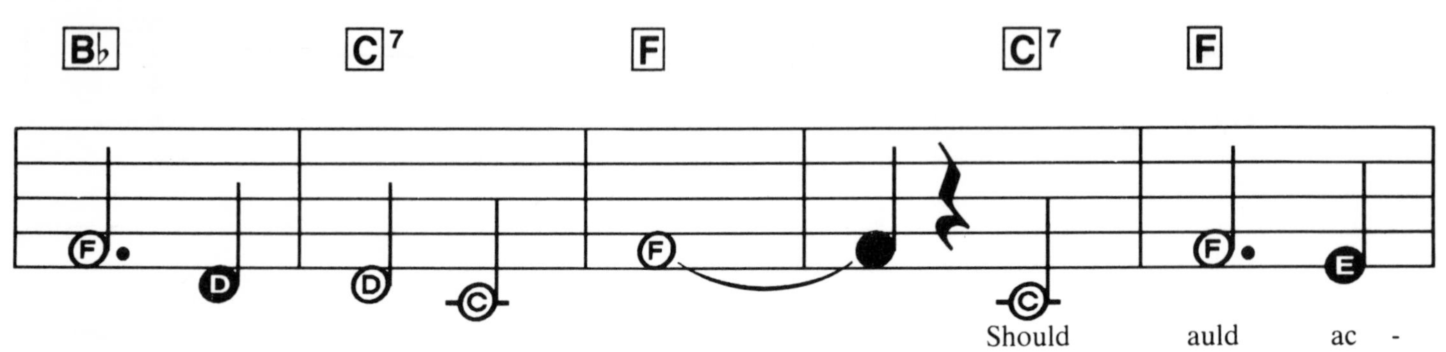
B♭
C7
F
C7
F
F
D
D
C
F
C
F
E
Should
auld
ac -

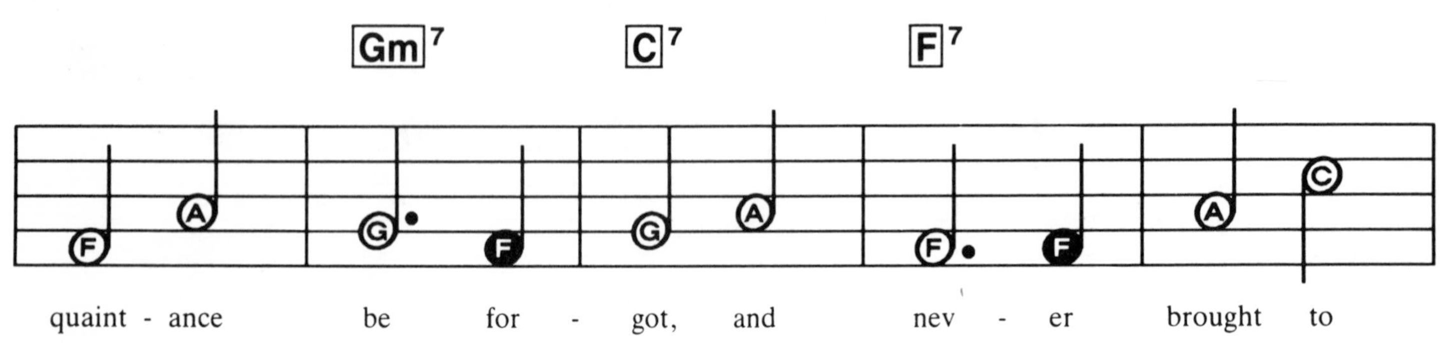
Gm7
C7
F7
F
A
G
F
G
A
F
F
A
C
quaint - ance
be
for -
got,
and
nev - er
brought
to

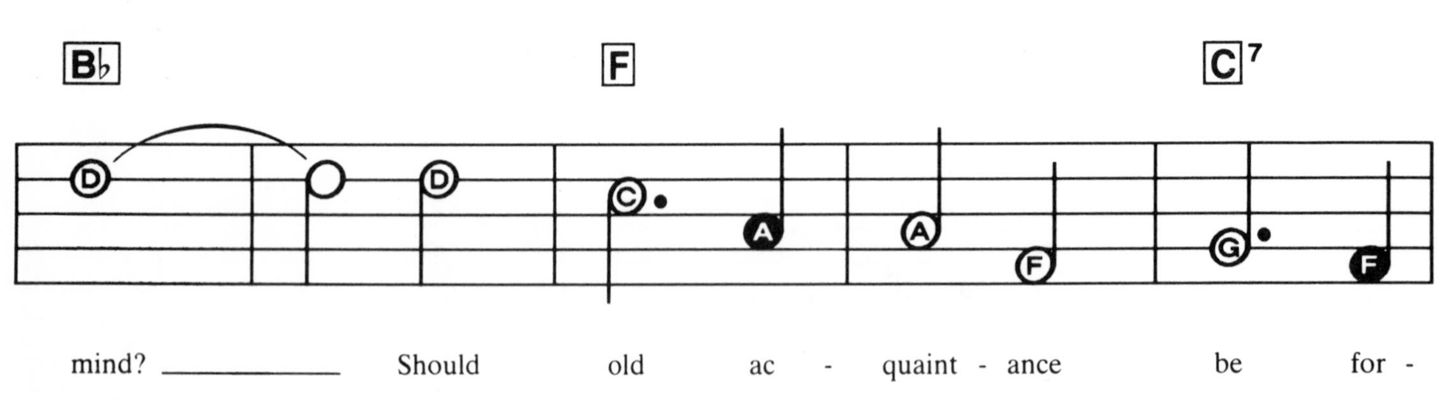
B♭
F
C7
D
D
C
A
A
F
G
F
mind? ___________
Should
old
ac - quaint - ance
be
for -

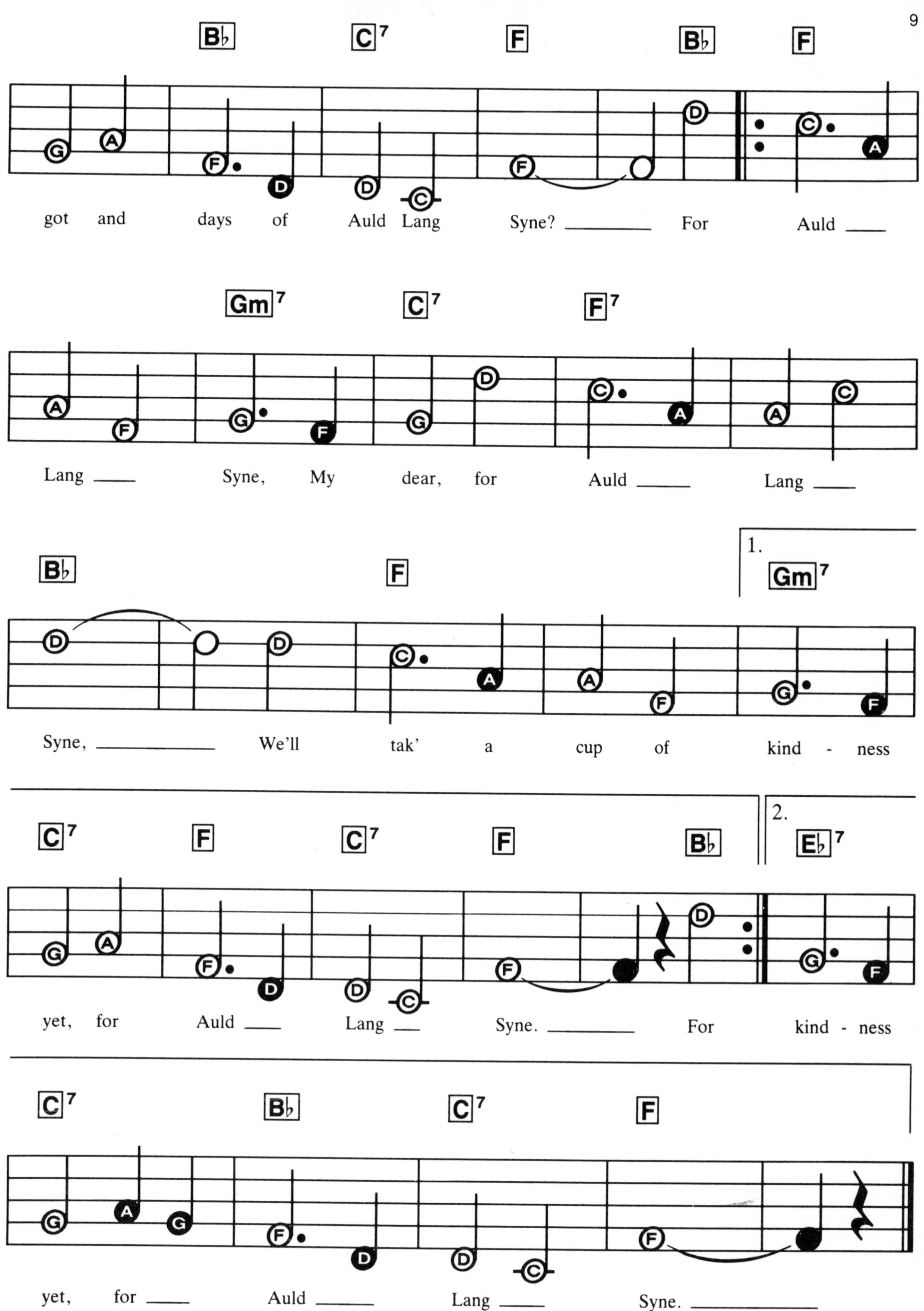
B♭ C7 F B♭ F
got and days of Auld Lang Syne? For Auld
Gm7 C7 F7
Lang Syne, My dear, for Auld Lang
1.
B♭ F Gm7
Syne, We'll tak' a cup of kind - ness
2.
C7 F C7 F B♭ E♭7
yet, for Auld Lang Syne. For kind - ness
C7 B♭ C7 F
yet, for Auld Lang Syne.

AVE MARIA

VIOLIN
CLASSICAL
No Rhythm

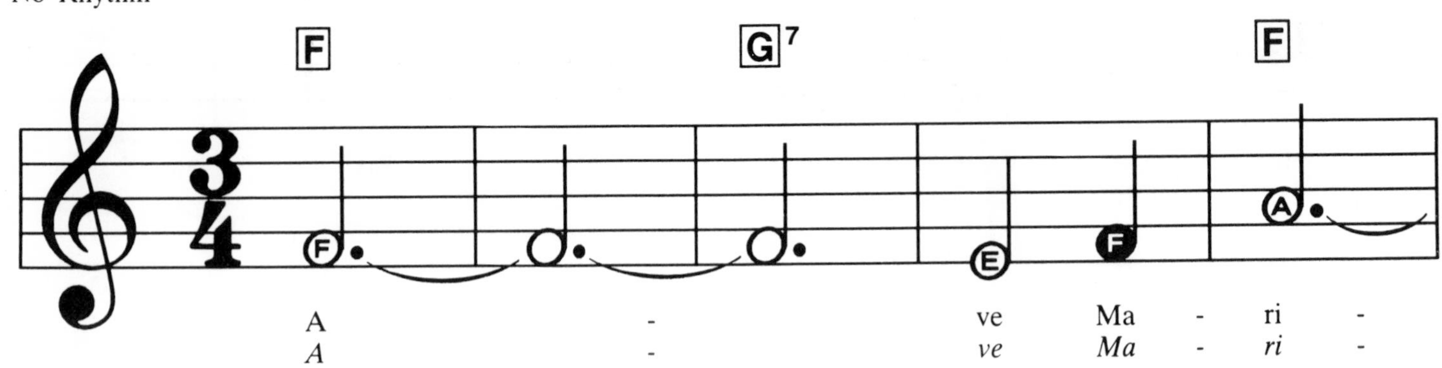

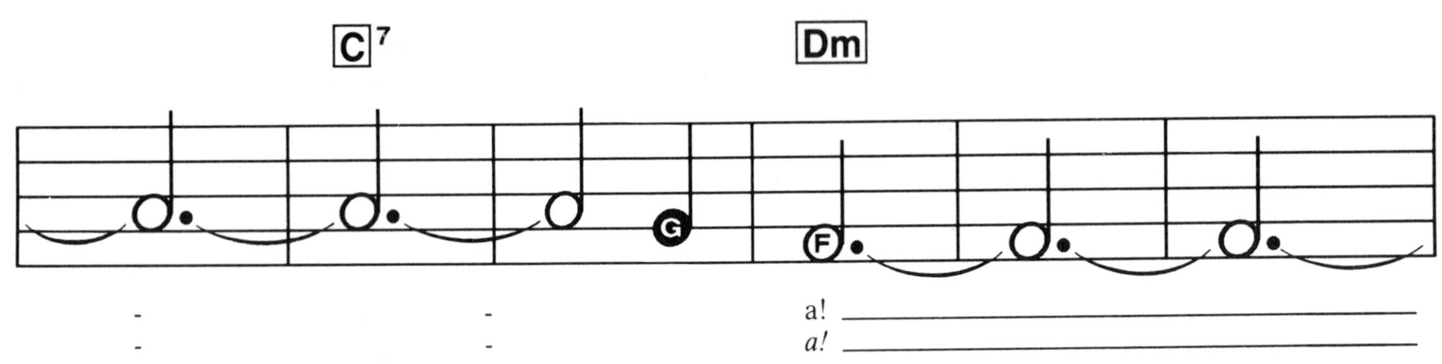

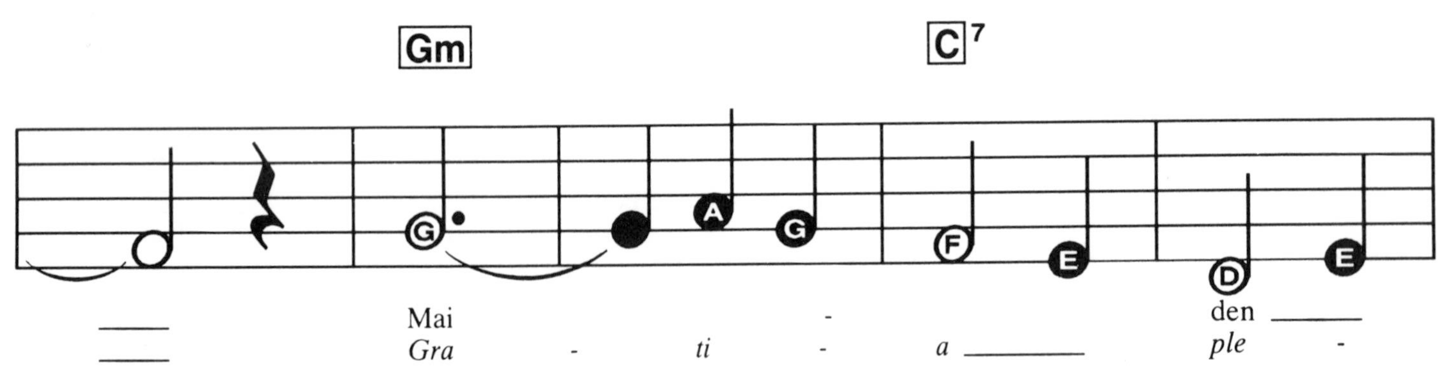

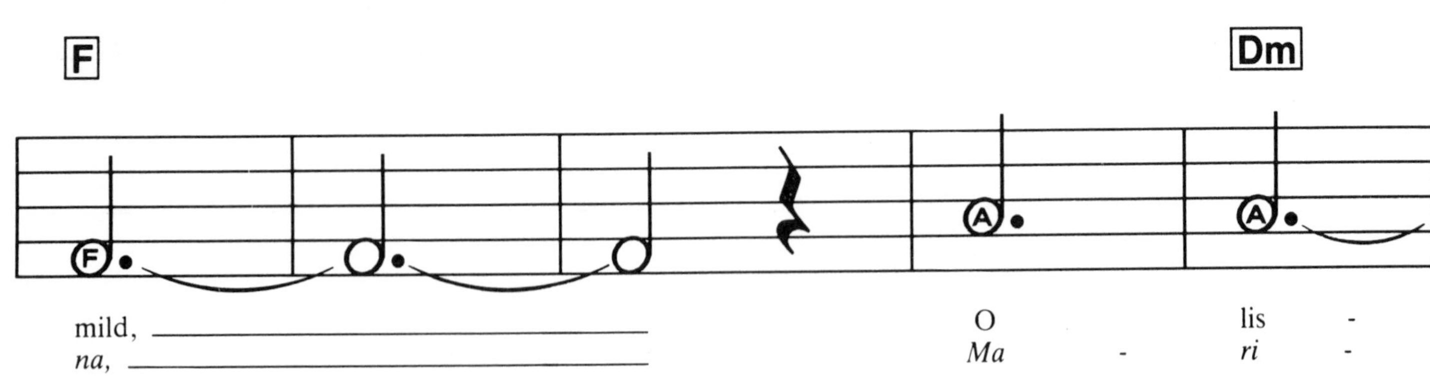

- ten ___ to a mai - den's pray -
- a ___ gra - ti - a ple -
E7
A7
er, ___ For Thou ___ canst hear ___ though
na, ___ Ma - ri - a gra - ti -
Dm
G7
from ___ the wild, ___ 'Tis ___
a ___ ple - na, ___ A -
C
D7
Thou, ___ 'tis Thou ___ canst save ___ a -
ve, ___ A - ve Do - mi -
C
G7
mid ___ de -
nus, ___ Do - mi - nus ___ te -

C
C7
spair. Safe may
cum. Be - ne - di -
F
we sleep be - neath Thy ten - der care,
- cta tu in mu - li - e - ri - bus,
C7
Tho' ban - ish'd, out - cast
et be - ne - di -
Dm
and re - viled. O
- - ctus, et
C
A
mai - den, See a mai - den's
be - ne - di - ctus, fru - ctus

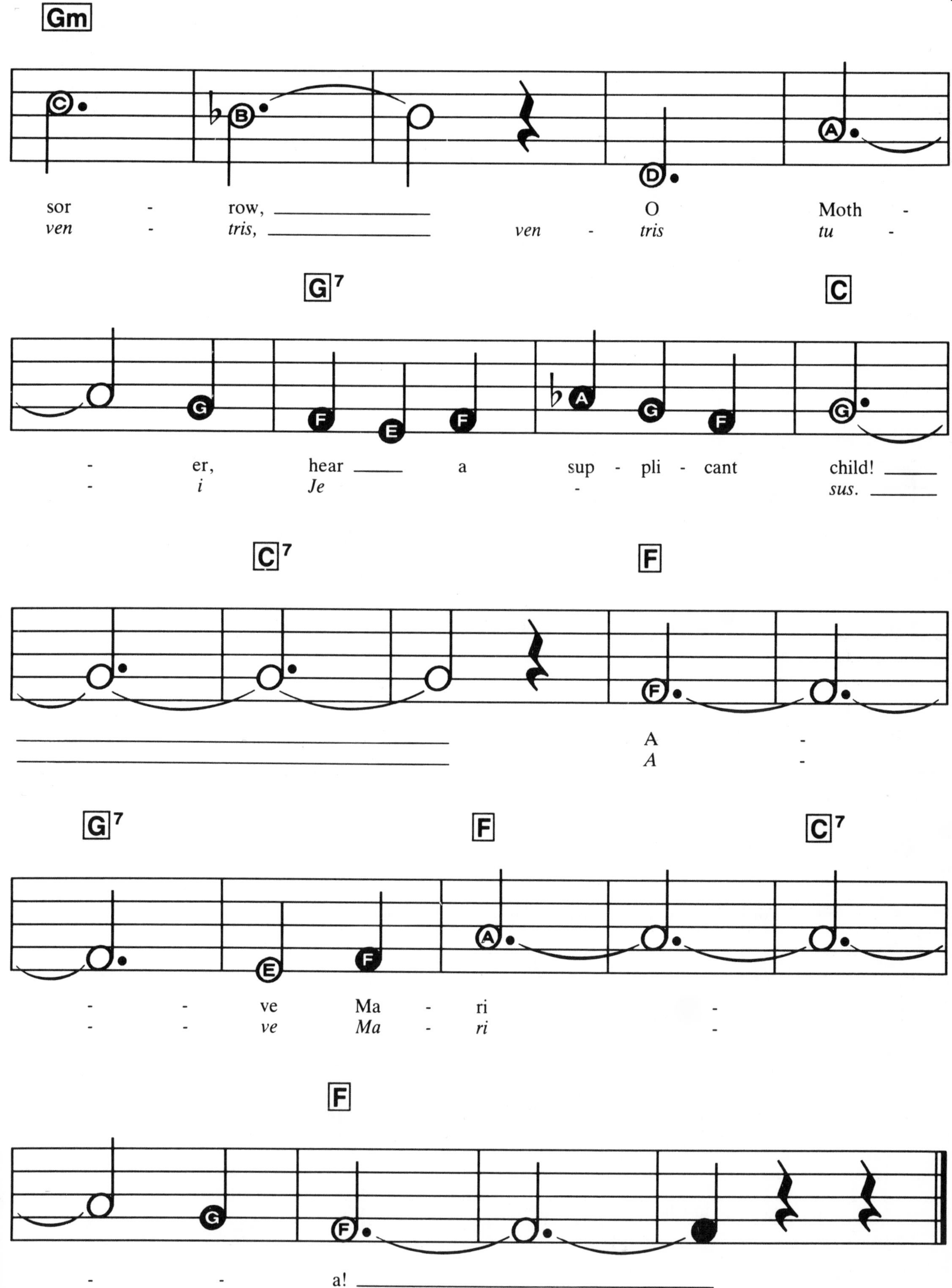
Gm
sor - row, O Moth -
ven - tris, ven - tris tu -
G7 C
- er, hear a sup - pli - cant child!
- i Je - sus.
C7 F
A -
A -
G7 F C7
- - ve Ma - ri -
- - ve Ma - ri -
F
- - a!
- - a!

AWAY IN A MANGER

PIANO
CLASSICAL
Medium WALTZ

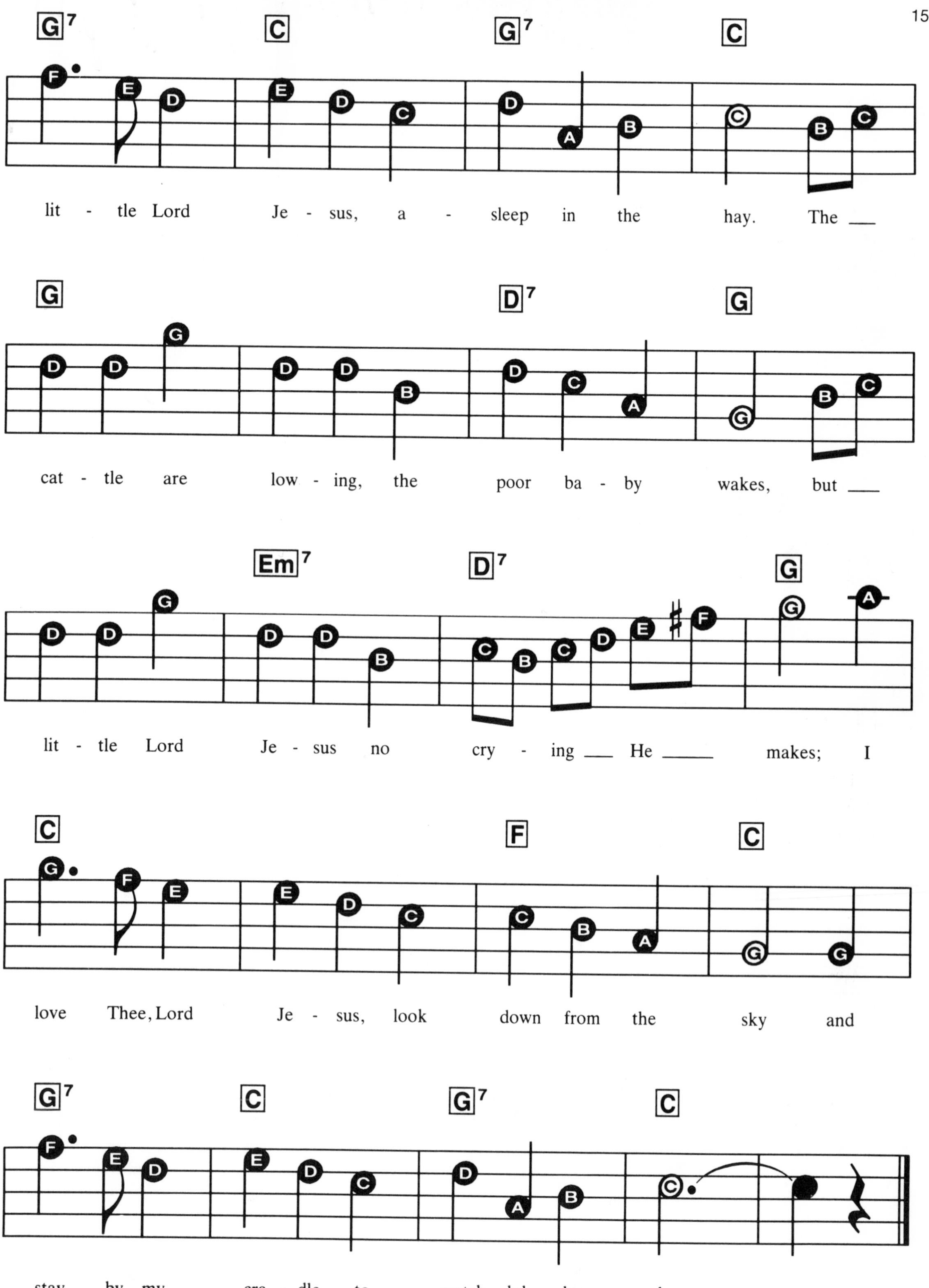
G7 C G7 C
lit - tle Lord Je - sus, a - sleep in the hay. The
G D7 G
cat - tle are low - ing, the poor ba - by wakes, but
Em7 D7 G
lit - tle Lord Je - sus no cry - ing He makes; I
C F C
love Thee, Lord Je - sus, look down from the sky and
G7 C G7 C
stay by my cra - dle to watch lul - la - by.

BABY BROTHER
(Santa Claus, Dear Santa Claus)

GUITAR
FULL 'N' MELLOW
Medium SWING

Words and Music by
VAUGHN HORTON
and WILLIE EVANS

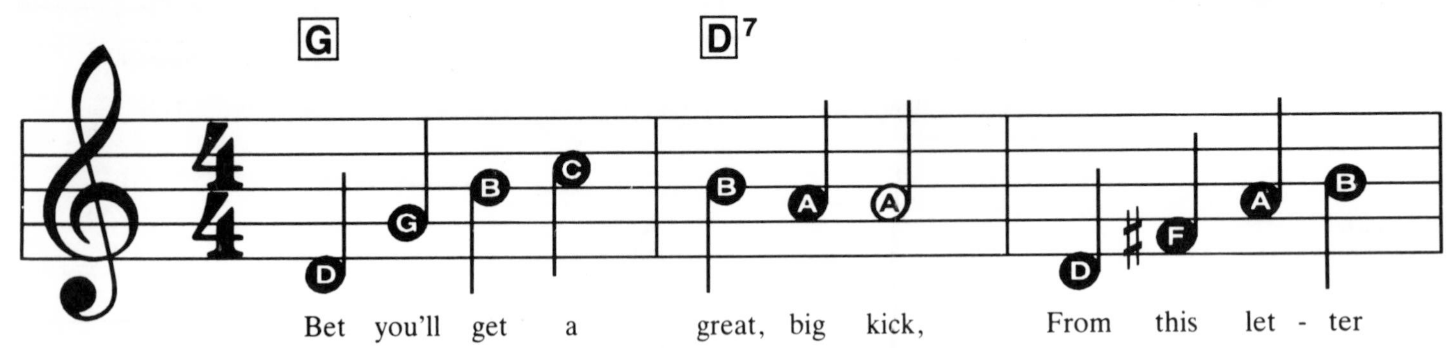

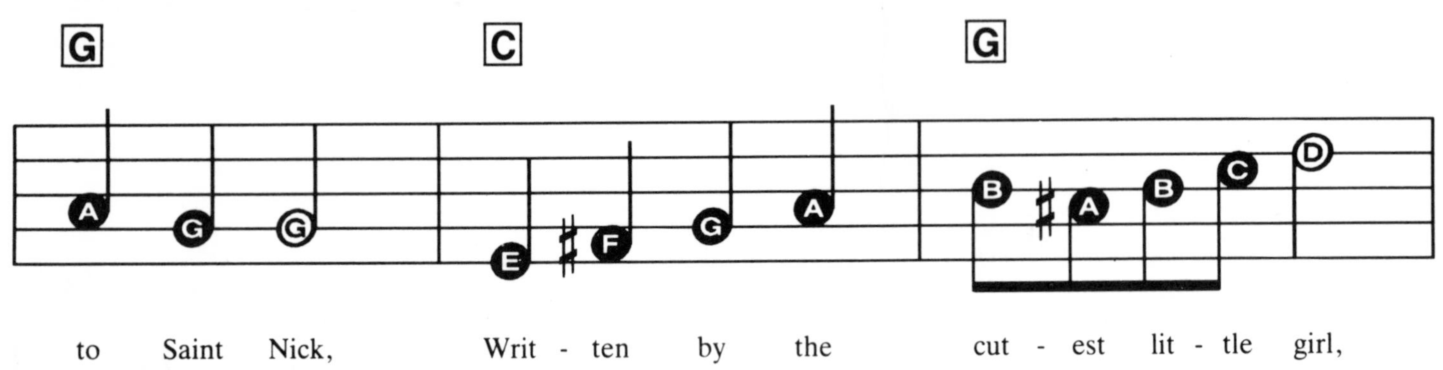

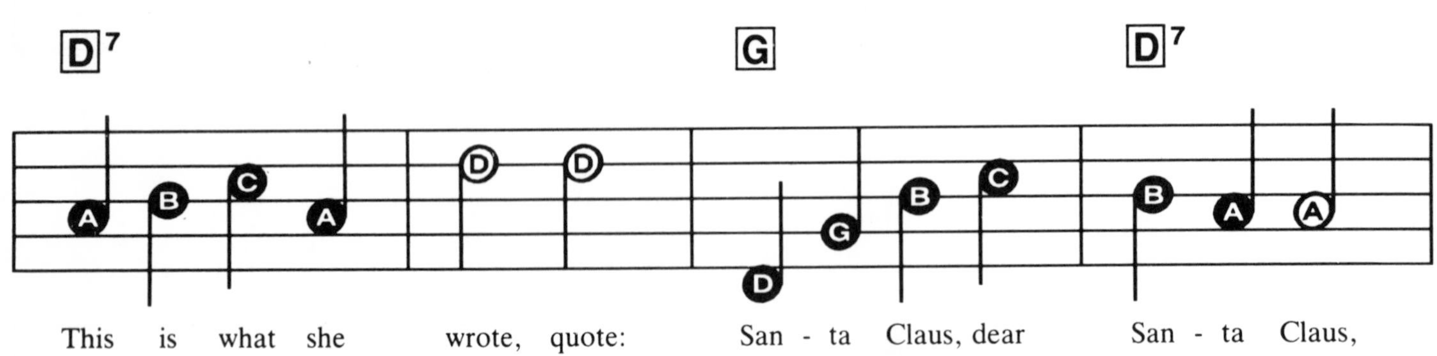

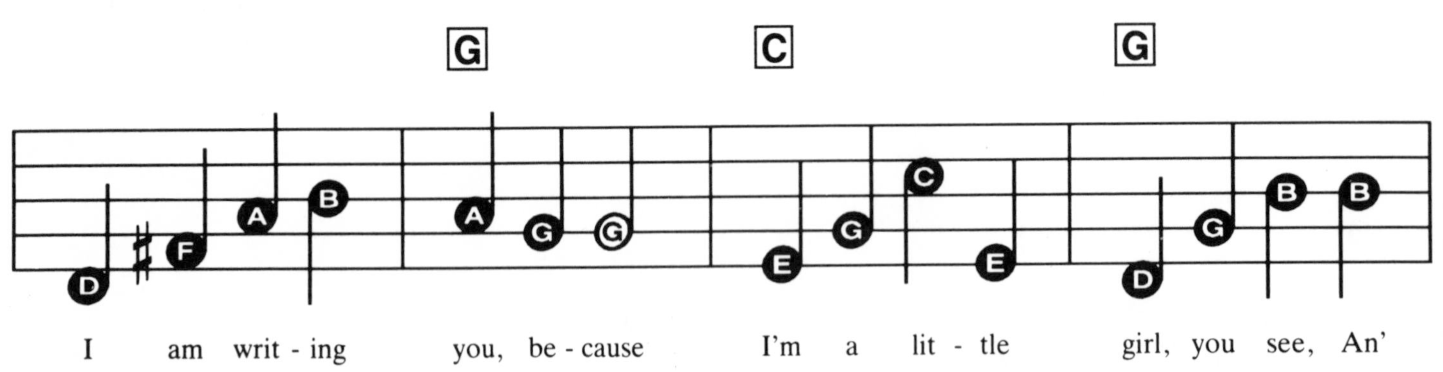

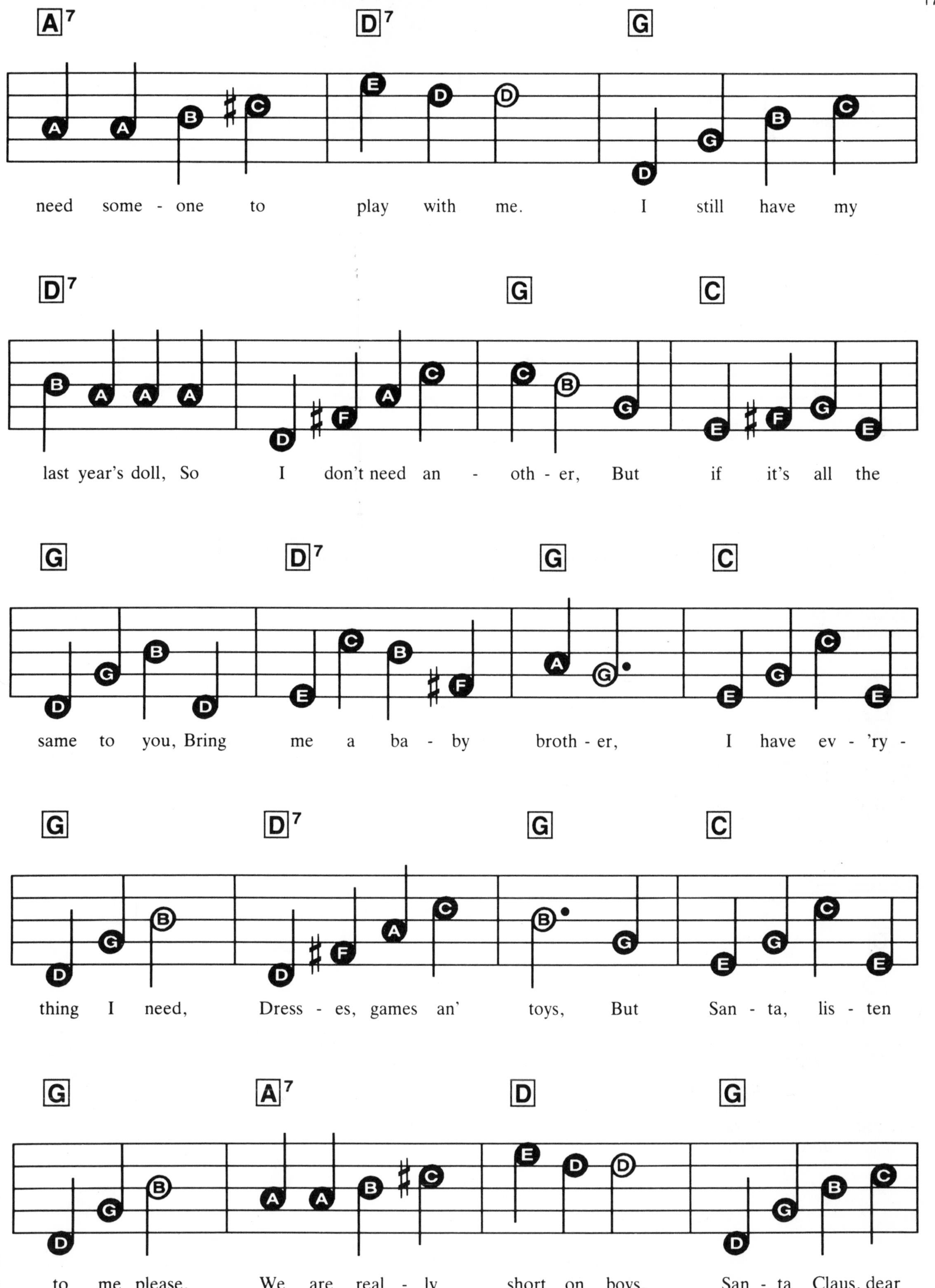
A7 D7 G
need some - one to play with me. I still have my
D7 G C
last year's doll, So I don't need an - oth - er, But if it's all the
G D7 G C
same to you, Bring me a ba - by broth - er, I have ev - 'ry -
G D7 G C
thing I need, Dress - es, games an' toys, But San - ta, lis - ten
G A7 D G
to me please, We are real - ly short on boys, San - ta Claus, dear

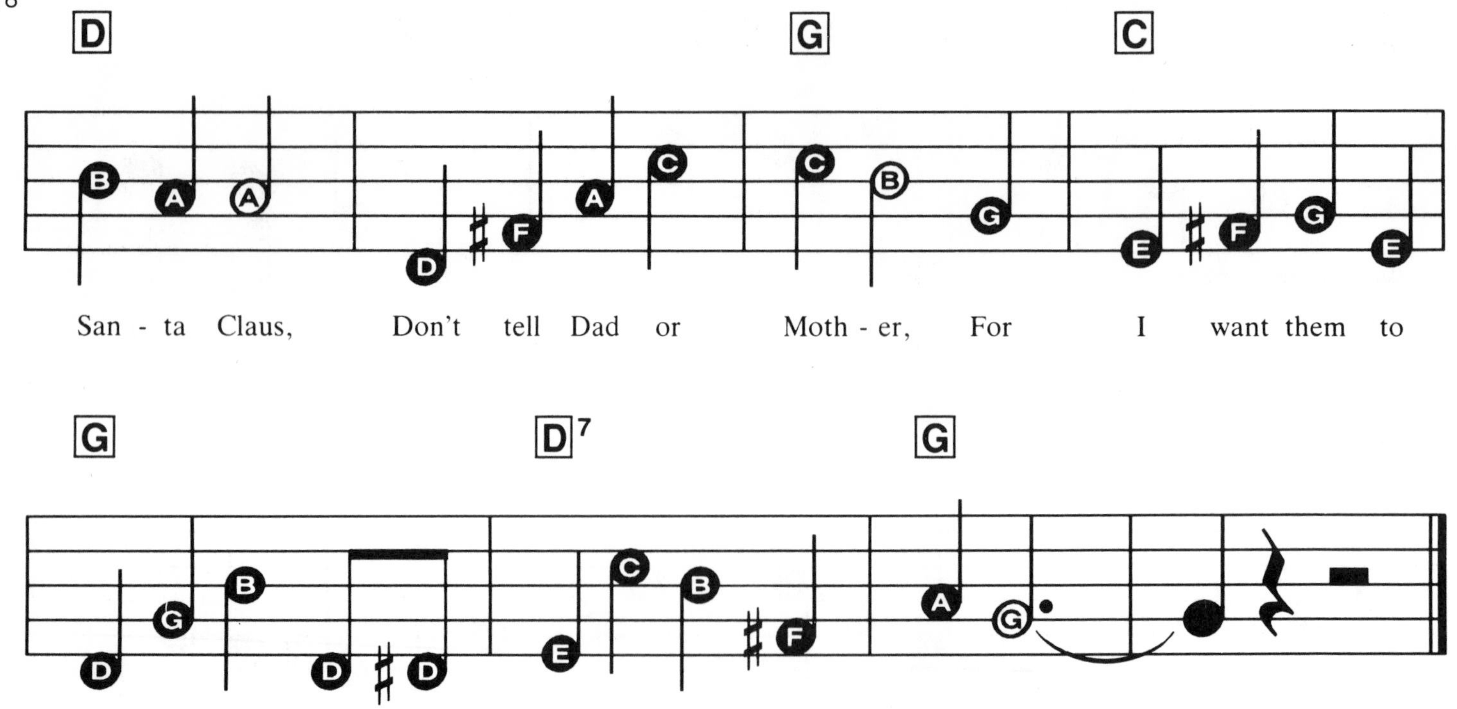
D G C
San - ta Claus, Don't tell Dad or Moth - er, For I want them to
G D7 G
be sur - prised, When they see my ba - by broth - er.

THE BABE OF BETHLEHEM

TRUMPET
BRILLIANT SOLO
No Rhythm

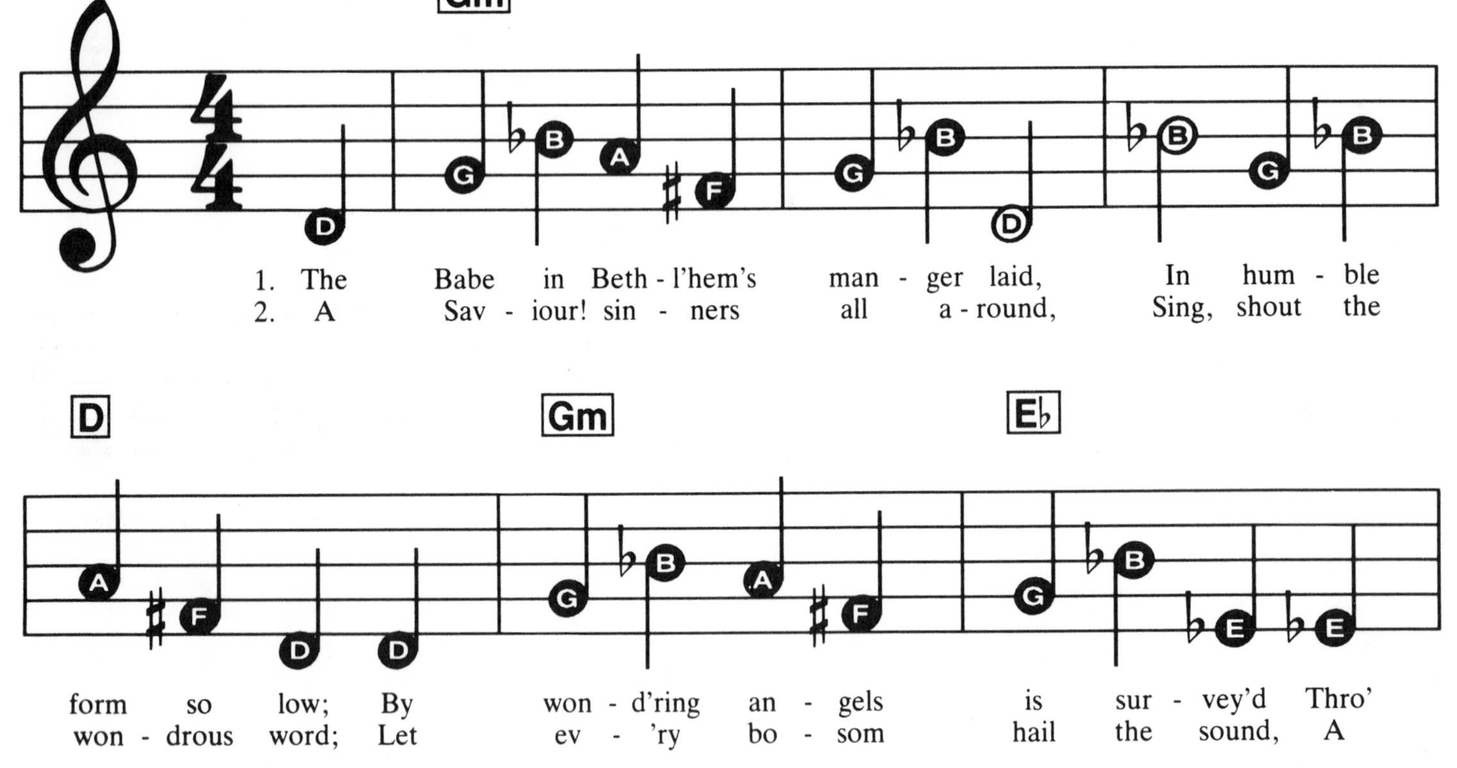
Gm
1. The Babe in Beth - l'hem's man - ger laid, In hum - ble
2. A Sav - iour! sin - ners all a - round, Sing, shout the
D Gm E♭
form so low; By won - d'ring an - gels is sur - vey'd Thro'
won - drous word; Let ev - 'ry bo - som hail the sound, A

Chorus
D
Gm
G
all His scenes of woe.
Sav - iour Christ the Lord.
No - el, No -

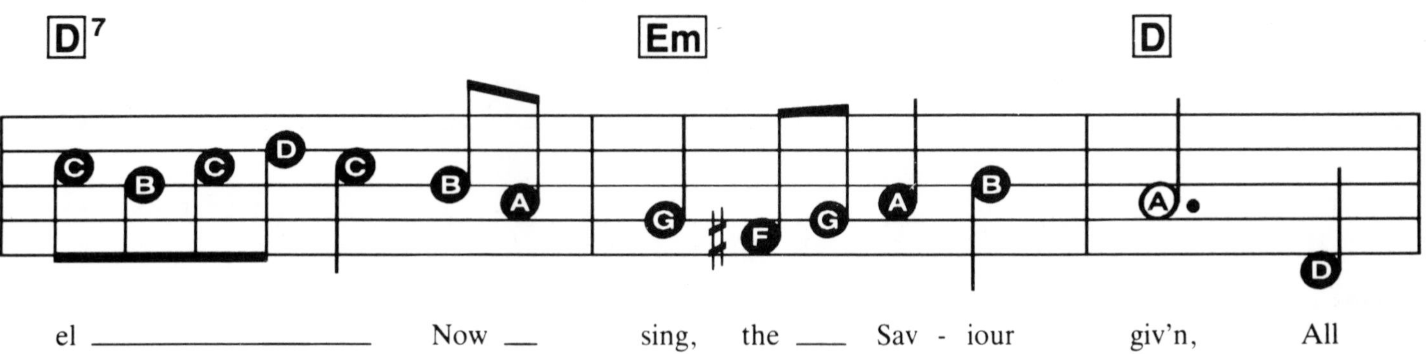
D7
Em
D
el Now sing, the Sav - iour giv'n, All

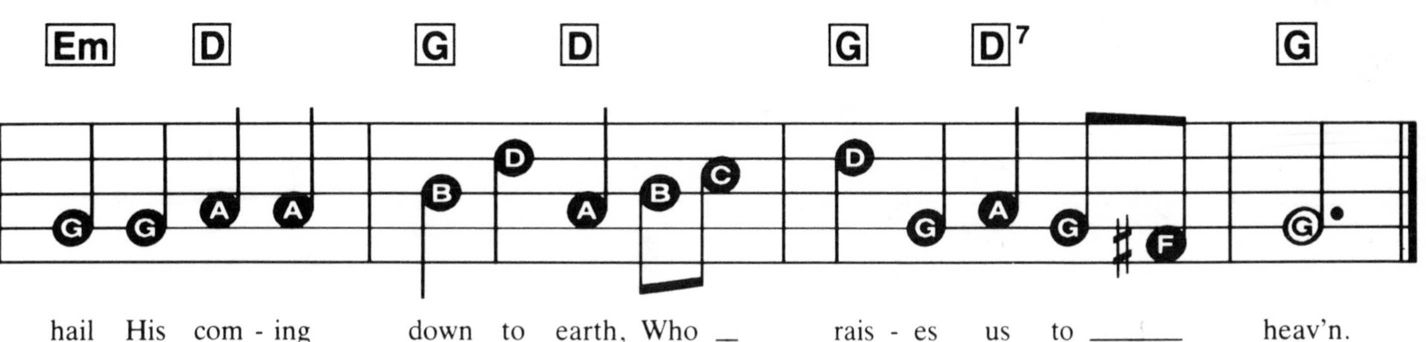
Em D G D G D7 G
hail His com - ing down to earth, Who rais - es us to heav'n.

3. For not to sit on David's throne
With worldly pomp and joy,
He came for sinners to atone
And Satan to destroy.
Chorus

4. Well may we sing a Saviour's birth,
Who need the grace so given,
And hail His coming down to earth,
Who raises us to heaven.
Chorus

AS LATELY WE WATCHED

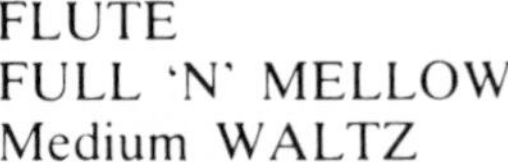

G D[7]

1. As late - ly we watch'd o'er ___ our ___ fields thro' the
2. A King of such beau - ty ___ was ___ ne'er be - fore

G D[7]

night, A star there was seen of ___ such ___ glo - ri - ous
seen, And Ma - ry his moth - er ___ so ___ like to a

G C A D

light; All thro' ___ the ___ night, an - gels ___ did ___ sing, In
queen. Blest be ___ the ___ hour, wel - come ___ the ___ morn, For

G D[7] G

car - ols so sweet of ___ the ___ birth of a King.
Christ our dear Sav - iour ___ on ___ earth now is born.

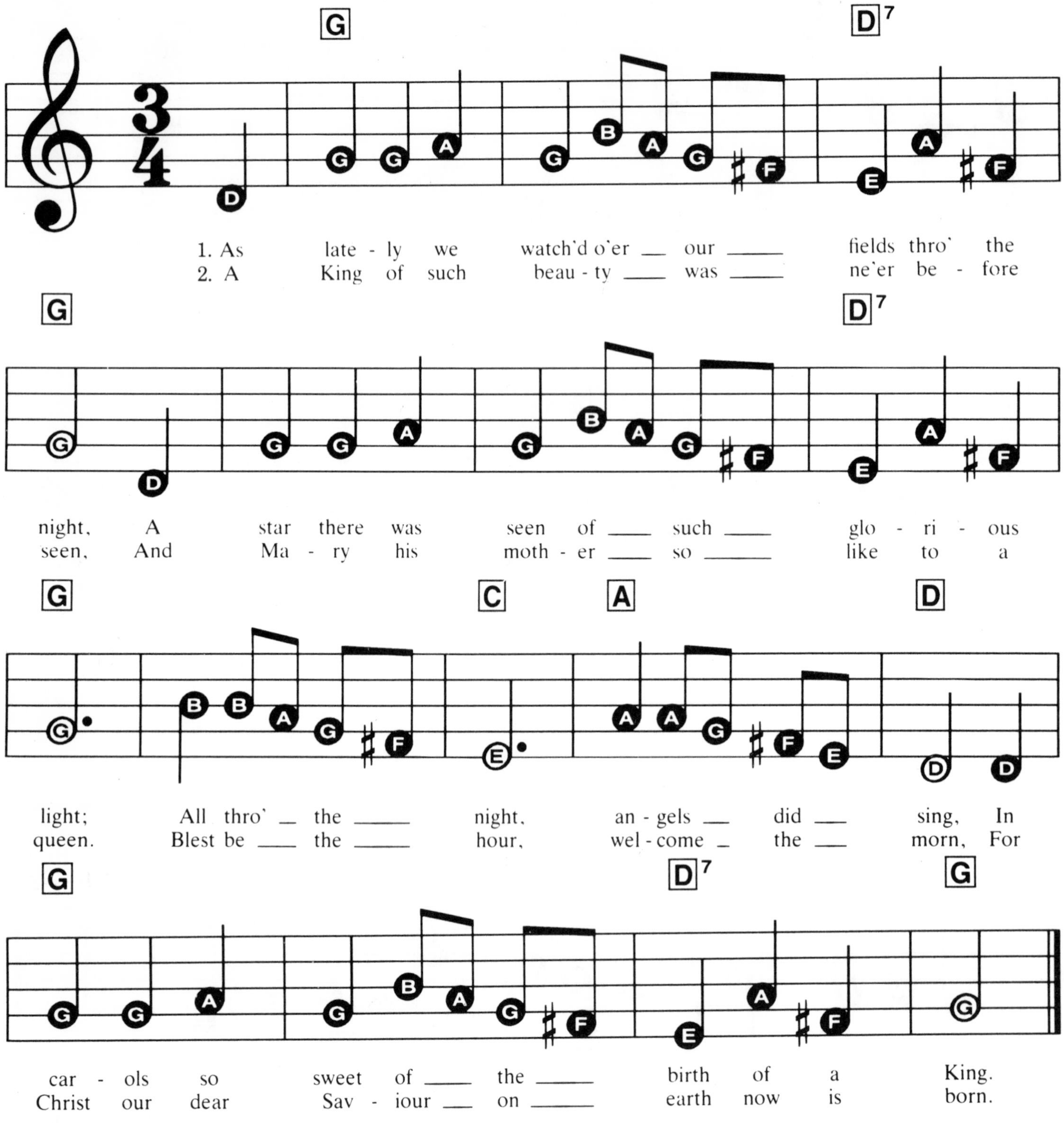

3. His throne is a manger, His court is a loft,
But troops of bright angels, in lays sweet and soft,
Him they proclaim, our Christ by name,
And earth, sky and air straight are fill'd with His fame.

4. Then shepherds, be joyful, salute your new King,
Let hills and dales ring to the song that ye sing,
Blest be the hour, welcome the morn,
For Christ our dear Saviour on earth now is born.

BIRTHDAY OF A KING

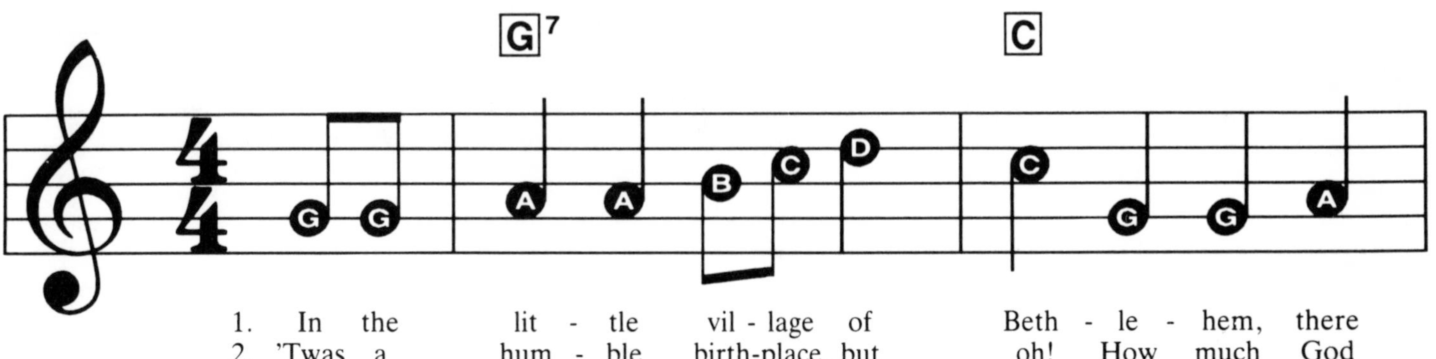

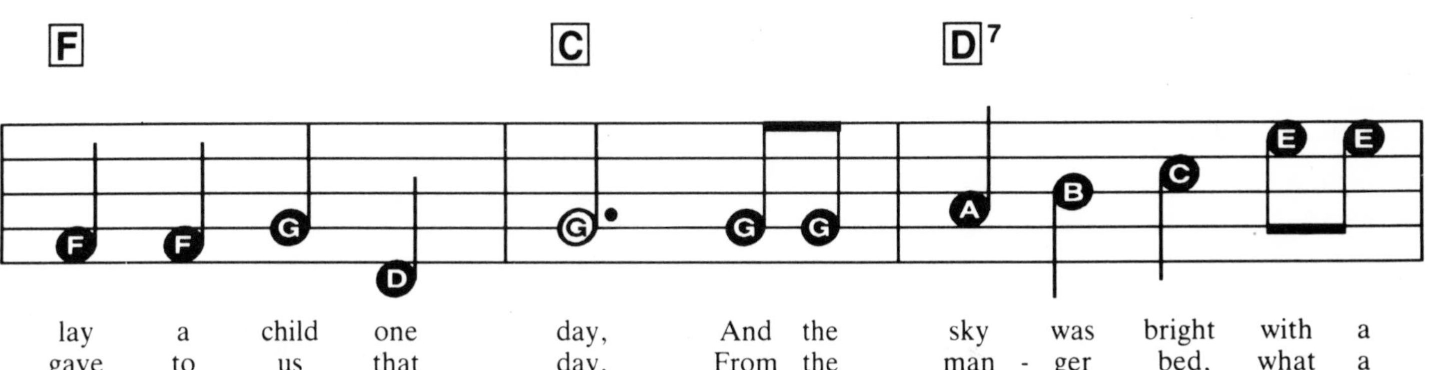

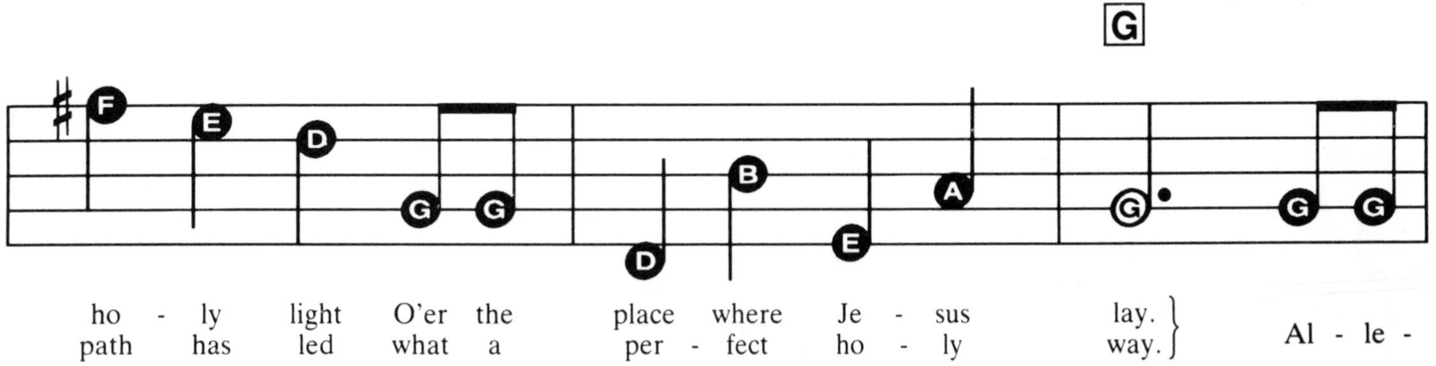

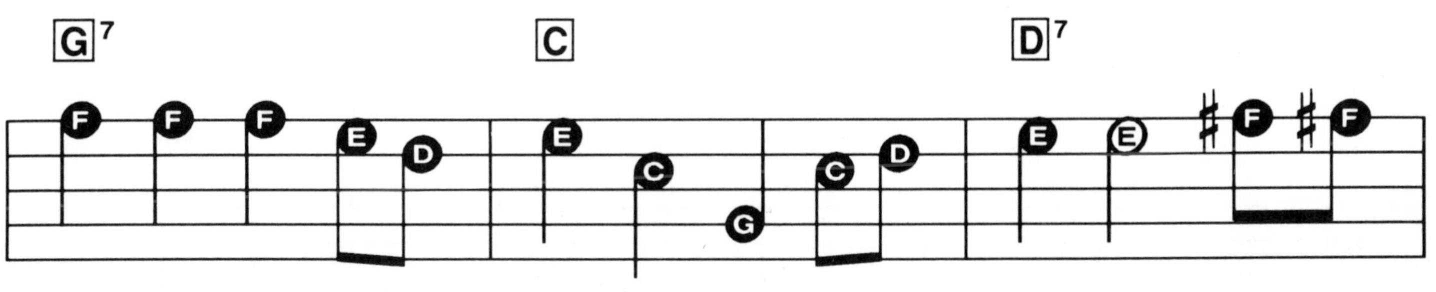

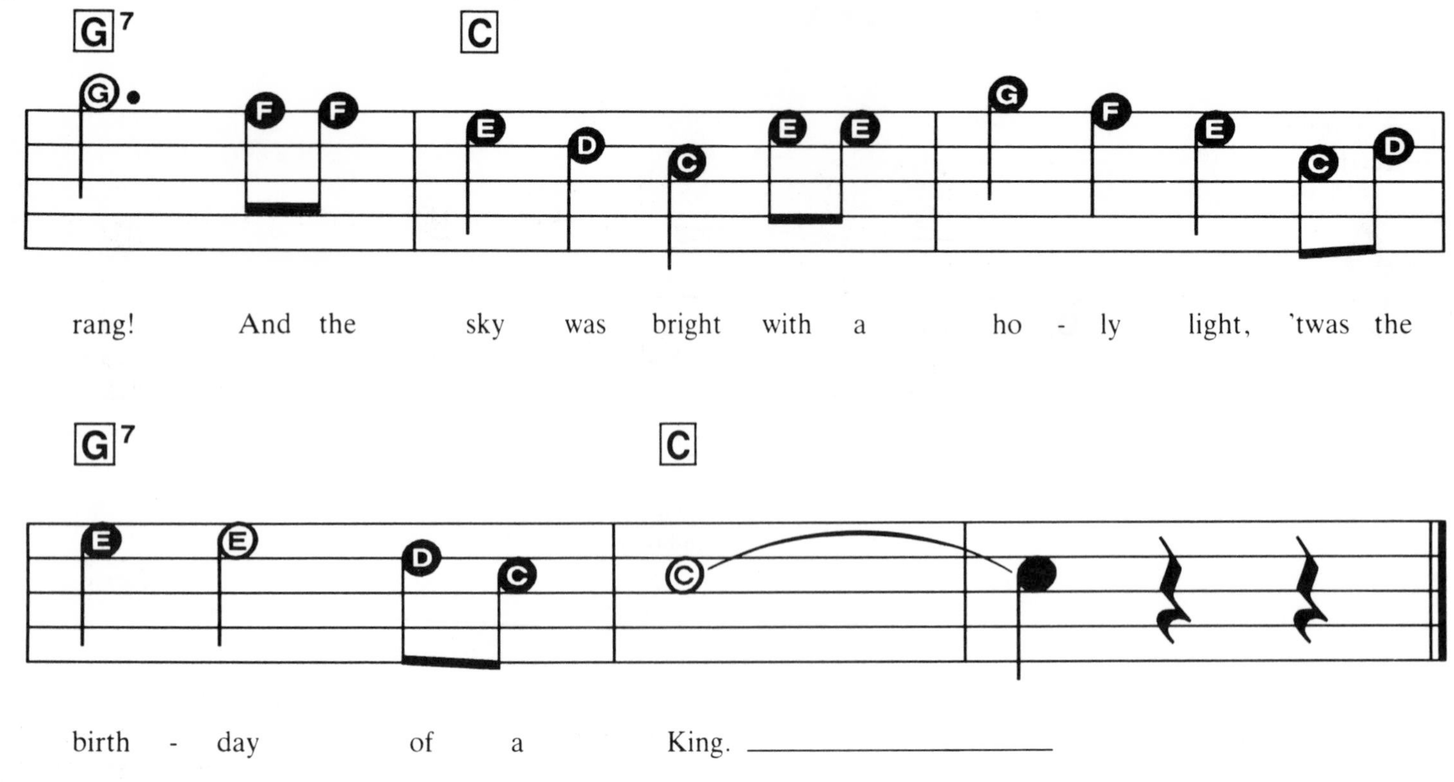
G7 C
rang! And the sky was bright with a ho - ly light, 'twas the
G7 C
birth - day of a King.

BRING A TORCH, JEANNETTE, ISABELLA

ORGAN
FULL 'N' BRILLIANT
Medium WALTZ

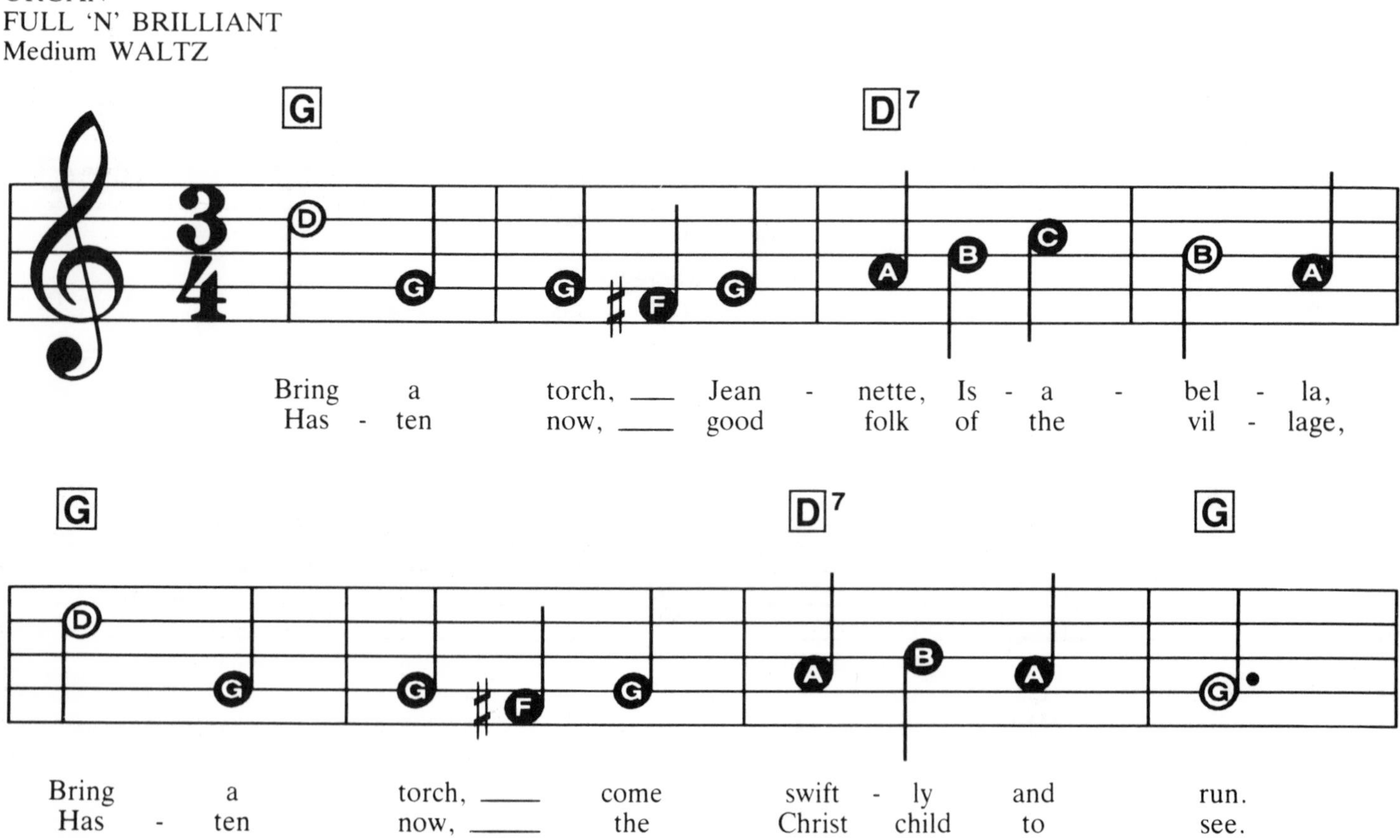
G D7
Bring a torch, Jean - nette, Is - a - bel - la,
Has - ten now, good folk of the vil - lage,
G D7 G
Bring a torch, come swift - ly and run.
Has - ten now, the Christ child to see.

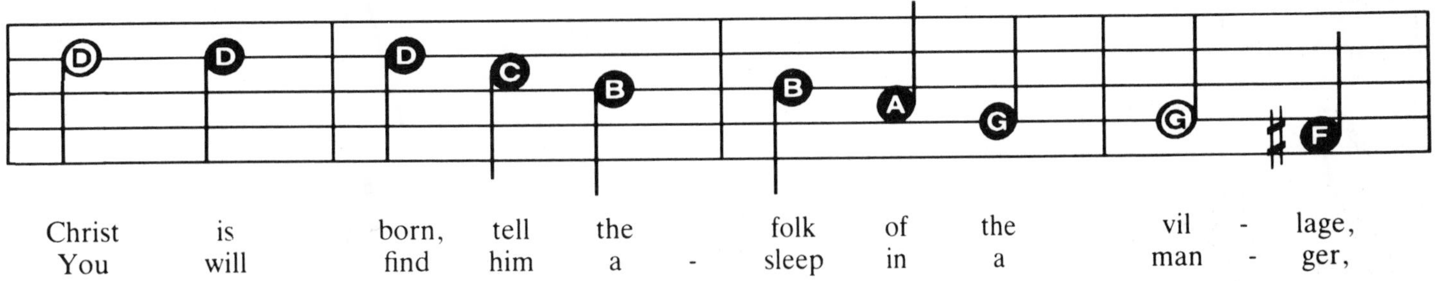
Christ is born, tell the folk of the vil - lage,
You will find him a - sleep in a man - ger,

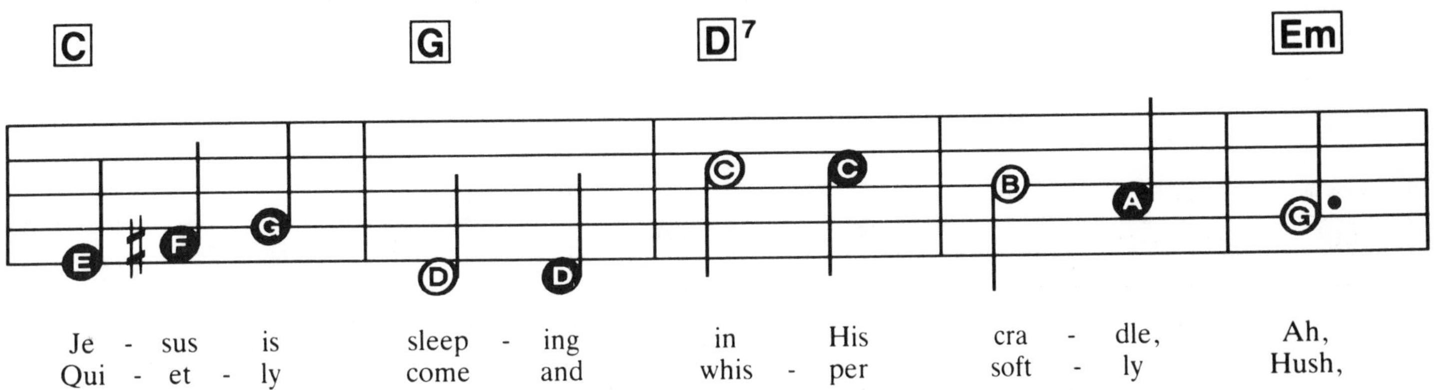
C G D7 Em
Je - sus is sleep - ing in His cra - dle, Ah,
Qui - et - ly come and whis - per soft - ly Hush,

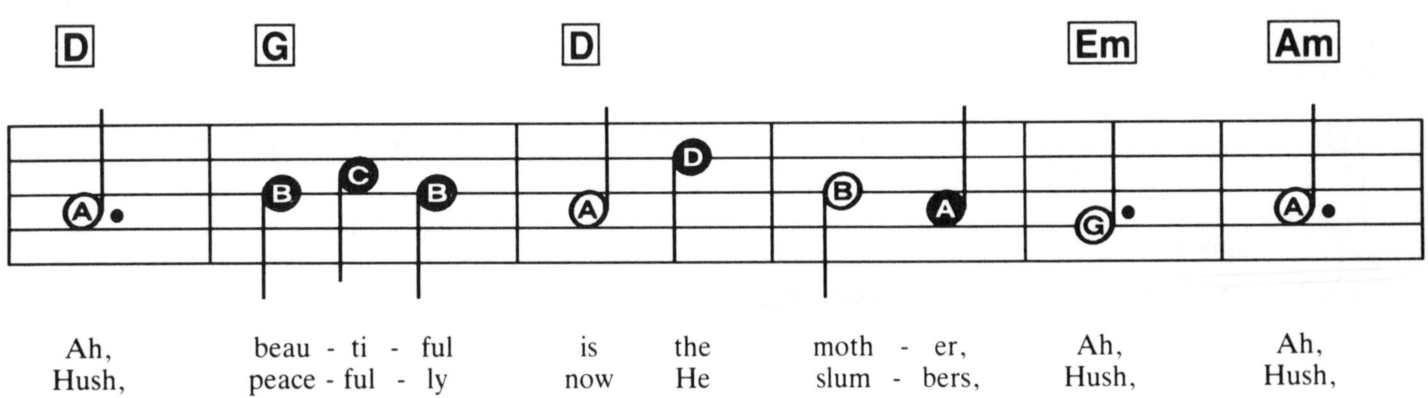
D G D Em Am
Ah, beau - ti - ful is the moth - er, Ah, Ah,
Hush, peace - ful - ly now He slum - bers, Hush, Hush,

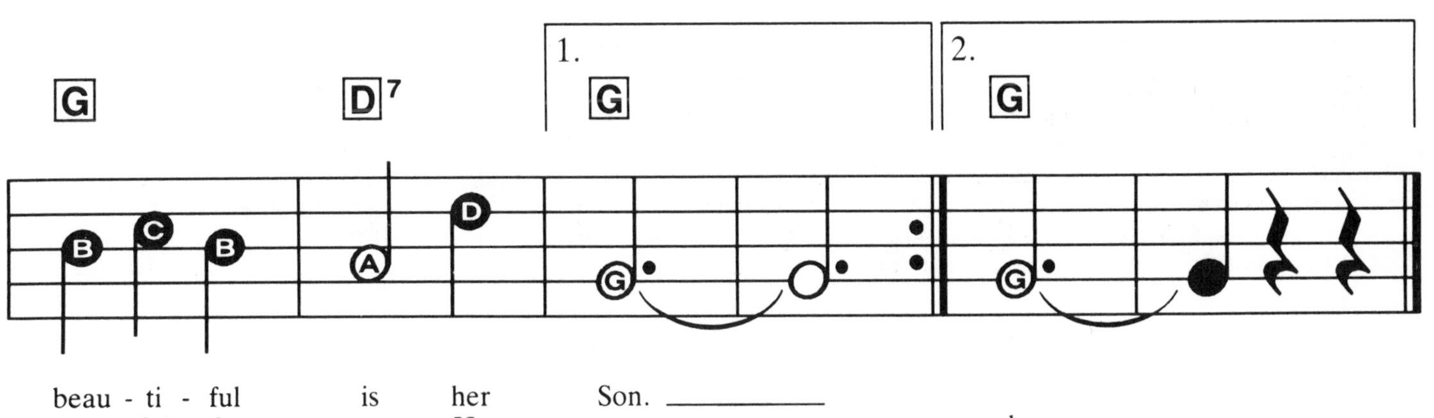
G D7 1. G 2. G
beau - ti - ful is her Son.
peace - ful - ly now He sleeps.

CAROL OF THE BELLS

TRUMPET
BRILLIANT SOLO
Medium WALTZ

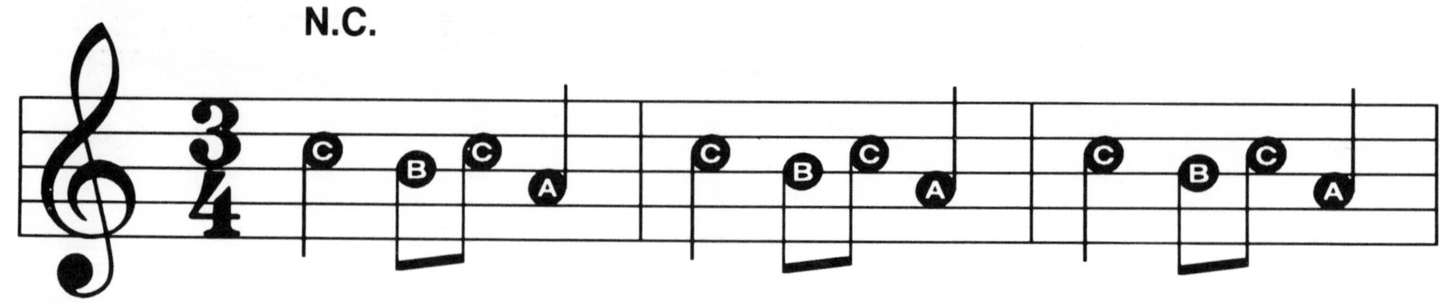
N.C.
C
B
C
A
Hark to the bells, Hark to the bells, Tell - ing us all

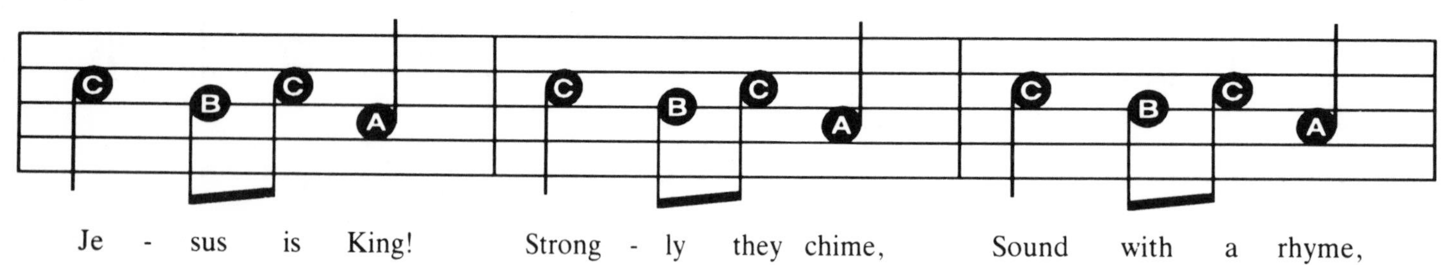
C
B
C
A
Je - sus is King! Strong - ly they chime, Sound with a rhyme,

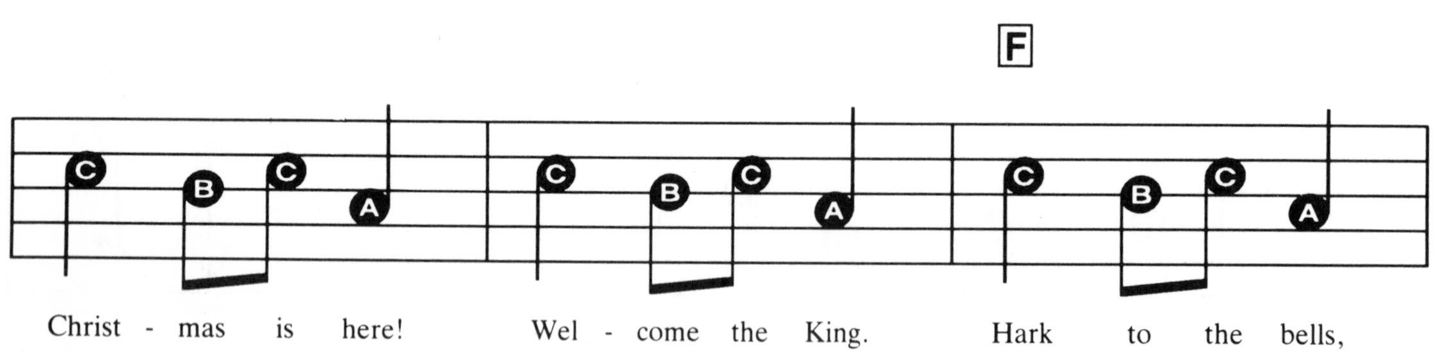
F
C
B
C
A
Christ - mas is here! Wel - come the King. Hark to the bells,

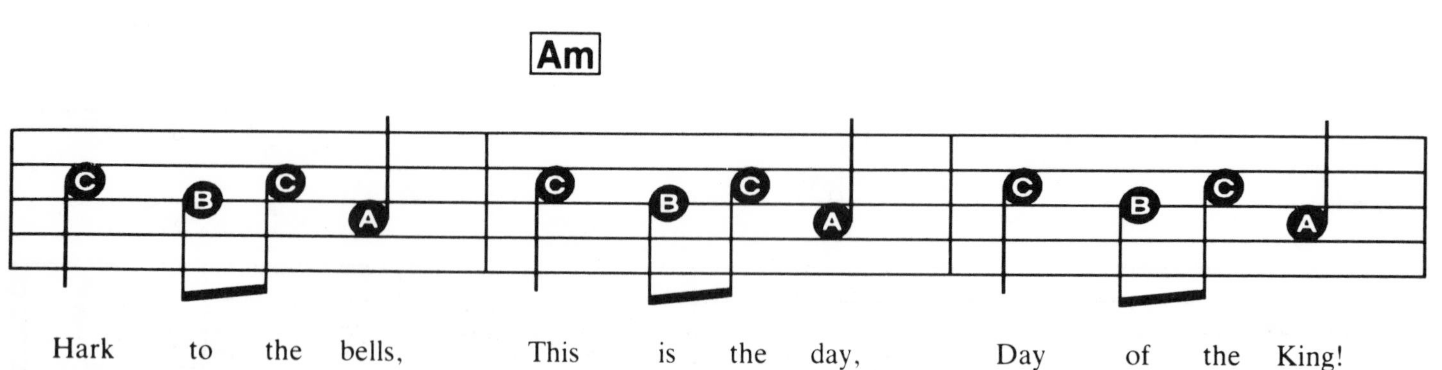
Am
C
B
C
A
Hark to the bells, This is the day, Day of the King!

Dm　　　　　　　　　　Am

Peal out the news o'er hill and dale, And 'round the town

tell - ing the tale. Hark! to the bells, Hark! to the bells,

Tell - ing us all Je - sus is King! Come, one and all ____

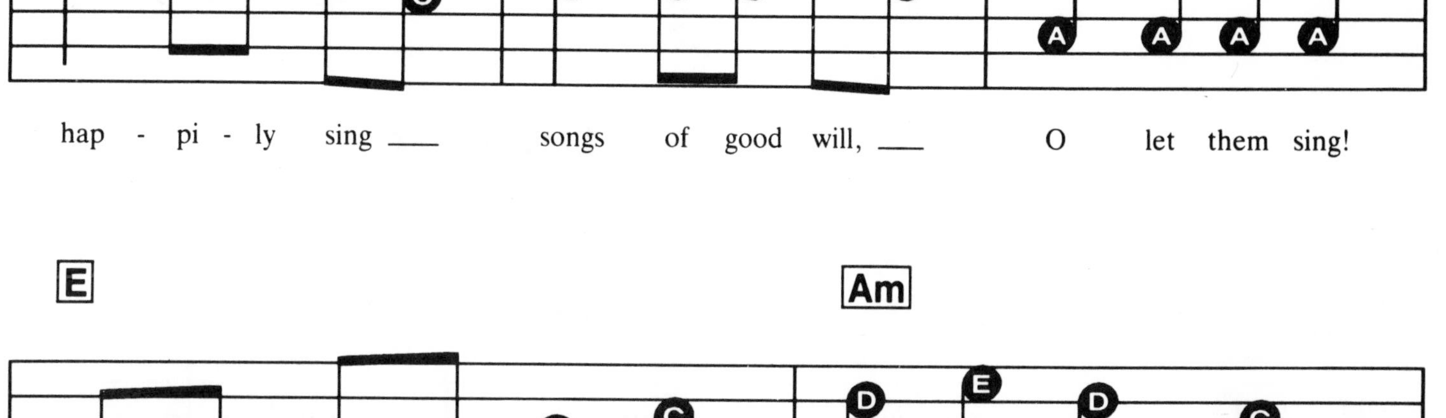
Dm
hap - pi - ly sing ___ songs of good will, ___ O let them sing!

E　　　　　　　　　　Am

ring, ______________________ silv - 'ry bells,

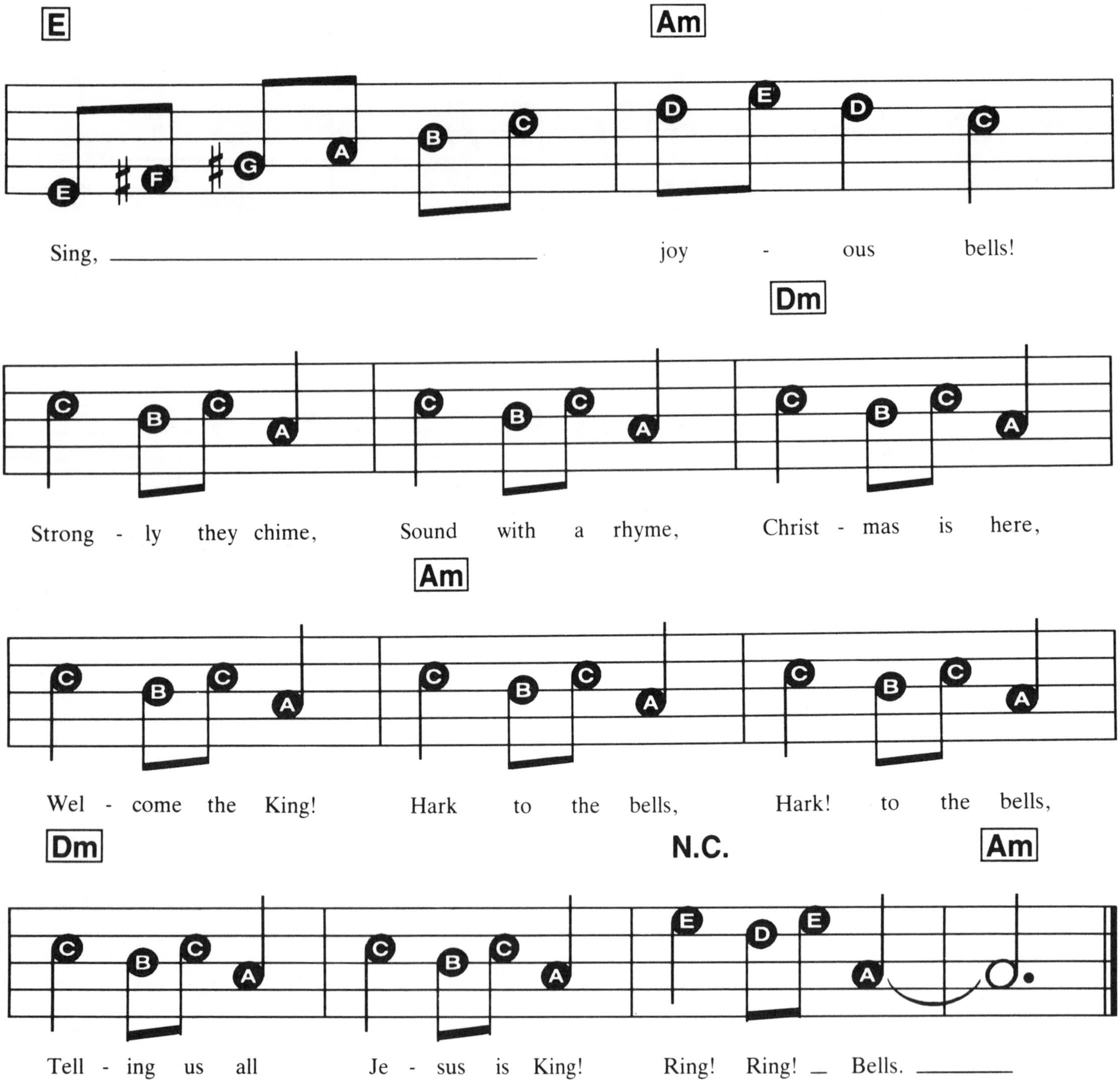

E Am
Sing, joy - ous bells!
Dm
Strong - ly they chime, Sound with a rhyme, Christ - mas is here,
Am
Wel - come the King! Hark to the bells, Hark! to the bells,
Dm N.C. Am
Tell - ing us all Je - sus is King! Ring! Ring! Bells.

THE BOAR'S HEAD CAROL

CLARINET
SOFT SOLO
No Rhythm

C G C G Dm
Ca - put a - pri de - fe - ro, Red - dens lau - des

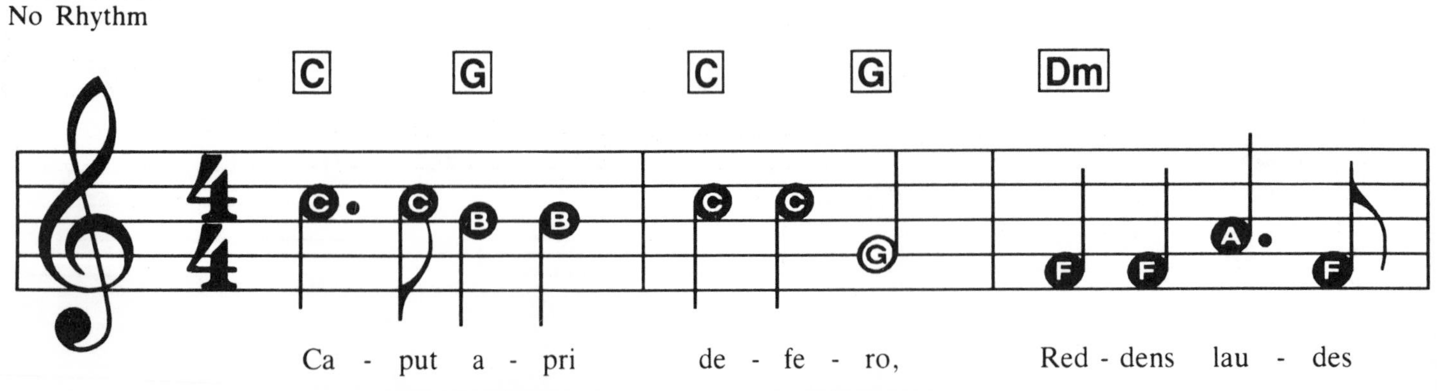

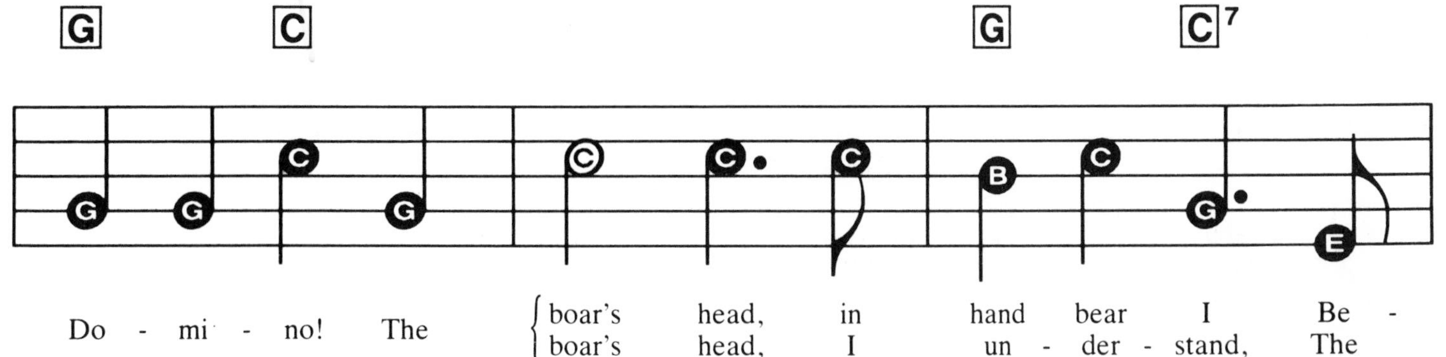
G
C
G
C7
C
C
C
G
G
C
G
C
C
B
C
G
E
Do - mi - no! The
boar's head, in hand bear I Be -
boar's head, I un - der - stand, The

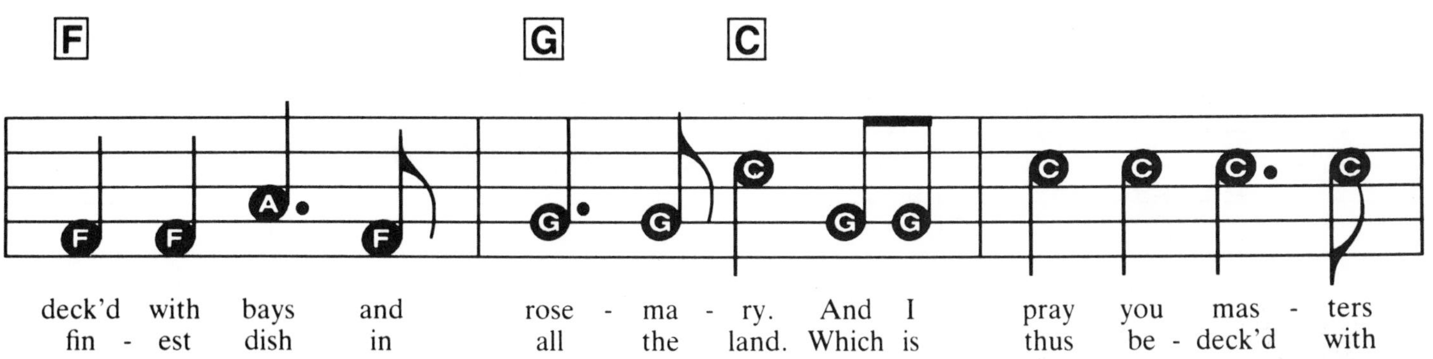
F
G
C
F
F
A
F
G
G
C
G
G
C
C
C
C
deck'd with bays and rose - ma - ry. And I pray you mas - ters
fin - est dish in all the land. Which is thus be - deck'd with

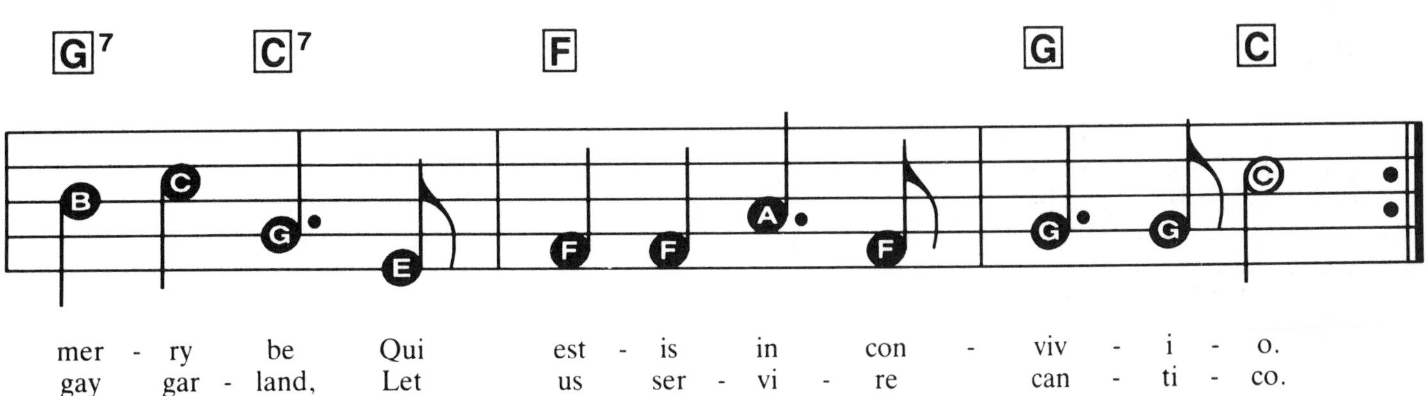
G7
C7
F
G
C
B
C
G
E
F
F
A
F
G
G
C
mer - ry be Qui est - is in con - viv - i - o.
gay gar - land, Let us ser - vi - re can - ti - co.

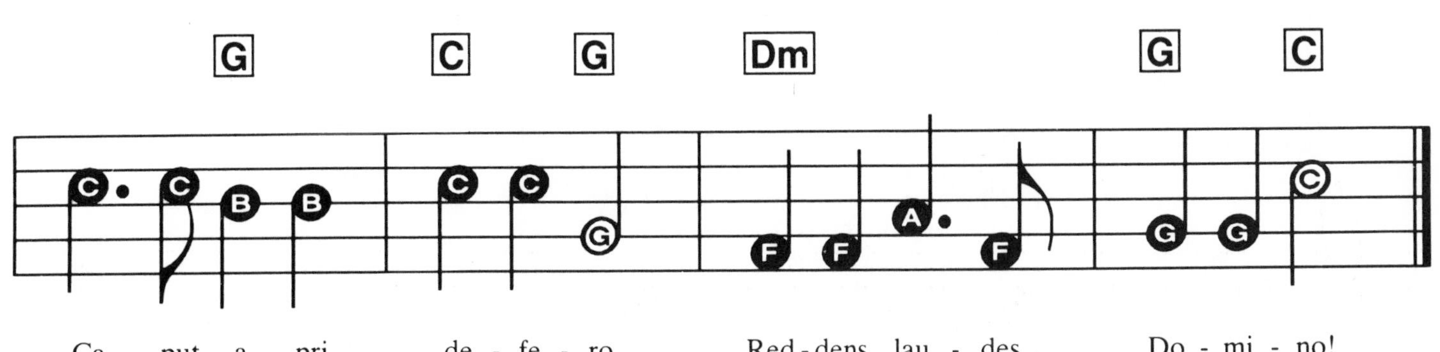
G
C
G
Dm
G
C
C
C
B
B
C
C
G
F
F
A
F
G
G
C
Ca - put a - pri de - fe - ro, Red - dens lau - des Do - mi - no!

CHRIST WAS BORN ON CHRISTMAS DAY

TRUMPET
CLASSICAL
Medium WALTZ

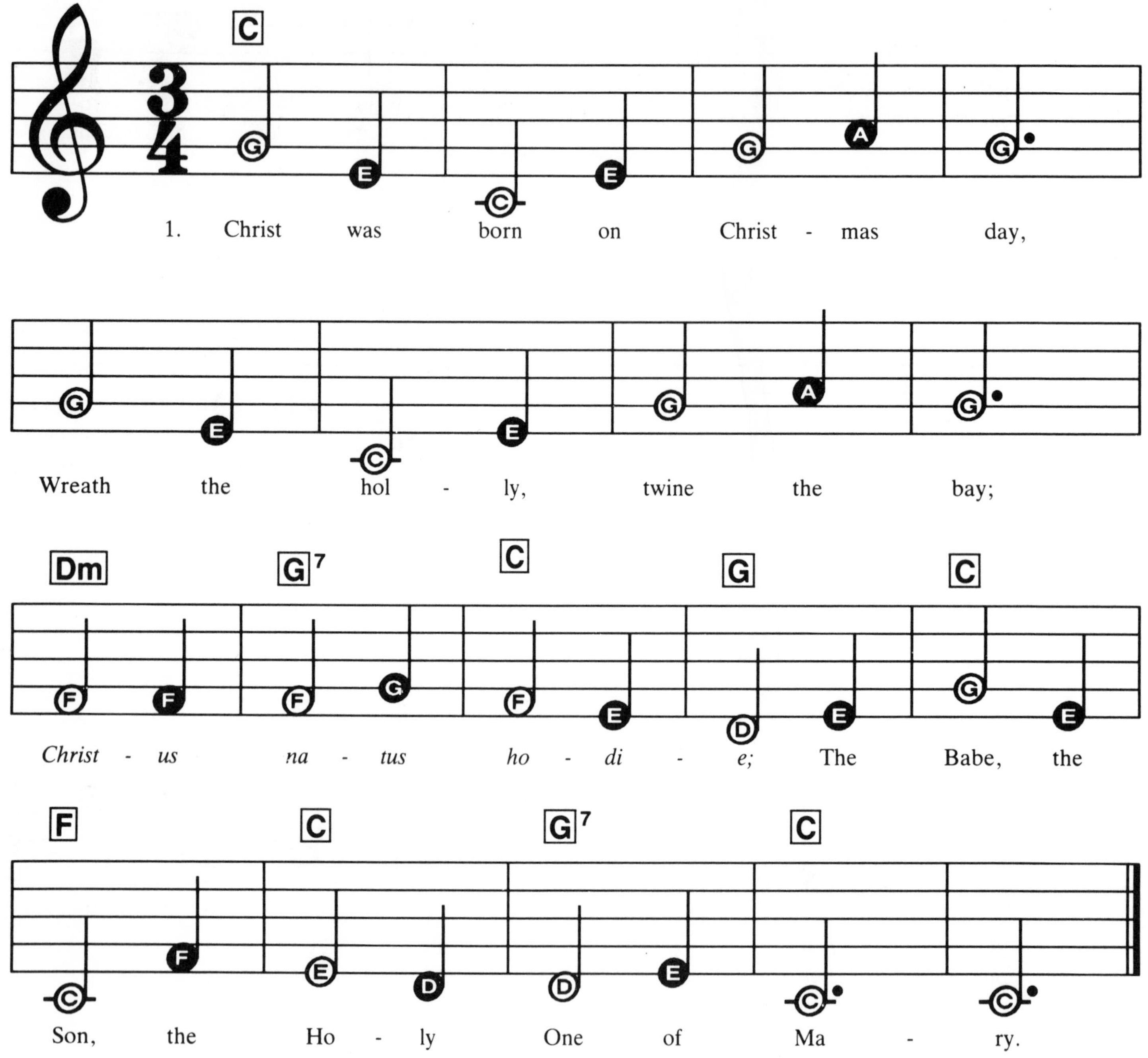

2. He is born to set us free,
He is born our Lord to be,
Ex Maria Virgine;
The God, the Lord, by all adored forever.

3. Let the bright red berries glow,
Everywhere in goodly show;
Christus natus hodie;
The Babe, the Son, the Holy One of Mary.

4. Christian men rejoice and sing,
'Tis the birthday of a King,
Ex Maria Virgine;
The God, the Lord, by all adored forever.

COME, THOU ALMIGHTY KING

ORGAN
FULL 'N' BRILLIANT
No Rhythm

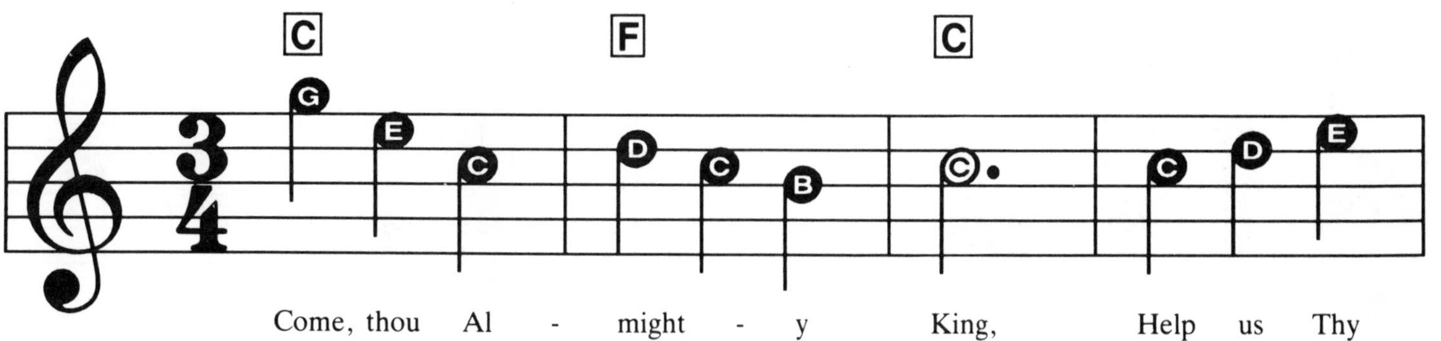

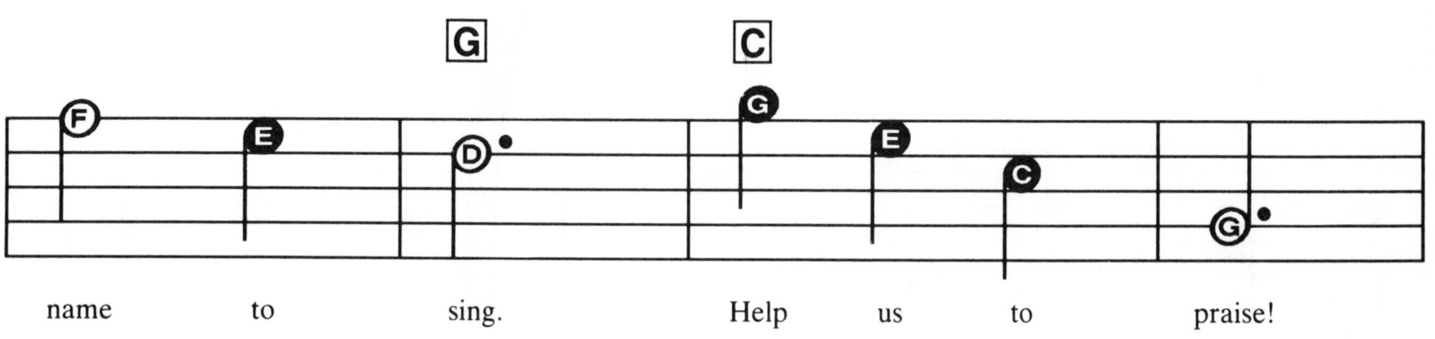

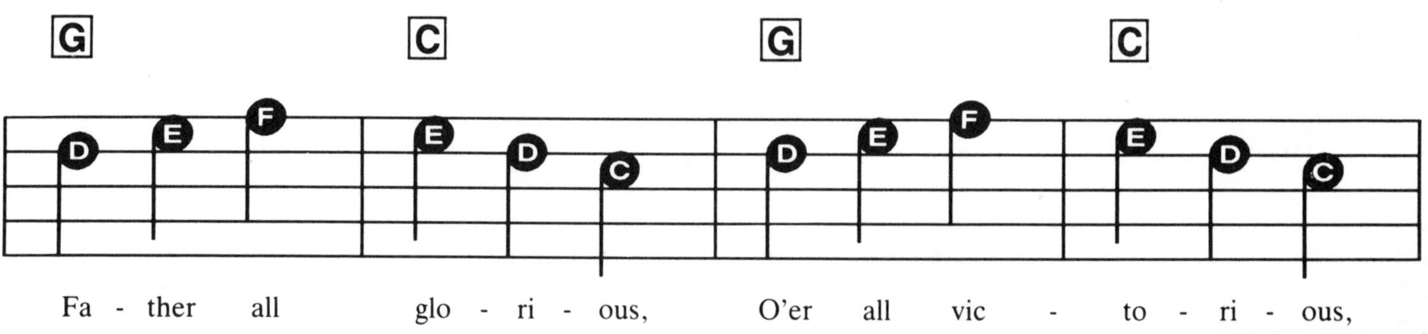

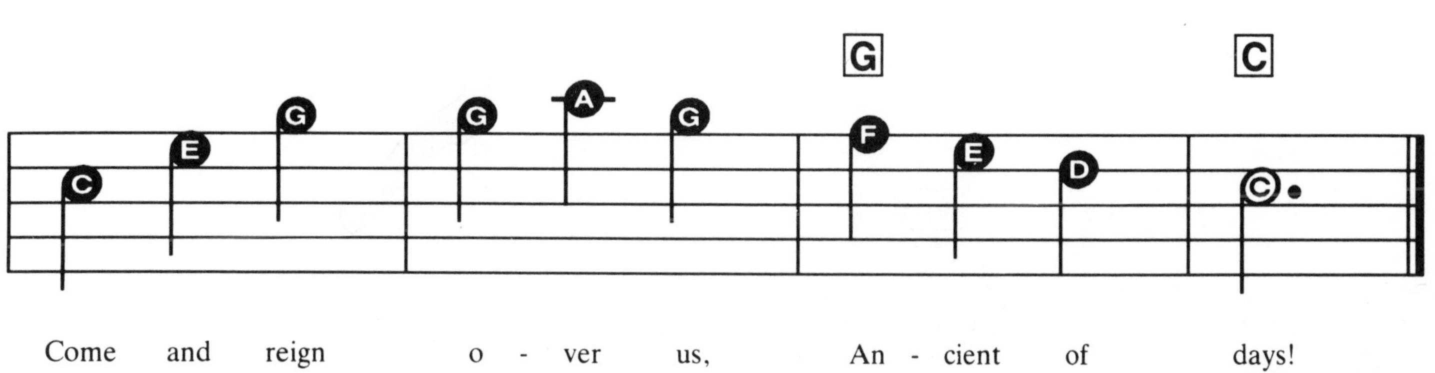

THE COVENTRY CAROL

OBOE
BRILLIANT SOLO
Slow WALTZ

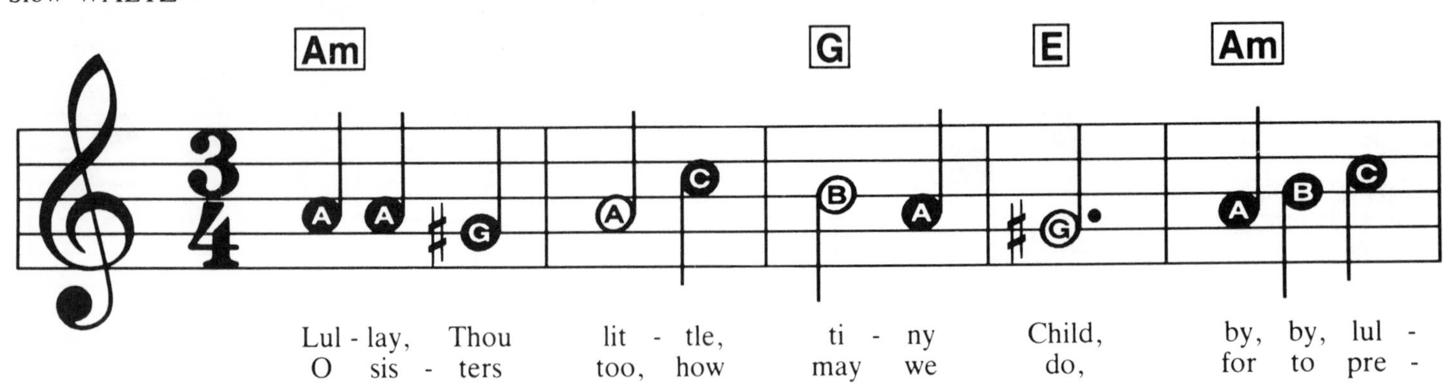
Am
G
E
Am
A A G A C B A G A B C
Lul - lay, Thou lit - tle, ti - ny Child, by, by, lul -
O sis - ters too, how may we do, for to pre -

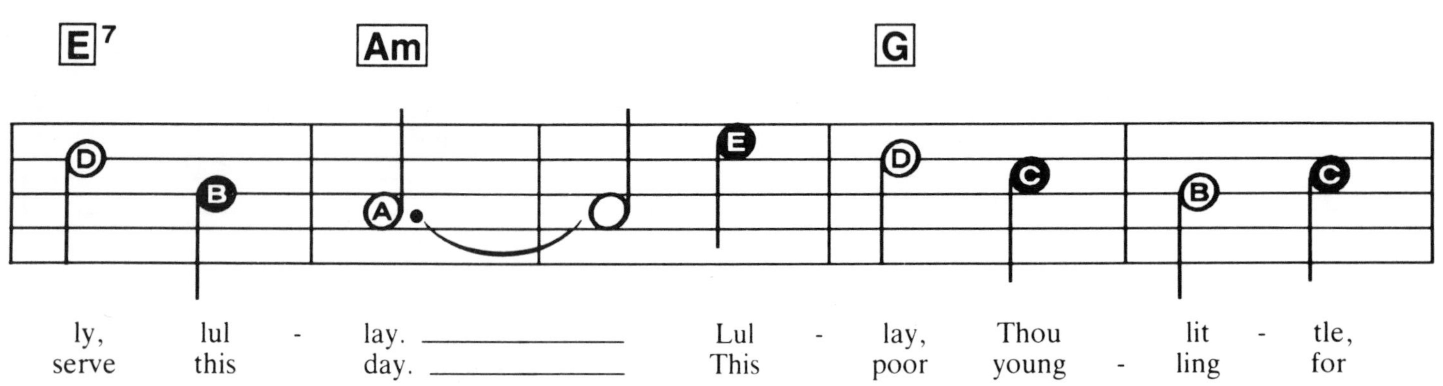
E7
Am
G
D B A E D C B C
ly, lul - lay.
serve this day.
Lul - lay, Thou lit - tle,
This poor young - ling for

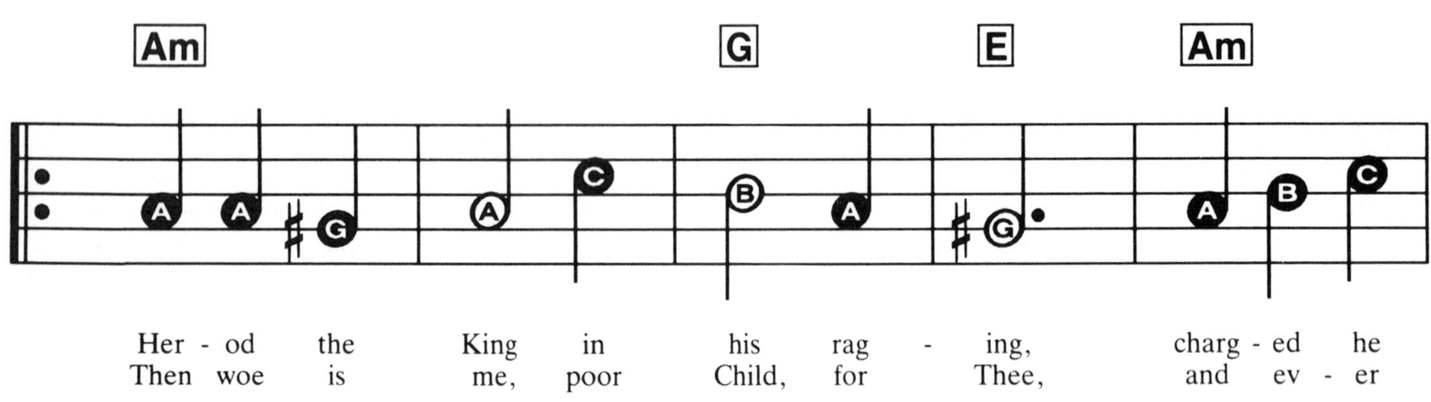
Am
G
E
Am
A A G A C B A G A B C
Her - od the King in his rag - ing, charg - ed he
Then woe is me, poor Child, for Thee, and ev - er

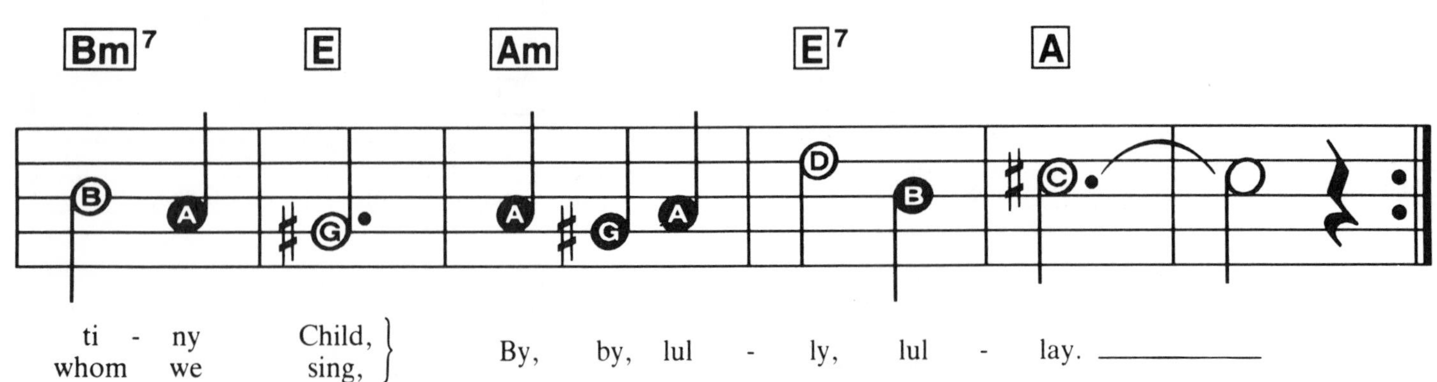
Bm7
E
Am
E7
A
B A G A G A D B C
ti - ny Child,
whom we sing,
By, by, lul - ly, lul - lay.

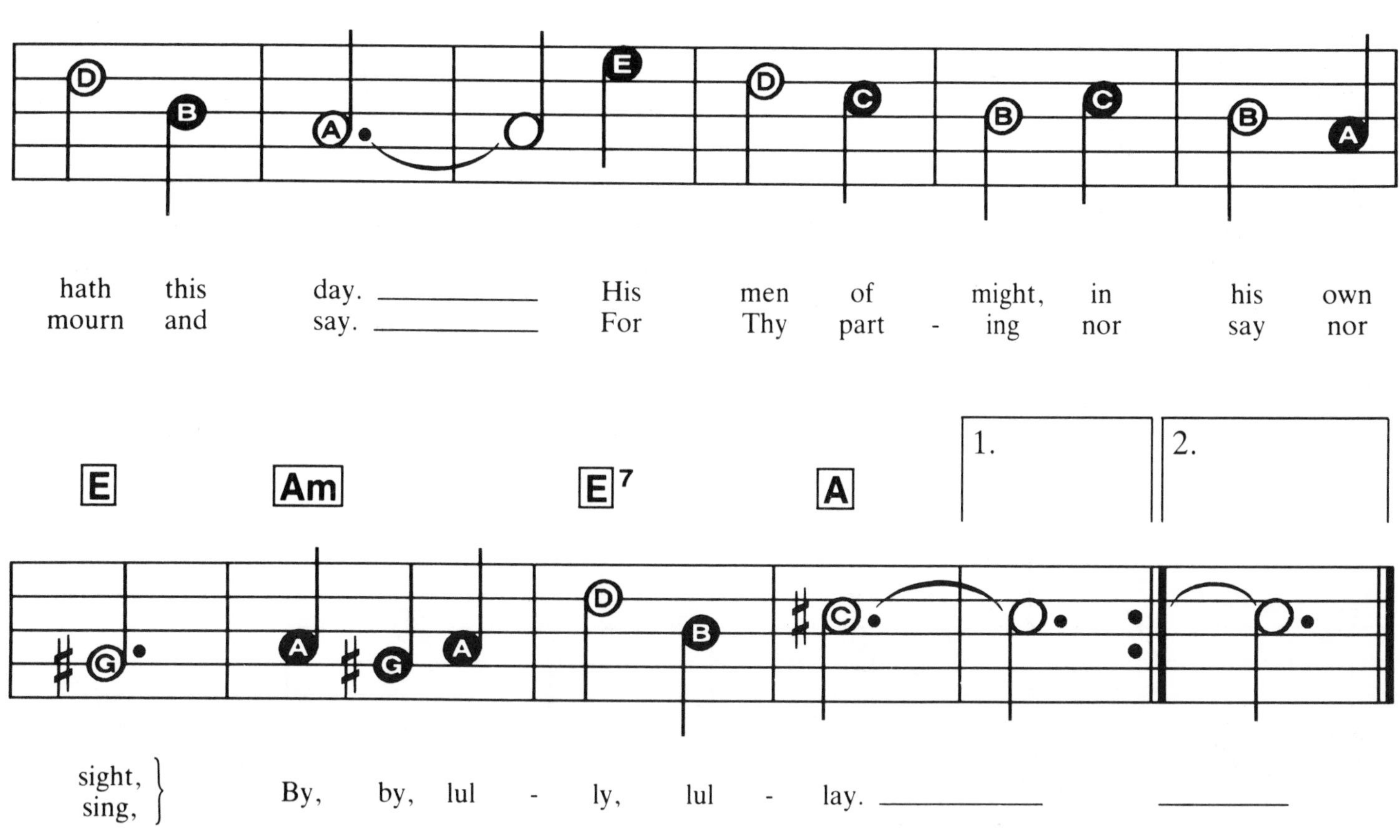

CHRISTIANS, AWAKE, SALUTE THE HAPPY MORN

TRUMPET
FULL 'N' BRILLIANT
Medium SLOW

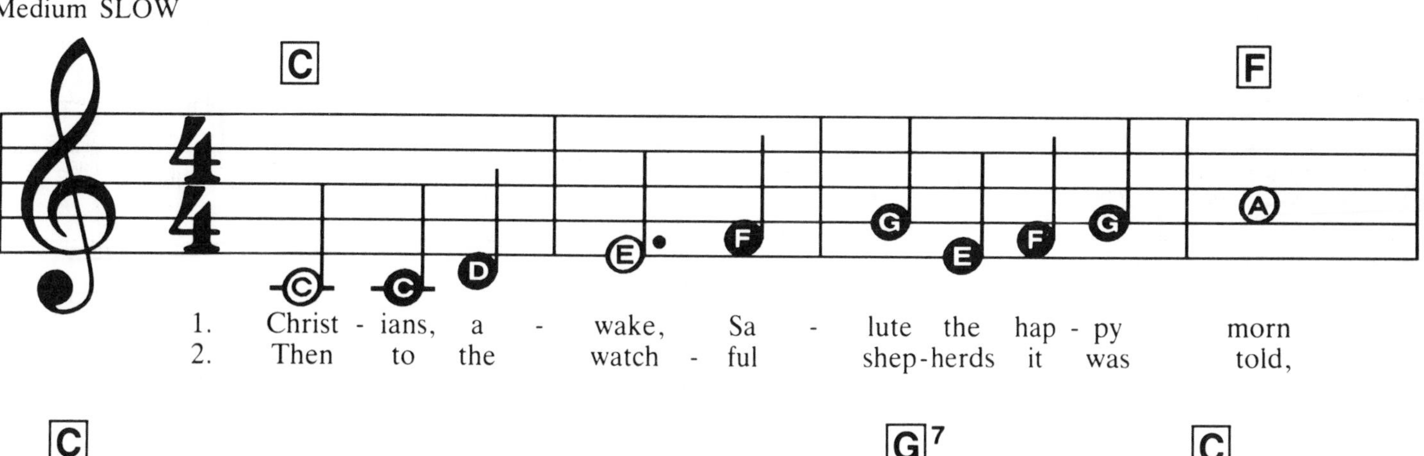

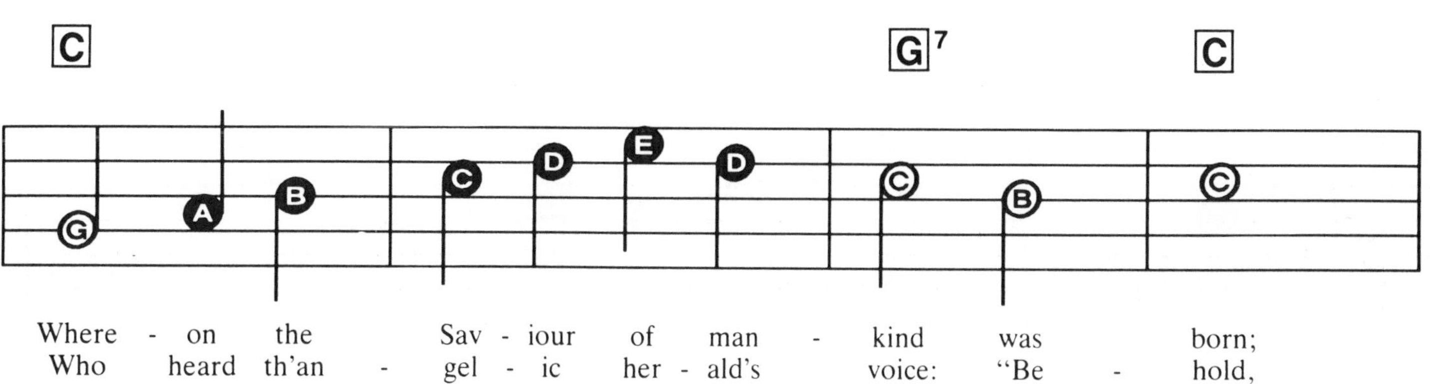

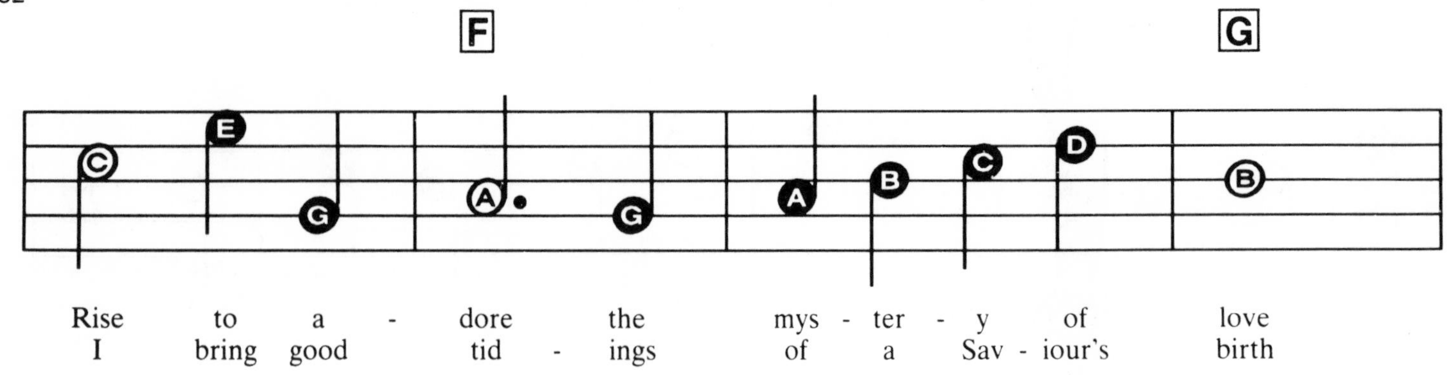
F
G
C E G
A G
A B C D
B
Rise to a - dore the mys - ter - y of love
I bring good tid - ings of a Sav - iour's birth

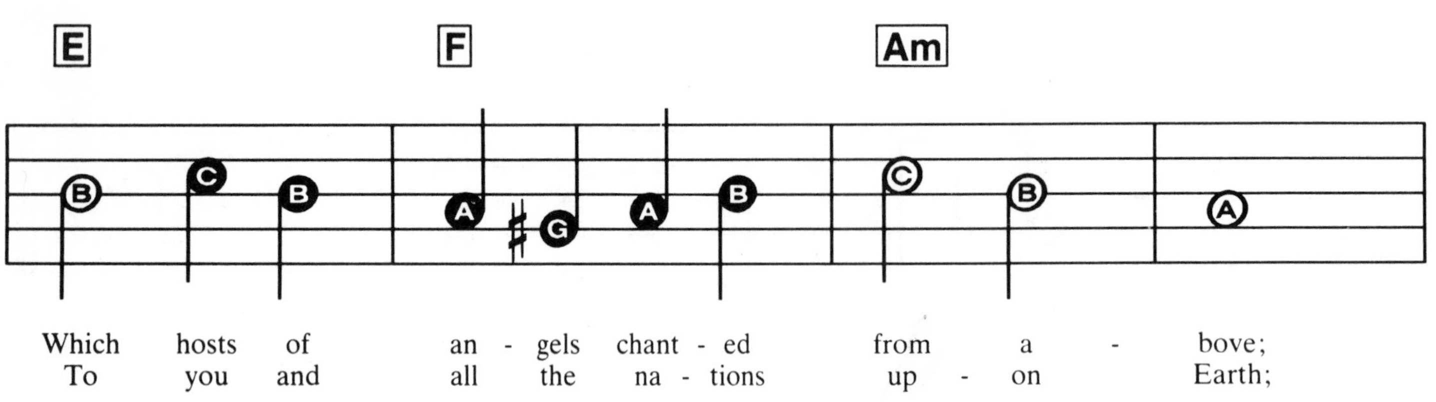
E
F
Am
B C B
A G A B
C B
A
Which hosts of an - gels chant - ed from a - bove;
To you and all the na - tions up - on Earth;

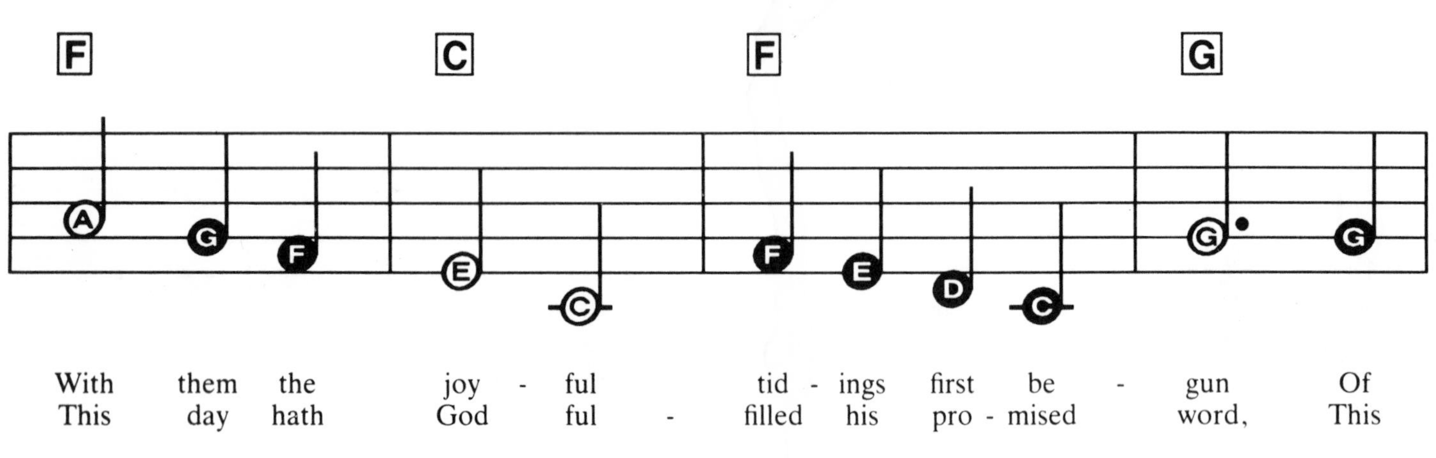
F
C
F
G
A G F
E C
F E D C
G G
With them the joy - ful tid - ings first be - gun Of
This day hath God ful - filled his pro - mised word, This

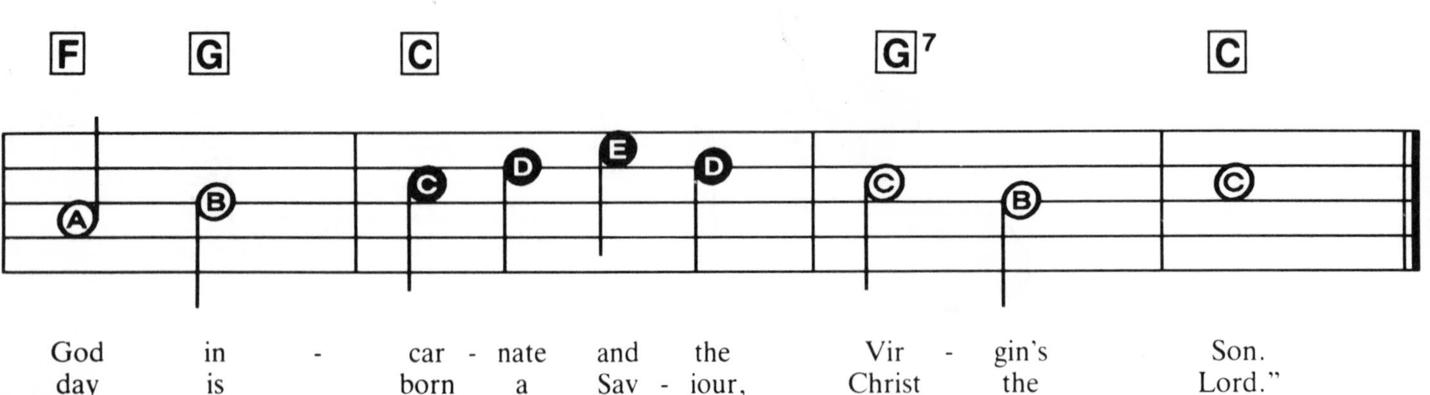
F
G
C
G7
C
A B
C D E D
C B
C
God in - car - nate and the Vir - gin's Son.
day is born a Sav - iour, Christ the Lord."

DING DONG! MERRILY ON HIGH

PIANO
SOFT SOLO
No Rhythm

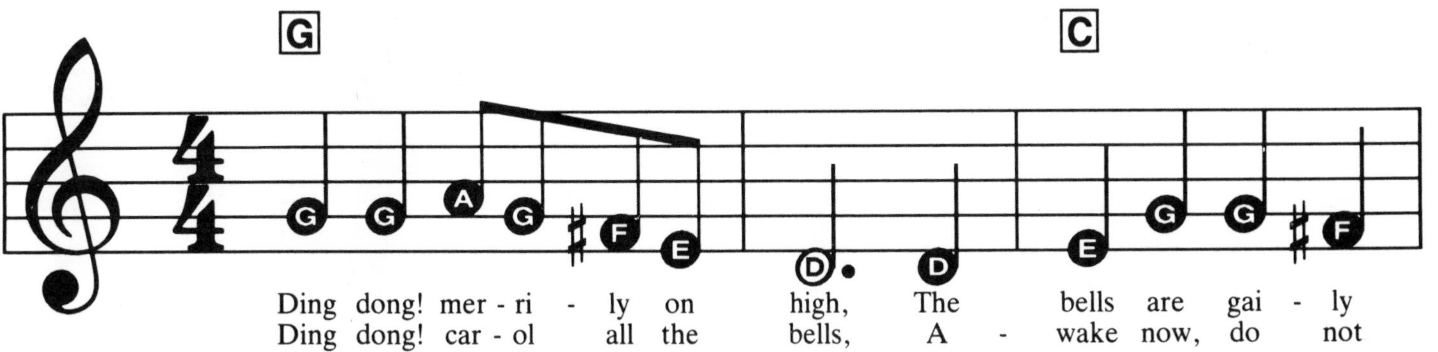
G
C
G G A G F E D D E G G F
Ding dong! mer - ri - ly on high, The bells are gai - ly
Ding dong! car - ol all the bells, A - wake now, do not

G
G G G G A G F E D D
ring - ing; Ding dong! hap - pi - ly re - ply, The
tar - ry! Sing out, sound the good now - ells, Je -

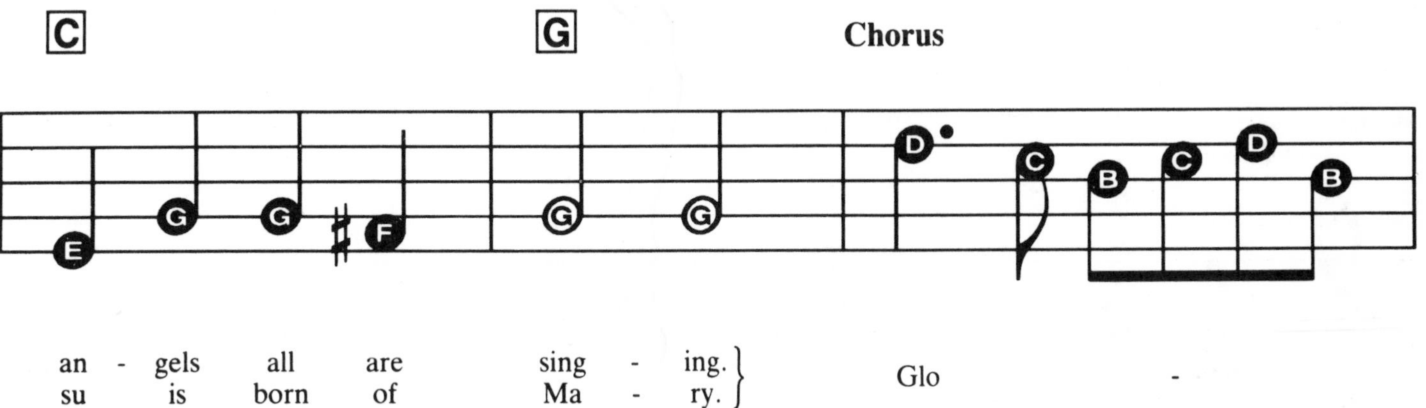
C
G
Chorus
E G G F G G D C B C D B
an - gels all are sing - ing.
su is born of Ma - ry.
Glo -

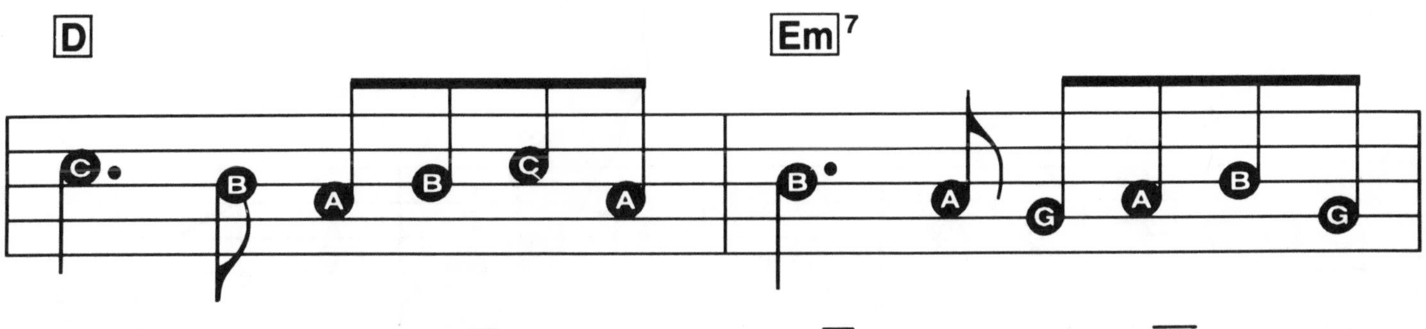
D
Em7
C B A B C A B A G A B G

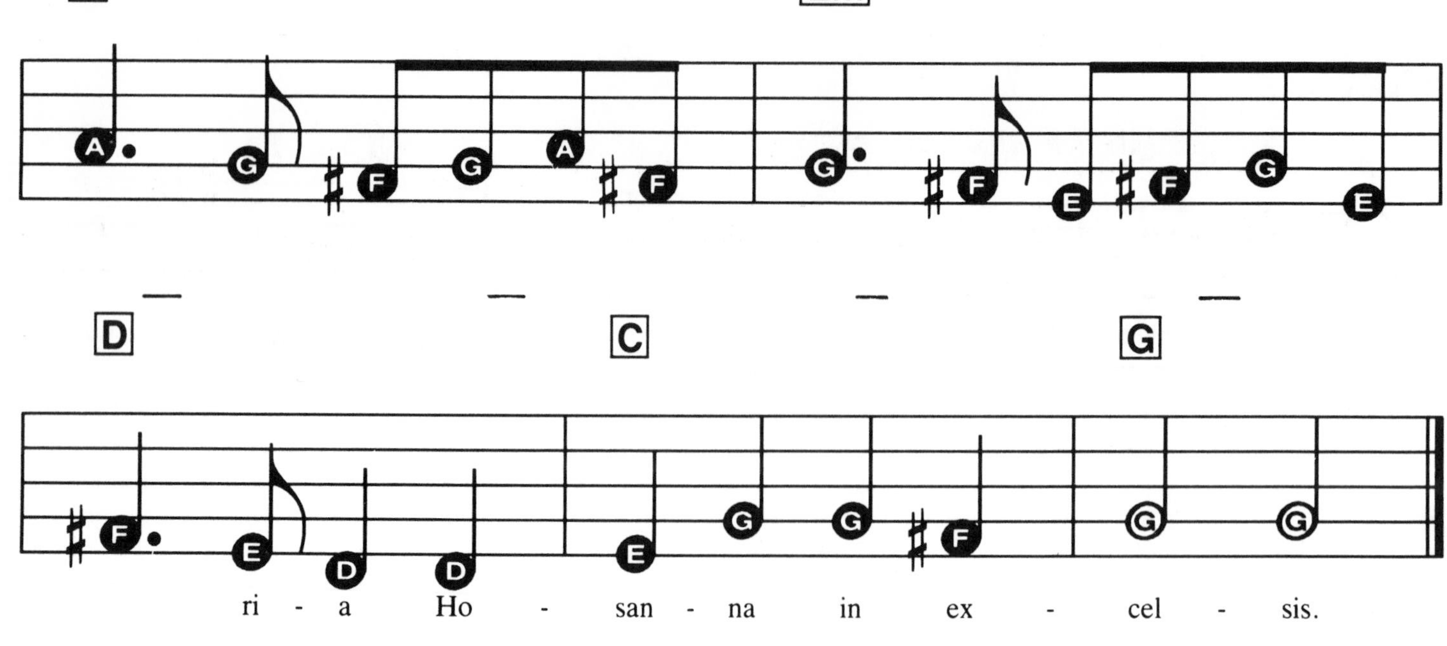

3. Ring out, merry, merry bells,
The angels all are singing;
Ding dong! swing the steeple bells,
Sound joyous news we're bringing!
Chorus

4. Hark now! happily we sing,
The angels wish us merry!
Ding dong! dancing as we bring
Good news from Virgin Mary.
Chorus

DANCE OF THE SUGAR-PLUM FAIRY

CELESTE
BRILLIANT SOLO
Medium MARCH

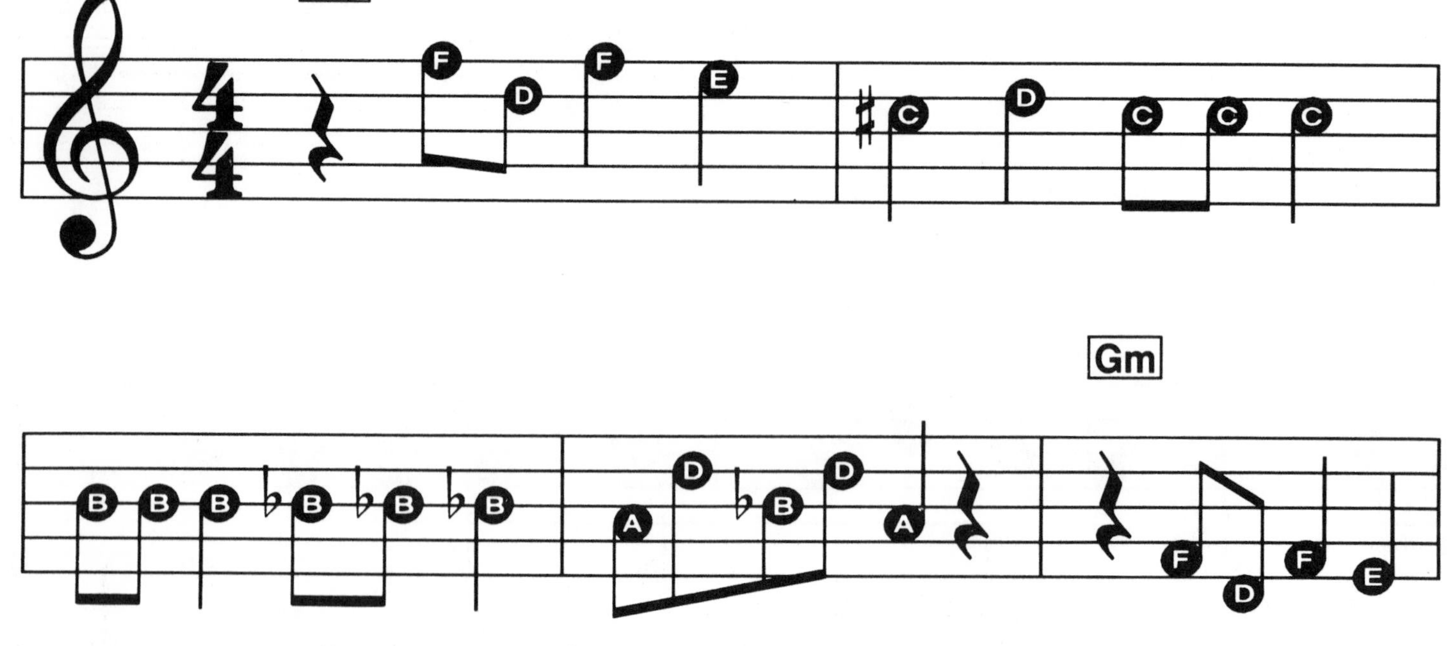

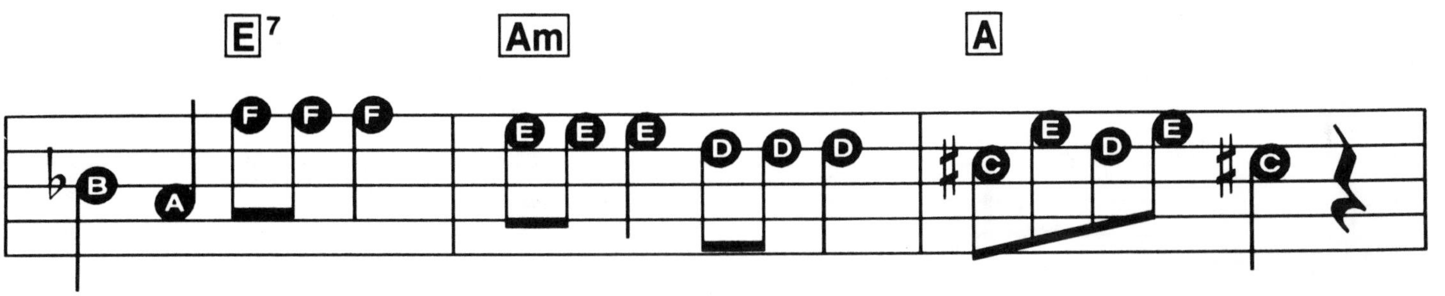
E7
Am
A
B A F F F
E E E D D D
C E D E C

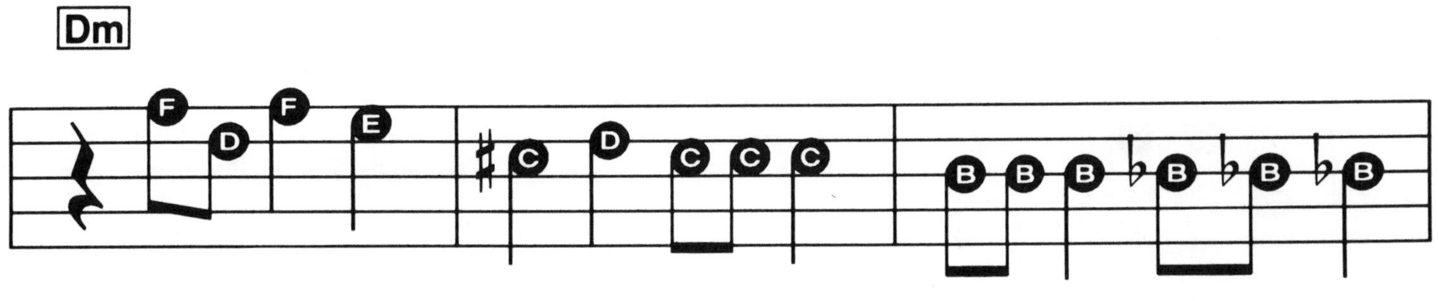
Dm
F D F E
C D C C C
B B B B B B

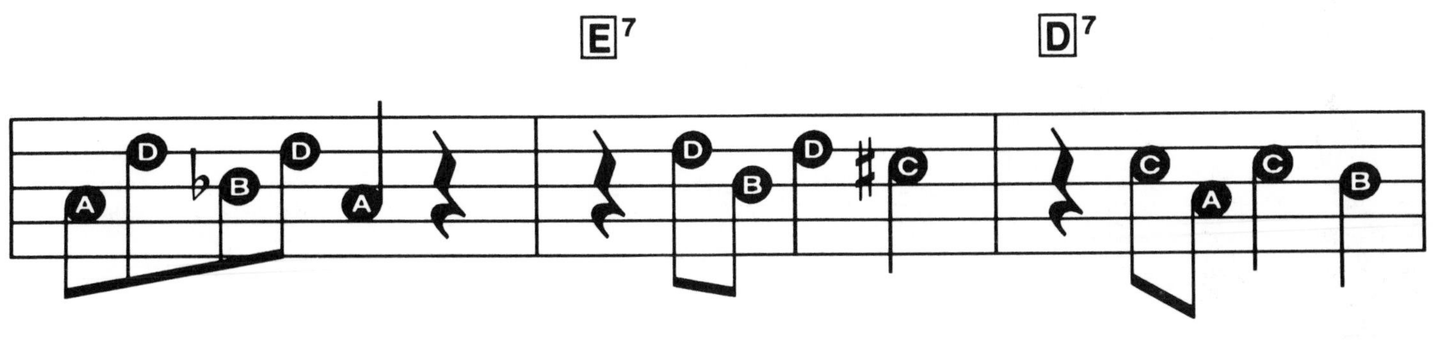
E7
D7
A D B D A
D B D C
C A C B

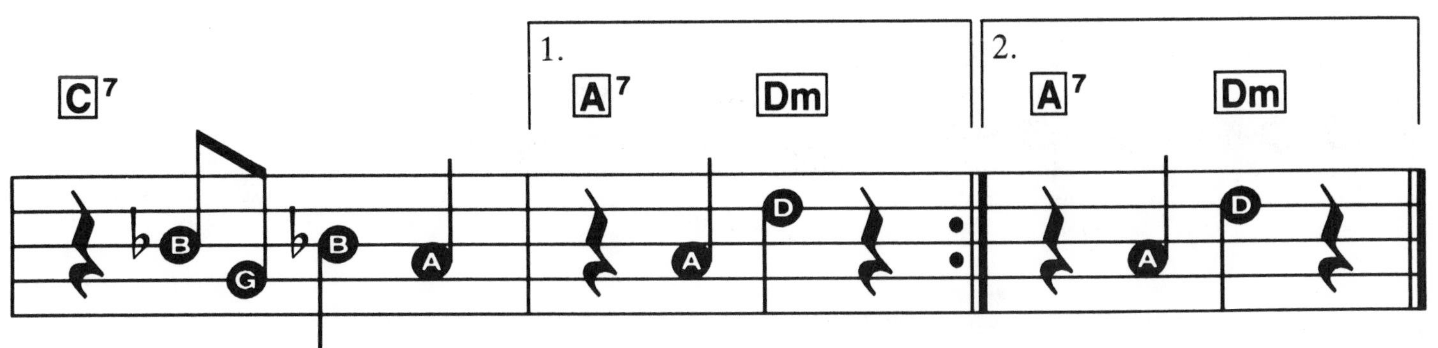
C7
1.
A7
Dm
2.
A7
Dm
B G B A
A D
A D

DO YOU HEAR WHAT I HEAR

VIBES
SOFT SOLO
Slow MARCH

Words and Music by
NOEL REGNEY and
GLORIA SHAYNE

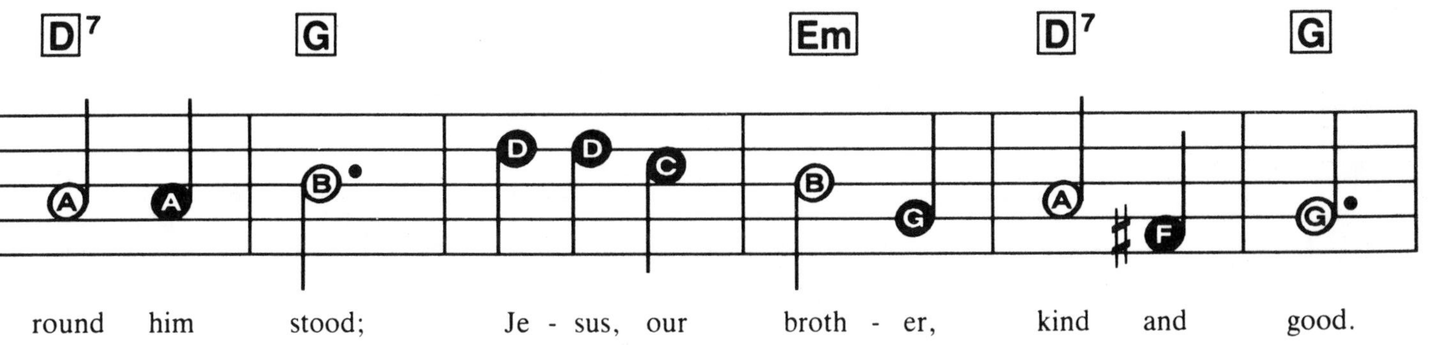
D7 G Em D7 G
A A B D D C B G A F G
round him stood; Je - sus, our broth - er, kind and good.

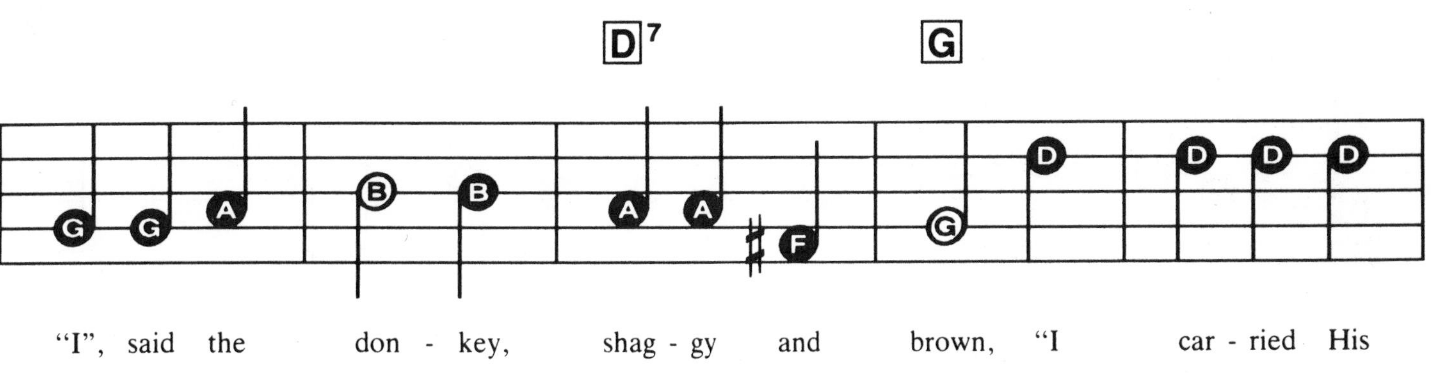
D7 G
G G A B B A A F G D D D D
"I", said the don - key, shag - gy and brown, "I car - ried His

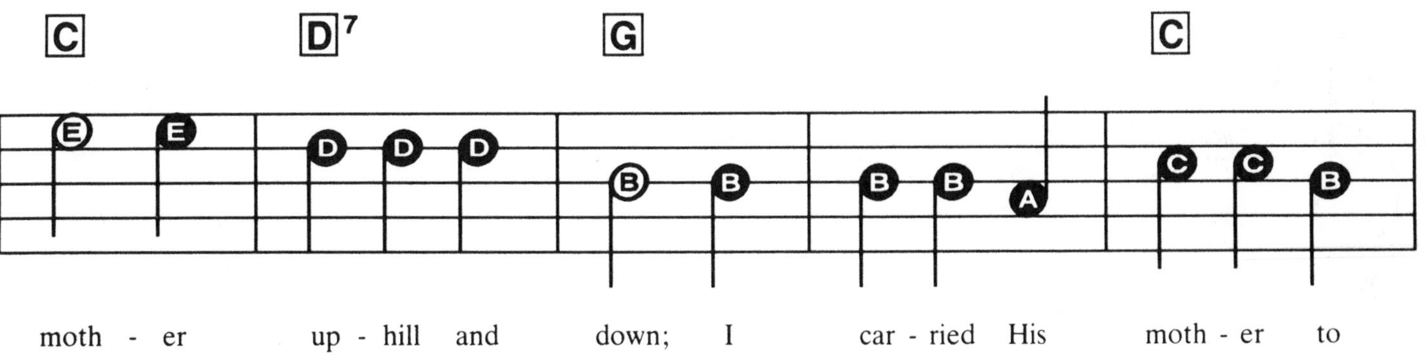
C D7 G C
E E D D D B B B B A C C B
moth - er up - hill and down; I car - ried His moth - er to

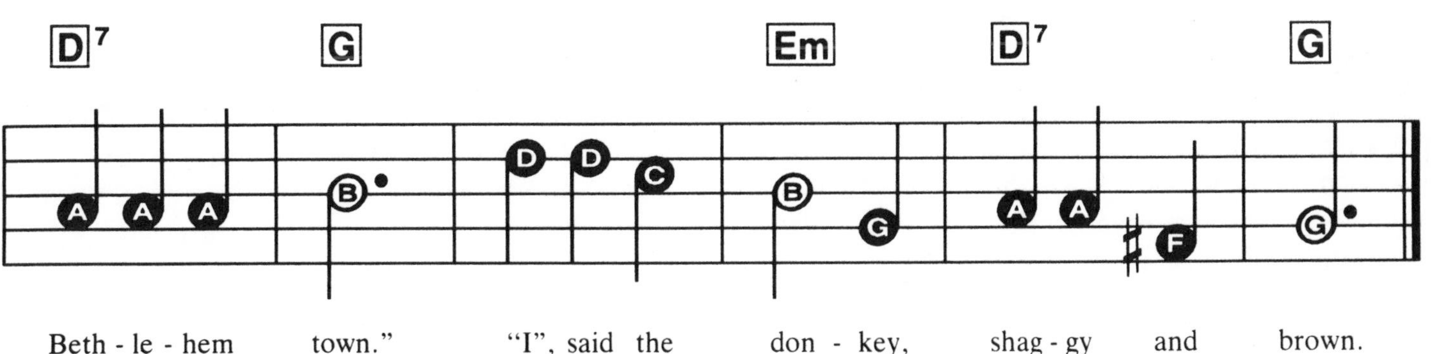
D7 G Em D7 G
A A A B D D C B G A A F G
Beth - le - hem town." "I", said the don - key, shag - gy and brown.

THE FIRST NOEL

CLARINET
CLASSICAL
Medium Slow WALTZ

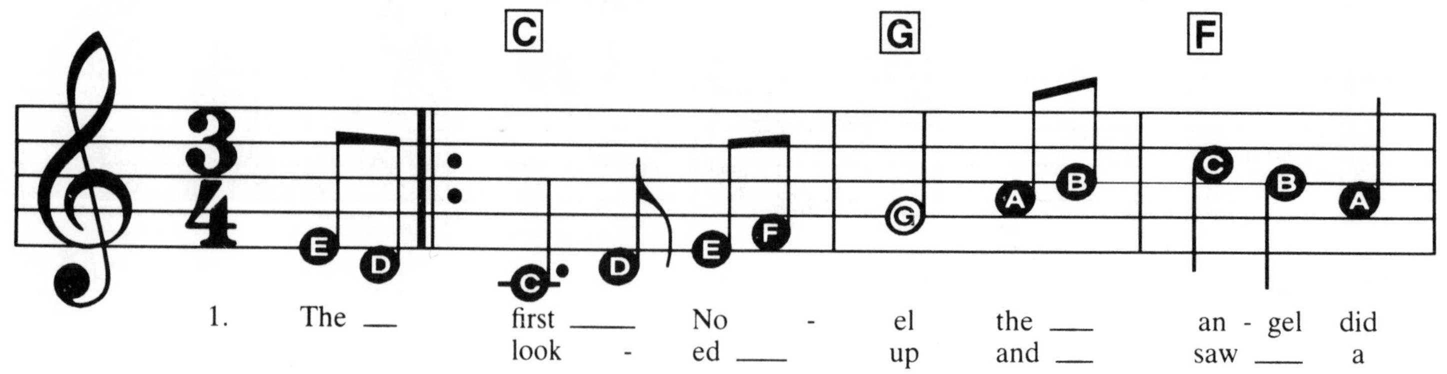

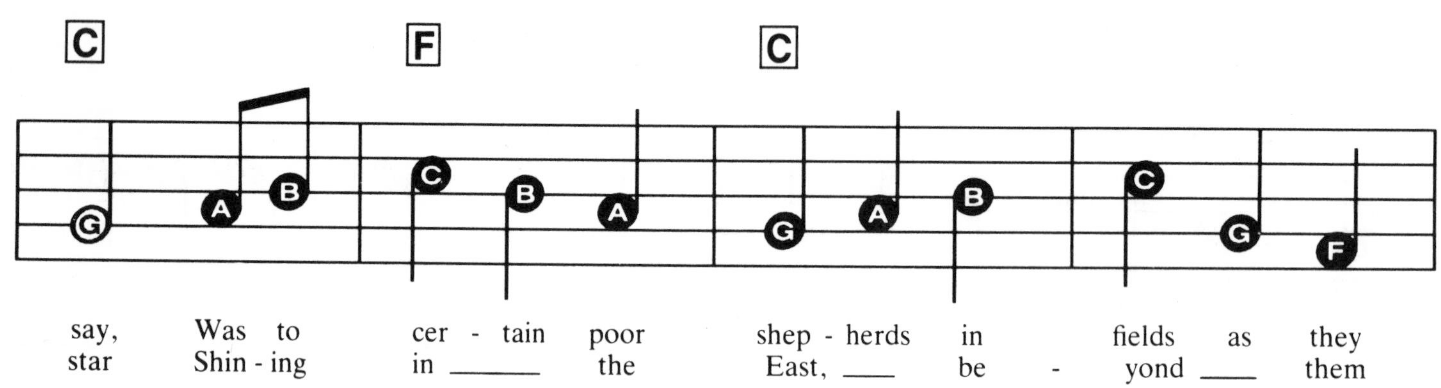

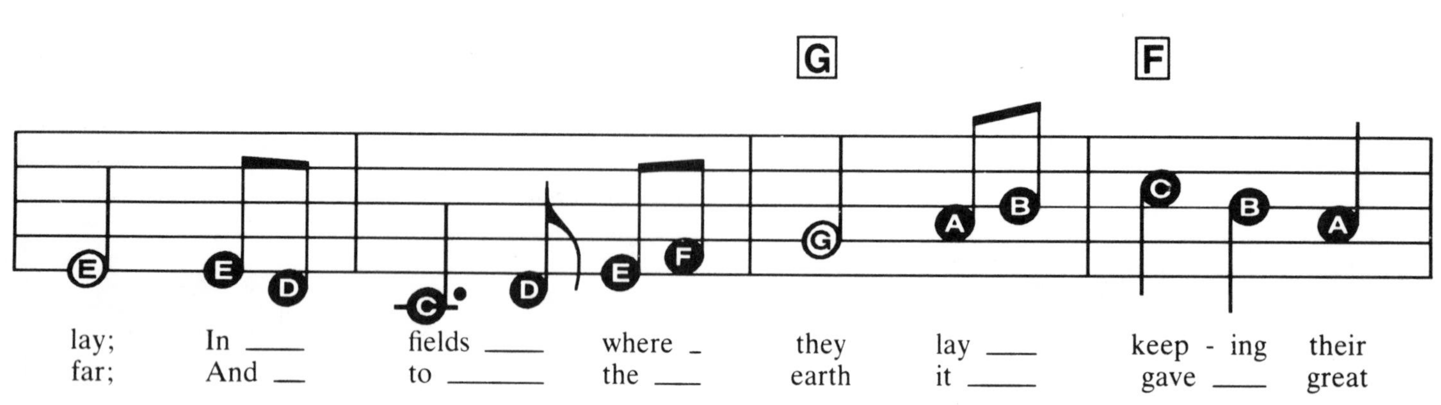

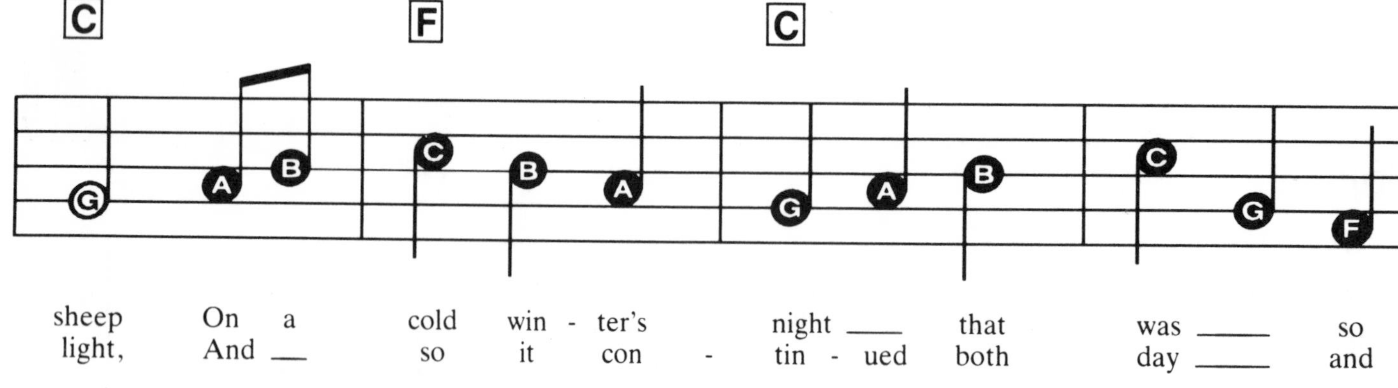

3. And by the light of that same star,
Three wise men came from country far;
To seek for a King was their intent,
And to follow the star wherever it went.
Refrain

4. This star drew nigh to the northwest,
O'er Bethlehem it took its rest;
And there it did both stop and stay,
Right over the place where Jesus lay.
Refrain

5. Then entered in those wise men three,
Full reverently upon their knee;
And offered there in His presence,
Their gold, and myrrh, and frankincense.
Refrain

FUM, FUM, FUM

OBOE
BRILLIANT SOLO
Medium MARCH

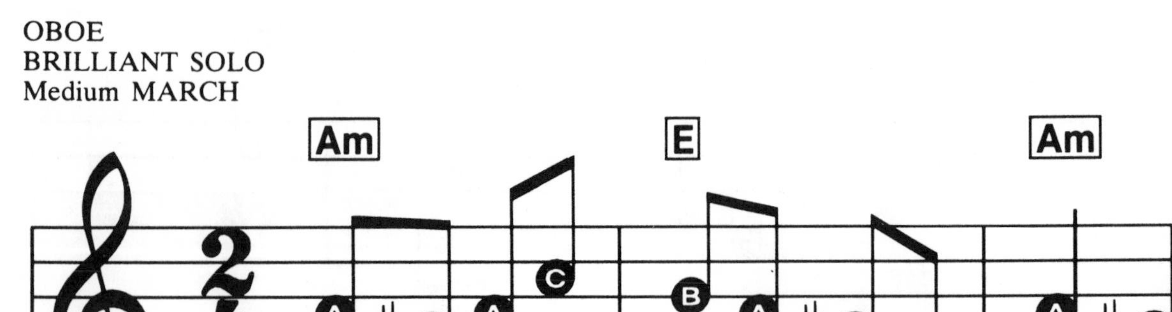
Am
E
Am

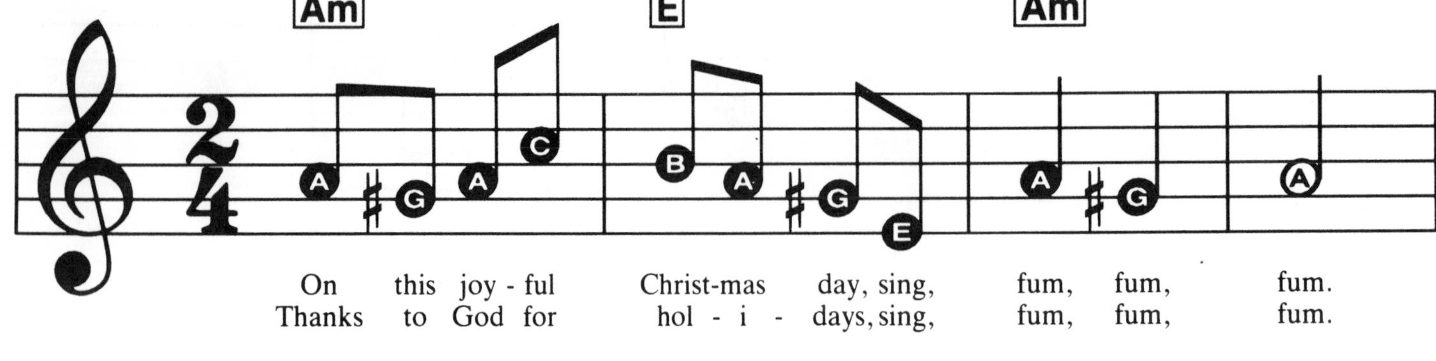
A G A C B A G E A G A
On this joy - ful Christ-mas day, sing, fum, fum, fum.
Thanks to God for hol - i - days, sing, fum, fum, fum.

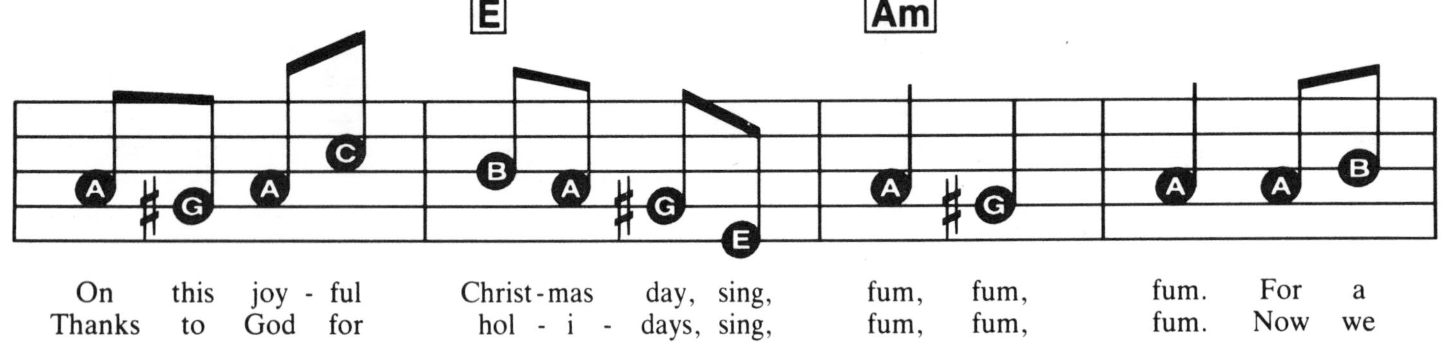
E
Am
A G A C B A G E A G A A B
On this joy - ful Christ-mas day, sing, fum, fum, fum. For a
Thanks to God for hol - i - days, sing, fum, fum, fum. Now we

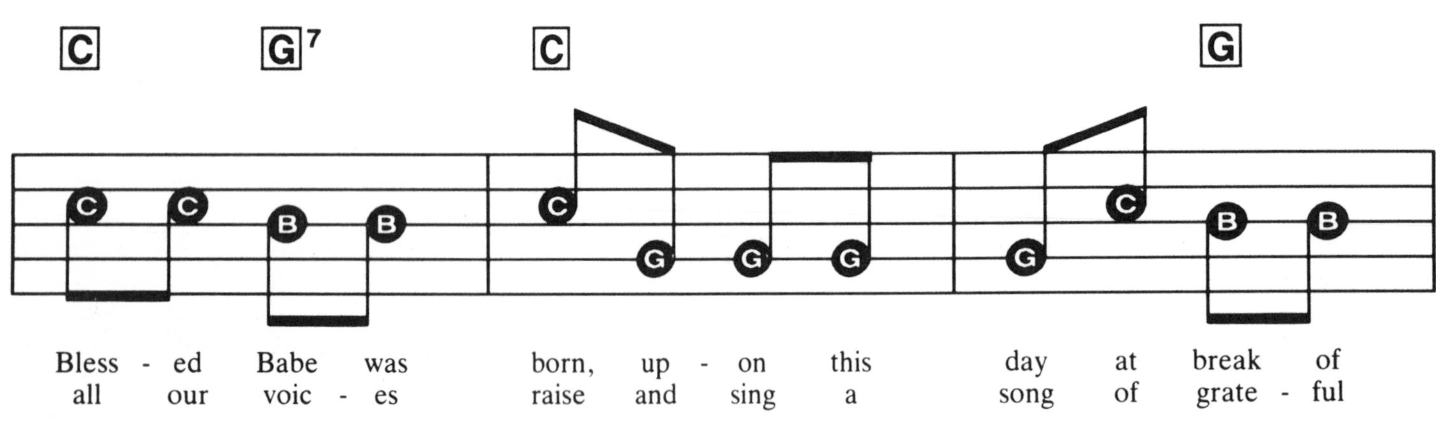
C
G7
C
G
C C B B C G G G G C B B
Bless - ed Babe was born, up - on this day at break of
all our voic - es raise and sing a song of grate - ful

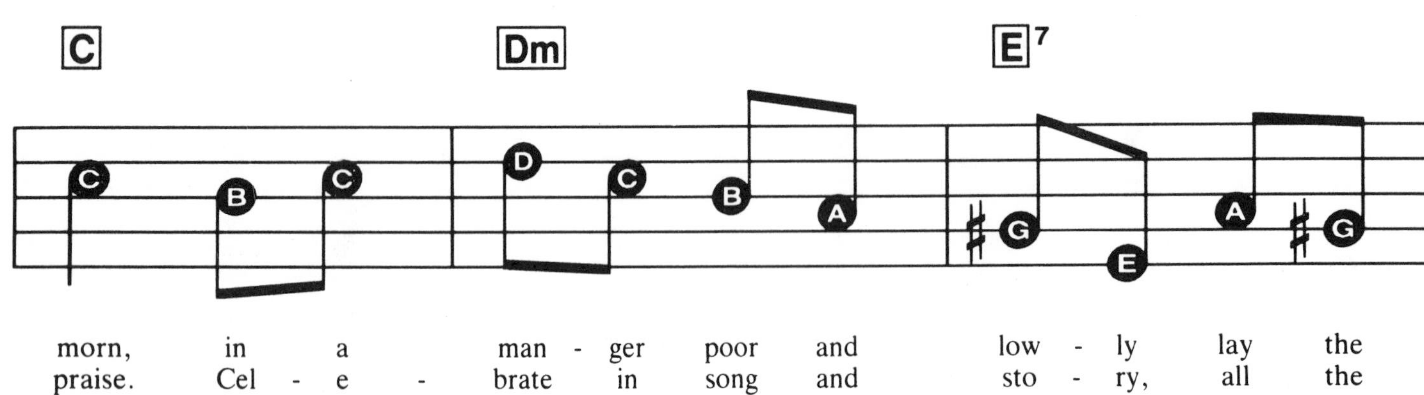
C
Dm
E7
C B C D C B A G E A G
morn, in a man - ger poor and low - ly lay the
praise. Cel - e - brate in song and sto - ry, all the

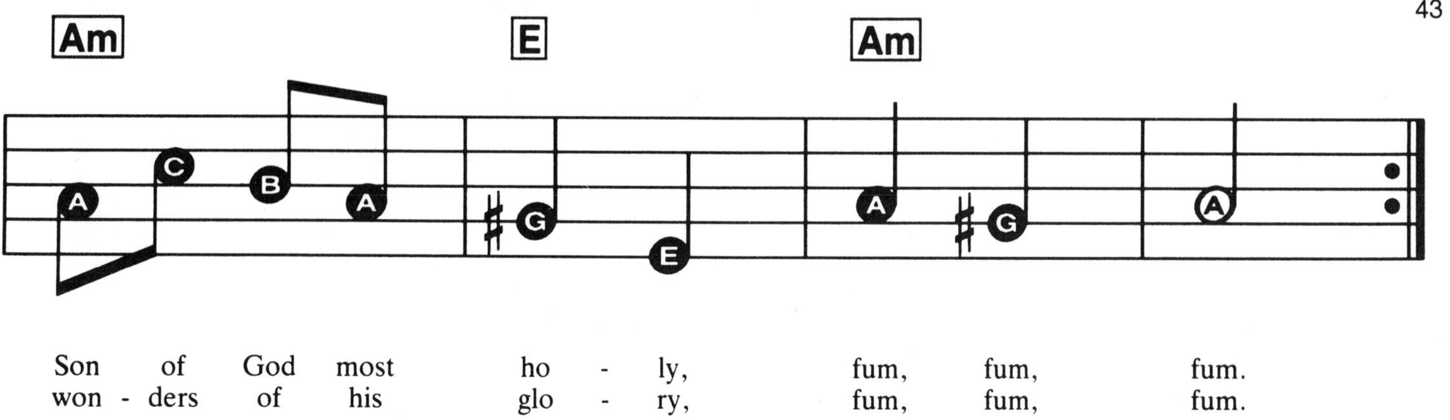

Son of God most ho - ly, fum, fum, fum.
won - ders of his glo - ry, fum, fum, fum.

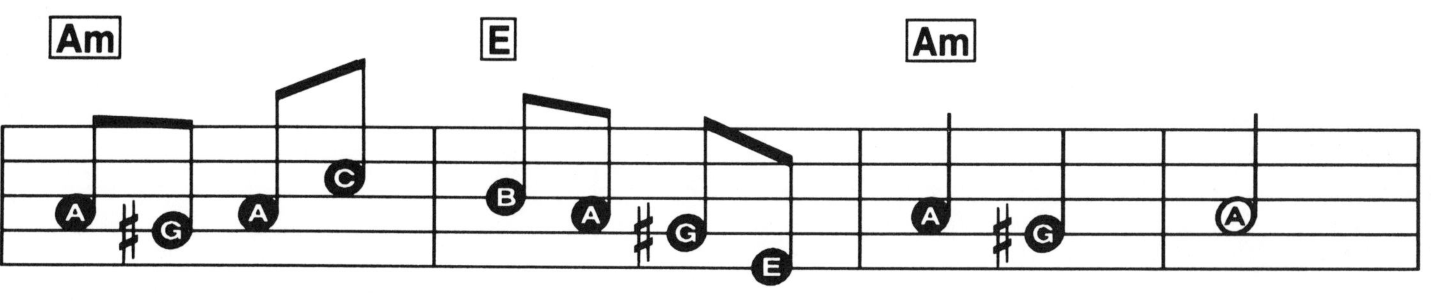

Praise we now the Lord a - bove, sing, fum, fum, fum.

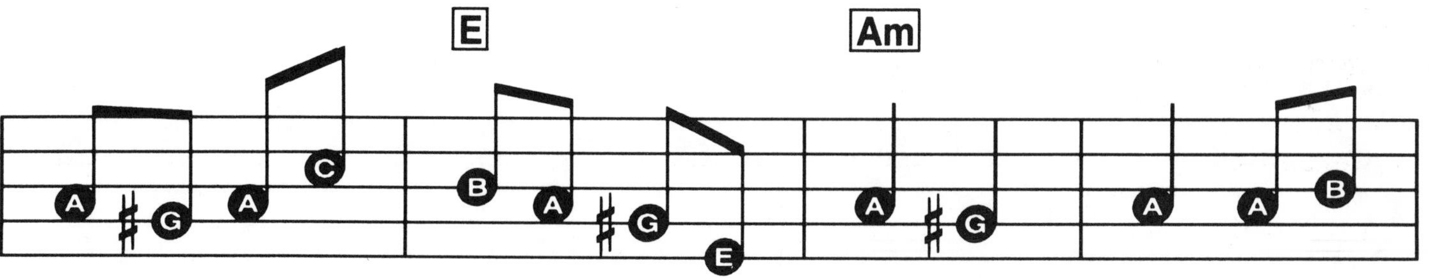

Praise we now the Lord a - bove, sing, fum, fum, fum. For up -

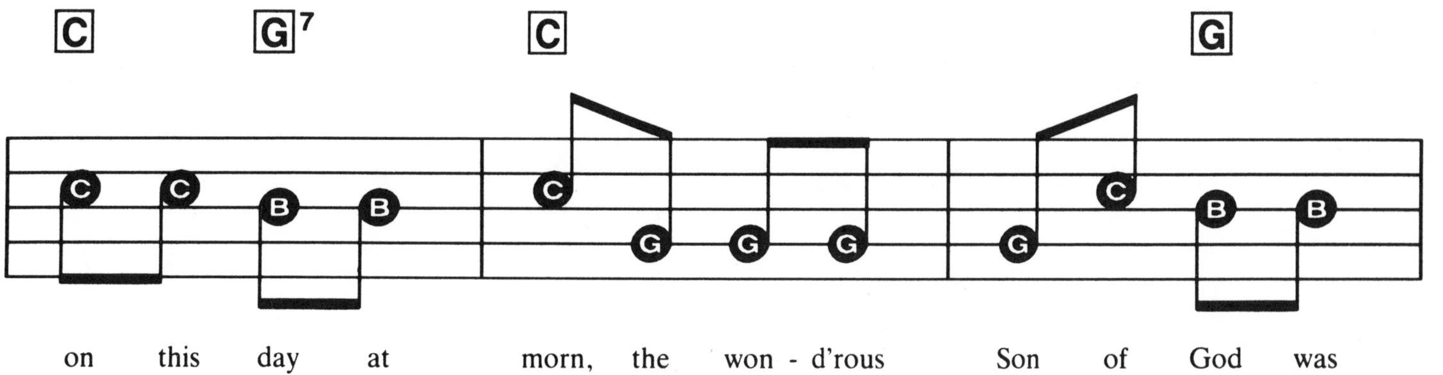

on this day at morn, the won - d'rous Son of God was

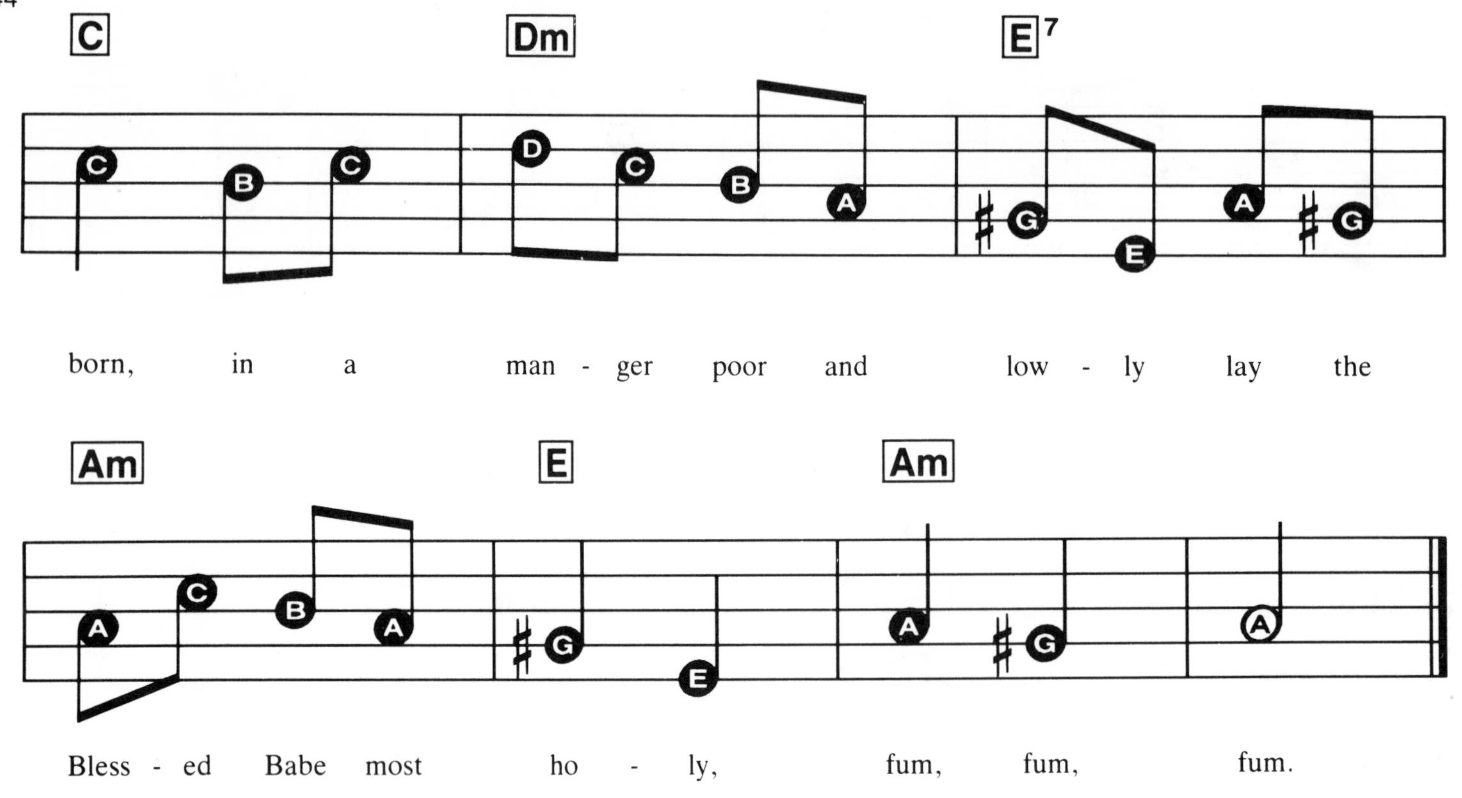
C
Dm
E7
born, in a man - ger poor and low - ly lay the
Am
E
Am
Bless - ed Babe most ho - ly, fum, fum, fum.

DECK THE HALL

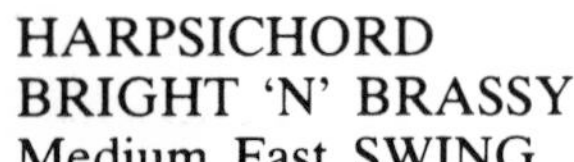
HARPSICHORD
BRIGHT 'N' BRASSY
Medium Fast SWING

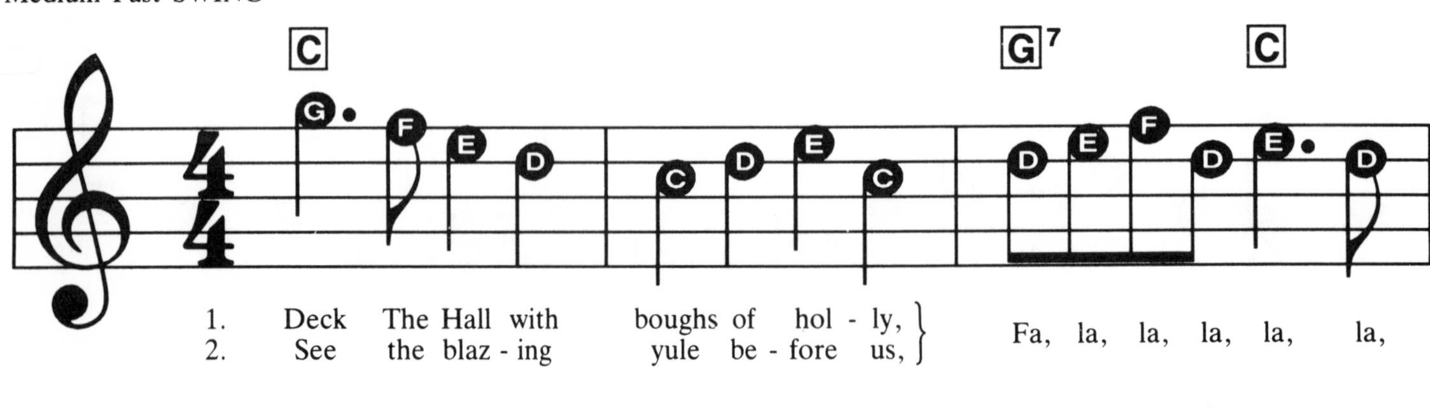
C
G7
C
1. Deck The Hall with boughs of hol - ly,
2. See the blaz - ing yule be - fore us,
Fa, la, la, la, la, la,

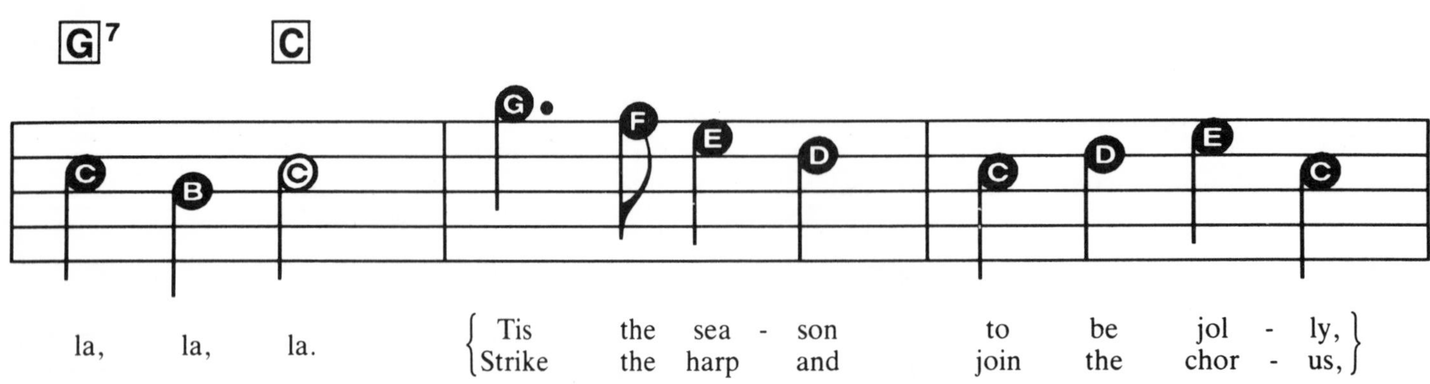
G7
C
la, la, la.
Tis the sea - son to be jol - ly,
Strike the harp and join the chor - us,

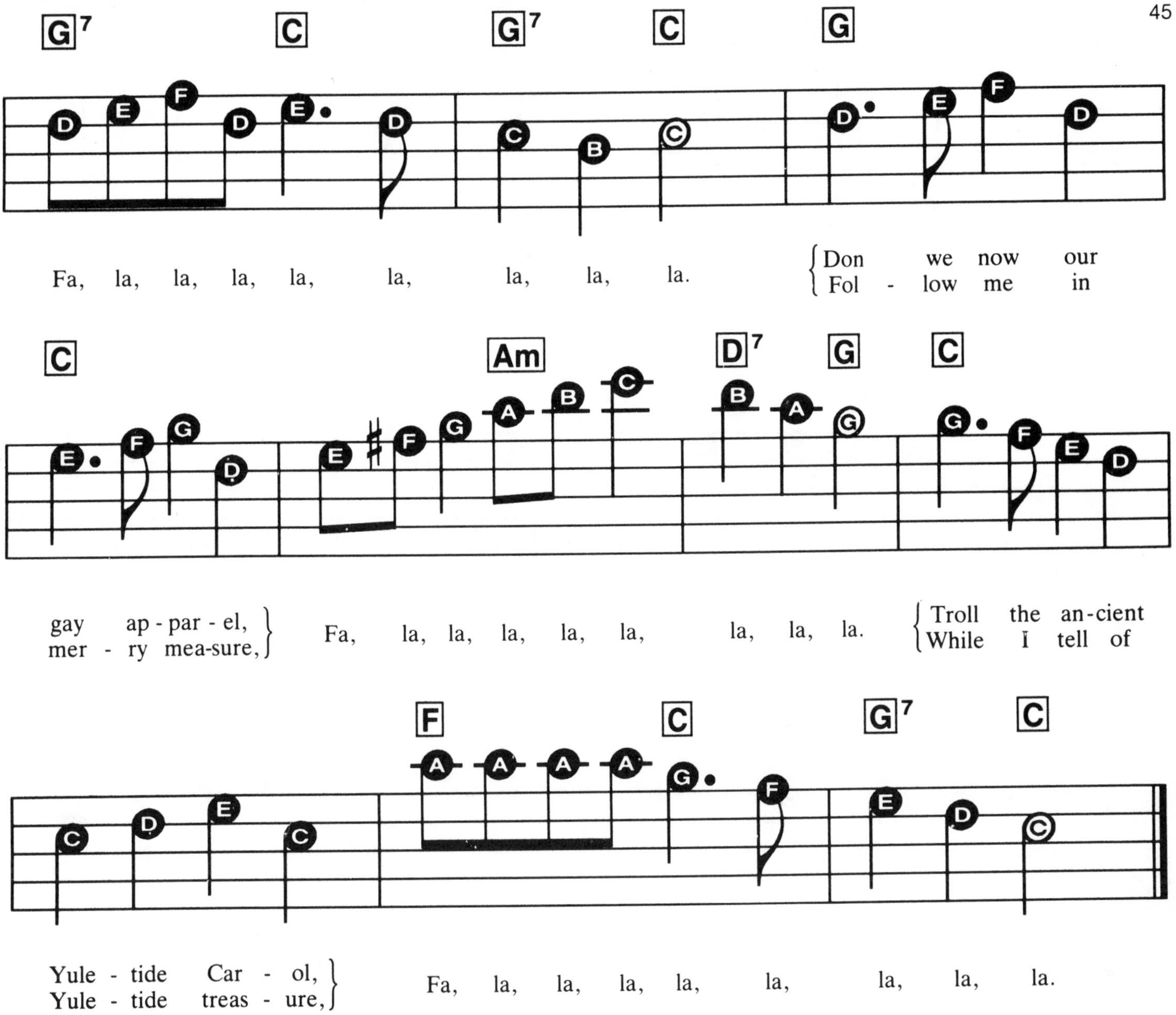

G7 C G7 C G

Fa, la, la, la, la, la, la, la, la.

{Don we now our
{Fol - low me in

C Am D7 G C

gay ap - par - el, / mer - ry mea-sure,

Fa, la, la, la, la, la, la, la, la.

{Troll the an-cient
{While I tell of

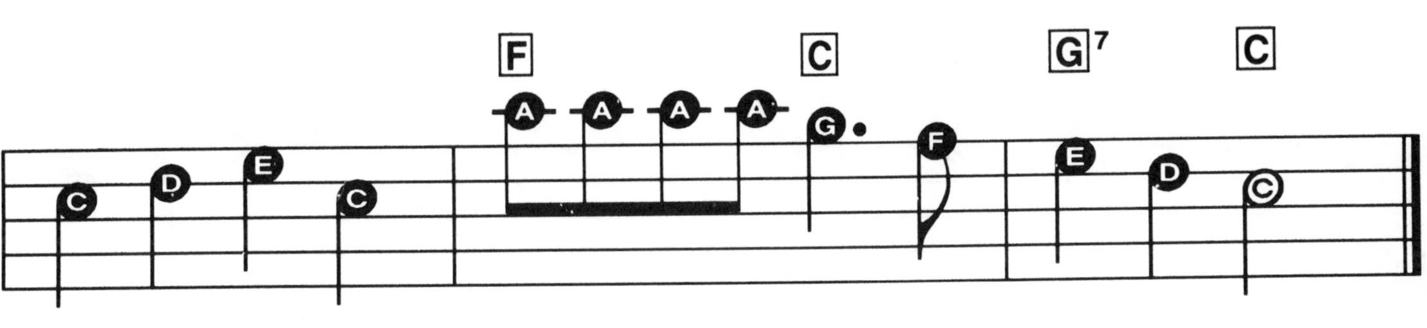
F
C
G7
C

Yule - tide Car - ol, / Yule - tide treas - ure,

Fa, la, la, la, la, la, la, la, la.

GOD REST YE MERRY, GENTLEMEN

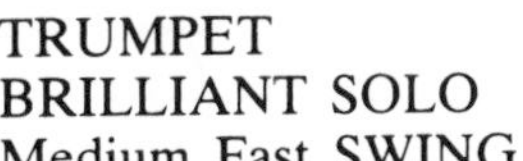
TRUMPET
BRILLIANT SOLO
Medium Fast SWING

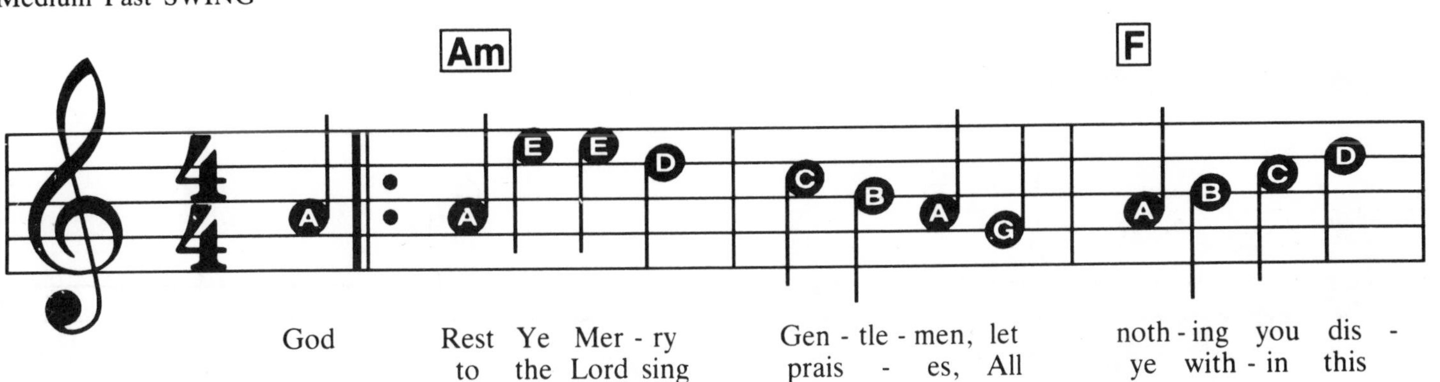
Am
F
God
Rest Ye Mer - ry
to the Lord sing
Gen - tle - men, let
prais - es, All
noth - ing you dis -
ye with - in this

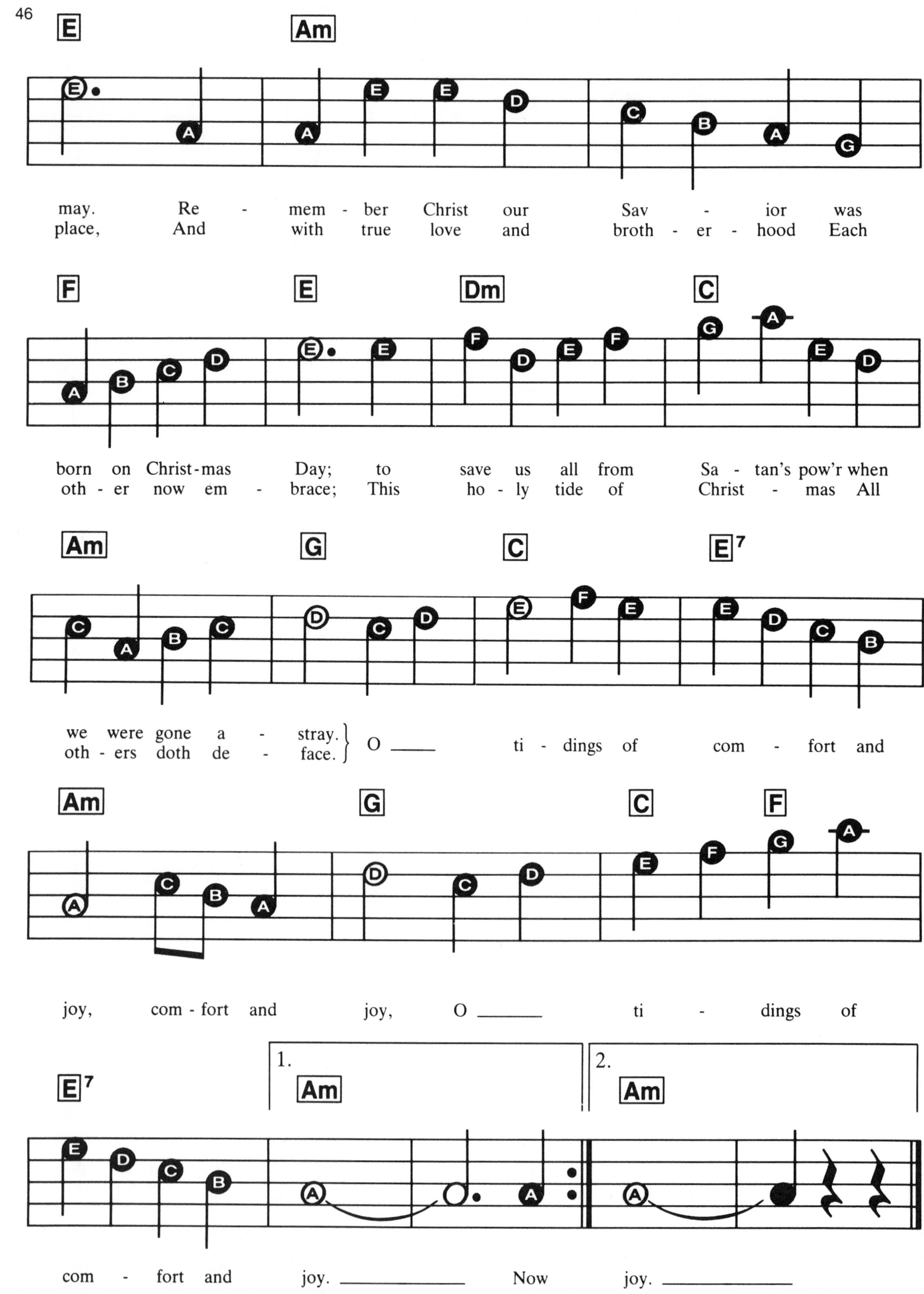
E Am
may. Re - mem - ber Christ our Sav - ior was
place, And with true love and broth - er - hood Each
F E Dm C
born on Christ-mas Day; to save us all from Sa - tan's pow'r when
oth - er now em - brace; This ho - ly tide of Christ - mas All
Am G C E7
we were gone a - stray.
oth - ers doth de - face.
O ___ ti - dings of com - fort and
Am G C F
joy, com - fort and joy, O ___ ti - dings of
E7
1. Am
2. Am
com - fort and joy. ___ Now joy. ___

FROM HEAVEN ABOVE TO EARTH I COME

ORGAN
FULL 'N' MELLOW
No Rhythm

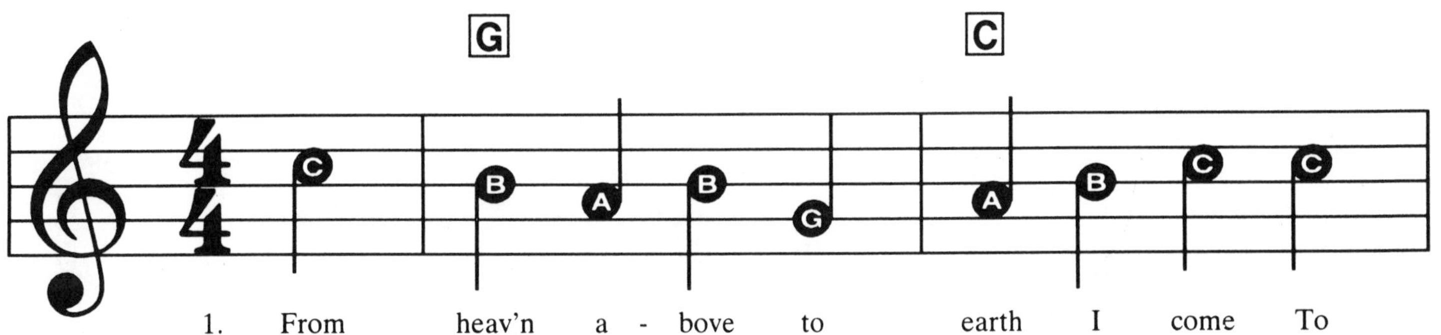

G
C
C
B
A
B
G
A
B
C
C
1. From heav'n a - bove to earth I come To

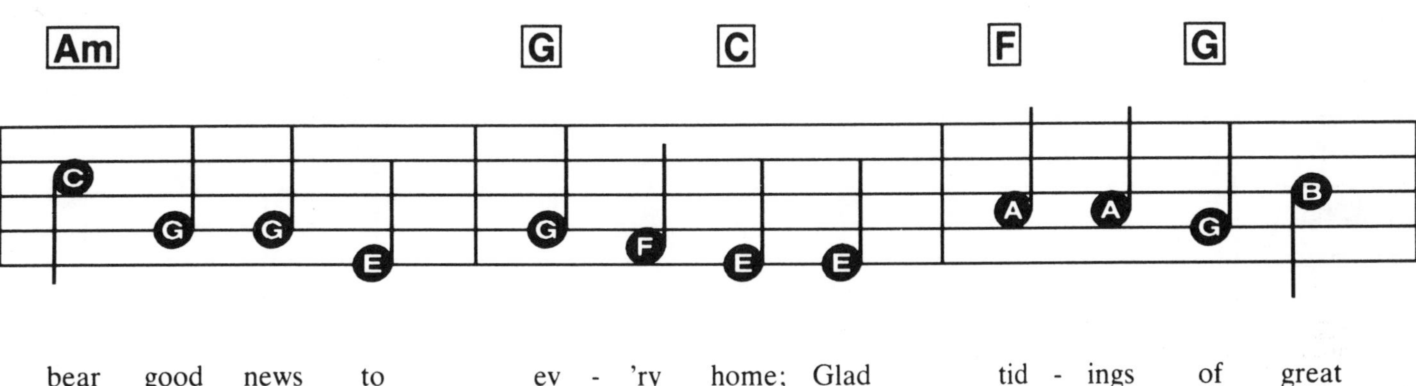

Am
G
C
F
G
C
G
G
E
G
F
E
E
A
A
G
B
bear good news to ev - 'ry home; Glad tid - ings of great

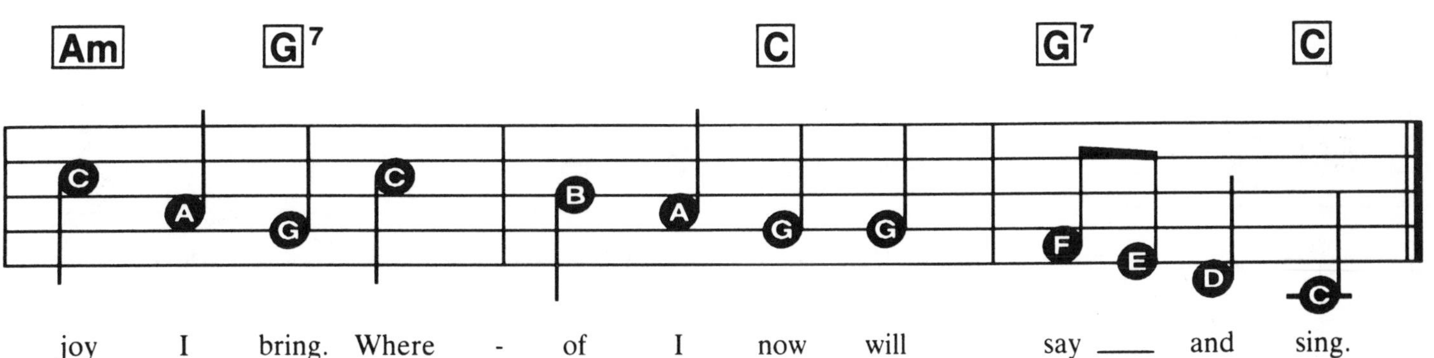

Am
G7
C
G7
C
C
A
G
C
B
A
G
G
F
E
D
C
joy I bring. Where - of I now will say ___ and sing.

2. To you this night is born a Child
Of mary, chosen virgin mild;
This little Child, of lowly birth,
Shall be the joy of all the earth.

3. This is Christ, our God and Lord,
Who in all need shall aid afford;
He will Himself your Saviour be
From all your sins to set you free.

4. Ah, dearest Jesus, holy Child,
Make Thee a bed, soft, undefiled,
Within my heart, that it may be
A quiet chamber kept for Thee.

5. Glory to God in highest heaven,
Who unto us His Son hath given!
While angels sing with pious mirth
A glad new year to all the earth.

GOOD CHRISTIAN MEN, REJOICE

FLUTE
FULL 'N' MELLOW
Medium WALTZ

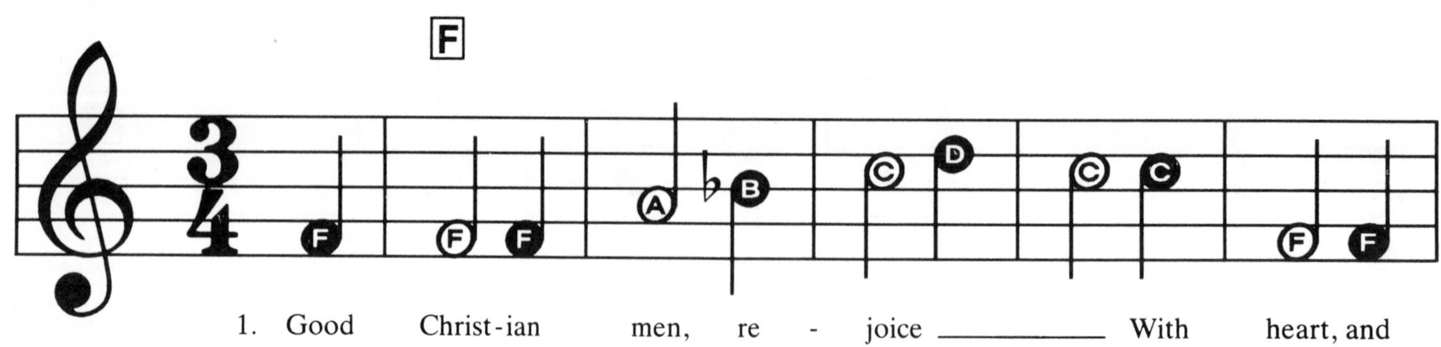
F
1. Good Christ-ian men, re - joice With heart, and

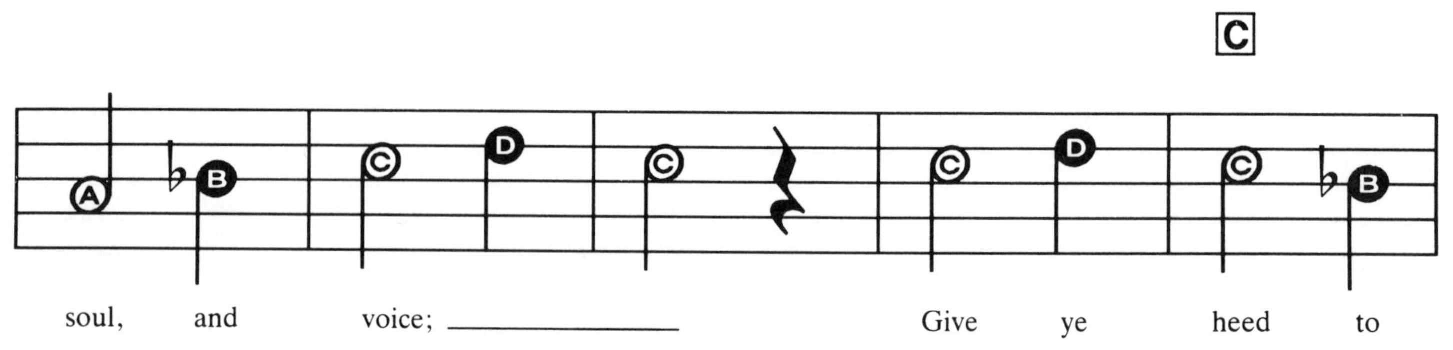
C
soul, and voice; Give ye heed to

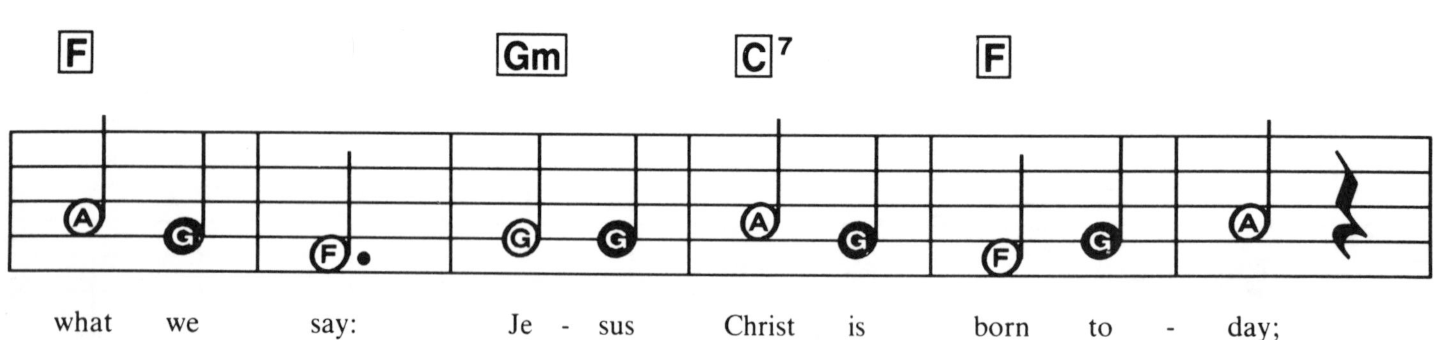
F
Gm
C7
F
what we say: Je - sus Christ is born to - day;

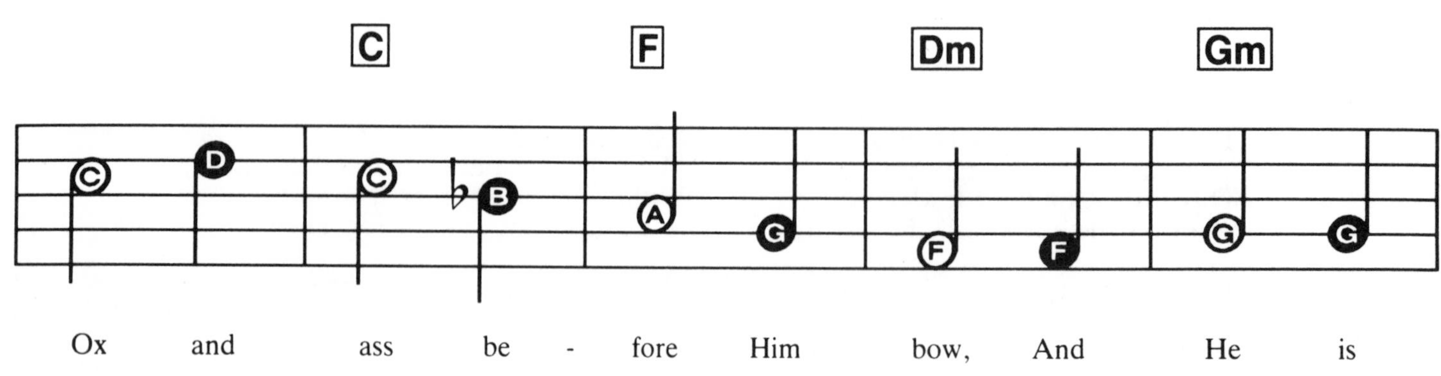
C
F
Dm
Gm
Ox and ass be - fore Him bow, And He is

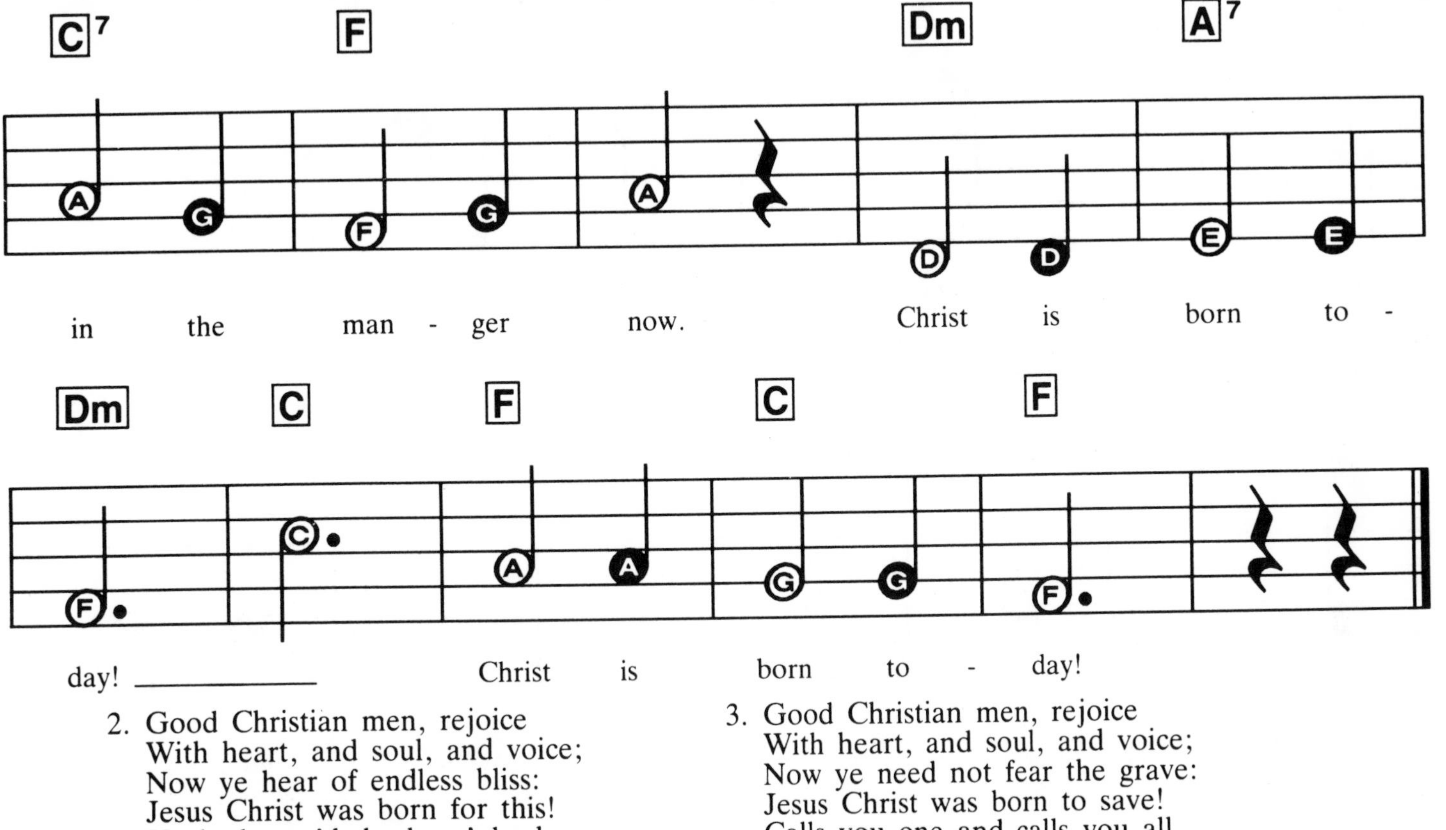
C7
F
Dm
A7
A
G
F
G
A
D
D
E
E
in the man - ger now. Christ is born to -
Dm
C
F
C
F
F
C
A
A
G
G
F
day! Christ is born to - day!

2. Good Christian men, rejoice
With heart, and soul, and voice;
Now ye hear of endless bliss:
Jesus Christ was born for this!
He hath ope'd the heav'nly door,
And man is blessed evermore.
Christ was born for this!
Christ was born for this!

3. Good Christian men, rejoice
With heart, and soul, and voice;
Now ye need not fear the grave:
Jesus Christ was born to save!
Calls you one and calls you all
To gain His everlasting hall.
Christ was born to save!
Christ was born to save!

GOOD KING WENCESLAS

FLUTE
FULL 'N' MELLOW
Medium MARCH

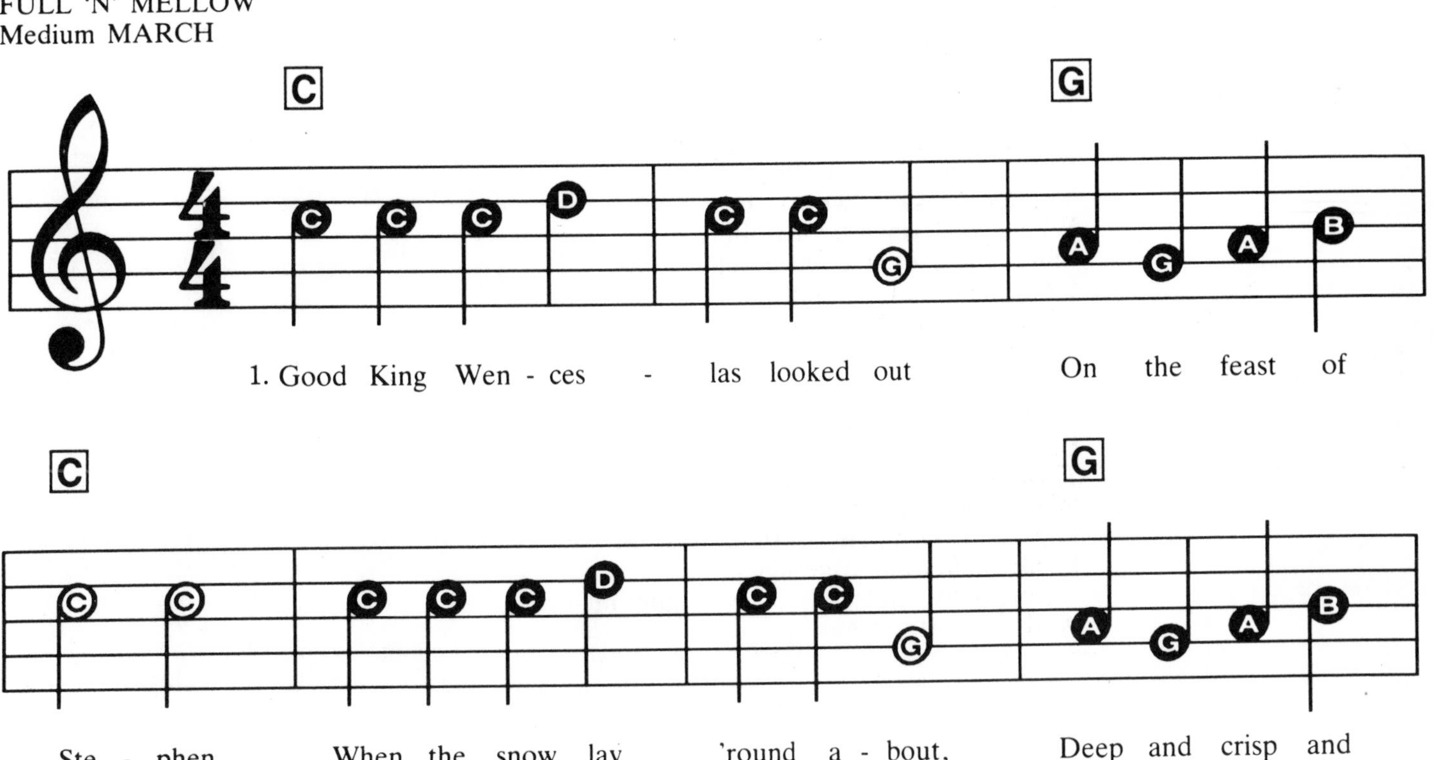
C
G
C
C
C
D
C
C
G
A
G
A
B
1. Good King Wen - ces - las looked out On the feast of
C
G
C
C
C
C
C
D
C
C
G
A
G
A
B
Ste - phen, When the snow lay 'round a - bout, Deep and crisp and

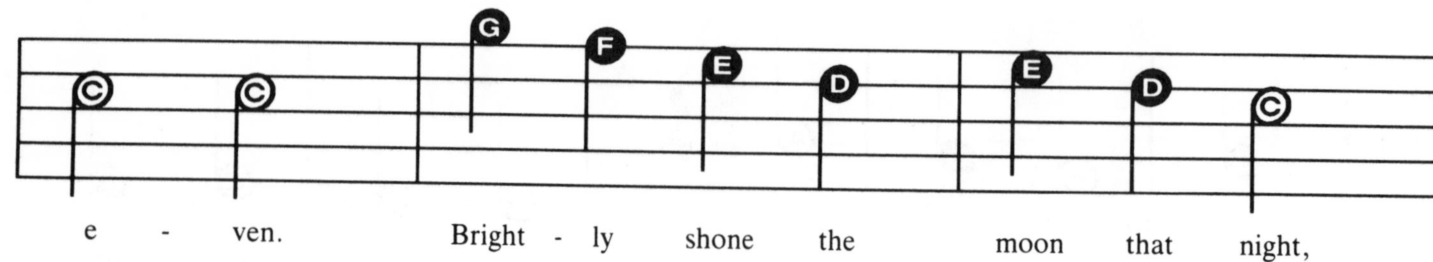
C
C C G F E D E D C
e - ven. Bright - ly shone the moon that night,

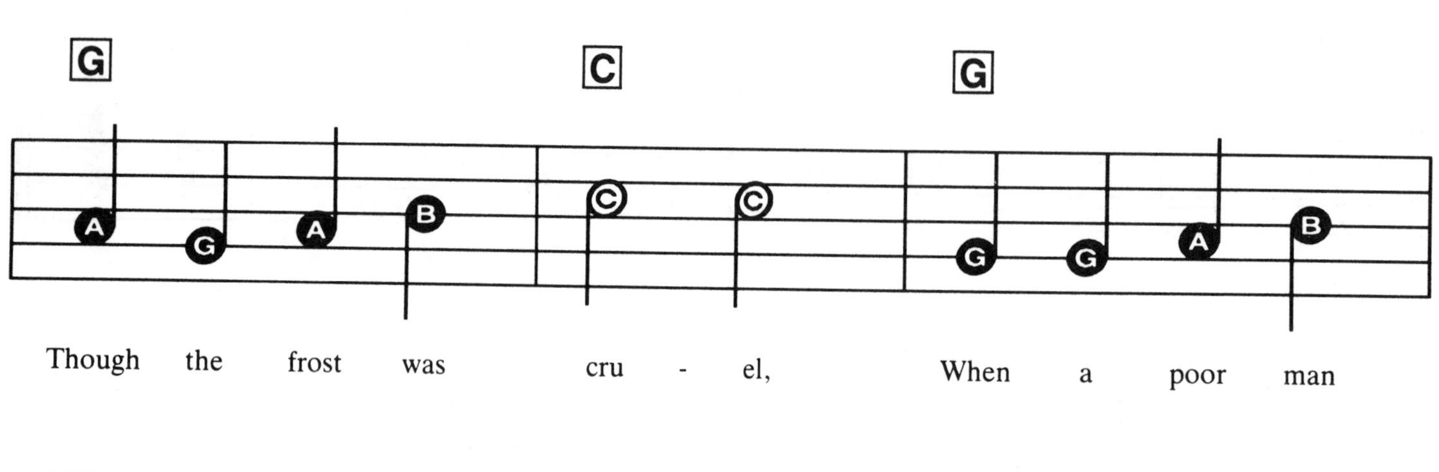
G C G
A G A B C C G G A B
Though the frost was cru - el, When a poor man

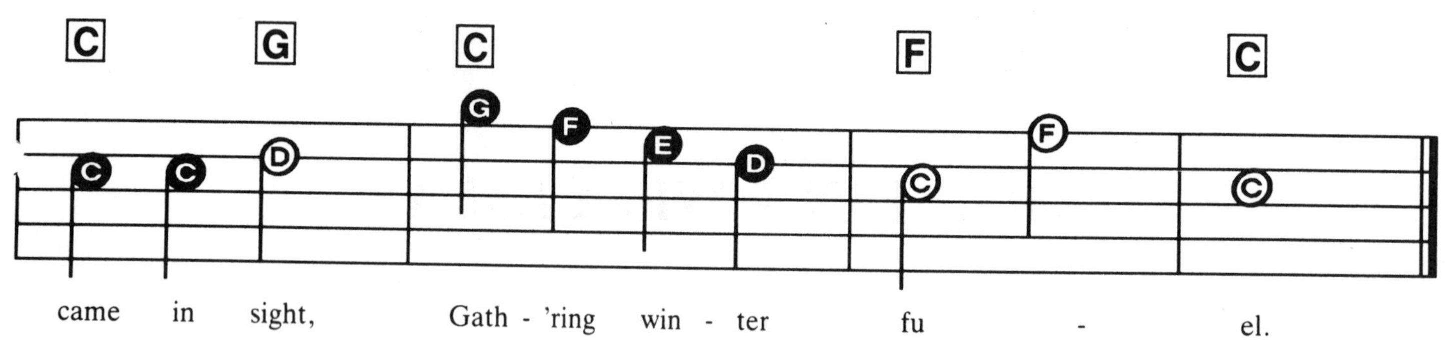
C G C F C
C C D G F E D C F C
came in sight, Gath - 'ring win - ter fu - el.

2. "Hither, page, and stand by me,
If thou know'st it telling,
Yonder peasant, who is he?
Where and what his dwelling?"
"Sire, he lives a good league hence,
Underneath the mountain,
Right against the forest fence,
By St. Agnes' fountain."

3. "Bring me flesh, and bring me wine,
Bring me pine logs hither;
Thou and I will see him dine,
When we bear them thither."
Page and monarch, forth they went,
Forth they went together;
Through the rude wind's wild lament,
And the bitter weather.

GO TELL IT ON THE MOUNTAIN

CLARINET
BRILLIANT SOLO
Medium SWING

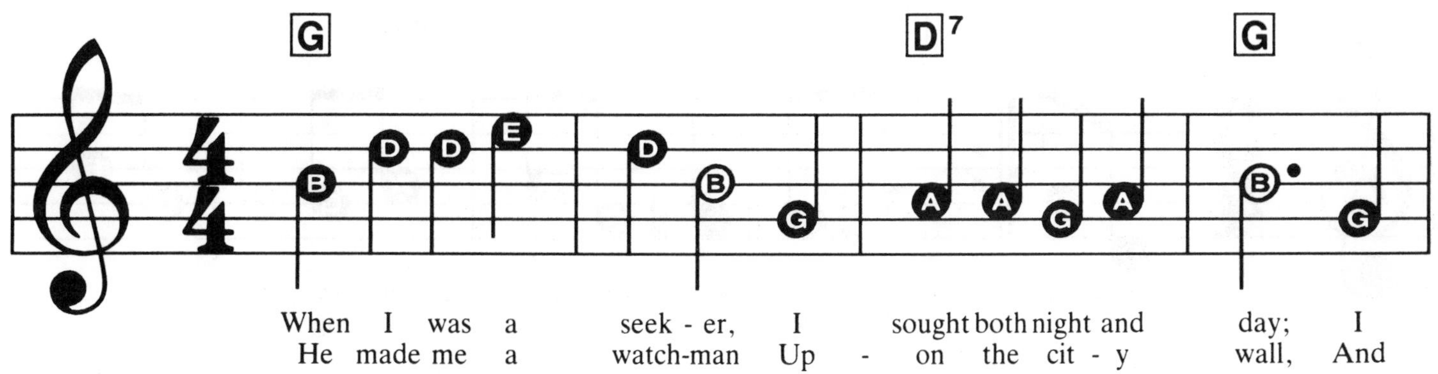
G
D7
G
When I was a seek - er, I sought both night and day; I
He made me a watch-man Up - on the cit - y wall, And

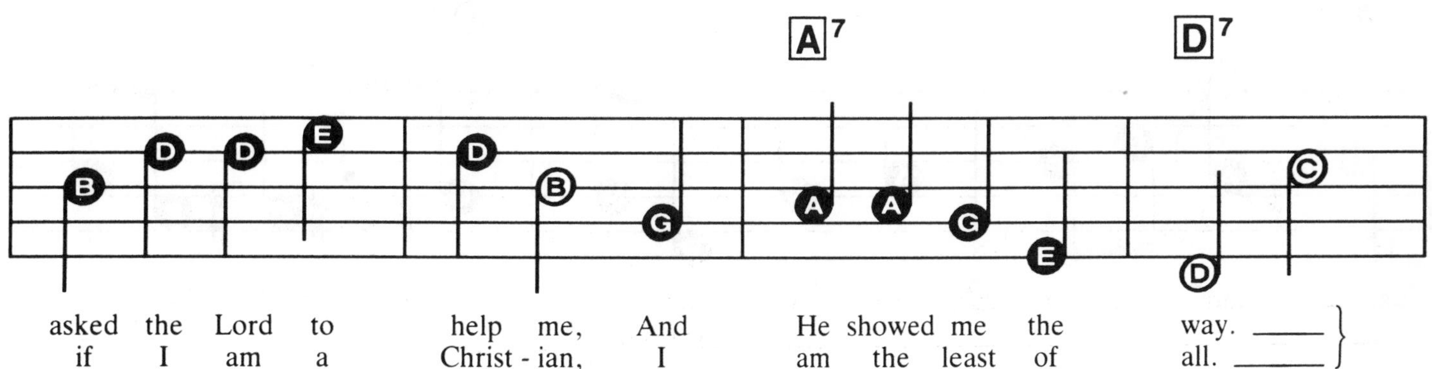
A7
D7
asked the Lord to help me, And He showed me the way.
if I am a Christ - ian, I am the least of all.

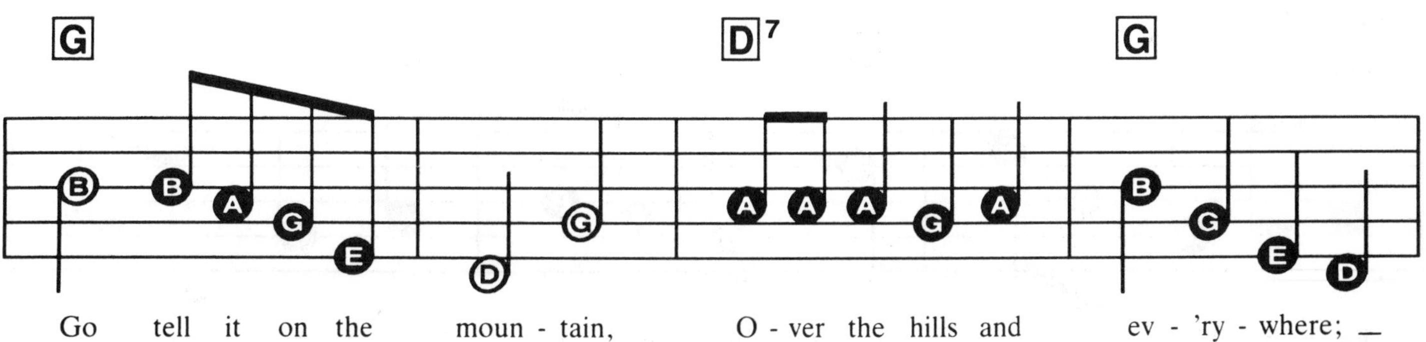
G
D7
G
Go tell it on the moun - tain, O - ver the hills and ev - 'ry - where;

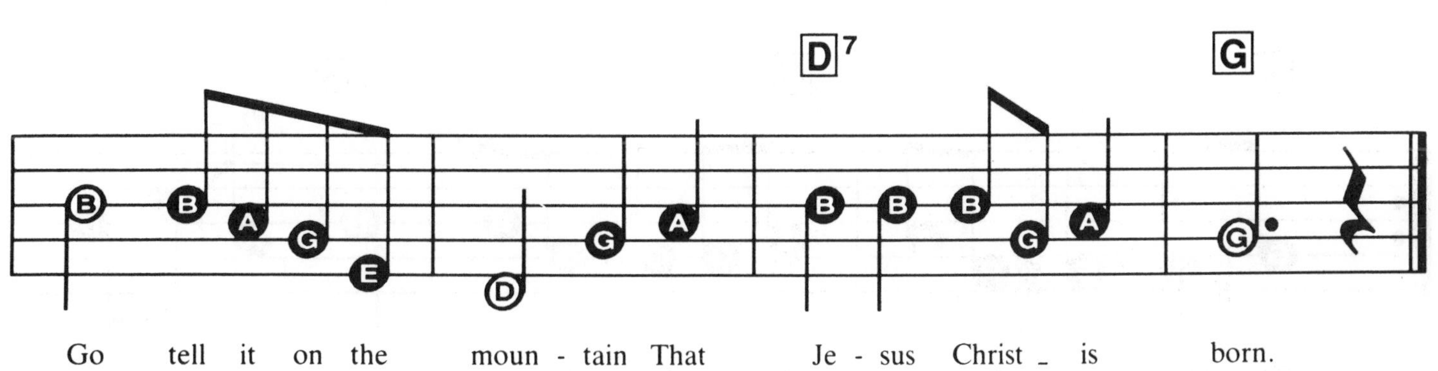
D7
G
Go tell it on the moun - tain That Je - sus Christ is born.

GLAD CHRISTMAS BELLS

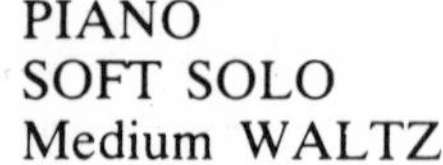
PIANO
SOFT SOLO
Medium WALTZ

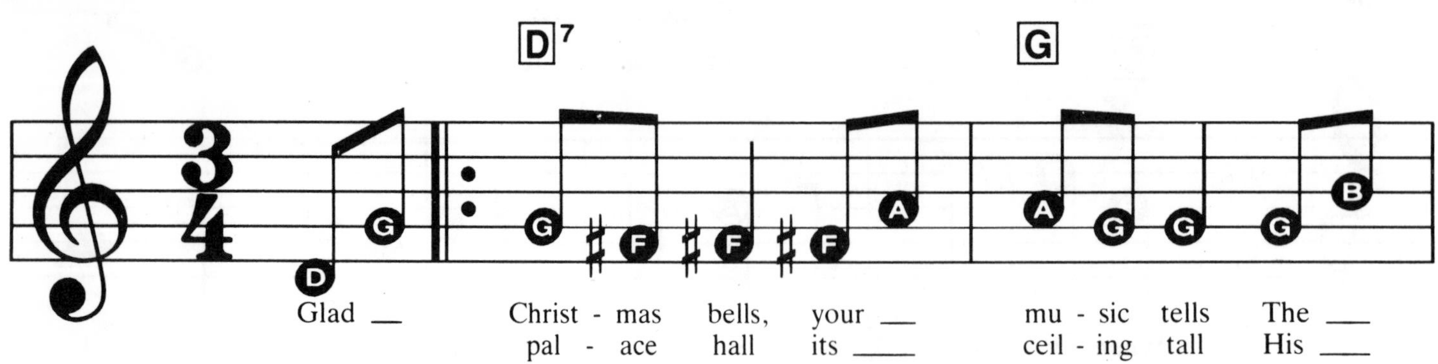
D7
G
Glad __ Christ - mas bells, your __ mu - sic tells The __
pal - ace hall its __ ceil - ing tall His __

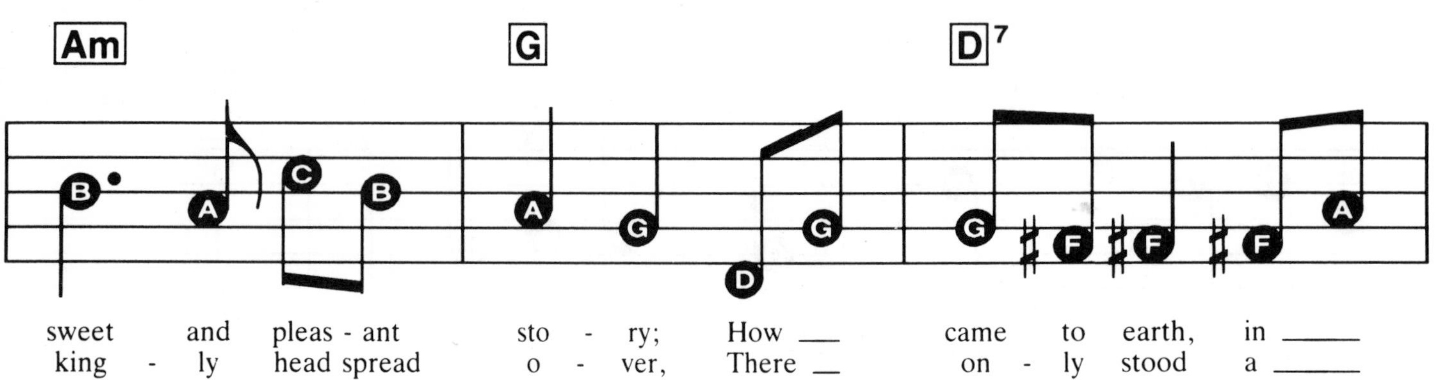
Am
G
D7
sweet and pleas - ant sto - ry; How __ came to earth, in __
king - ly head spread o - ver, There __ on - ly stood a __

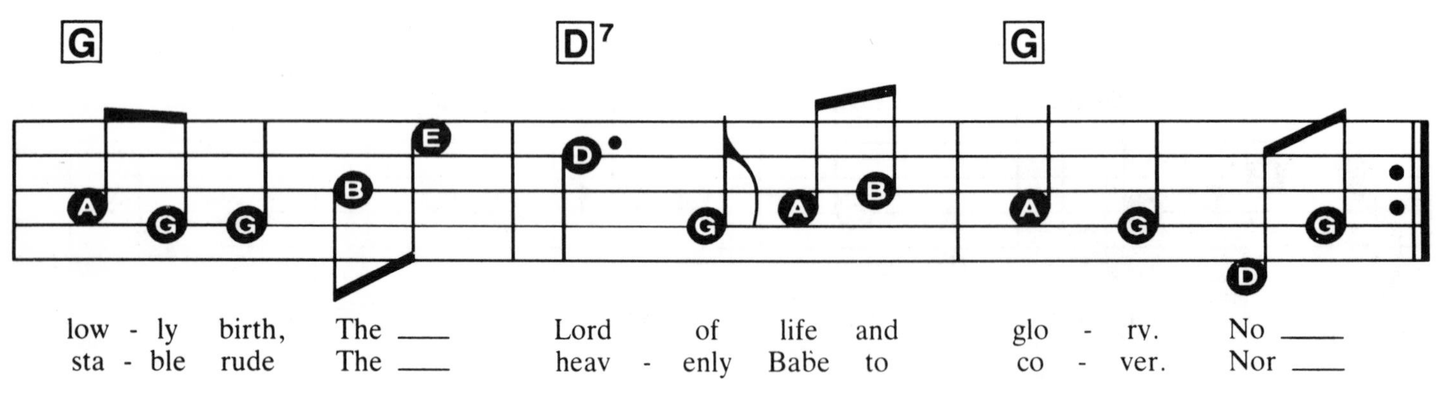
G
D7
G
low - ly birth, The __ Lord of life and glo - ry. No __
sta - ble rude The __ heav - enly Babe to co - ver. Nor __

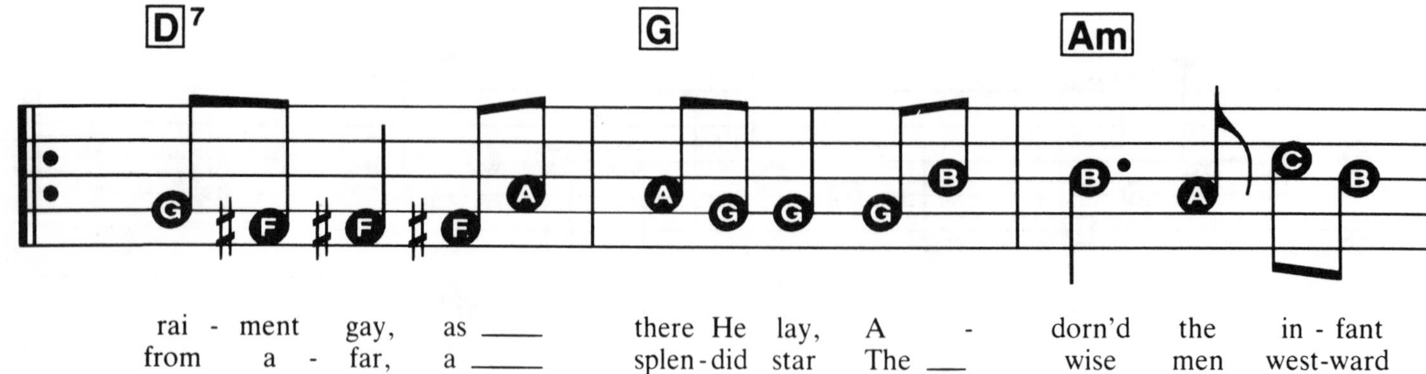
D7
G
Am
rai - ment gay, as __ there He lay, A - dorn'd the in - fant
from a - far, a __ splen - did star The __ wise men west-ward

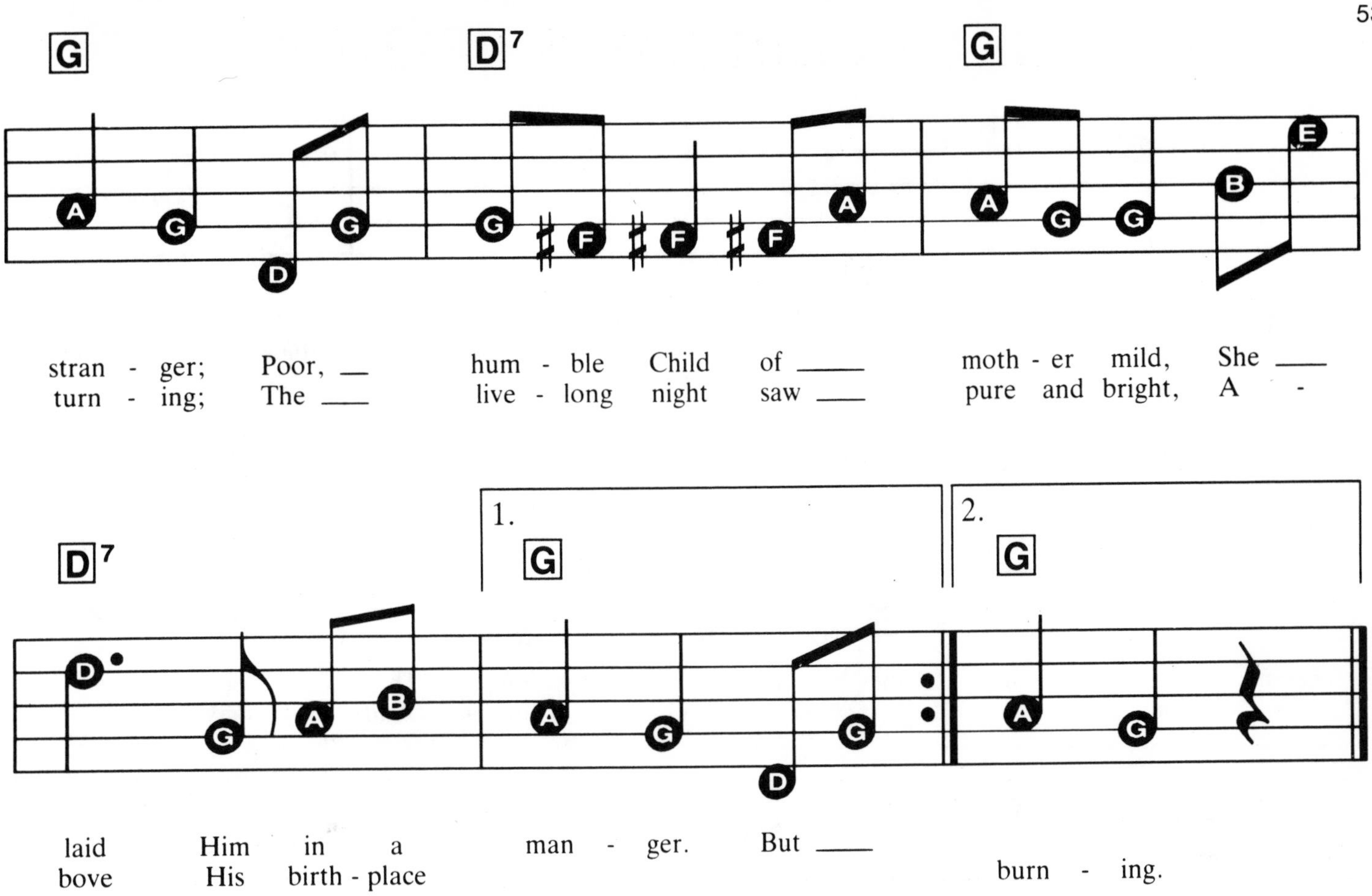

G D7 G

stran - ger; Poor, ___ hum - ble Child of ___ moth - er mild, She ___
turn - ing; The ___ live - long night saw ___ pure and bright, A -

D7 1. G 2. G

laid Him in a man - ger. But ___
bove His birth - place burn - ing.

THE GOLDEN CAROL

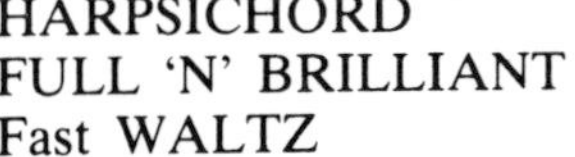
HARPSICHORD
FULL 'N' BRILLIANT
Fast WALTZ

Cm
Ab
1. We saw a light shine out a -
2. Oh, ev - er thought be of his
Cm
G
Cm
far, On Christ - mas in the morn - ing, And
name, On Christ - mas in the morn - ing, Who

A♭ Cm
straight we knew it was Christ's star, Bright
bore for us both grief and shame, Af -
G Cm Fm
beam - ing in the morn - ing, Then did we
flic - tions sharp - est scorn - ing, And may we
Cm G A♭
fall on bend - ed knee, On Christ - mas in the
die, when death shall come, On Christ - mas in the
Cm G G7 Cm
morn - ing, And praised the Lord, who'd let us
morn - ing, And see in heav'n, our glo - rious
G Fm G7 Cm
see his glo - ry at the dawn - ing.
home, That Star of Christ - mas morn - ing.

GRANDMA GOT RUN OVER BY A REINDEER

GUITAR
FULL 'N' BRILLIANT
Medium SWING or ROCK

Words and Music by
RANDY BROOKS

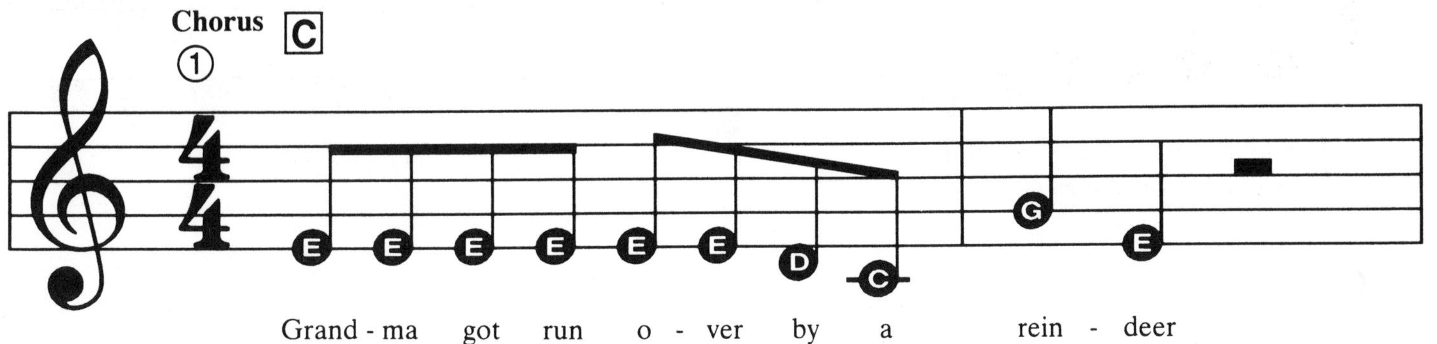

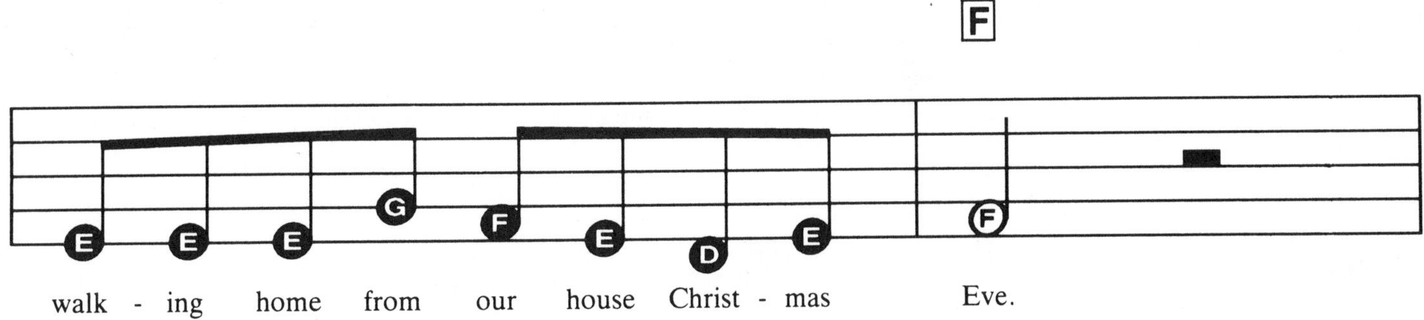

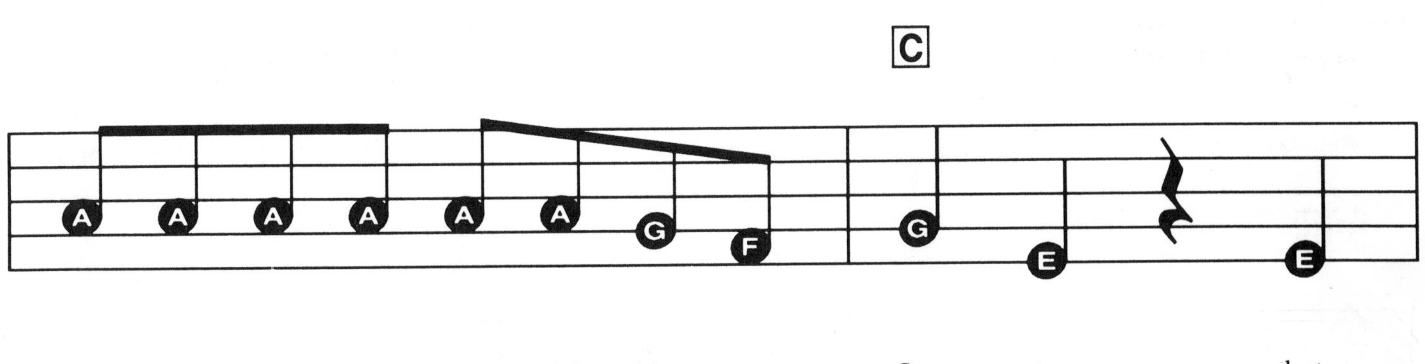

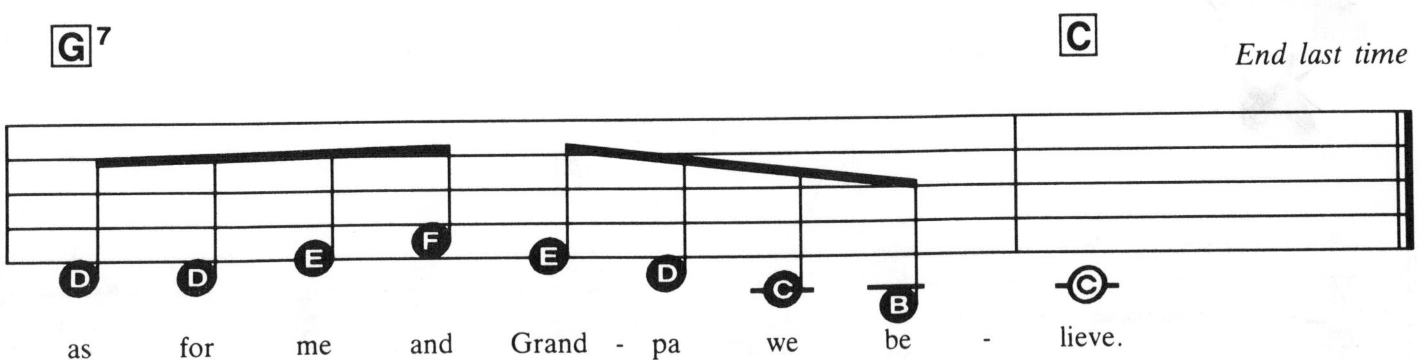

Verse
G7
1. She'd been drink-ing too much egg nog, and we begged her not to
2. 3. (See additional lyrics)
C
F
go, but she for - got her med - i - ca - tion, and she
G7
C
Am
stag-gered out the door in - to the snow. When we found her Christ-mas
Em
G7
C
morn - ing at the scene of the at - tack,
F
she had hoof - prints on her fore - head, and in -

Return to ① for additional lyrics.
Last time, return to ① and play to End.

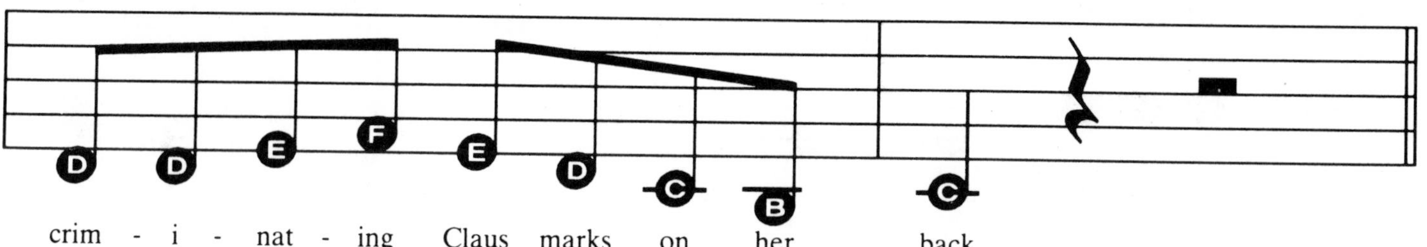
G7
D D E F E D C B C
crim - i - nat - ing Claus marks on her back.

Verse 2:
Now we're all so proud of Grandpa,
He's been taking this so well.
See him in there watching football,
Drinking beer and playing cards with Cousin Mel.
It's not Christmas without Grandma.
All the family's dressed in black,
And we just can't help but wonder:
Should we open up her gifts or send them back?

(To Chorus:)

Verse 3:
Now the goose is on the table,
And the pudding made of fig,
And the blue and silver candles,
That would just have matched the hair in Grandma's wig.
I've warned all my friends and neighbors,
Better watch out for yourselves.
They should never give a license
To a man who drives a sleigh and plays with elves.

(To Chorus:)

HARK! THE HERALD ANGELS SING

ORGAN
CLASSICAL
Medium Fast SWING

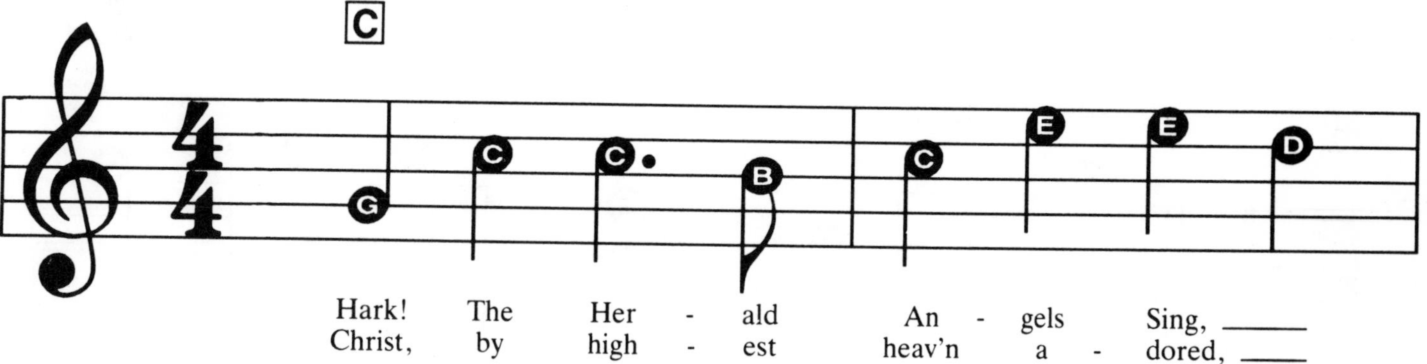
C
G C C B C E E D
Hark! The Her - ald An - gels Sing,
Christ, by high - est heav'n a - dored,

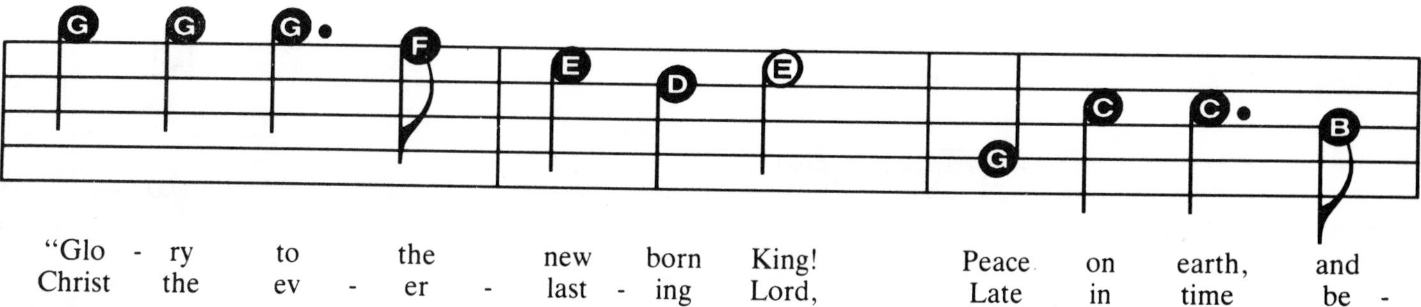
G G G F E D E G C C B
"Glo - ry to the new born King! Peace on earth, and
Christ the ev - er - last - ing Lord, Late in time be -

G
mer - cy mild, God and sin - ners re - con - ciled."
hold Him come, Off - spring of the Vir - gin's womb.
C G7 C
Joy - ful all ye na - tions rise, join the tri - umph
Veiled in flesh the God - head see. Hail th'in - car - nate
G7 F Dm
of the skies; with th'an - gel - ic host pro - claim,
De - i - ty Pleased as man with man to dwell,
G7 C F
"Christ is born in Beth - le - hem."
Je - sus our Im - man - u - el.
Hark! The Her - ald
Dm G7 C G7 C
An - gels Sing, "Glo - ry to the new born King."

HERE COMES SANTA CLAUS
(Right Down Santa Claus Lane)

TRUMPET
BIG 'N' BOLD
Fast SWING

Words and Music by
GENE AUTRY and
OAKLEY HALDEMAN

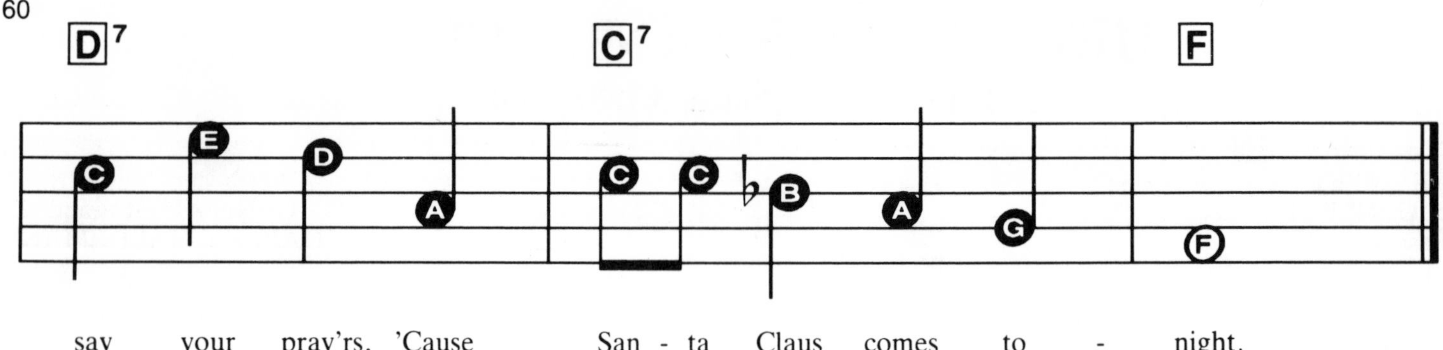
D7
C7
F
C E D A C C B A G F
say your pray'rs, 'Cause San - ta Claus comes to - night.

THE HOLLY AND THE IVY

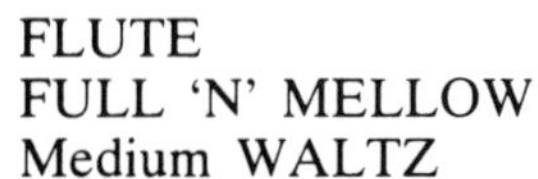
FLUTE
FULL 'N' MELLOW
Medium WALTZ

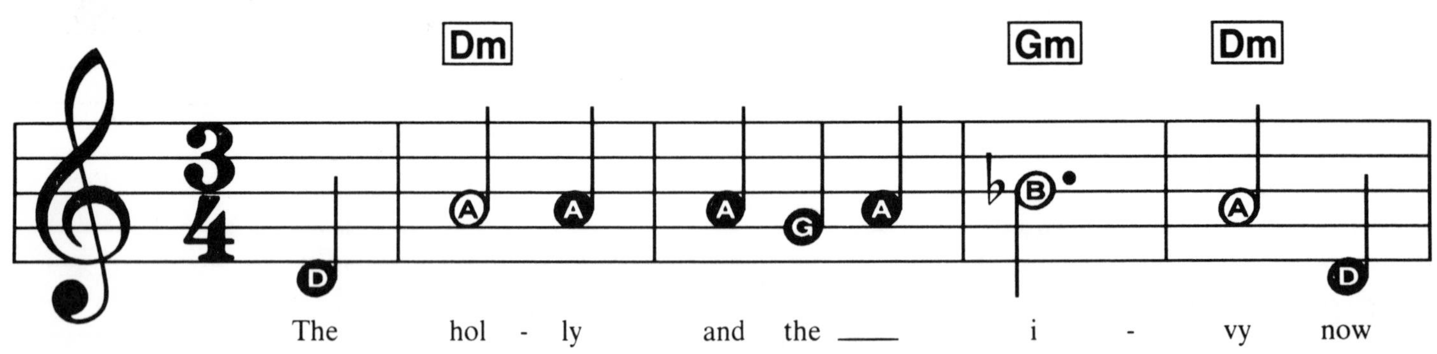
Dm
Gm
Dm
D A A A G A B A D
The hol - ly and the ___ i - vy now

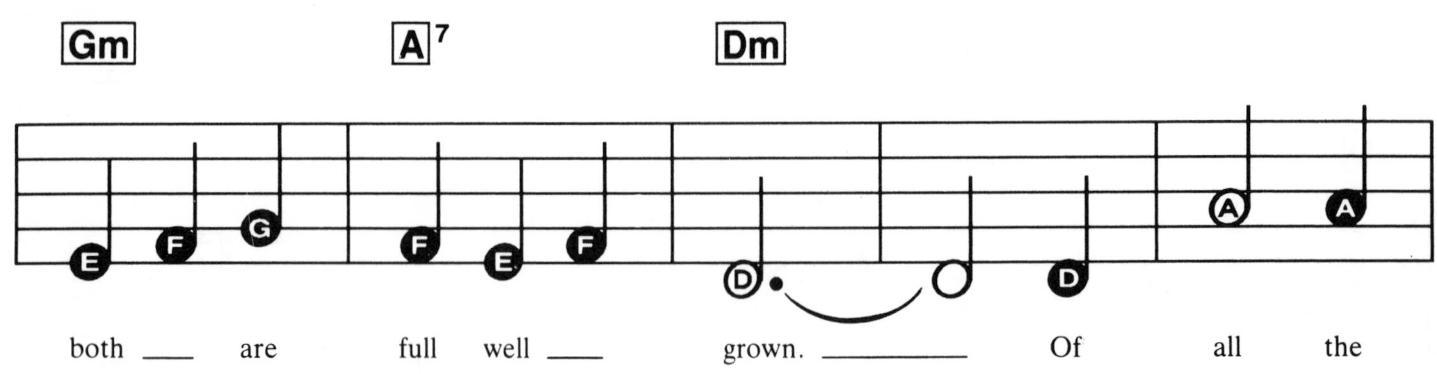
Gm
A7
Dm
E F G F E F D D A A
both ___ are full well ___ grown. _________ Of all the

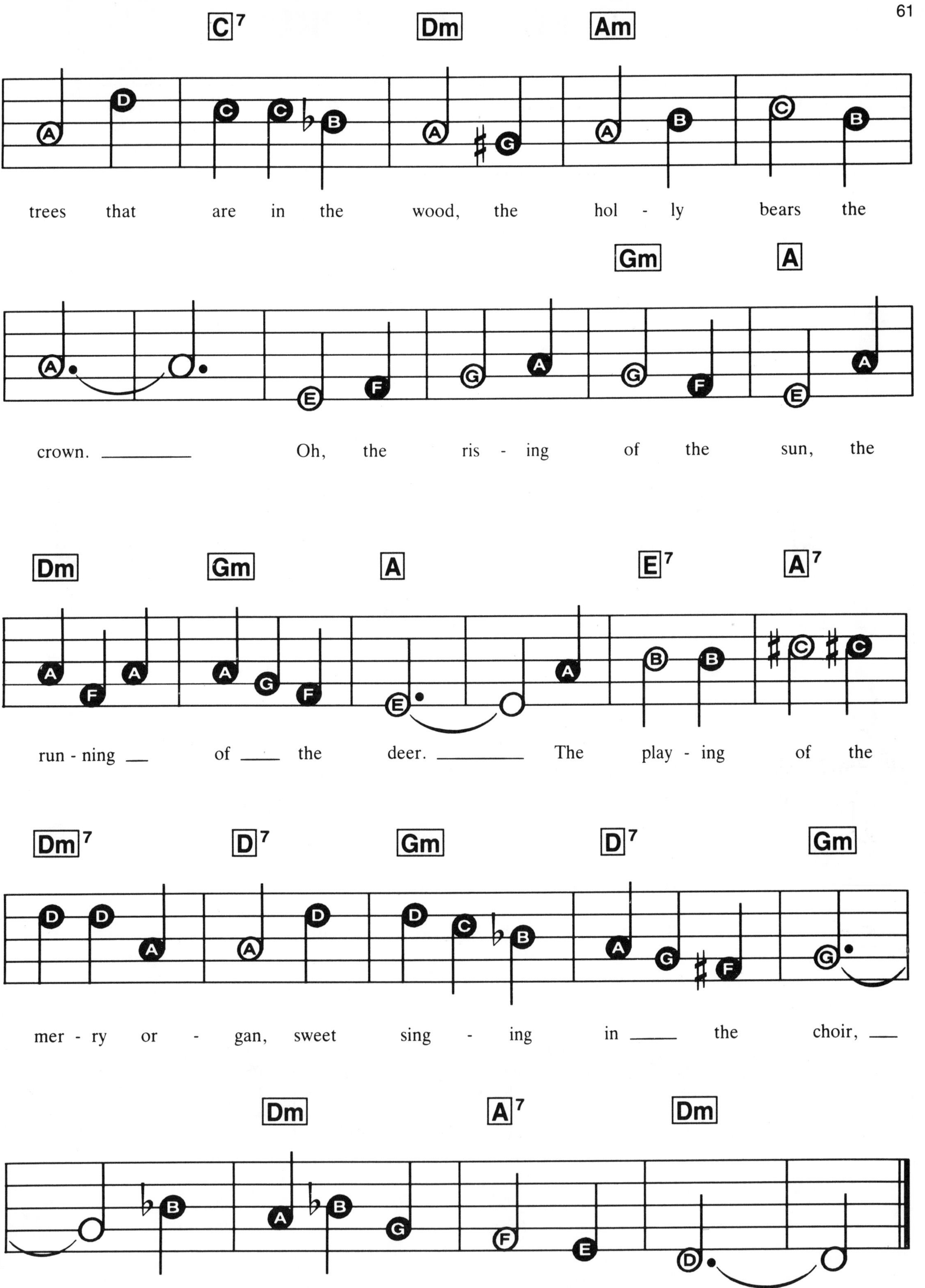
C7 Dm Am
trees that are in the wood, the hol - ly bears the
Gm A
crown. Oh, the ris - ing of the sun, the
Dm Gm A E7 A7
run - ning of the deer. The play - ing of the
Dm7 D7 Gm D7 Gm
mer - ry or - gan, sweet sing - ing in the choir,
Dm A7 Dm
sweet sing - ing in the choir.

HALLELUJAH CHORUS

TRUMPET
BRIGHT 'N' BRASSY
No Rhythm

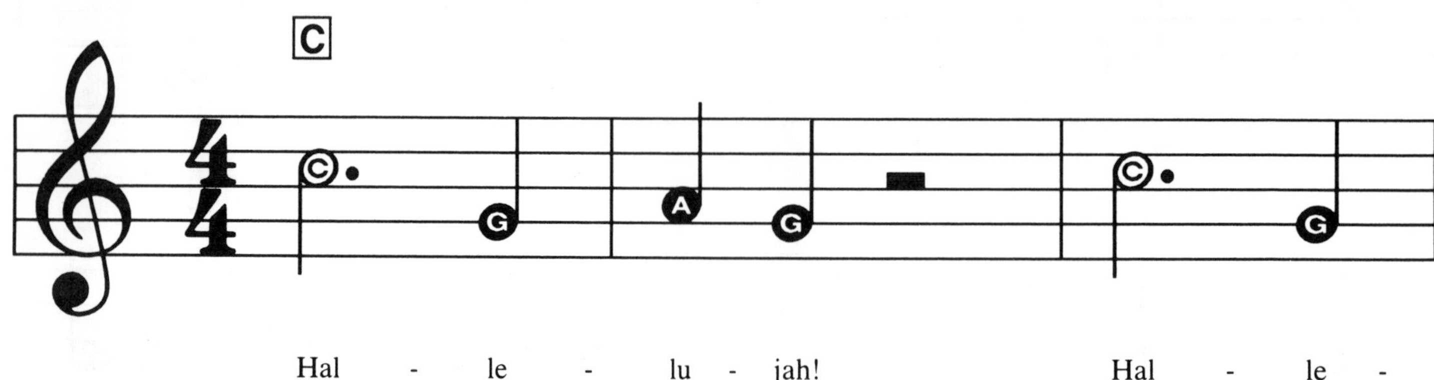
C
Hal - le - lu - jah! Hal - le -

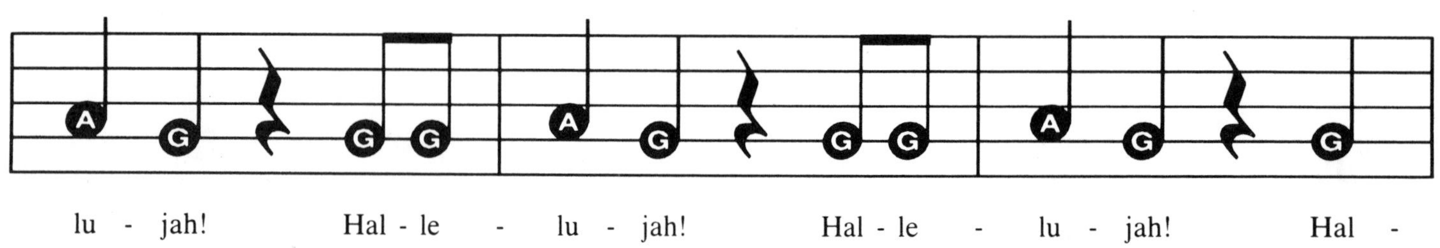
lu - jah! Hal - le - lu - jah! Hal - le - lu - jah! Hal -

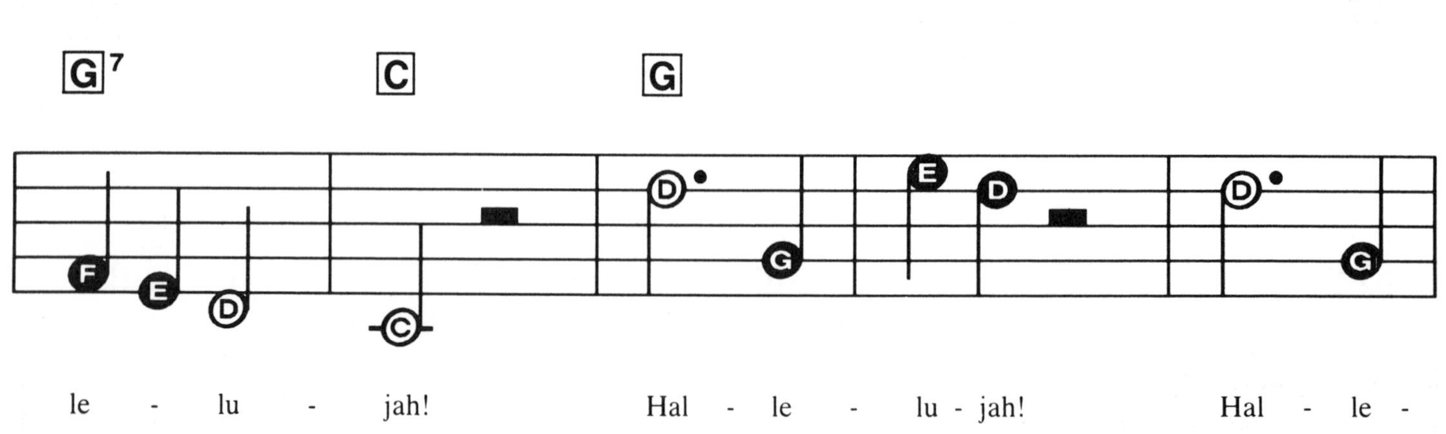
G7
C
G
le - lu - jah! Hal - le - lu - jah! Hal - le -

lu - jah! Hal - le - lu - jah! Hal - le - lu - jah! Hal -

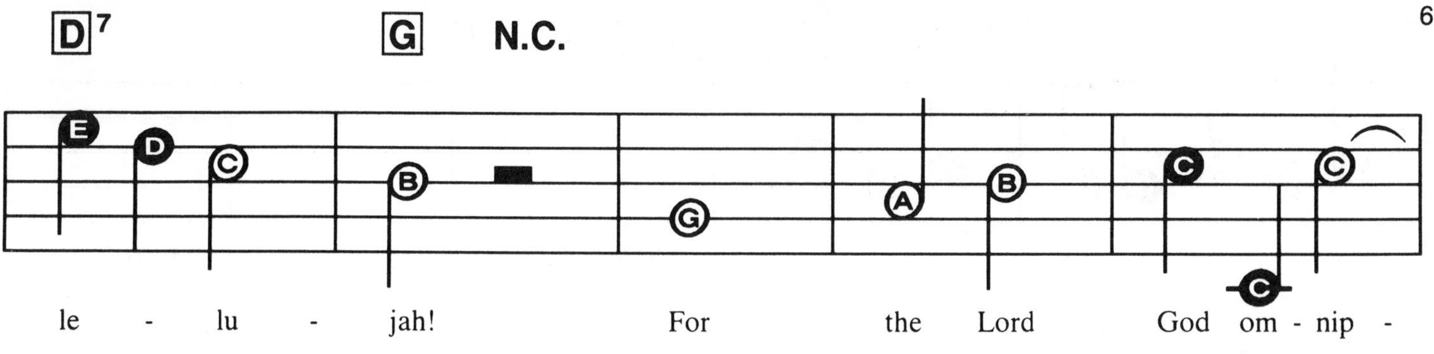
D7
G
N.C.
E D C B G A B C C C
le - lu - jah! For the Lord God om - nip -

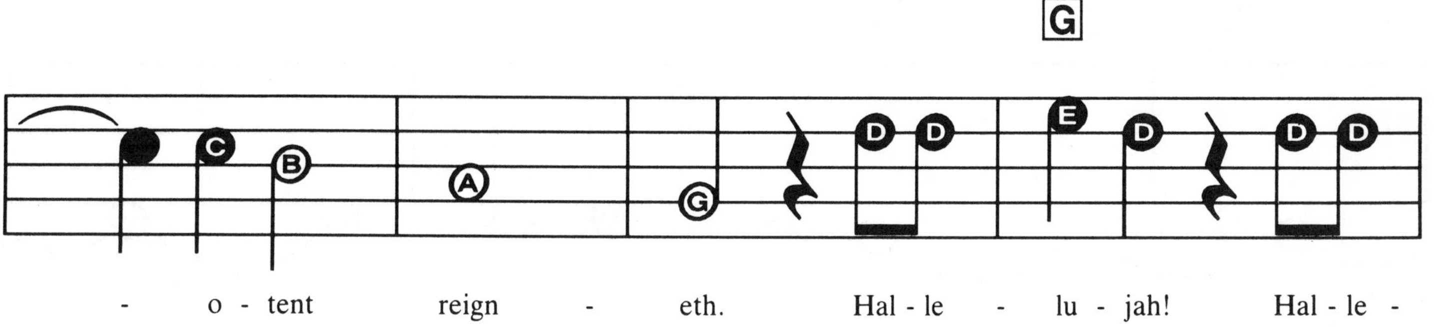
G
C B A G D D E D D D
- o - tent reign - eth. Hal - le - lu - jah! Hal - le -

E D D D E D D D E D
lu - jah! Hal - le - lu - jah! Hal - le - lu - jah!

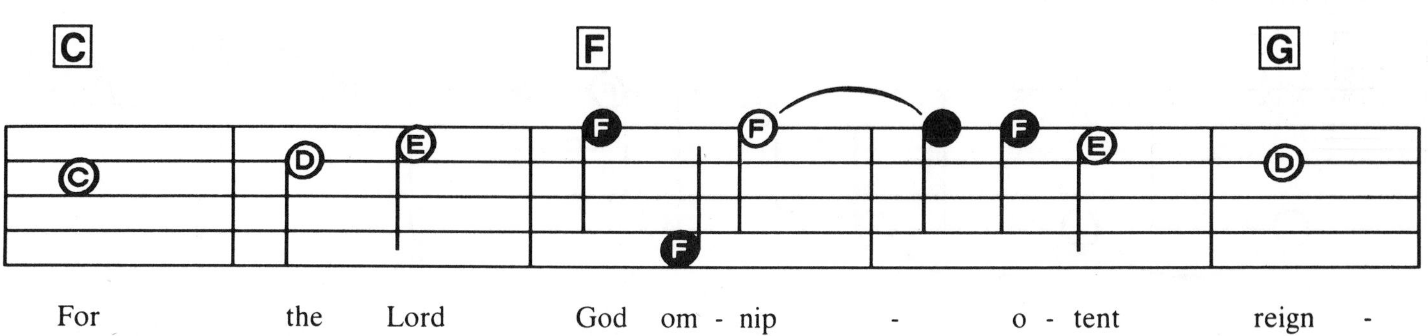
C
F
G
C D E F F F F E D
For the Lord God om - nip - o - tent reign -

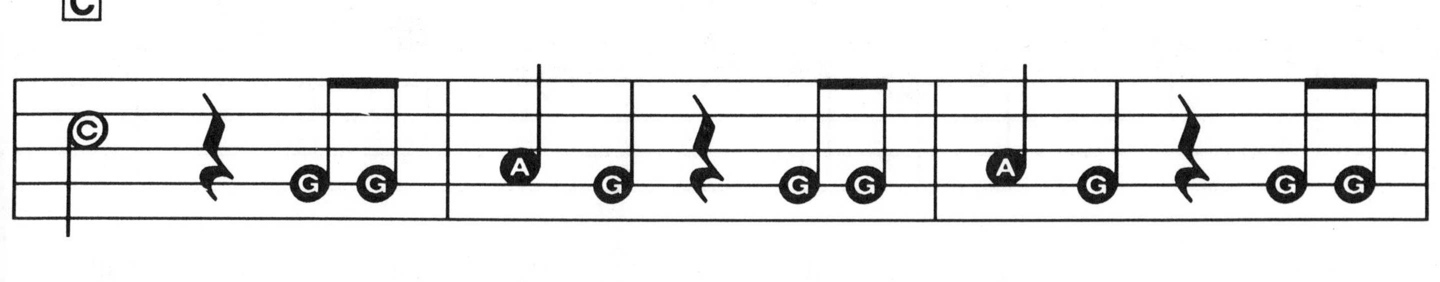
C
C G G A G G G A G G G
eth. Hal - le - lu - jah! Hal - le - lu - jah! Hal - le -

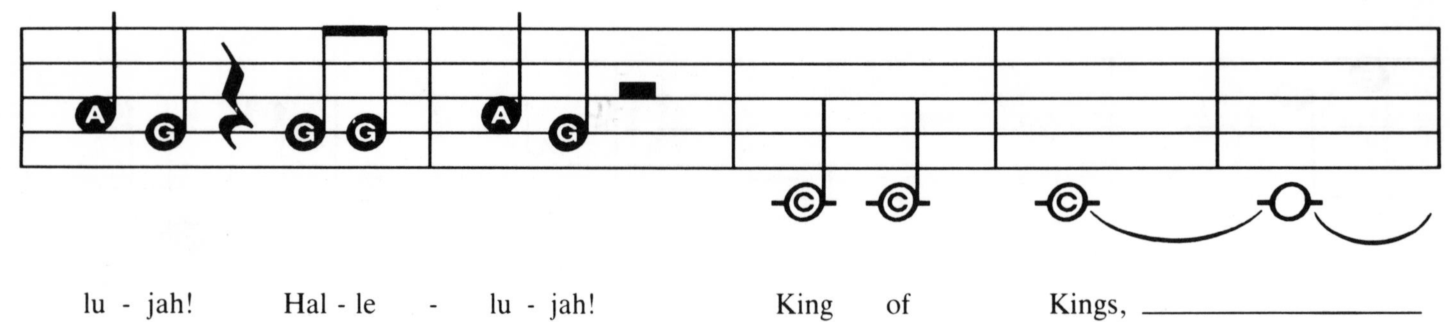
N.C.
lu - jah! Hal - le - lu - jah! King of Kings,

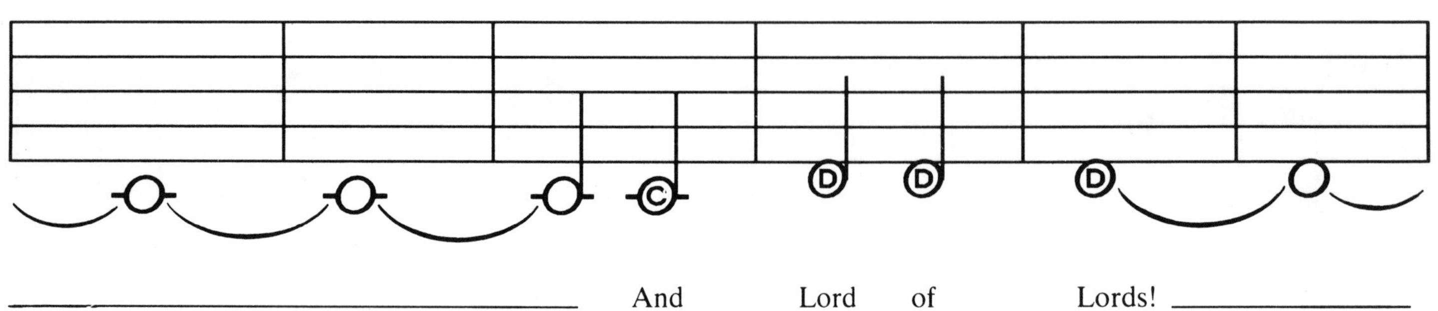
And Lord of Lords!

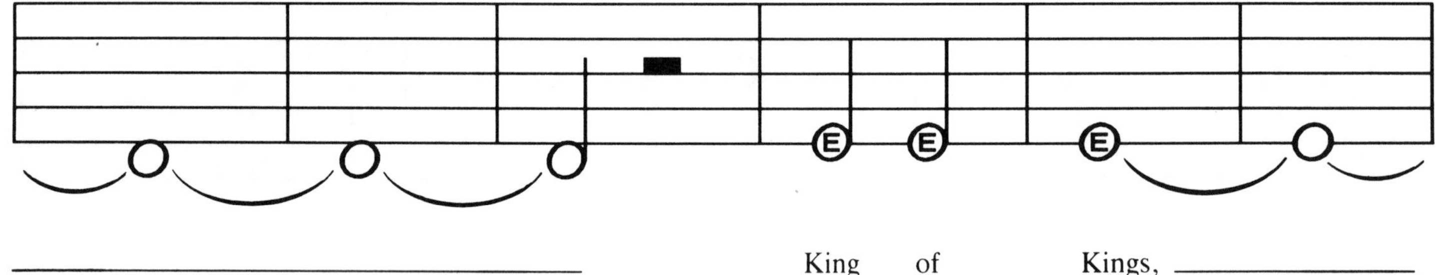
King of Kings,

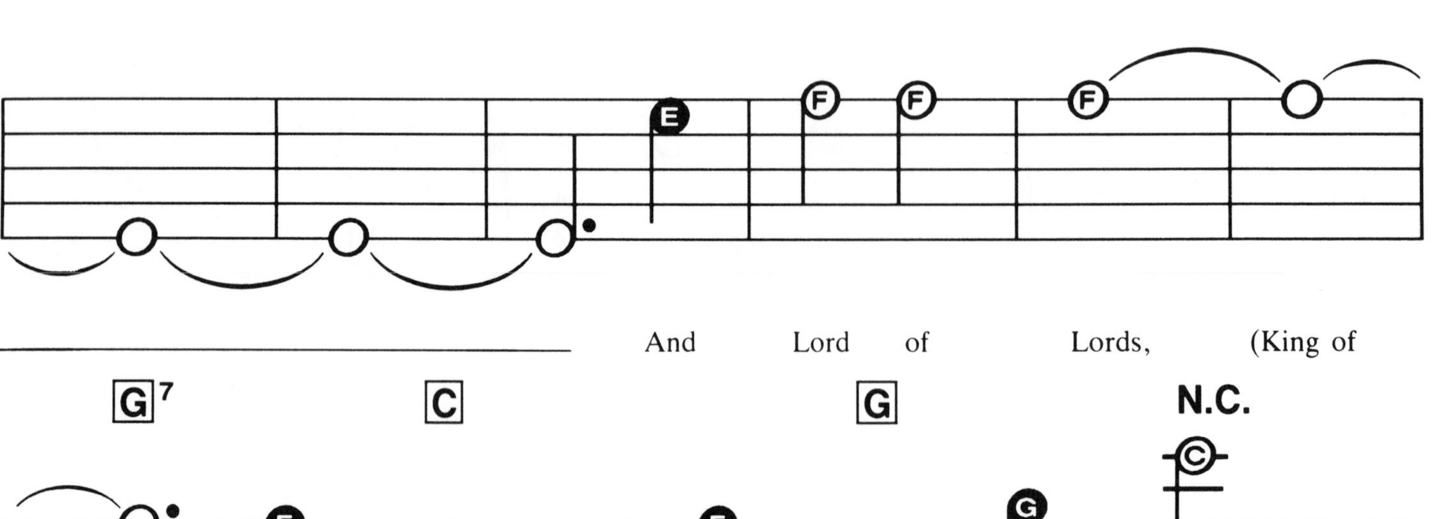
And Lord of Lords, (King of
G7
C
G
N.C.
Kings,) And Lord of Lords! And He shall

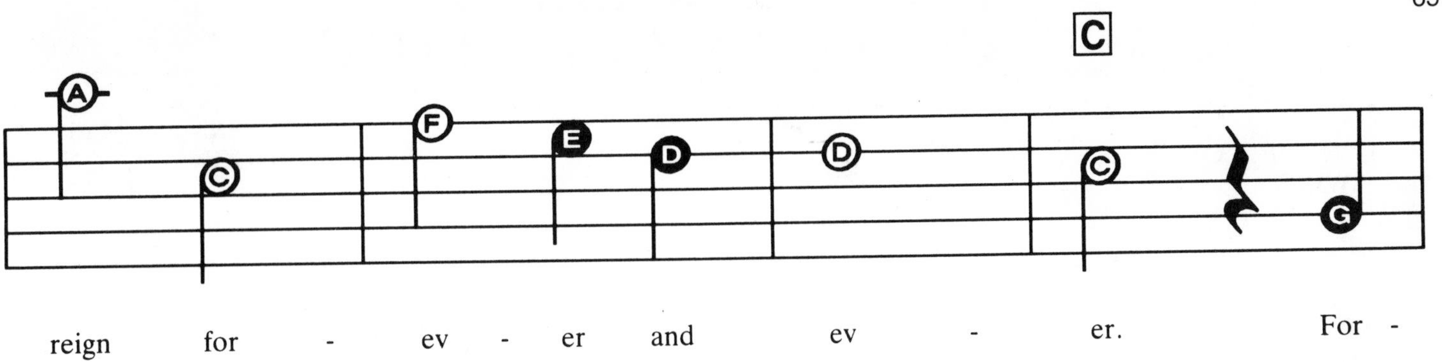
C
reign for - ev - er and ev - er. For -

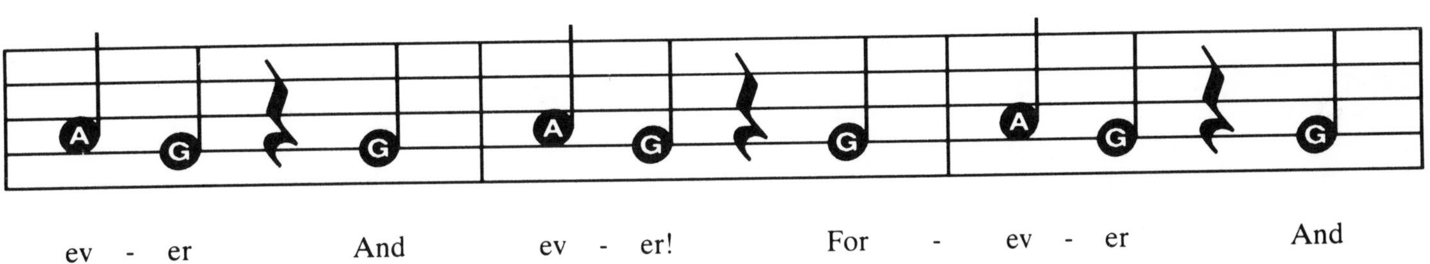
ev - er And ev - er! For - ev - er And

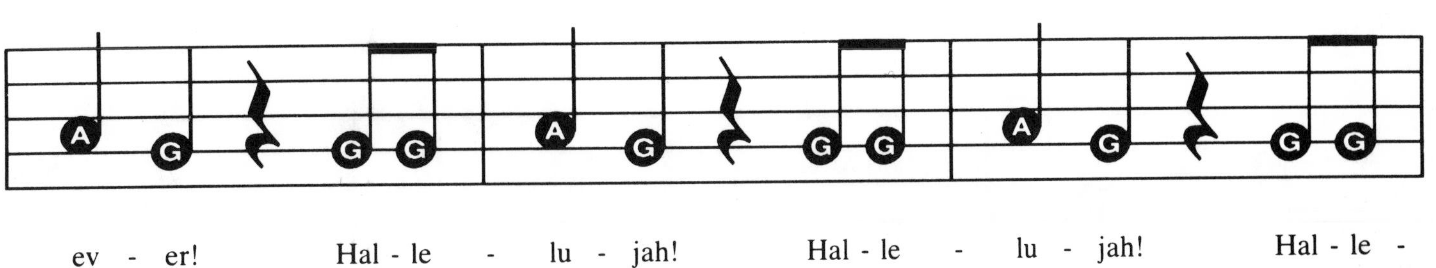
ev - er! Hal - le - lu - jah! Hal - le - lu - jah! Hal - le -

F
C
lu - jah! Hal - le - lu - jah! Hal - le - lu - jah!

HAVE YOURSELF A MERRY LITTLE CHRISTMAS

PIANO
FULL 'N' MELLOW
Slow SWING
Words and Music by
HUGH MARTIN and
RALPH BLANE
①
C
Dm7
Have your - self a mer - ry lit - tle Christ - mas,
Have your - self a mer - ry lit - tle Christ - mas
Through the years we all will be to - geth - er,
C
G7
Am
②
let your heart be light. From now on, our
make the Yule - tide gay. From now on, our
if the Fates al - low, Hang a shin - ing
1.
Dm
E7
G7
trou - bles will be out of sight.
2.
Dm
E
Am
C7
trou - bles will be miles a - way.

F
C
Here we are as in old - en days, hap - py
Dm7
Em
Am
gold - en days of yore,
Faith - ful friends who are
Em
D7
G
Return to ①
Play to ②
Skip to ③
dear to us gath - er near to us once more.
③
Dm
Am
C7
F
Star up - on the high - est bough,
And have your - self a
G7
C
mer - ry lit - tle Christ - mas now.

A HOLLY, JOLLY CHRISTMAS

SAXOPHONE
BIG 'N' BOLD
Medium SWING

Words and Music by
JOHNNY MARKS

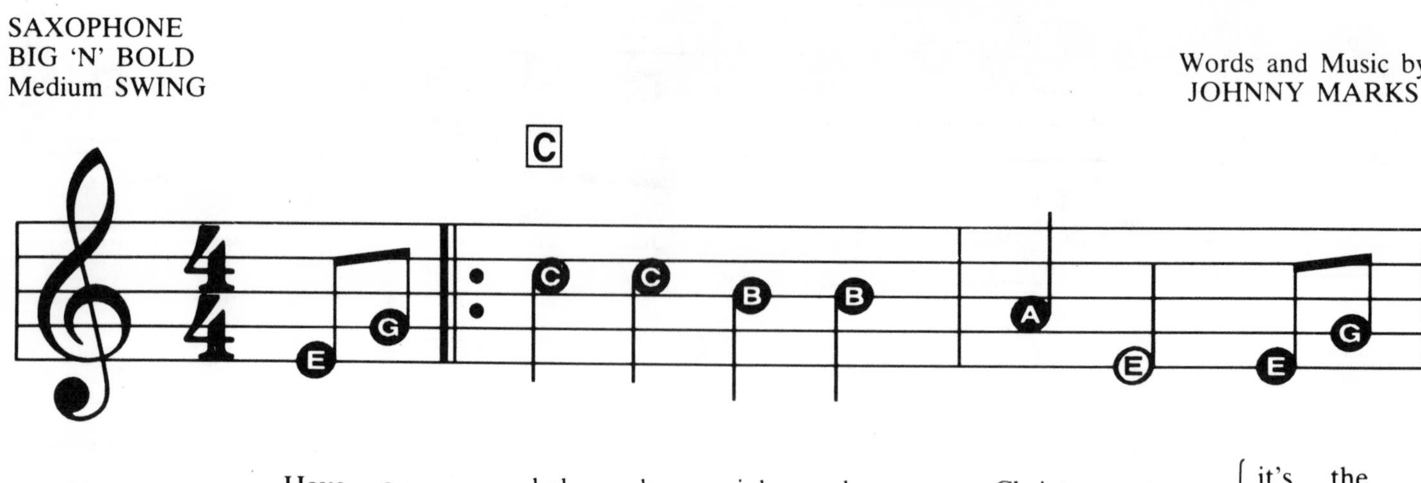
C
E G C C B B A E E G
Have a hol - ly jol - ly Christ - mas, it's the
And when

G7
A A G G B B B B A G G G E
best time of the year. I don't know if there'll be snow, but
you walk down the street Say hel - lo to friends you know and

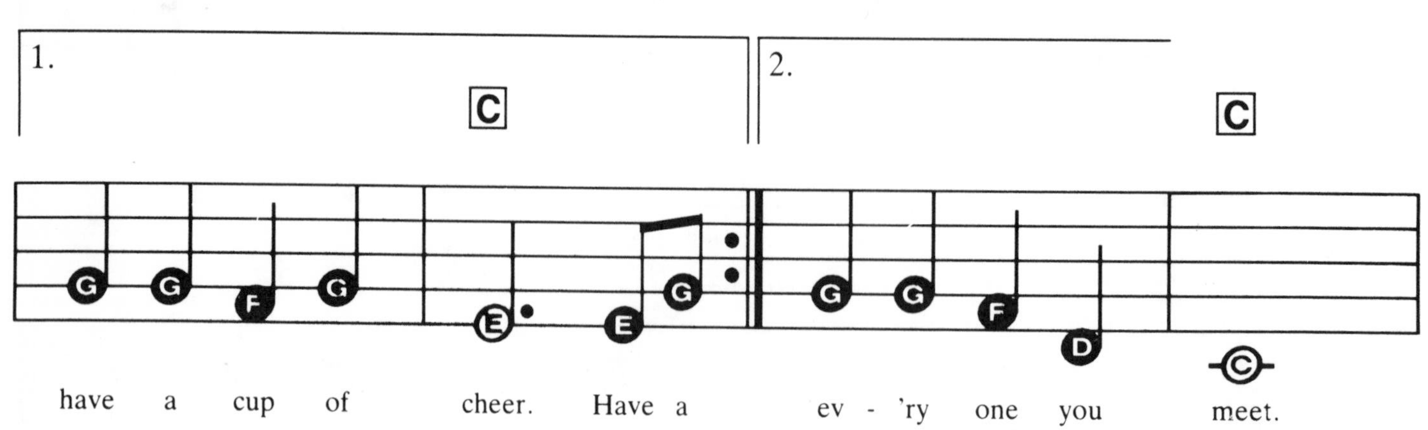
1. C 2. C
G G F G E E G G G F D C
have a cup of cheer. Have a ev - 'ry one you meet.

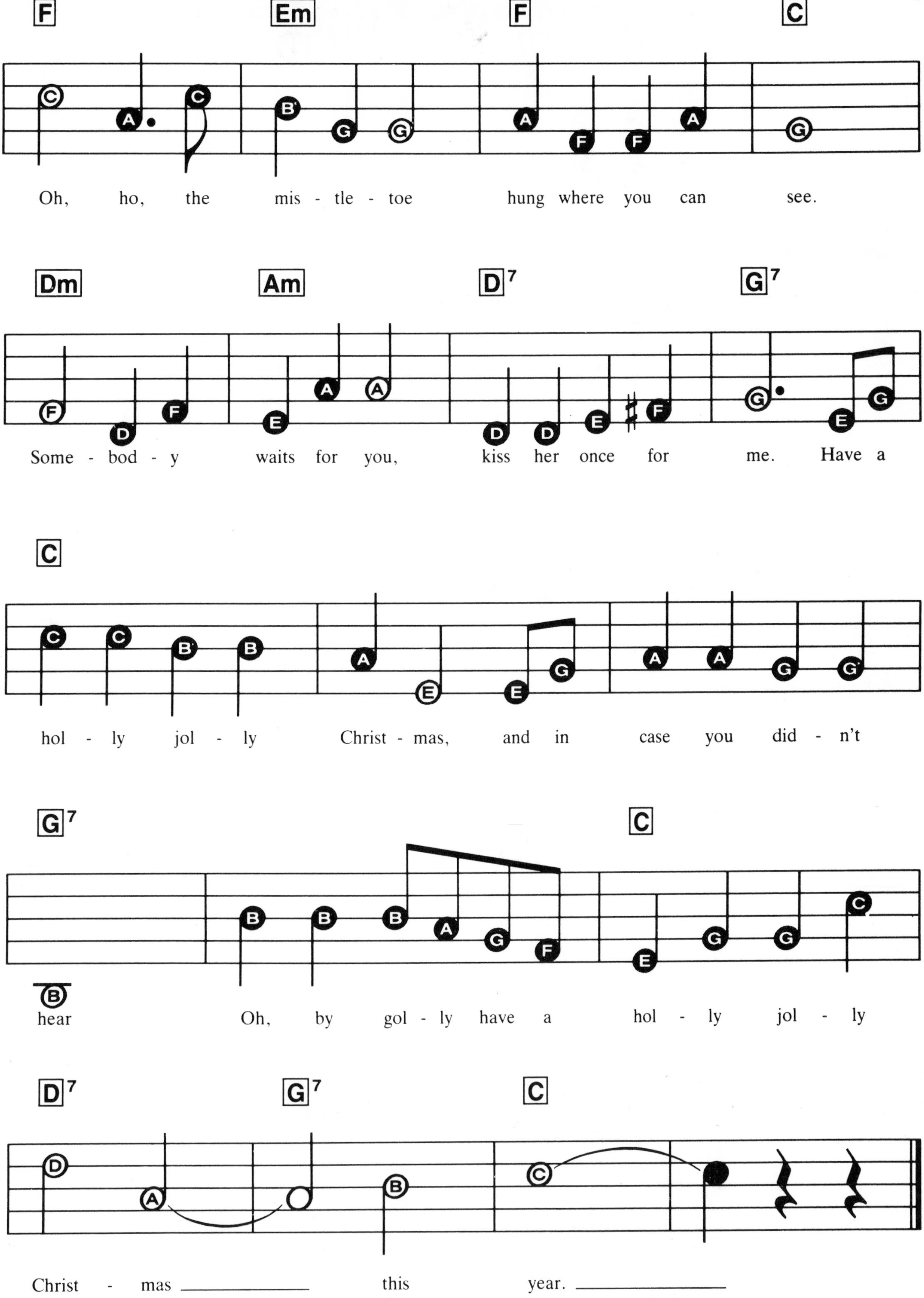

F Em F C

Oh, ho, the mis - tle - toe hung where you can see.

Dm Am D7 G7

Some - bod - y waits for you, kiss her once for me. Have a

C

hol - ly jol - ly Christ - mas, and in case you did - n't

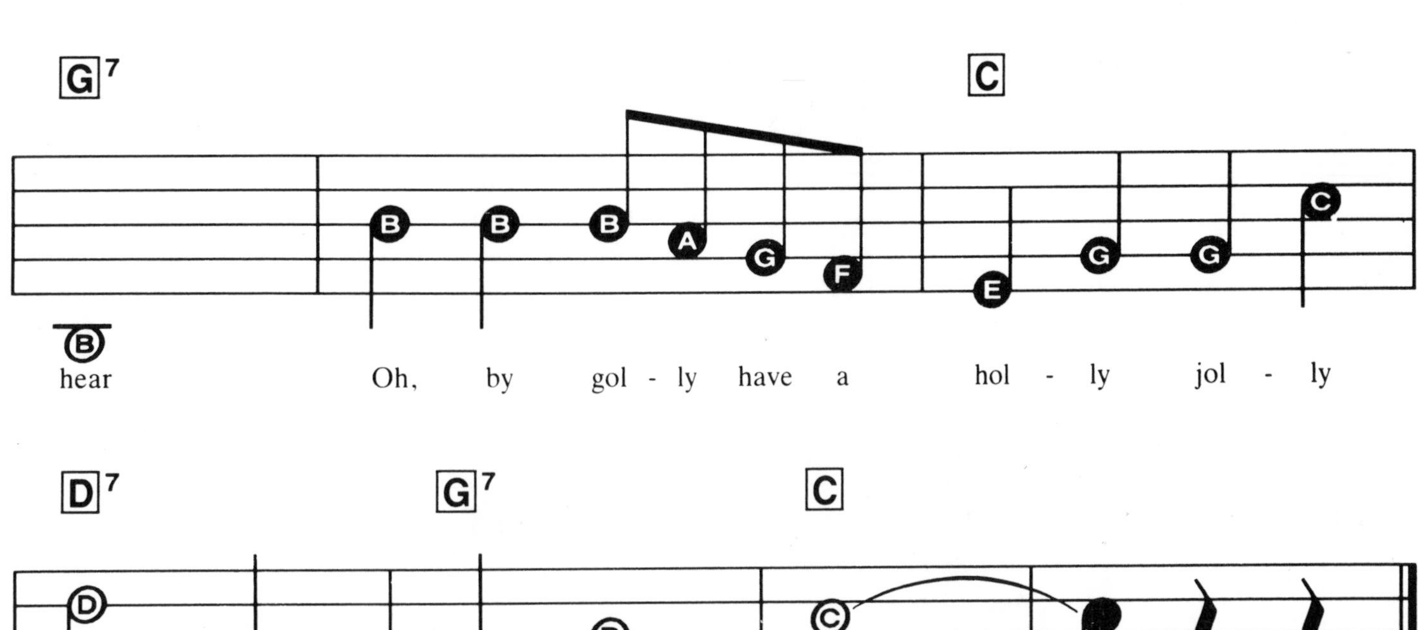

Christ - mas ______ this year. ______

(THERE'S NO PLACE LIKE)

HOME FOR THE HOLIDAYS

ORGAN
FULL 'N' BRILLIANT
Medium SWING
Words by AL STILLMAN
Music by ROBERT ALLEN
① C F C
E F G E C C B A G F E
Oh, there's no place like home for the hol - i - days, __
G7
C D E C E A G F E D
'Cause no mat - ter how far a - way you roam, ___
C F C
E F G E C D C B A C E G
when you pine for the sun - shine of a friend - ly gaze, _
If you want to be hap - py in a mil - lion ways, _
G7 C ②
D C B G A F G E F D C
For the hol - i - days you can't beat home, sweet home ___

F
I met a man who lives in Ten - nes - see and
C G7
he was head - in' for Penn - syl - van - ia and some home-made pump - kin
C F
pie; From Penn - syl - van - ia folks are trav - lin' down to
C G7
Dix - ie's sun - ny shores; From At - lan - tic to Pa -
D7 G7
Return to ①
Play to ②
cif - ic, Gee, the traf - fic is ter - rif - ic, Oh, there's

HERE WE COME A-WASSAILING

ORGAN
FULL 'N' BRILLIANT
No Rhythm

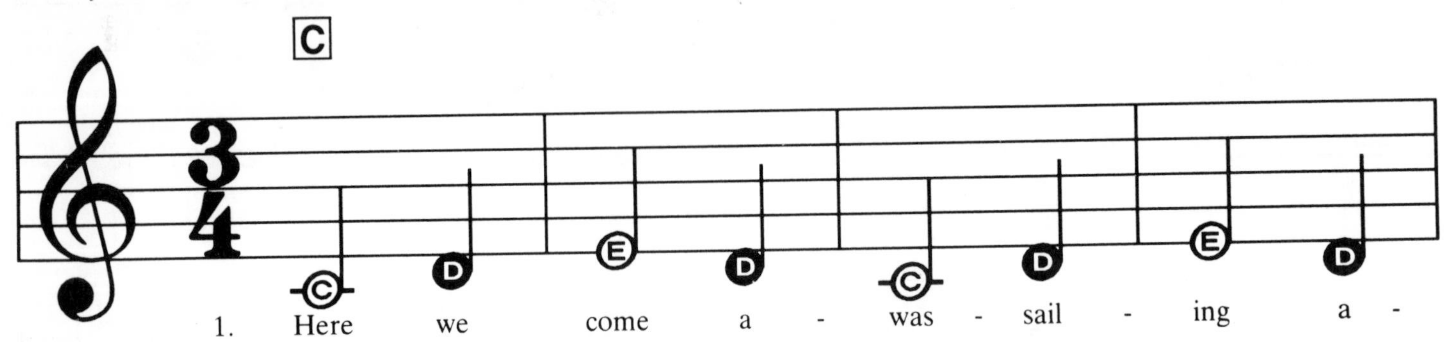

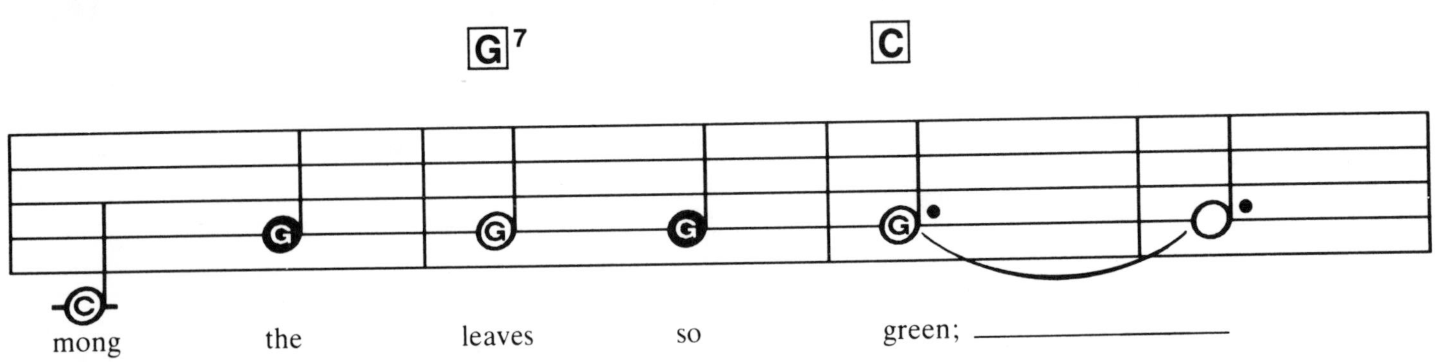

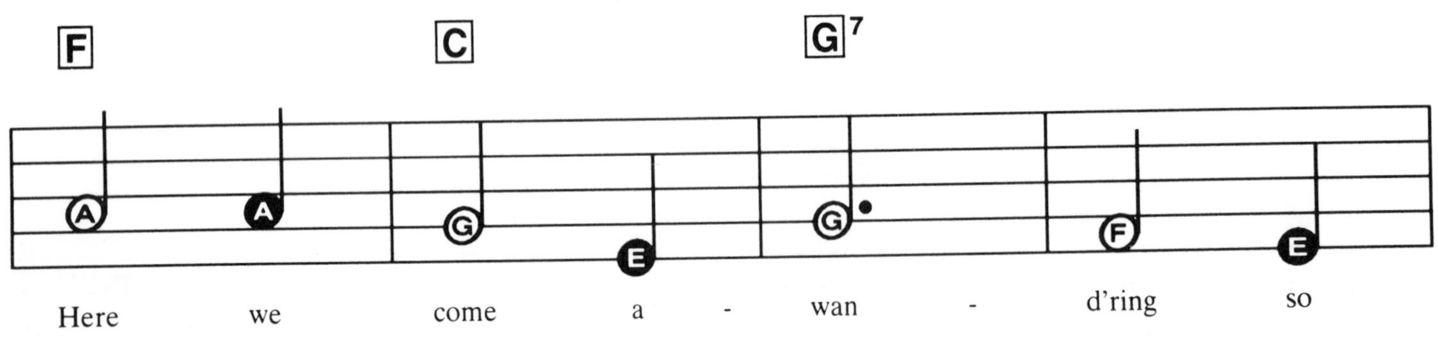

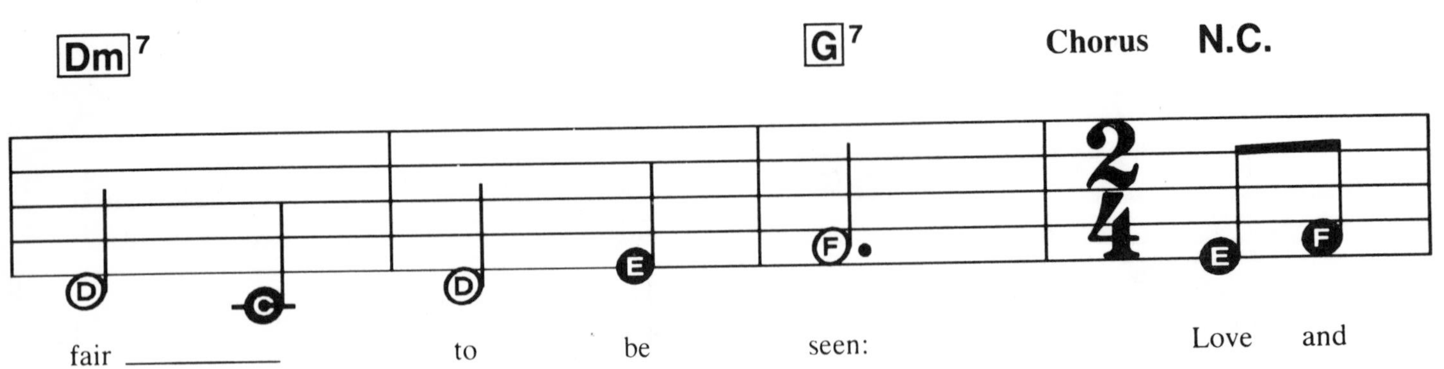

C

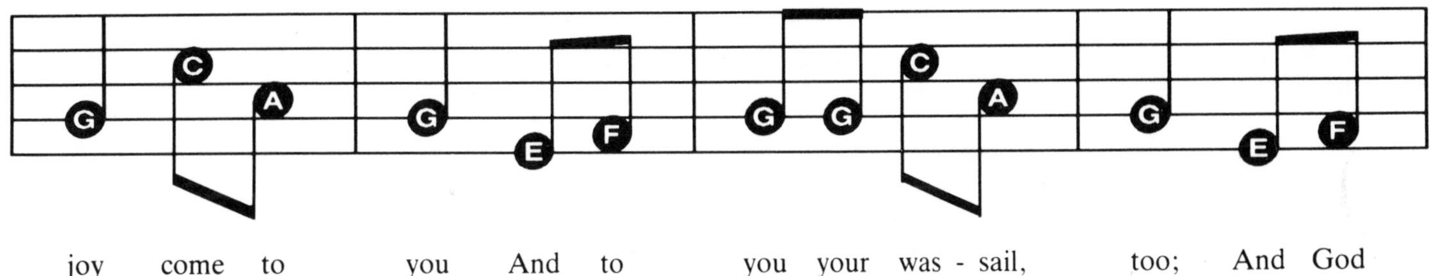
joy come to you And to you your was - sail, too; And God

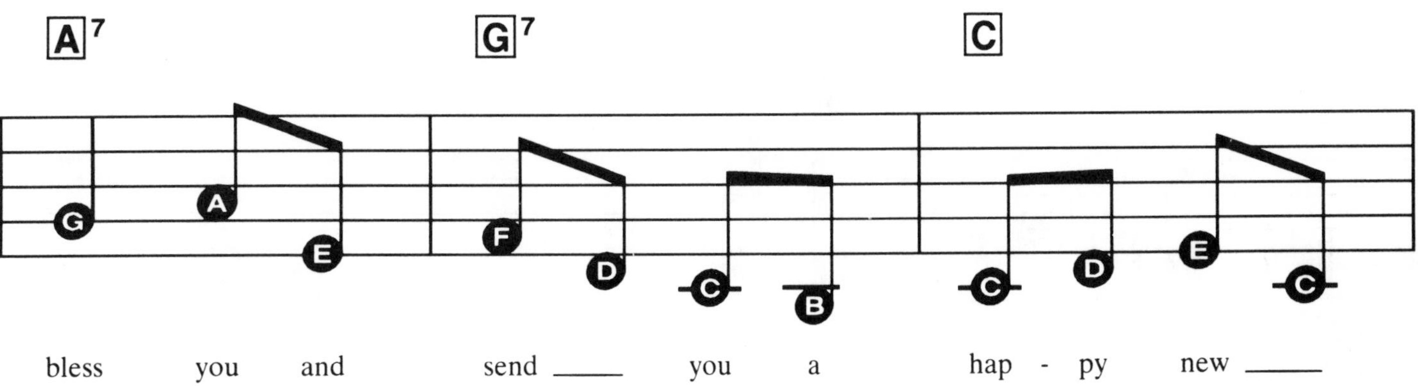
A7
G7
C
bless you and send ___ you a hap - py new ___

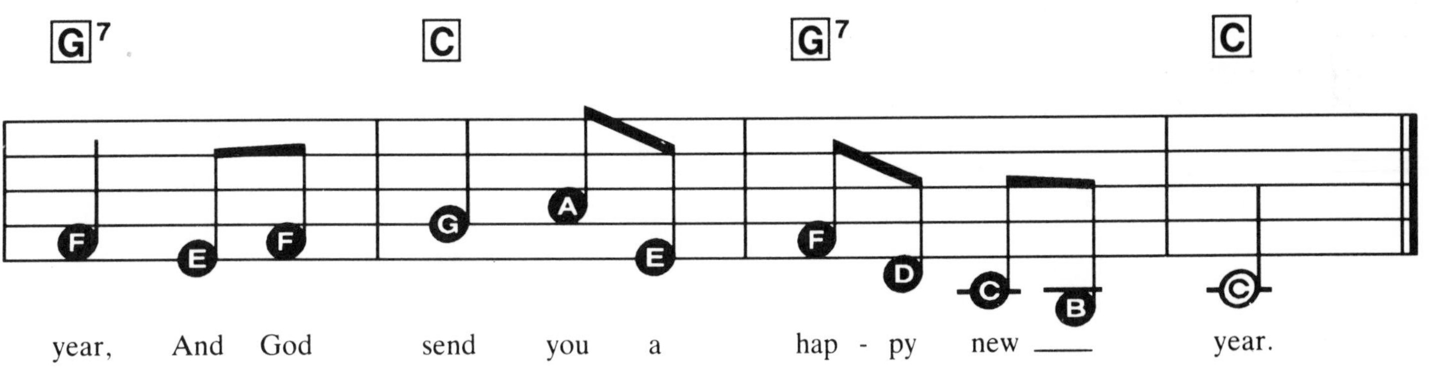
G7
C
G7
C
year, And God send you a hap - py new ___ year.

2. We are not daily beggars
   That beg from door to door;
   But we are neighbors' children
   Whom you have seen before.
   (Chorus)

3. We have got a little purse
   Of stretching leather skin;
   We want a little of your money
   To line it well within.
   (Chorus)

4. Bring us out a table,
   And spread it with a cloth;
   Bring us out a mouldy cheese,
   And some of your Christmas loaf.
   (Chorus)

5. God bless the master of this house,
   Likewise the mistress too;
   And all the little children
   That round the table go.
   (Chorus)

(Il est Ne, Le Divin Enfant)

HE IS BORN

VIOLIN
FULL 'N' MELLOW
No Rhythm

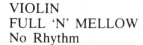

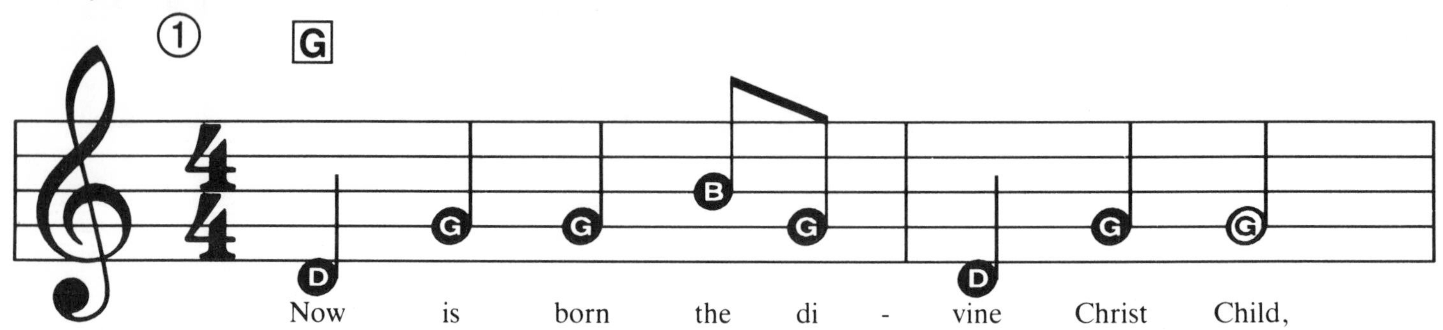
①
G
D G G B G D G G
Now is born the di - vine Christ Child,

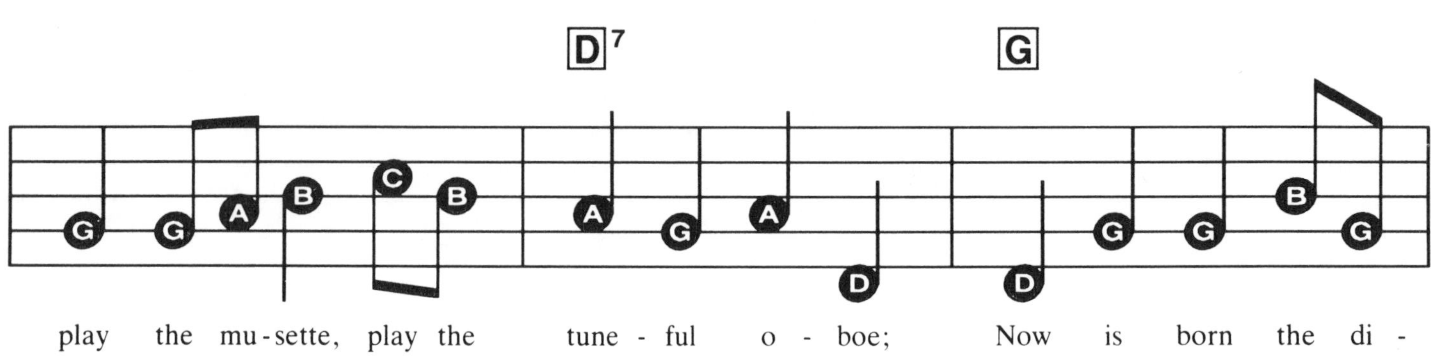
D7
G
G G A B C B A G A D D G G B G
play the mu-sette, play the tune - ful o - boe; Now is born the di -

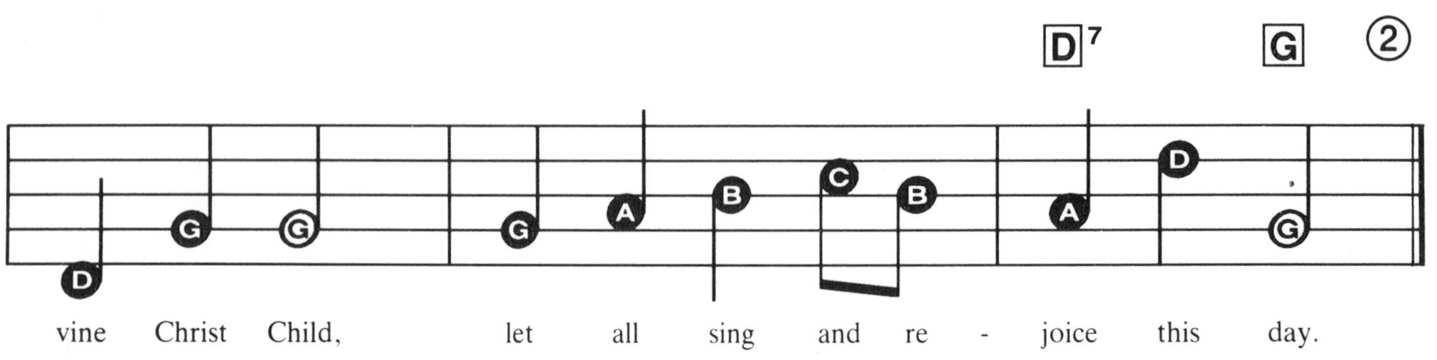
D7
G
②
D G G G A B C B A D G
vine Christ Child, let all sing and re - joice this day.

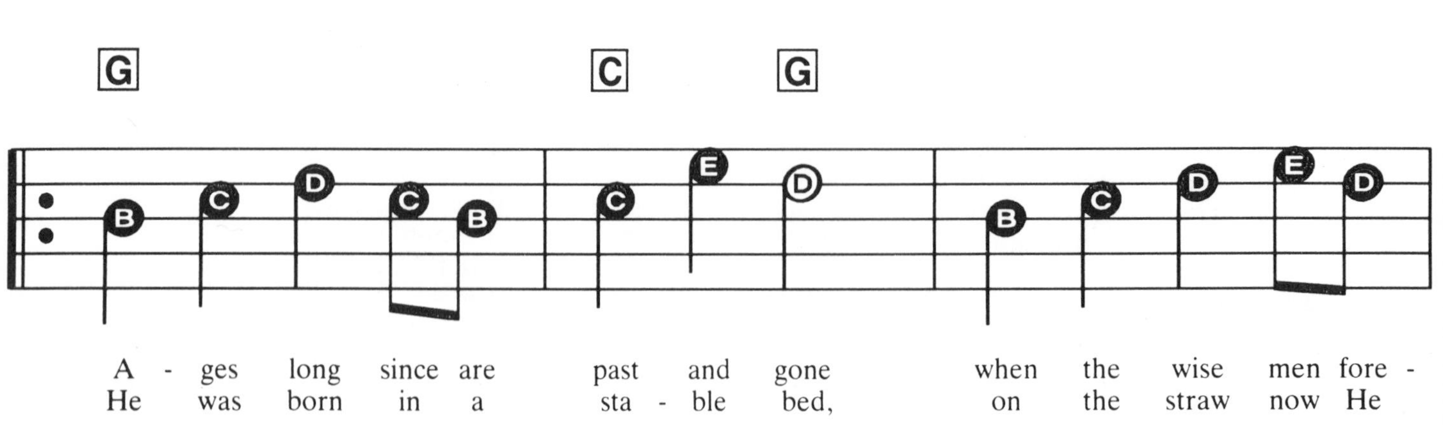
G
C
G
B C D C B C E D B C D E D
A - ges long since are past and gone when the wise men fore -
He was born in a sta - ble bed, on the straw now He

D G C G
told His com - ing; A - ges long since are past and gone.
sleeps so sound - ly; He was born in a sta - ble bed,
1. D7
2. D7
Return to ①
Play to ②
No - el, no - el, let us sing!
bow in hom - age to Him now.
I SAW THREE SHIPS
SAXOPHONE
FULL 'N' MELLOW
Medium WALTZ
G D7 G D7
I saw three ships come sail - ing in On
G D7 G
Christ - mas day, on Christ - mas day; I saw three
D7 G D7 G
ships come sail - ing in On Christ - mas day in the

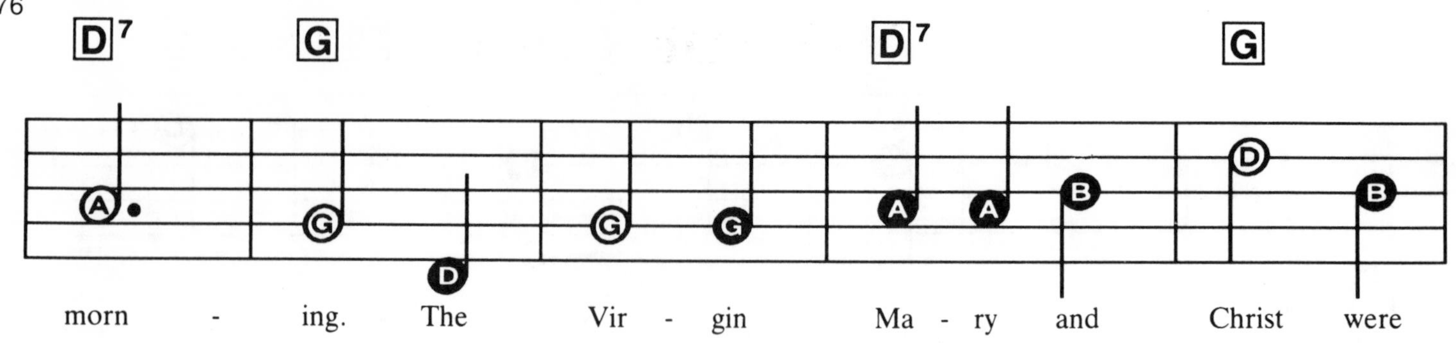
D7
G
D7
G
A
G
D
G
G
A
A
B
D
B
morn - ing. The Vir - gin Ma - ry and Christ were

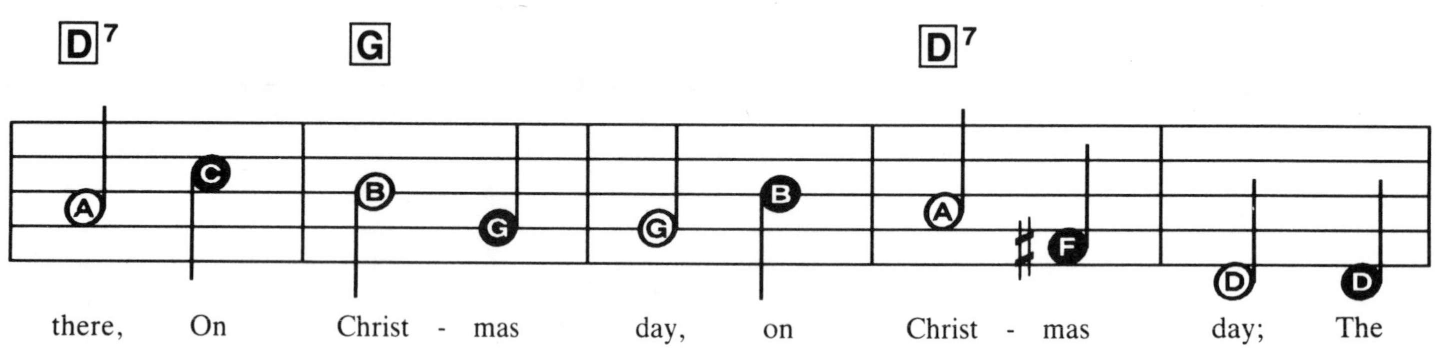
D7
G
D7
A
C
B
G
G
B
A
F
D
D
there, On Christ - mas day, on Christ - mas day; The

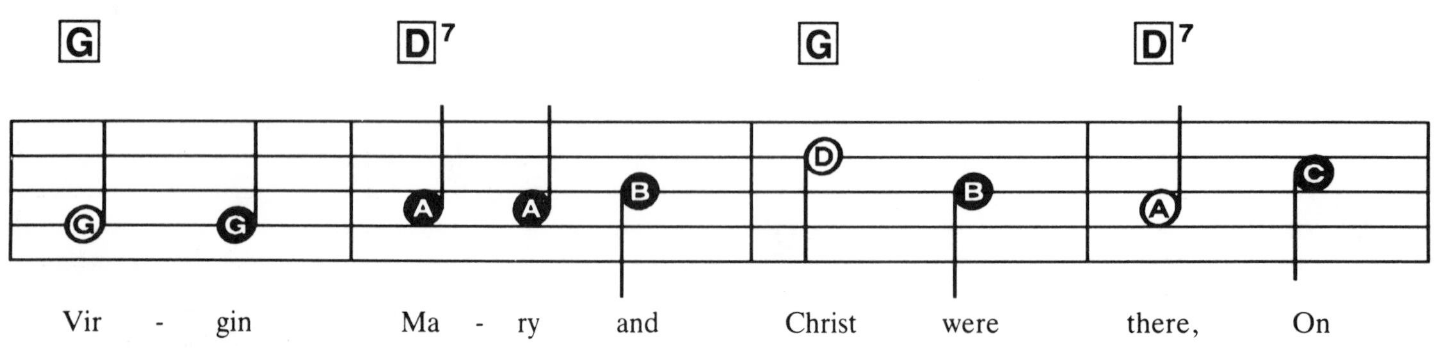
G
D7
G
D7
G
G
A
A
B
D
B
A
C
Vir - gin Ma - ry and Christ were there, On

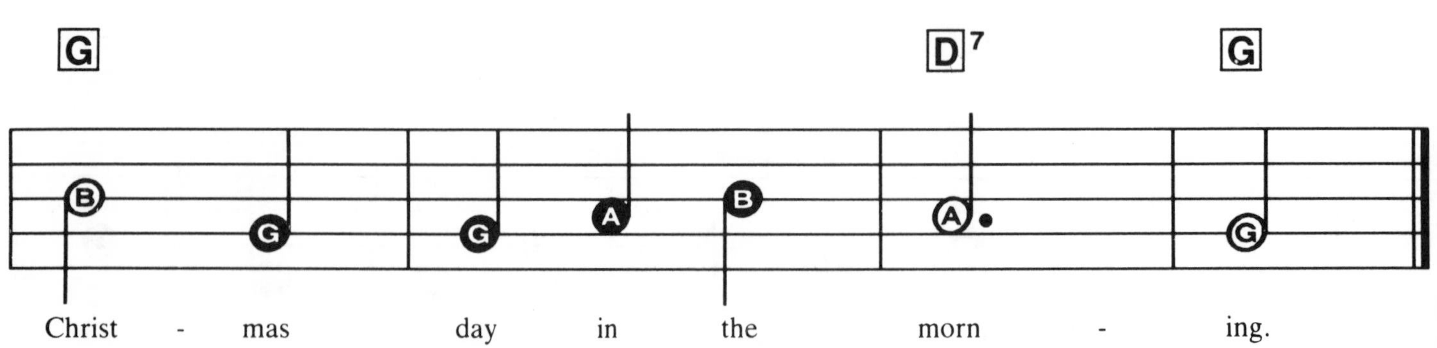
G
D7
G
B
G
G
A
B
A
G
Christ - mas day in the morn - ing.

I'LL BE HOME FOR CHRISTMAS

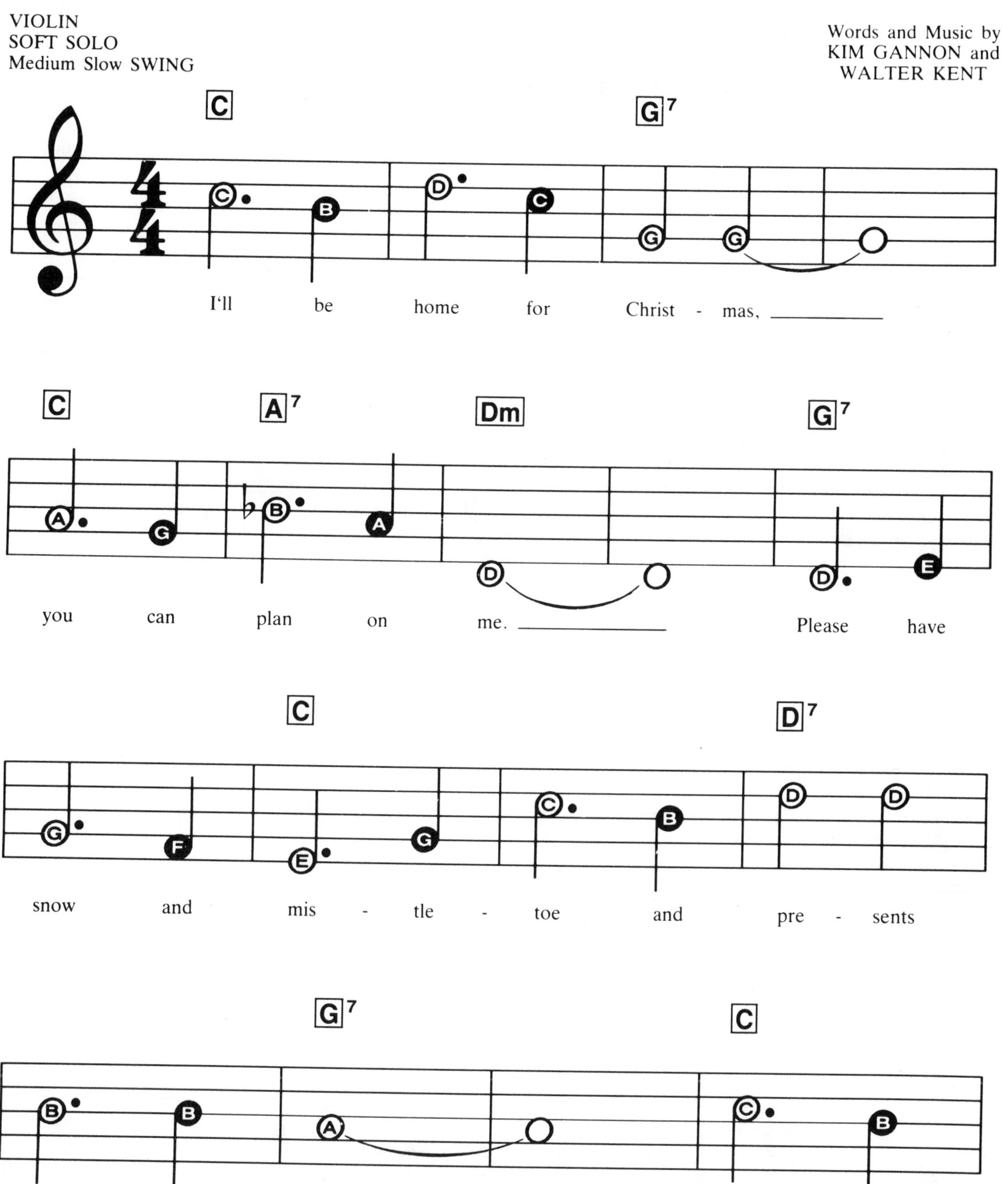

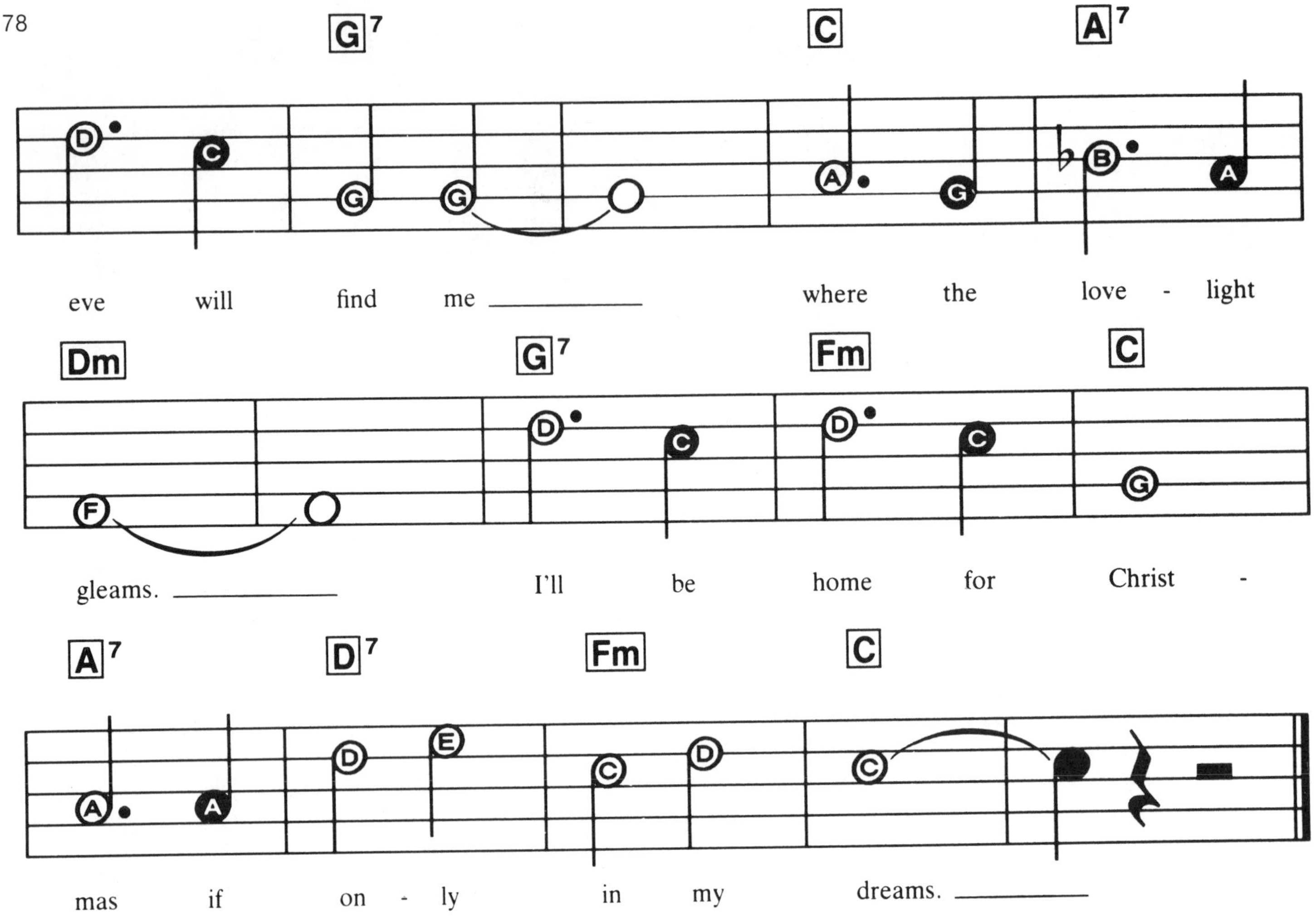

G7 C A7

eve will find me ___ where the love - light

Dm G7 Fm C

gleams. ___ I'll be home for Christ -

A7 D7 Fm C

mas if on - ly in my dreams. ___

From the Videocraft TV Musical Spectacular "RUDOLPH THE RED-NOSED REINDEER"

I HEARD THE BELLS ON CHRISTMAS DAY

WOODWINDS
FULL 'N' MELLOW
Medium SWING

Words by HENRY WADSWORTH LONGFELLOW
Adapted by JOHNNY MARKS
Music by JOHNNY MARKS

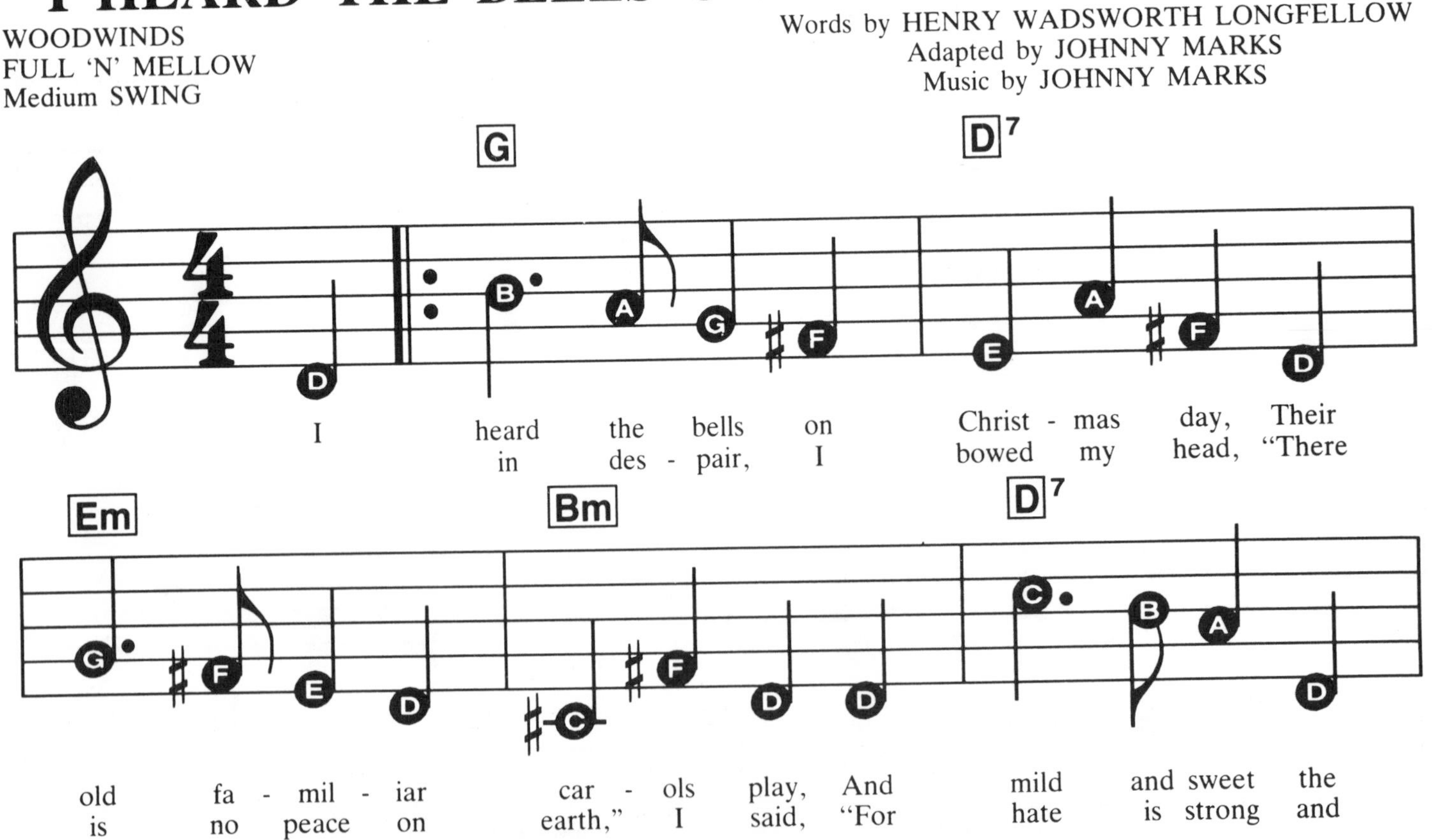
G D7
I heard the bells on Christ - mas day, Their
in des - pair, I bowed my head, "There
Em Bm D7
old fa - mil - iar car - ols play, And mild and sweet the
is no peace on earth," I said, "For hate is strong and

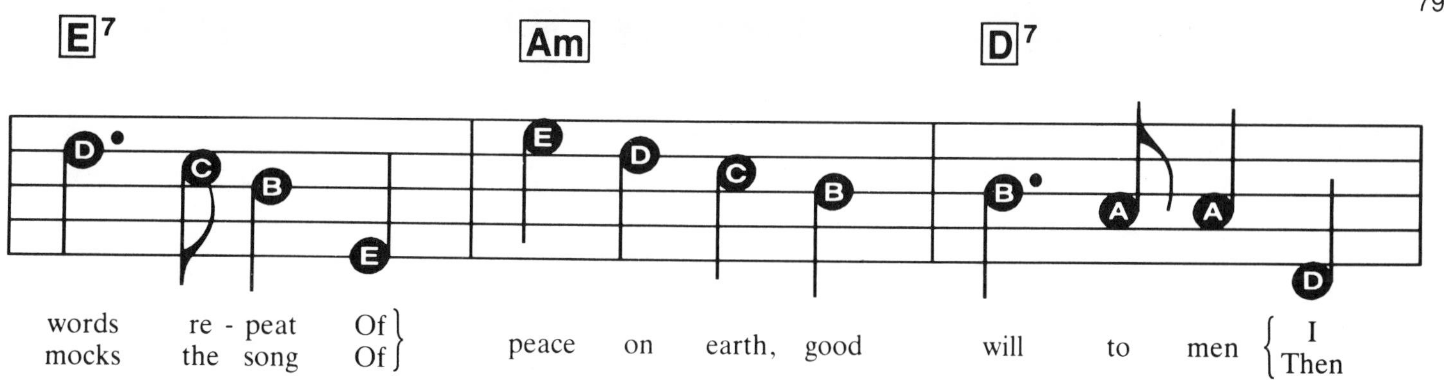
E7 Am D7
words re - peat Of peace on earth, good will to men I
mocks the song Of Then

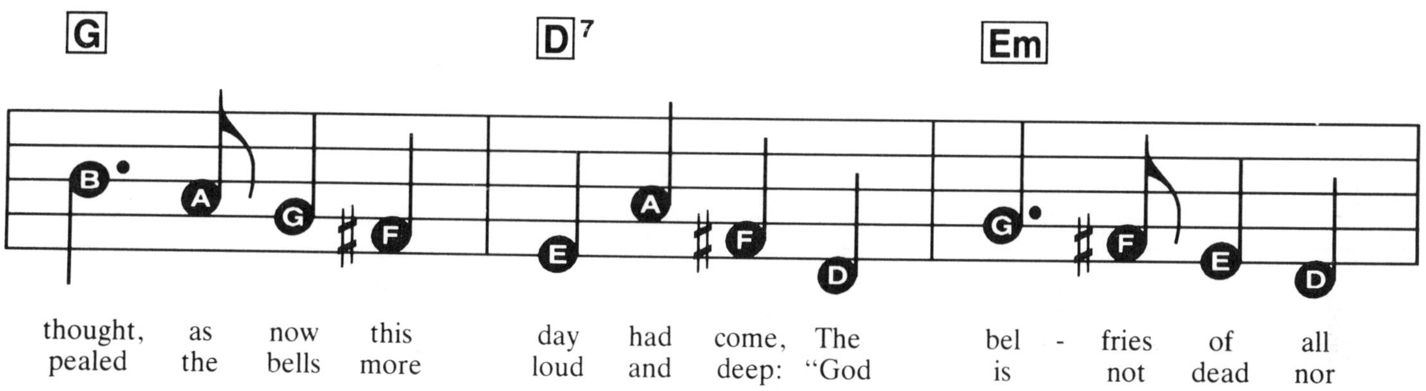
G D7 Em
thought, as now this day had come, The bel - fries of all
pealed the bells more loud and deep: "God is not dead nor

Bm D7 E7
christ - en - dom Had sung so long the un - bro - ken song Of
doth he sleep; The wrong shall fail, the ___ right pre - vail, With

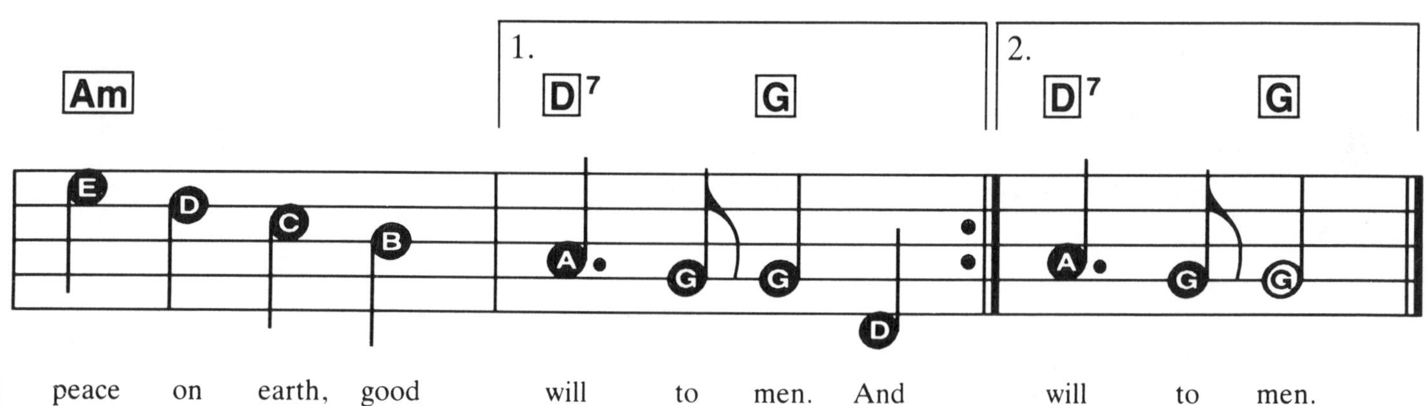
Am 1. D7 G 2. D7 G
peace on earth, good will to men. And will to men.

I SAW MOMMY KISSING SANTA CLAUS

TRUMPET
BRIGHT 'N' BRASSY
Medium SWING

Words and Music by
TOMMIE CONNOR

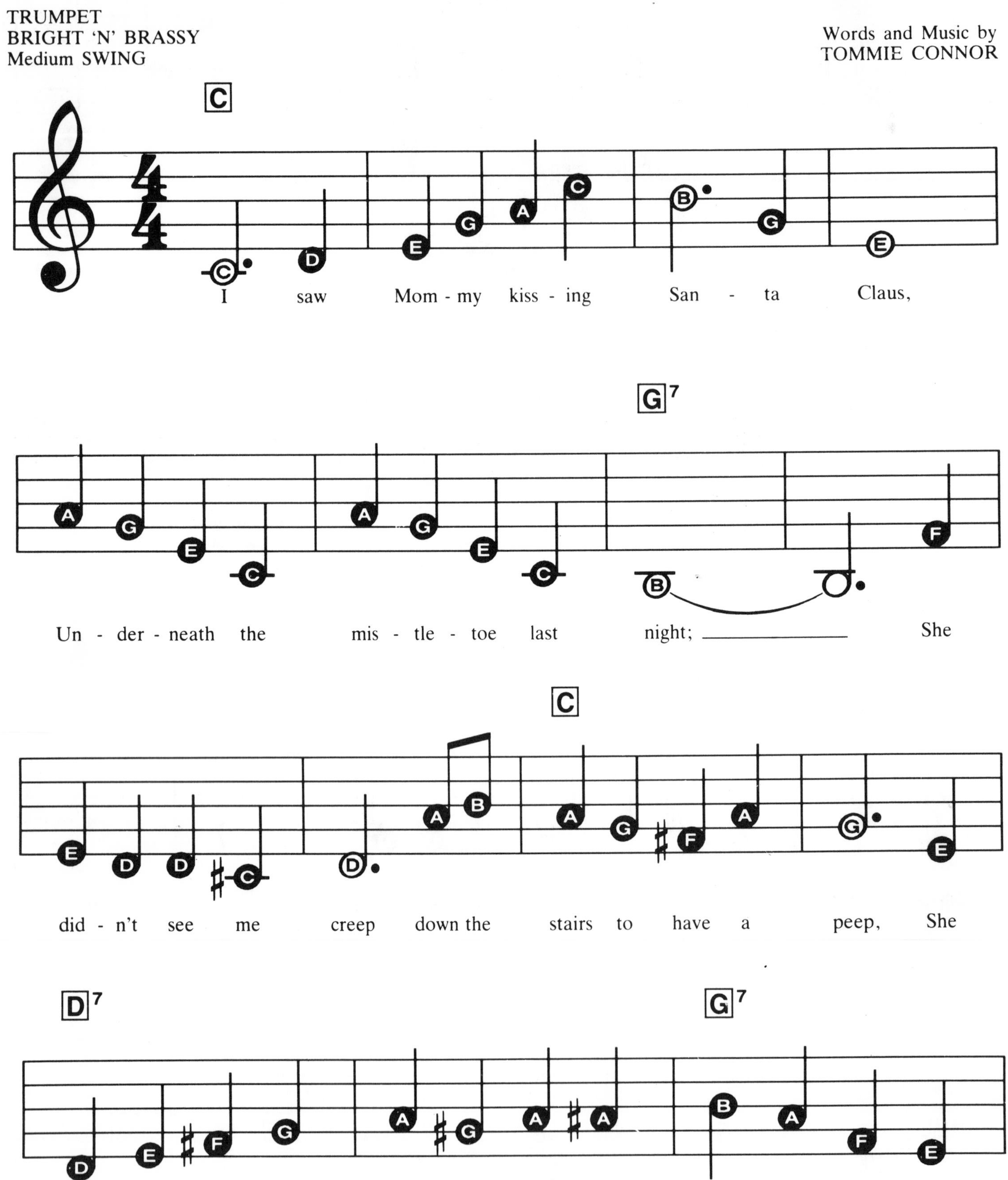

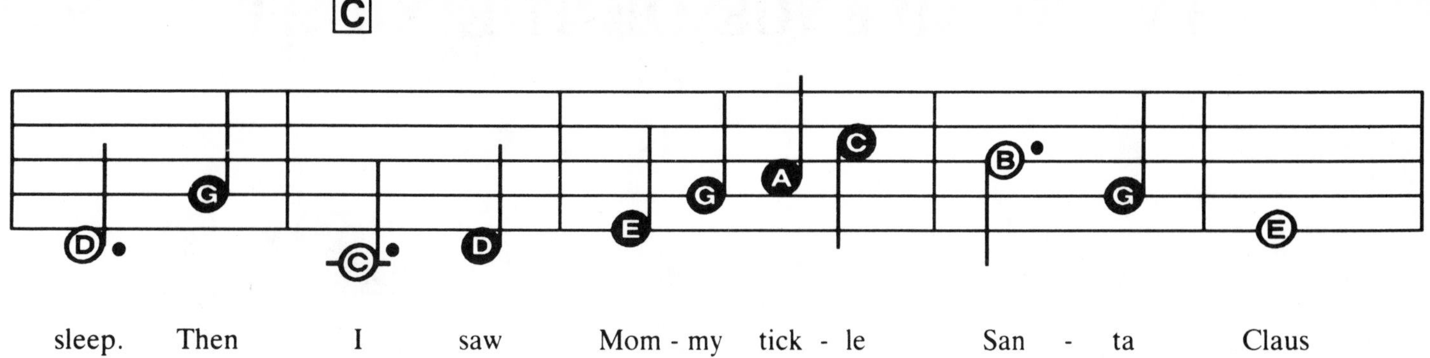
C
D G C D E G A C B G E
sleep. Then I saw Mom - my tick - le San - ta Claus

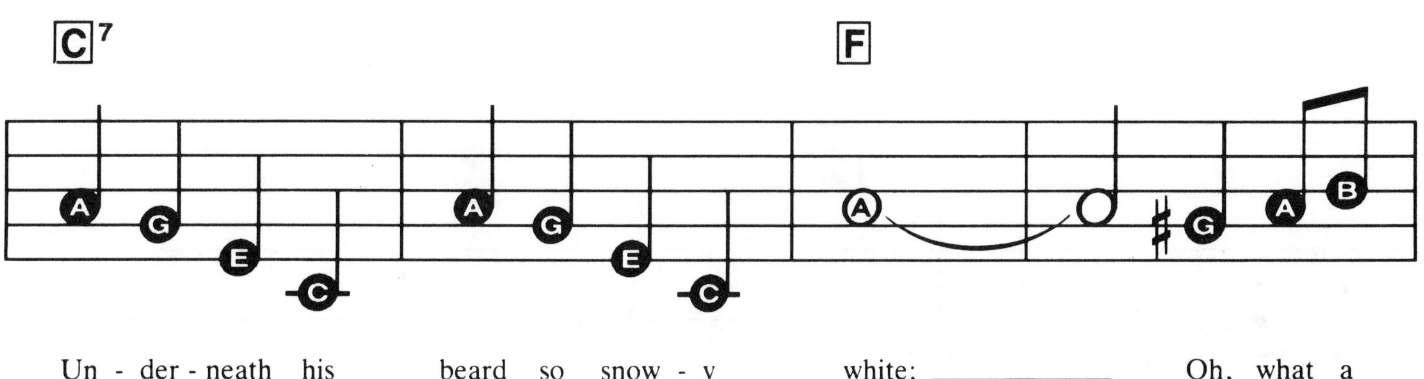
C7
F
A G E C A G E C A G A B
Un - der - neath his beard so snow - y white; Oh, what a

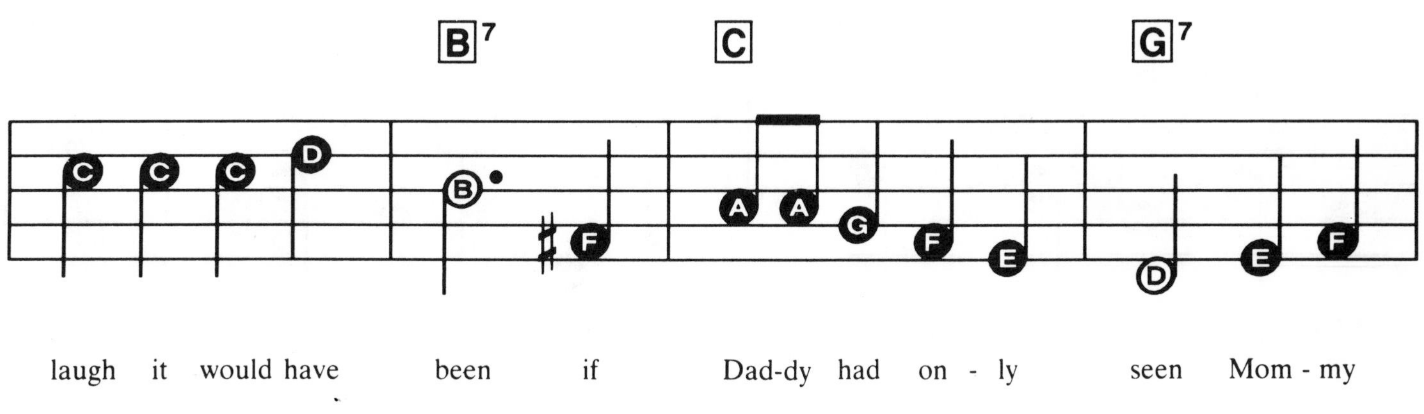
B7
C
G7
C C C D B F A A G F E D E F
laugh it would have been if Dad-dy had on - ly seen Mom - my

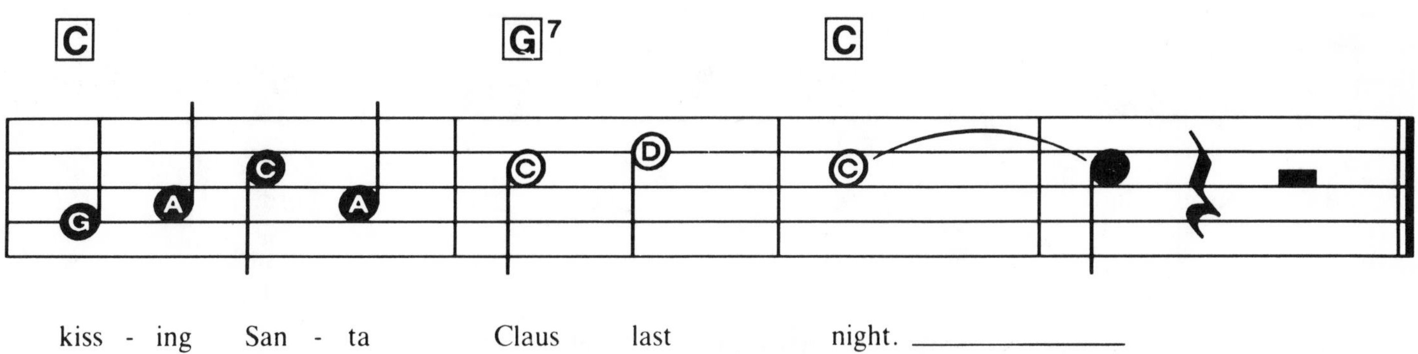
C
G7
C
G A C A C D C
kiss - ing San - ta Claus last night.

IN THE SILENCE OF THE NIGHT

SAXOPHONE
FULL 'N' MELLOW
No Rhythm

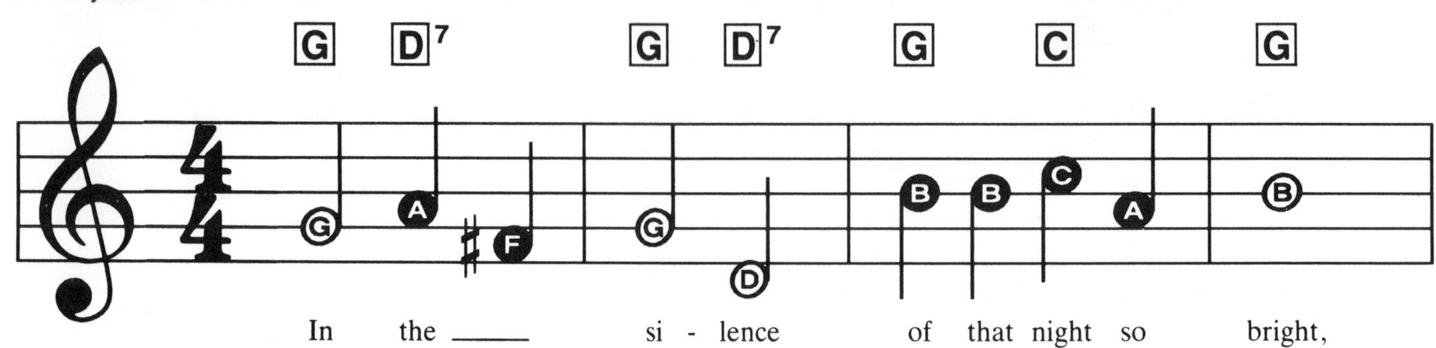
G D7 G D7 G C G
In the ___ si - lence of that night so bright,

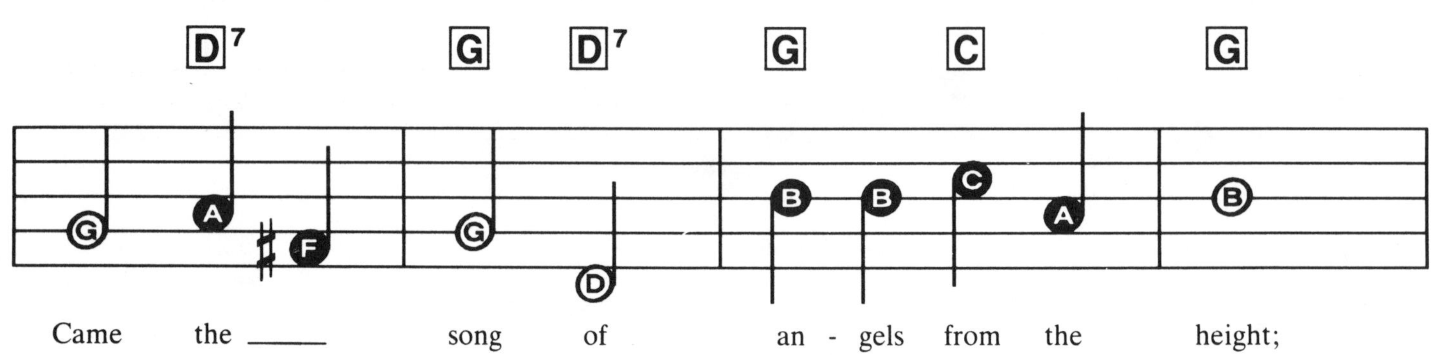
D7 G D7 G C G
Came the ___ song of an - gels from the height;

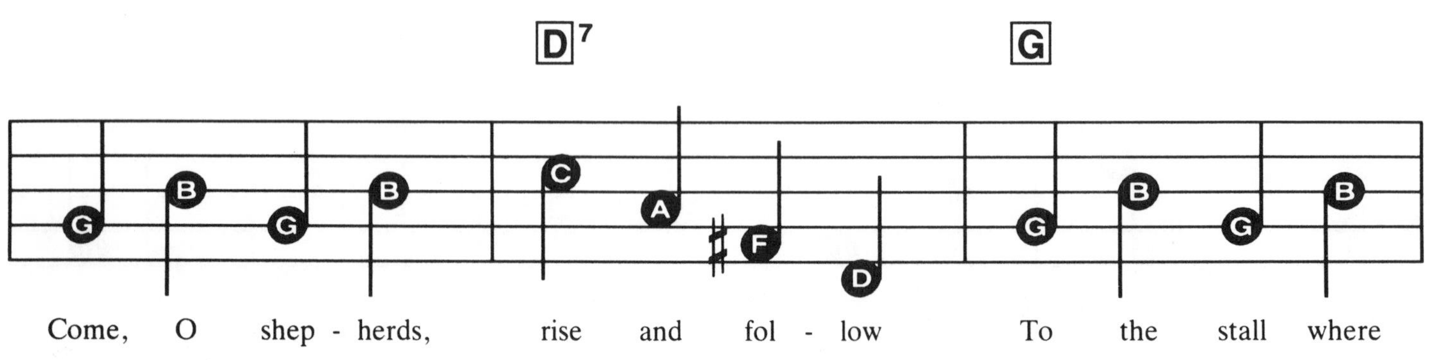
D7 G
Come, O shep - herds, rise and fol - low To the stall where

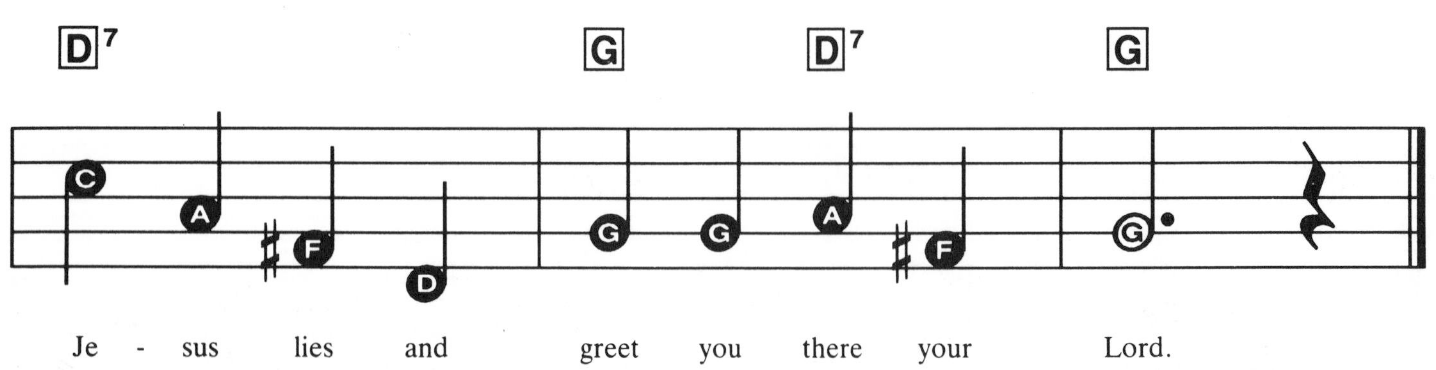
D7 G D7 G
Je - sus lies and greet you there your Lord.

INFANT IN THE MANGER

WOODWINDS
FULL 'N' MELLOW
Medium WALTZ

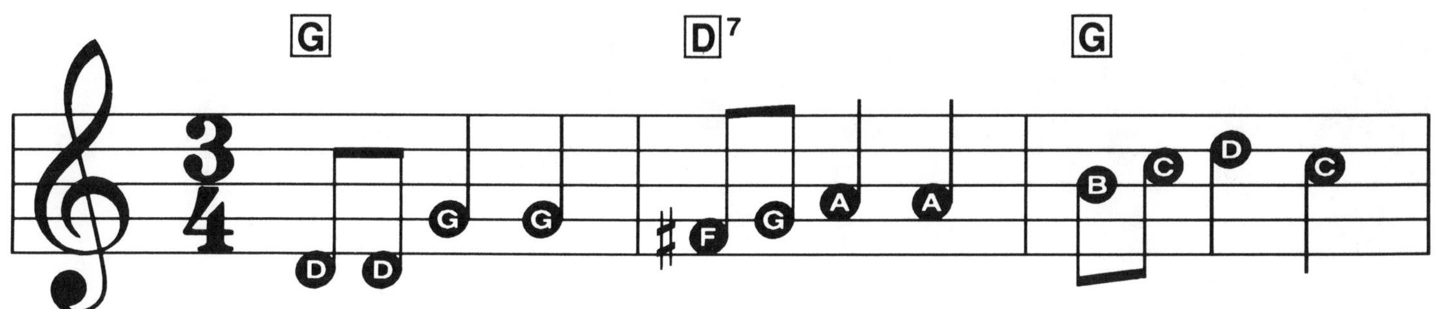

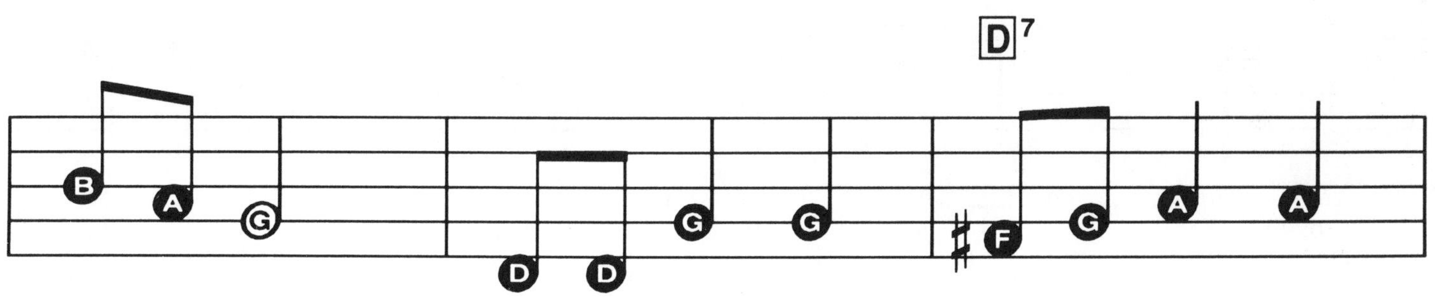

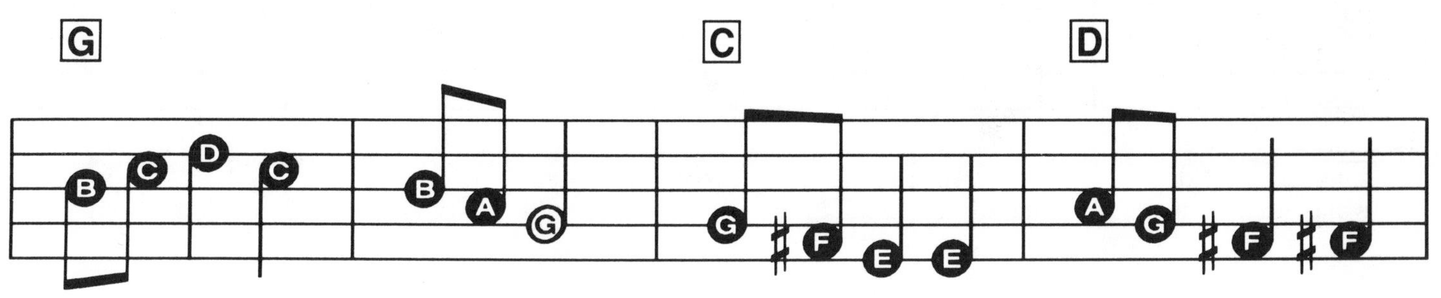

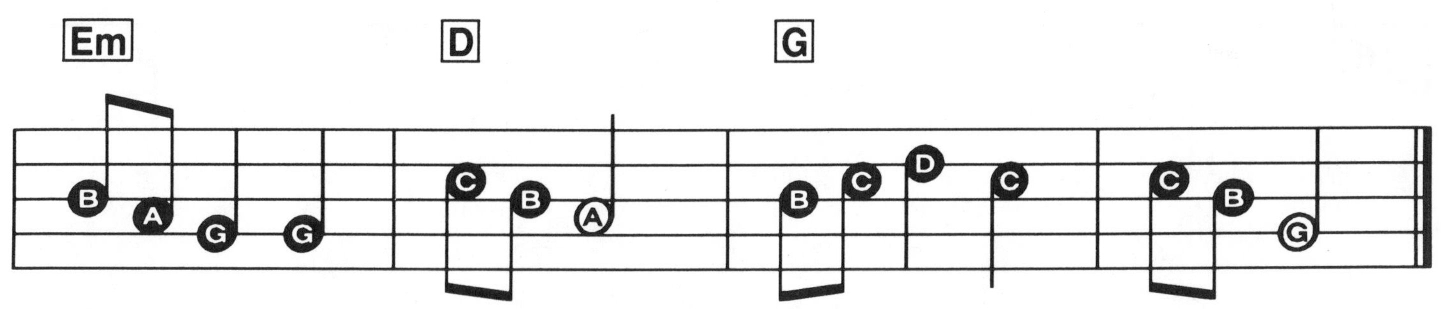

IT CAME UPON THE MIDNIGHT CLEAR

HARPSICHORD
FULL 'N' MELLOW
Medium WALTZ

F
G7
C
N.C.
Instr.
It
C
F
C
F
came up - on the mid - night clear, that glo - ri - ous
through the clo - ven skies they come, with peace - ful
D7
G7
C
F
song of old from an - gels bend - ing
wings un - furled; And still their heav - en - ly
C
F
G7
C
near the earth to touch their harps of gold.
mu - sic floats o'er all the wear - y world:

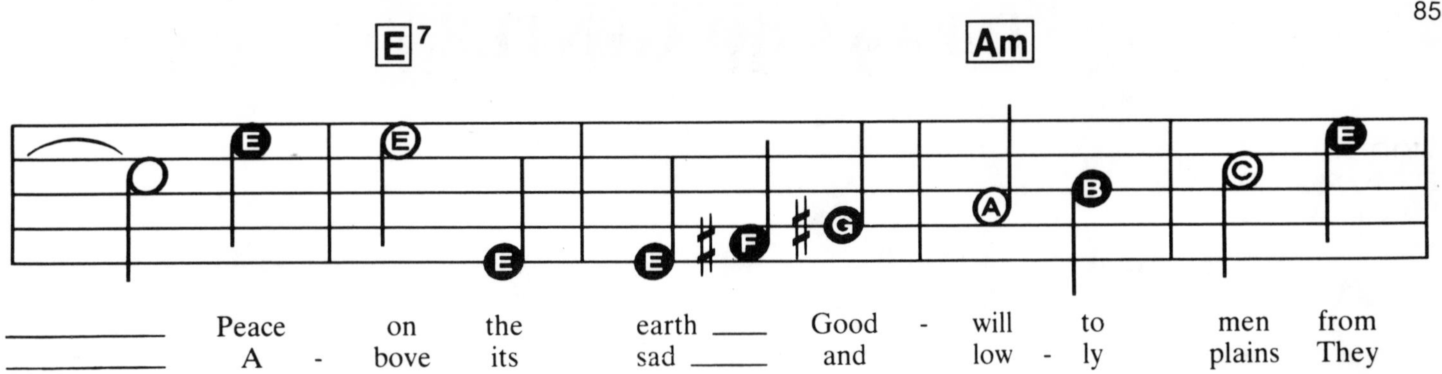
E7
Am
Peace on the earth Good - will to men from
A - bove its sad and low - ly plains They

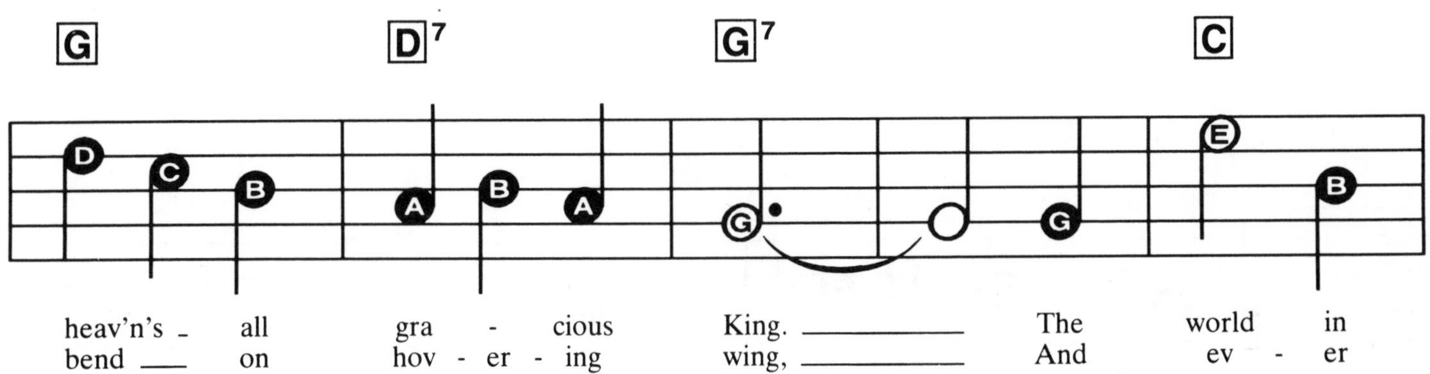
G
D7
G7
C
heav'n's all gra - cious King. The world in
bend on hov - er - ing wing, And ev - er

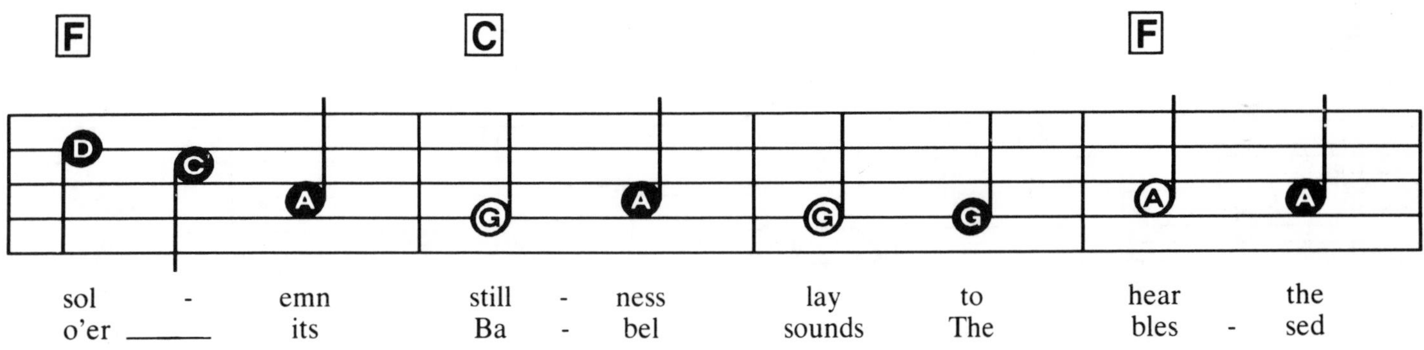
F
C
F
sol - emn still - ness lay to hear the
o'er its Ba - bel sounds The bles - sed

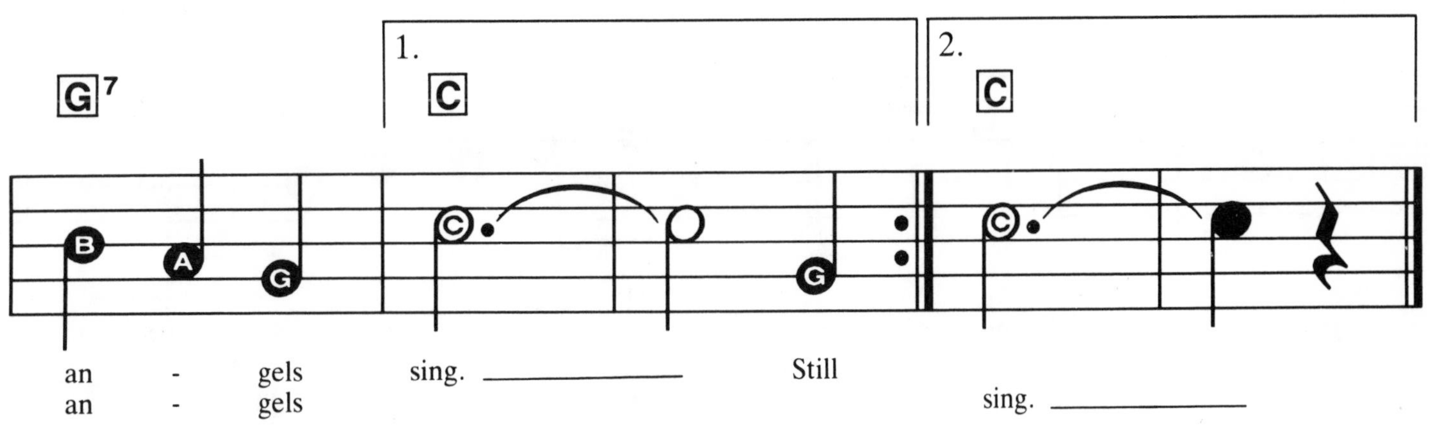
G7
1.
C
2.
C
an - gels sing. Still
an - gels sing.

INFANT SO GENTLE

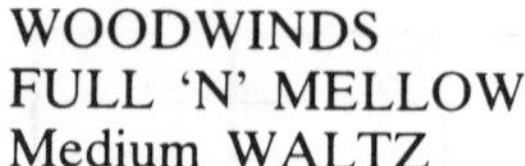

F C7

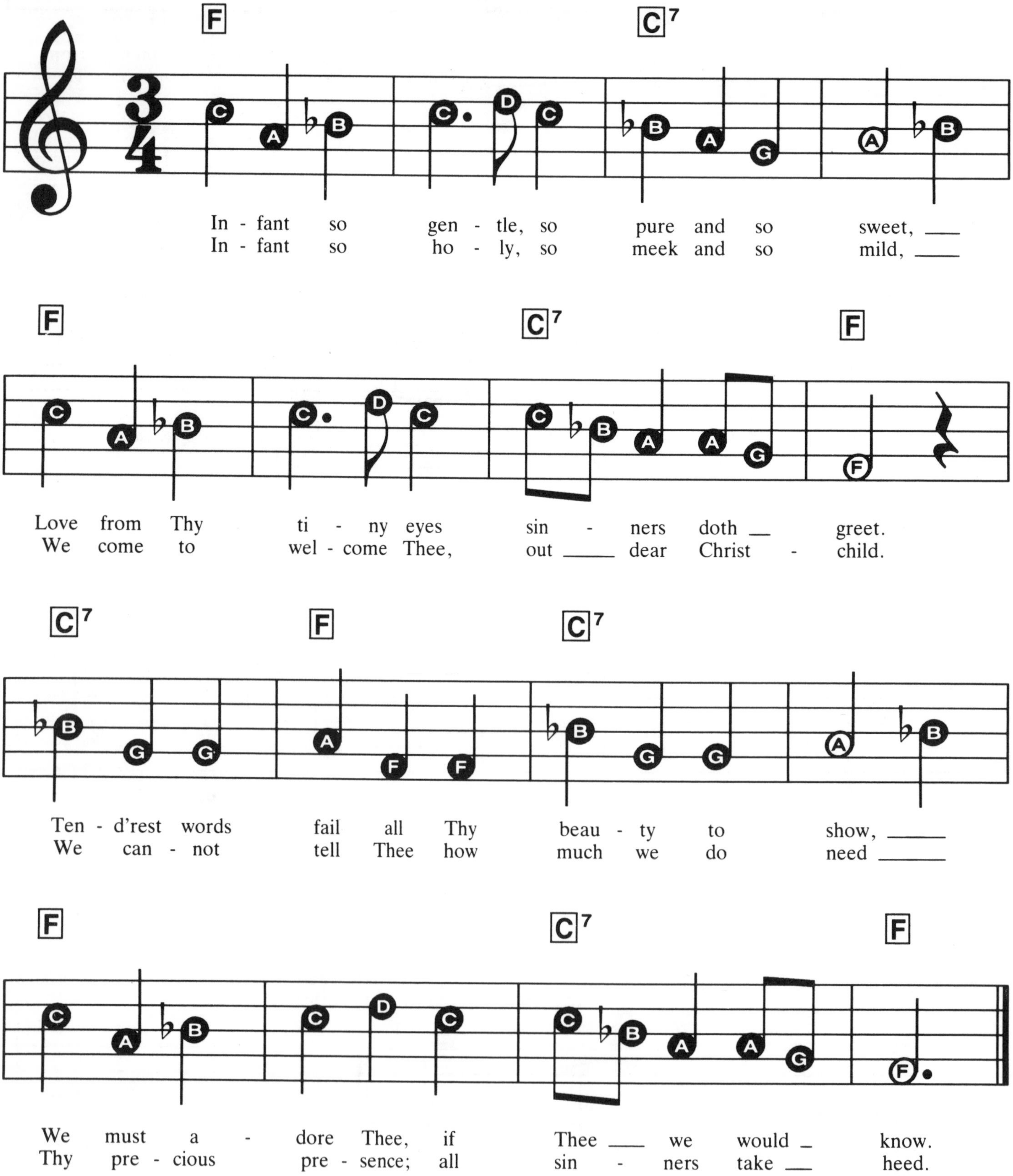

In - fant so gen - tle, so pure and so sweet, ___
In - fant so ho - ly, so meek and so mild, ___

F C7 F

Love from Thy ti - ny eyes sin - ners doth __ greet.
We come to wel - come Thee, out ____ dear Christ - child.

C7 F C7

Ten - d'rest words fail all Thy beau - ty to show, ____
We can - not tell Thee how much we do need ____

F C7 F

We must a - dore Thee, if Thee ___ we would _ know.
Thy pre - cious pre - sence; all sin - ners take __ heed.

JOLLY OLD SAINT NICHOLAS

C | G7 | Am | Em7

E E E E | D D D | C C C C | E

1. Jol - ly Old Saint Ni - cho - las, lean your ear this way!
2. When the clock is strik - ing twelve, when I'm fast a - sleep,

F | C | G7

A A A A | G G C | B C D E | D

Don't you tell a sin - gle soul what I'm going to say;
Down the chim - ney broad and black with your pack you'll creep;

C | G7 | Am | Em7

E E E E | D D D | C C C C | E

Christ - mas Eve is com - ing soon; now you dear old man,
All the stock - ings you will find hang - ing in a row,

F | C | G7 | C

A A A A | G G C | D C D E | C

whis - per what you'll bring to me; tell me if you can.
Mine will be the short - est one, you'll be sure to know.

JINGLE BELLS

TRUMPET
BRIGHT 'N' BRASSY
Medium Fast SWING

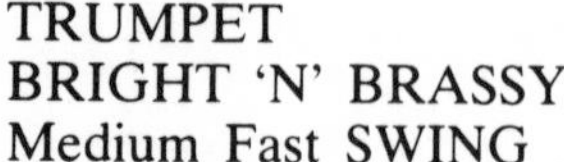

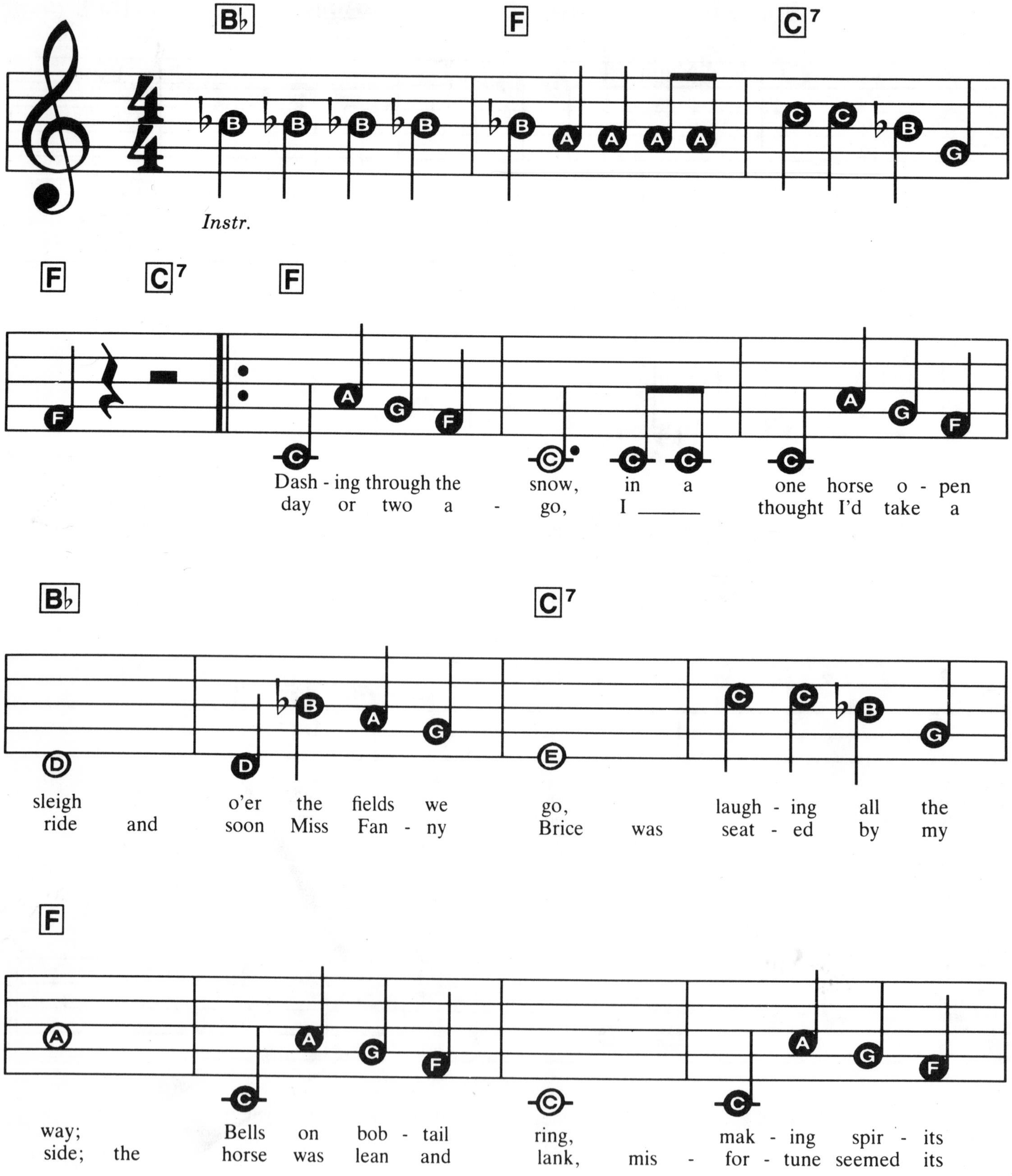

B♭
F
C7
Instr.
F
C7
F
Dash - ing through the snow, in a one horse o - pen
day or two a - go, I ___ thought I'd take a
B♭
C7
sleigh o'er the fields we go, laugh - ing all the
ride and soon Miss Fan - ny Brice was seat - ed by my
F
way; Bells on bob - tail ring, mak - ing spir - its
side; the horse was lean and lank, mis - for - tune seemed its

B♭
Gm
F
C7
D D D B A G C C C C D C B G
bright, what fun it is to ride and sing a sleigh - ing song to -
lot, we got in - to a drift - ed bank and we, we got up -
F
F
F A A A A A A A C F G
night!
sot!
Jin - gle Bells! Jin - gle Bells! Jin - gle all the
F7
B♭
F
A B B B B B A A A A
way. Oh what fun it is to ride in a
1.
G7
C
2.
C7
A G G A G C C C B G
one horse o - pen sleigh, Hey! one horse o - pen
F
3.
C7
F
F C C C B G F
sleigh. 2. A one horse o - pen sleigh.

From the Videocraft TV Musical Spectacular, "RUDOLPH THE RED-NOSED REINDEER"

JINGLE-JINGLE-JINGLE

TROMBONE
BRIGHT 'N' BRASSY
Medium SWING

Words and Music by
JOHNNY MARKS

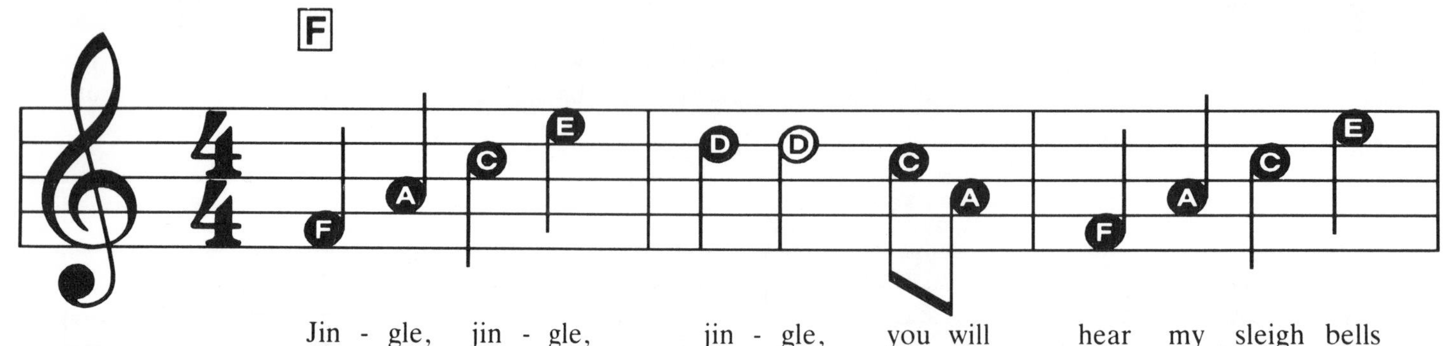

F
F A C E D D C A F A C E
Jin - gle, jin - gle, jin - gle, you will hear my sleigh bells

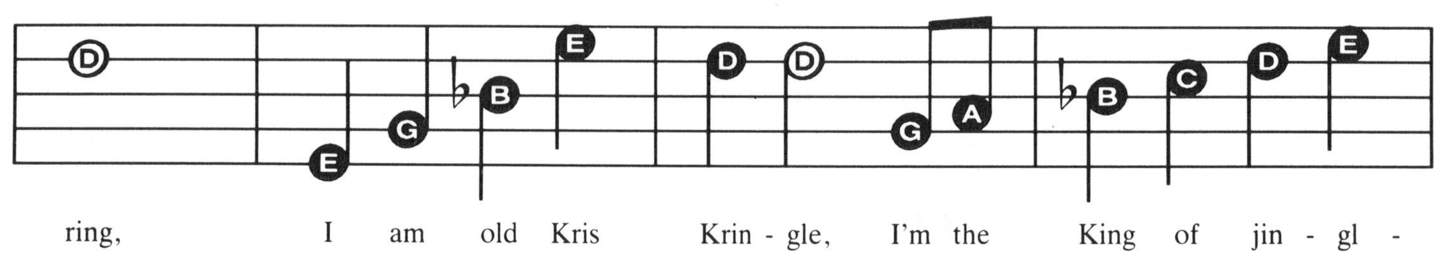

C7
D E G B E D D G A B C D E
ring, I am old Kris Krin - gle, I'm the King of jin - gl -

F

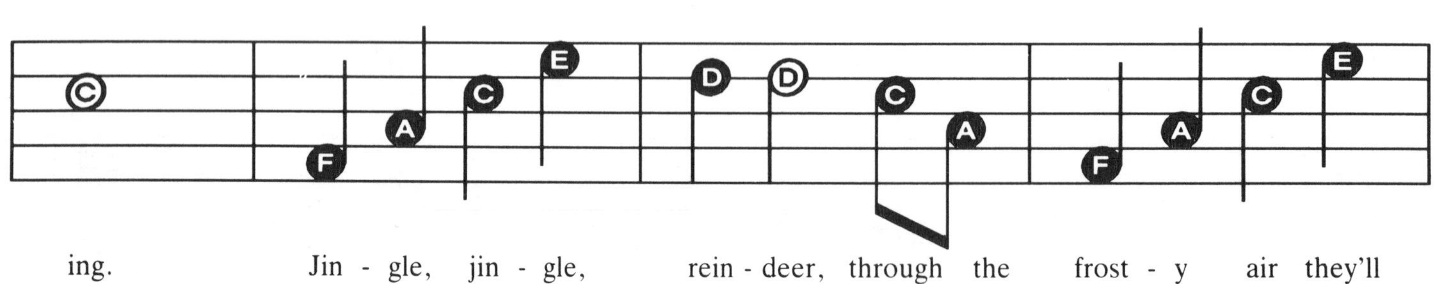

C F A C E D D C A F A C E
ing. Jin - gle, jin - gle, rein - deer, through the frost - y air they'll

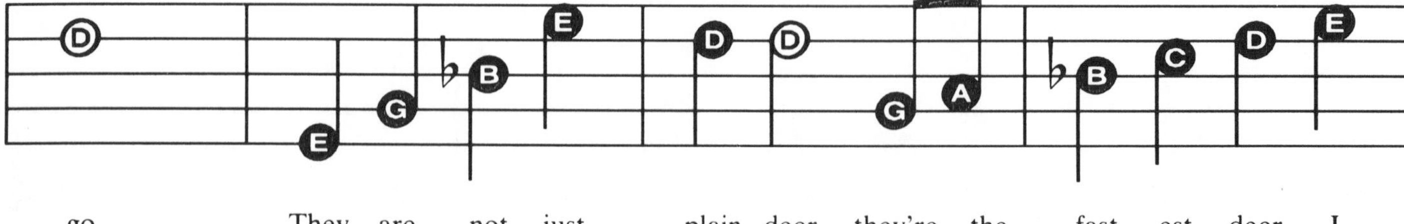

C7
D E G B E D D G A B C D E
go, They are not just plain deer, they're the fast - est deer I

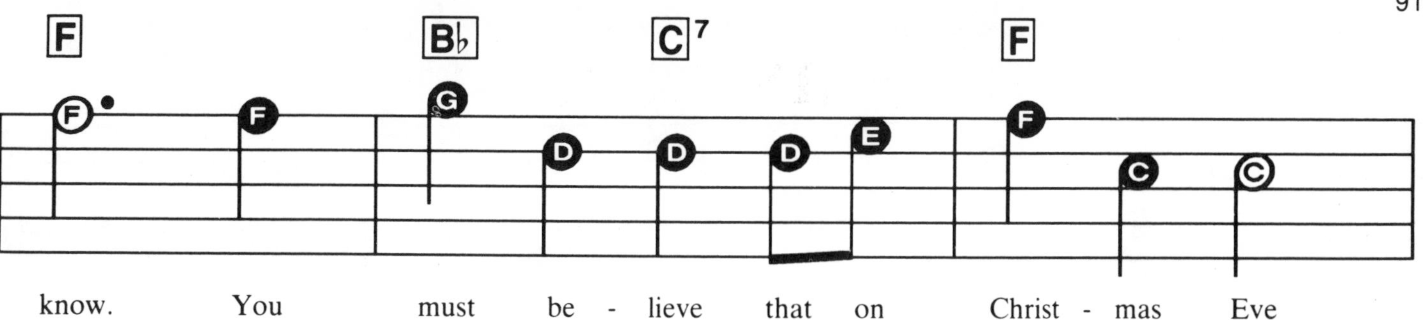
F
B♭
C7
F
F
F
G
D
D
D
E
F
C
C
know. You must be - lieve that on Christ - mas Eve

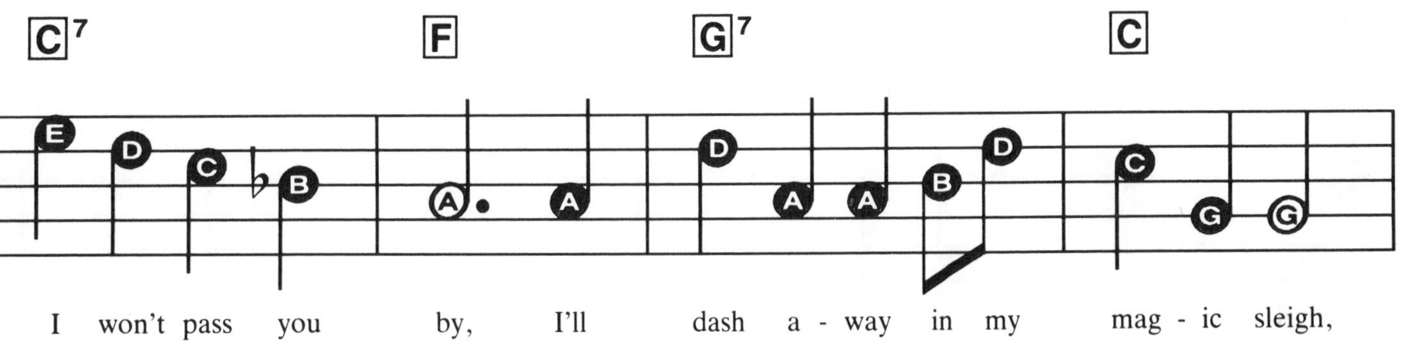
C7
F
G7
C
E
D
C
B
A
A
D
A
A
B
D
C
G
G
I won't pass you by, I'll dash a - way in my mag - ic sleigh,

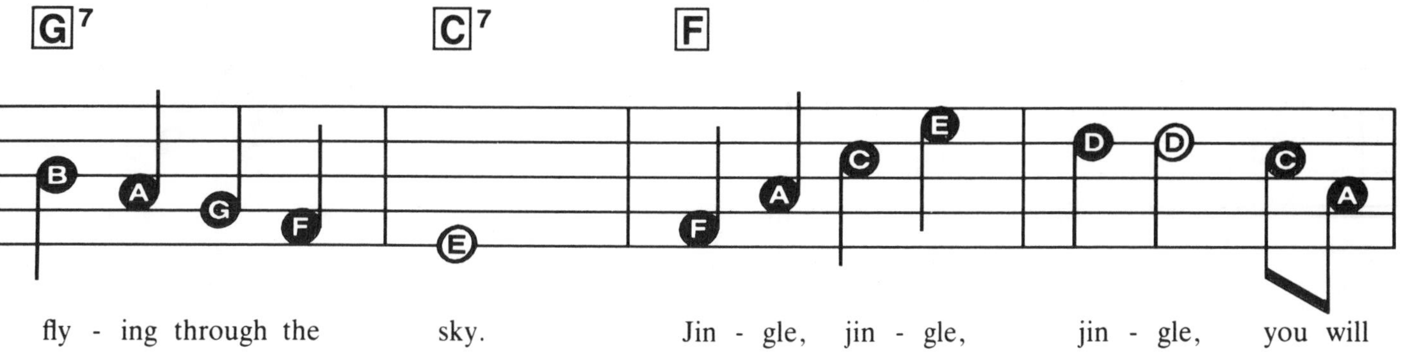
G7
C7
F
B
A
G
F
E
F
A
C
E
D
D
C
A
fly - ing through the sky. Jin - gle, jin - gle, jin - gle, you will

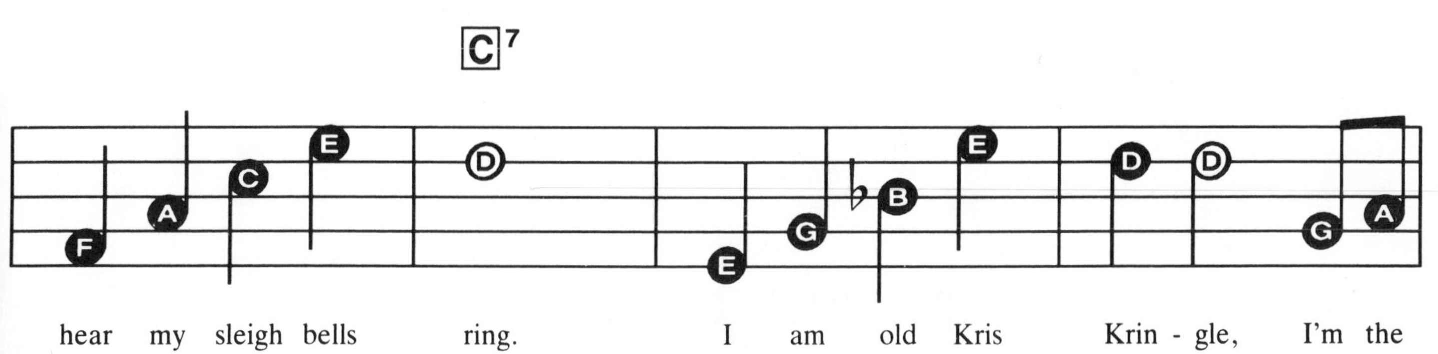
C7
F
A
C
E
D
E
G
B
E
D
D
G
A
hear my sleigh bells ring. I am old Kris Krin - gle, I'm the

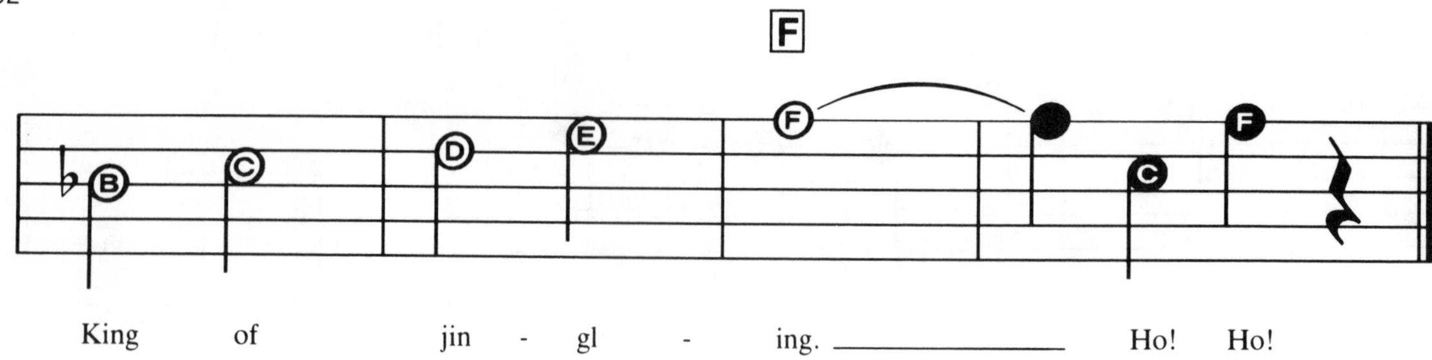
F
King of jin - gl - ing. ______ Ho! Ho!

JOY TO THE WORLD

ORGAN
CLASSICAL
Medium Fast SWING

C G7 C F

1. Joy to the world! The Lord is come! Let earth re -
2. Joy to the earth, the Sa - vior reigns! Let men their

G7 C F C

ceive her King; Let ev - 'ry ____ heart ________ pre -
songs em - ploy while fields __ and ____ floods, ________ rocks,

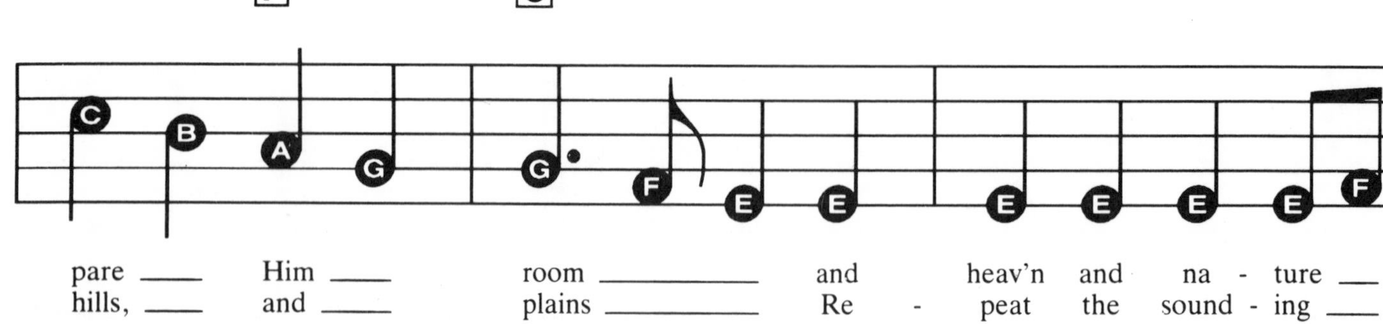
F C
pare ____ Him ____ room ________ and heav'n and na - ture ___
hills, ____ and ____ plains ________ Re - peat the sound - ing ___

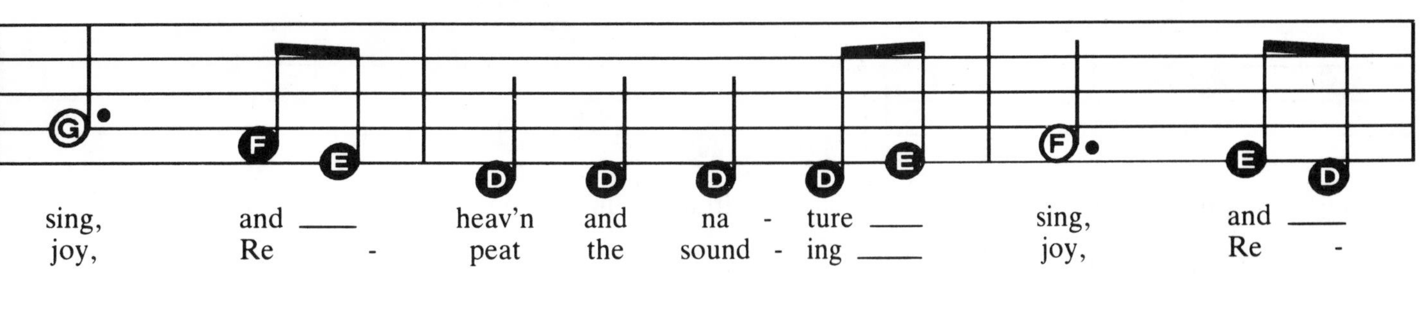
G7
sing, and heav'n and na - ture sing, and
joy, Re - peat the sound - ing joy, Re -

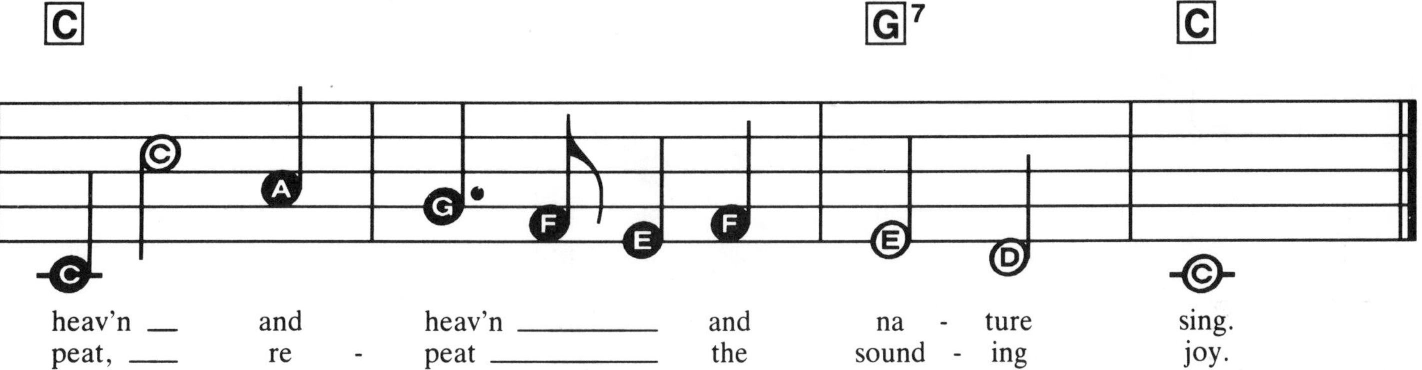
C G7 C
heav'n and heav'n and na - ture sing.
peat, re - peat the sound - ing joy.

JOYOUS CHRISTMAS

TRUMPET
BRILLIANT SOLO
Medium SWING

Words and Music by
JOHNNY MARKS

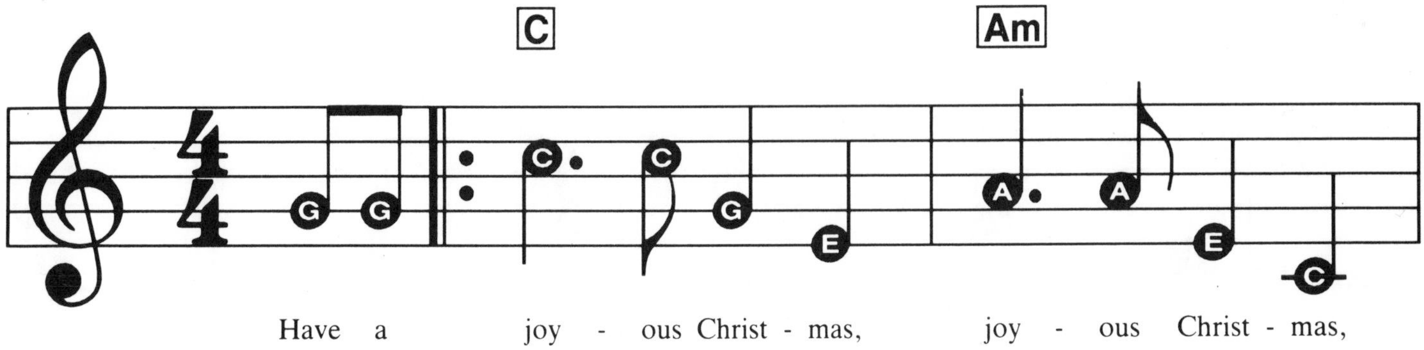

C Am

Have a joy - ous Christ - mas, joy - ous Christ - mas,

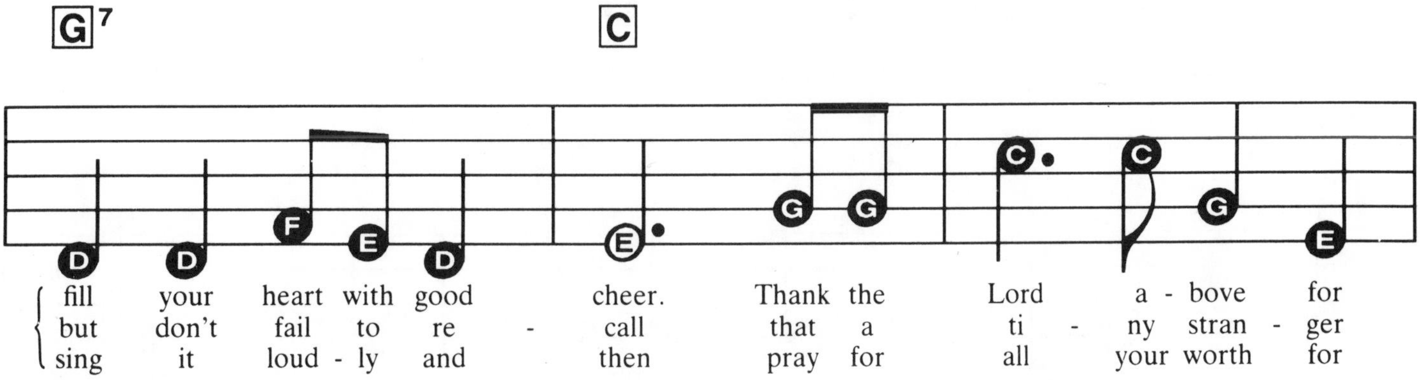

G7 C

fill your heart with good cheer. Thank the Lord a - bove for
but don't fail to re - call that a ti - ny stran - ger
sing it loud - ly and then pray for all your worth for

Am G7 C

all the love you have from those you hold dear.
in a man - ger was the start of it all.
peace on earth and for good will ___ to men.

F C D7

Let the Christ - mas bells ring out, pro - claim - ing loud and

G7 C Am

clear: Have a joy - ous Christ - mas, joy - ous Christ - mas

G7 | 1. C | 2. C

and ___ a hap - py New Year. Have a Year.

A MARSHMALLOW WORLD

OBOE
BRILLIANT SOLO
Medium SWING

Music by PETER DE ROSE
Words by CARL SIGMAN

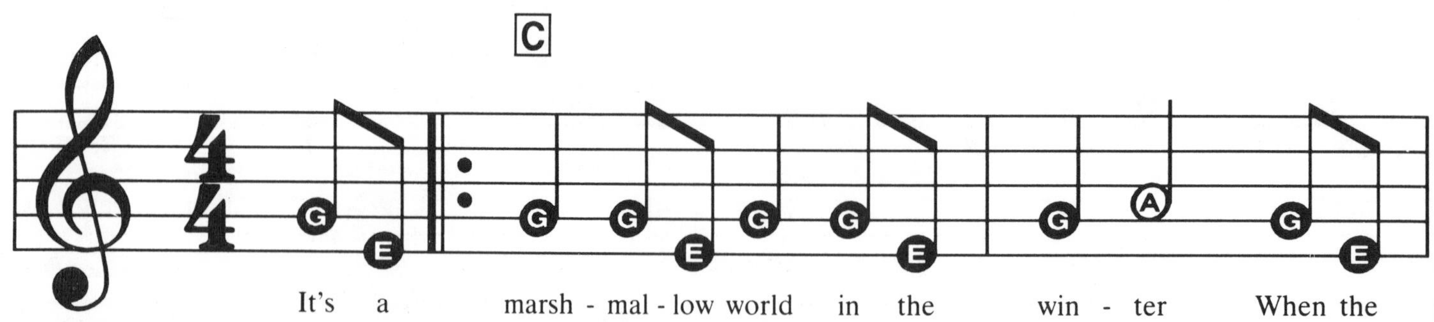
C
It's a marsh - mal - low world in the win - ter When the

G7
snow comes to cov - er the ground. It's the time for play It's a
Am7 D7
whipped cream day, I wait for it the whole year
G7 C
round. Those are marsh - mal - low clouds be - ing friend - ly In the
G7
arms of the ev - er - green trees And the sun is red Like a
Am7 G7 C
pump - kin head It's shin - ing so your nose won't freeze. The
Gm7 Dm7 C7
world is your snow - ball, see how it grows That's how it goes When -

F
D7
ev - er it snows The world is your snow - ball
Em7
D7
G7
Just for a song Get out and roll it a - long. It's a
C
yum - yum - my world made for sweet - hearts Take a walk with your fav - o - rite
G7
C
girl. It's a sug - ar date What if spring is late In
G7
1.
C
G7
2.
C
win - ter it's a marsh - mal - low world. It's a world.

LITTLE JESUS, DO NOT WAKE

SAXOPHONE
BRILLIANT SOLO
Medium MARCH

LET IT SNOW! LET IT SNOW! LET IT SNOW!

SAXOPHONE
FULL 'N' MELLOW
Medium SWING

Lyrics by SAMMY CAHN
Music by JULE STYNE

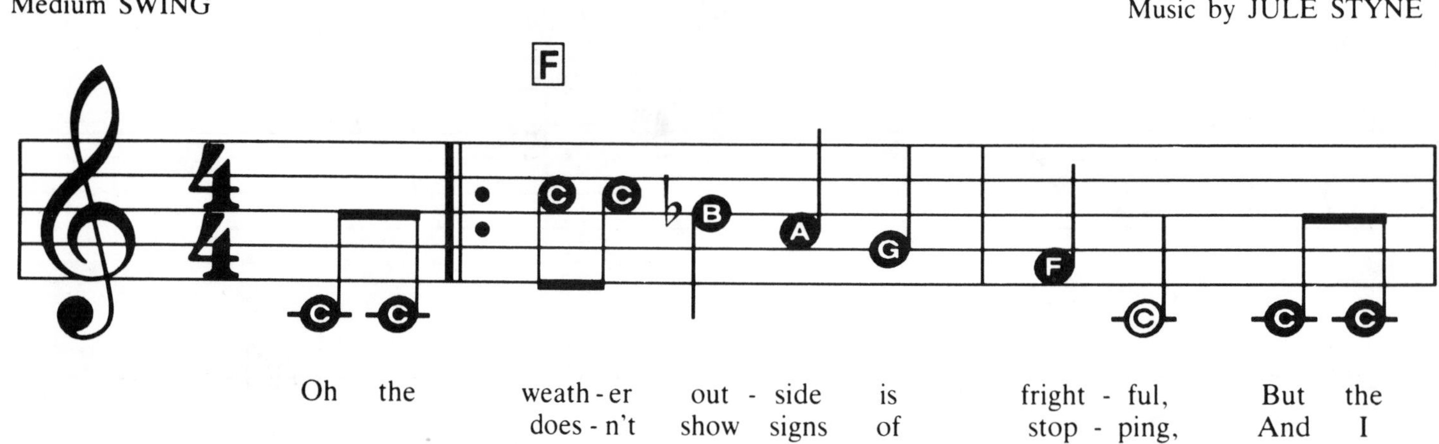
F
Oh the weath - er out - side is fright - ful, But the
does - n't show signs of stop - ping, And I

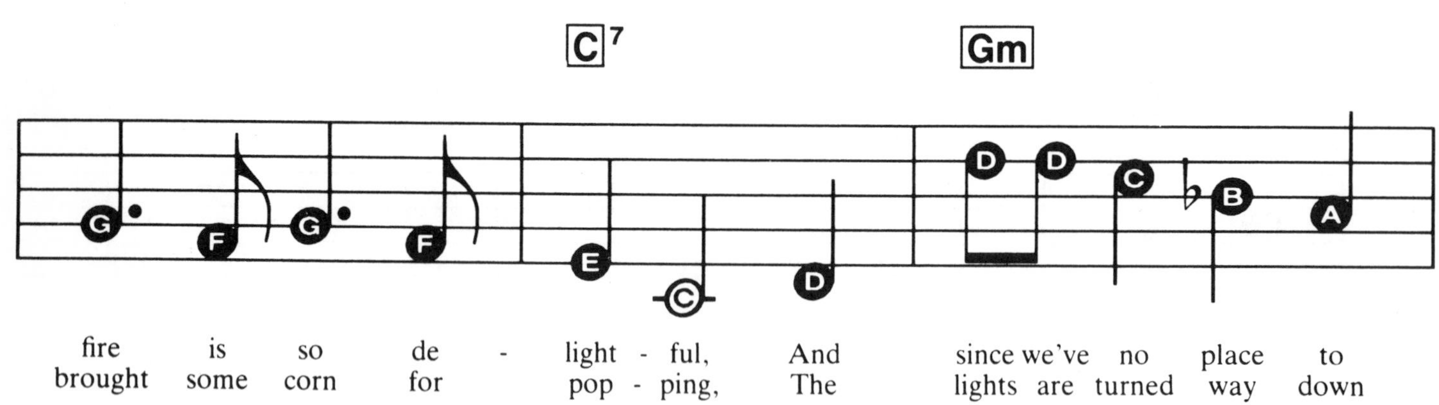
C7
Gm
fire is so de - light - ful, And since we've no place to
brought some corn for pop - ping, The lights are turned way down

C7
1.
F
2.
F
go; low. Let it snow! Let it snow! Let it snow! It snow! When we

C G7
fin - al - ly kiss good - night, How I'll hate go - ing out in the
C G7
storm! But if you'll real - ly hold me tight, All the way home I'll be
C7 F
warm. The fire ___ is slow - ly dy - ing And my
C7 Gm
dear, we're still good - bye - ing, But as long as you love me
C7 F
so, Let it snow! Let it snow! Let it snow!

THE LITTLE DRUMMER BOY

OBOE
CLASSICAL
Medium MARCH

Words and Music by
KATHERINE DAVIS, HENRY ONORATI
and HARRY SIMEONE

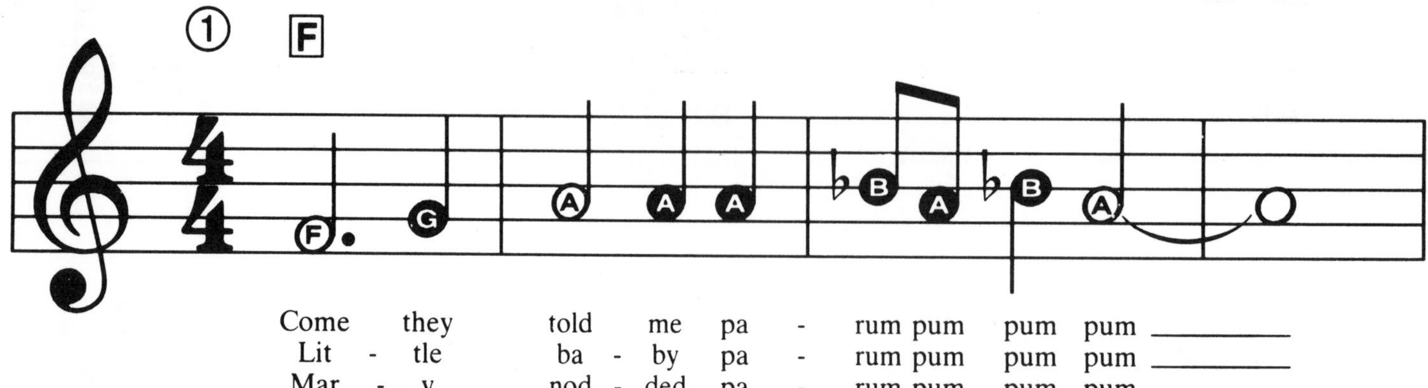
1
F
Come they told me pa - rum pum pum pum
Lit - tle ba - by pa - rum pum pum pum
Mar - y nod - ded pa - rum pum pum pum

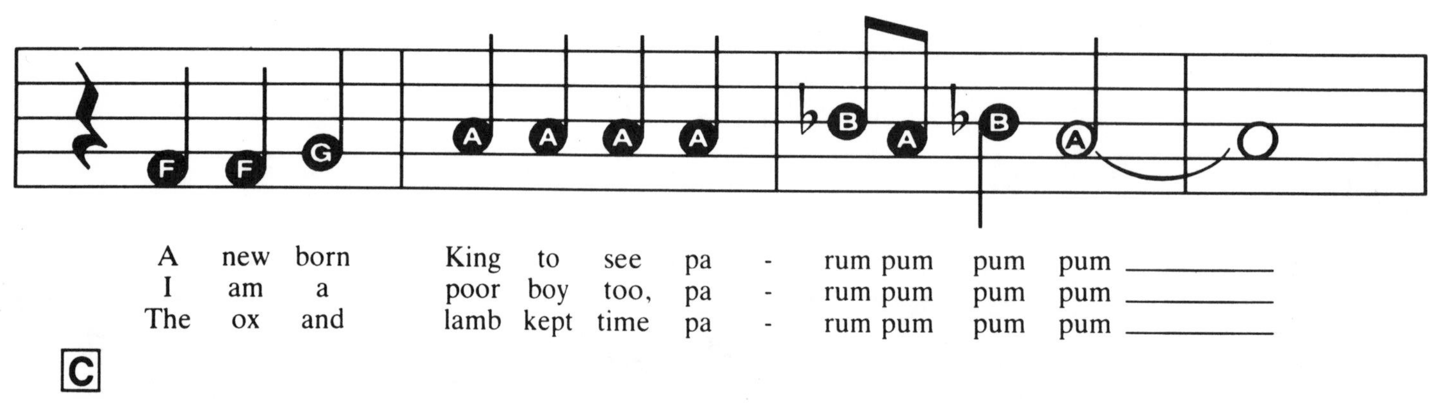
A new born King to see pa - rum pum pum pum
I am a poor boy too, pa - rum pum pum pum
The ox and lamb kept time pa - rum pum pum pum

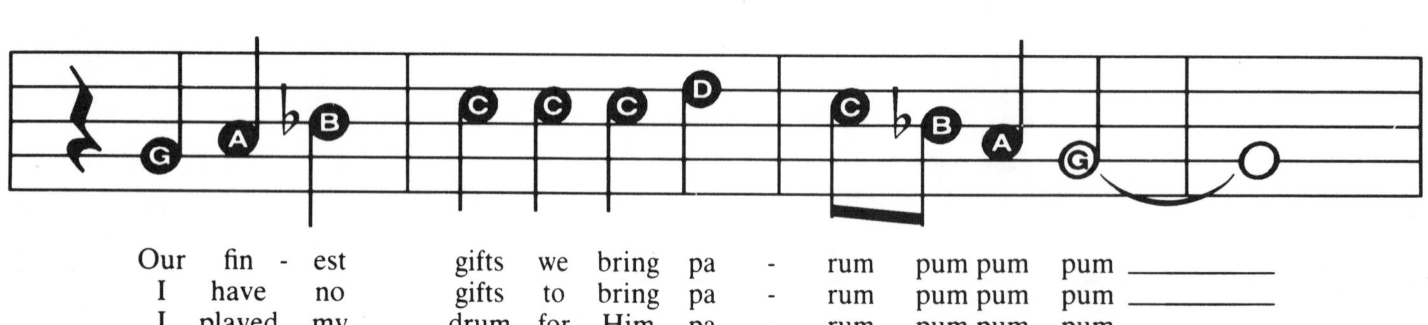
C
Our fin - est gifts we bring pa - rum pum pum pum
I have no gifts to bring pa - rum pum pum pum
I played my drum for Him pa - rum pum pum pum

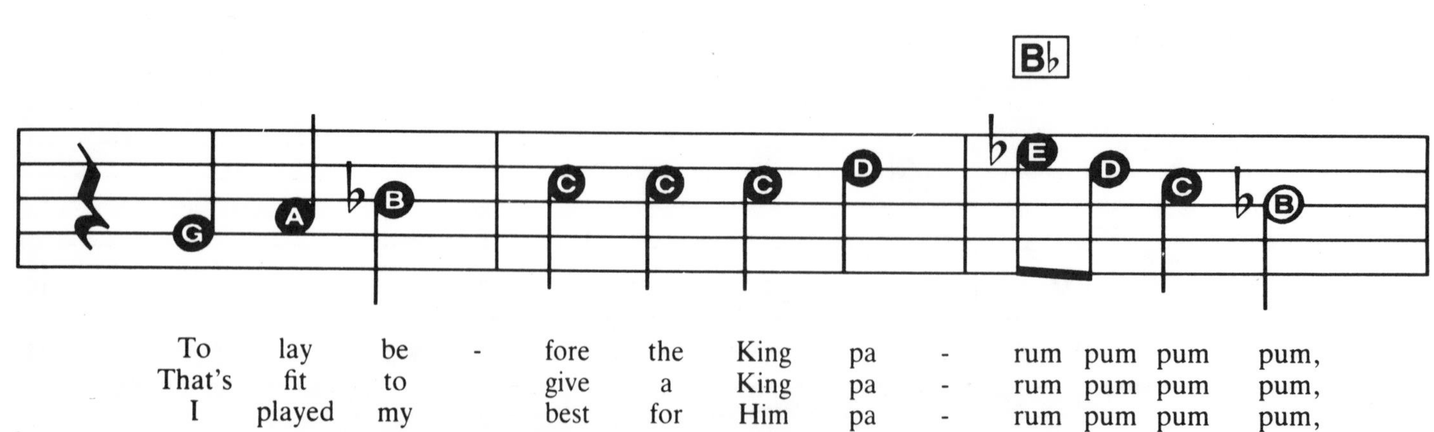
B♭
To lay be - fore the King pa - rum pum pum pum,
That's fit to give a King pa - rum pum pum pum,
I played my best for Him pa - rum pum pum pum,

②
F
C
rum pum pum pum, rum pum pum pum.
rum pum pum pum, rum pum pum pum.
rum pum pum pum, rum pum pum pum.
F
So to hon - or Him pa - rum pum pum pum
1.
when we come.
2.
C
Return to ①
Play to ②
Skip to ③
on my drum.
③
F
Then He smiled at me pa rum pum pum pum
me and my drum.

MARCH OF THE THREE KINGS

ORGAN
FULL 'N' BRILLIANT
No Rhythm

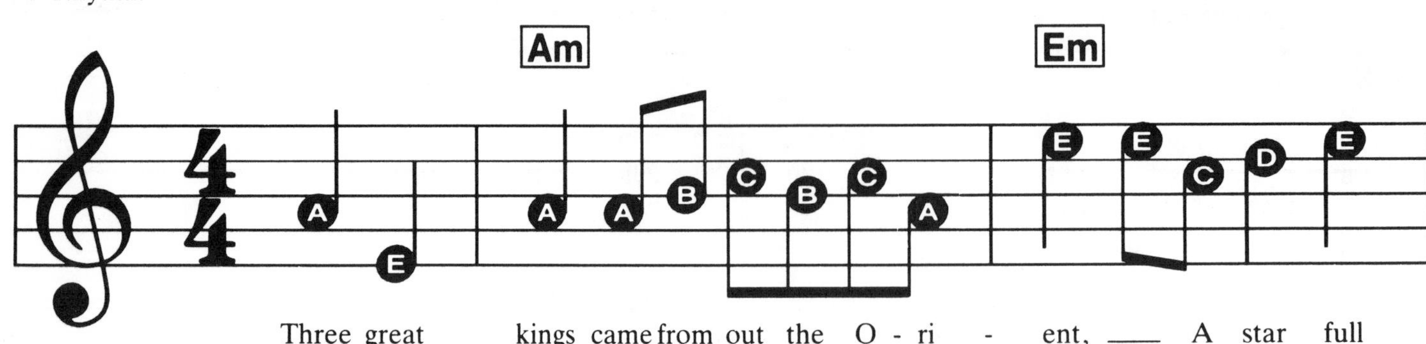

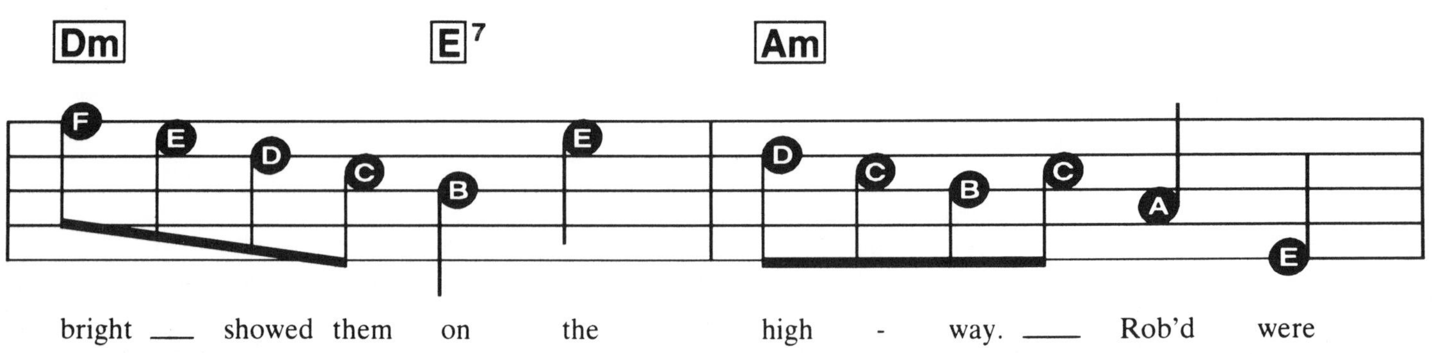

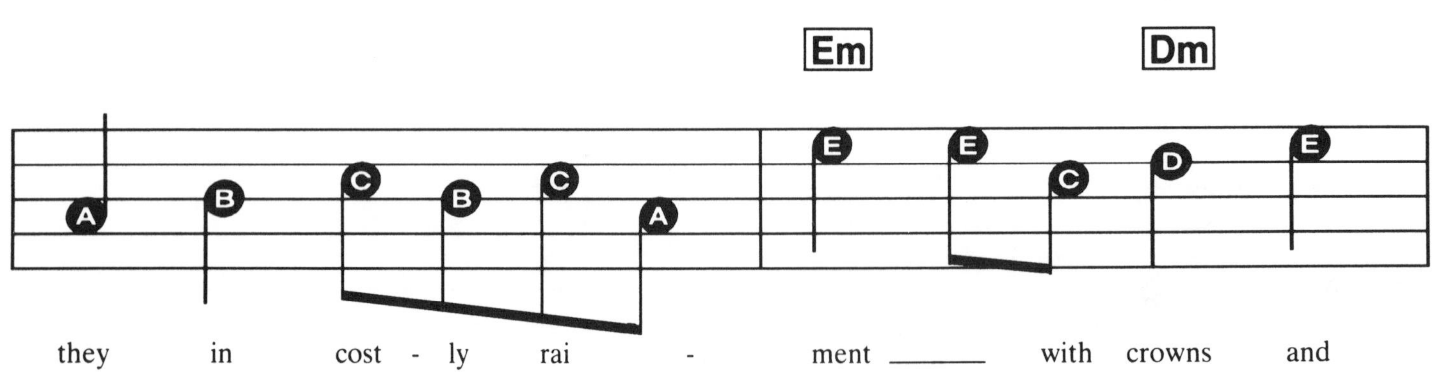

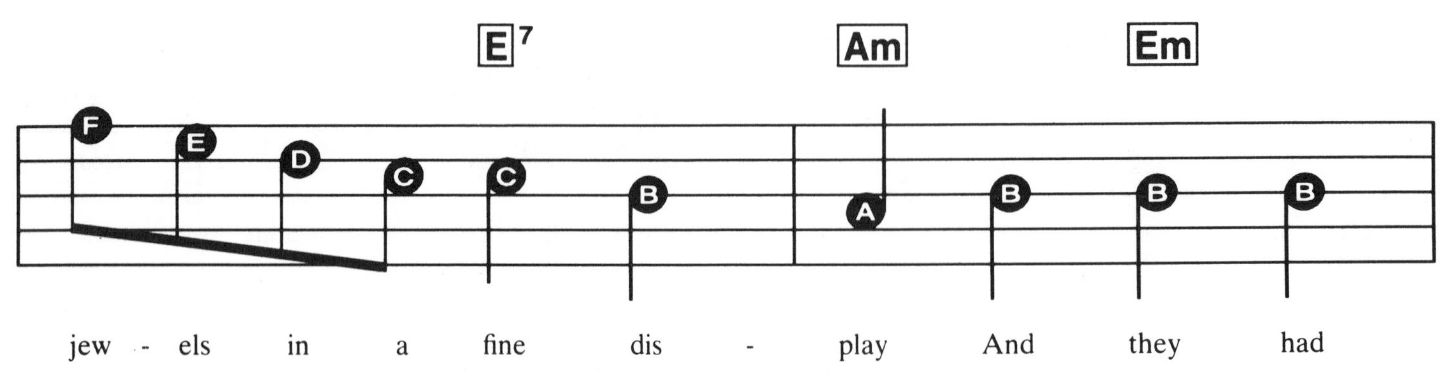

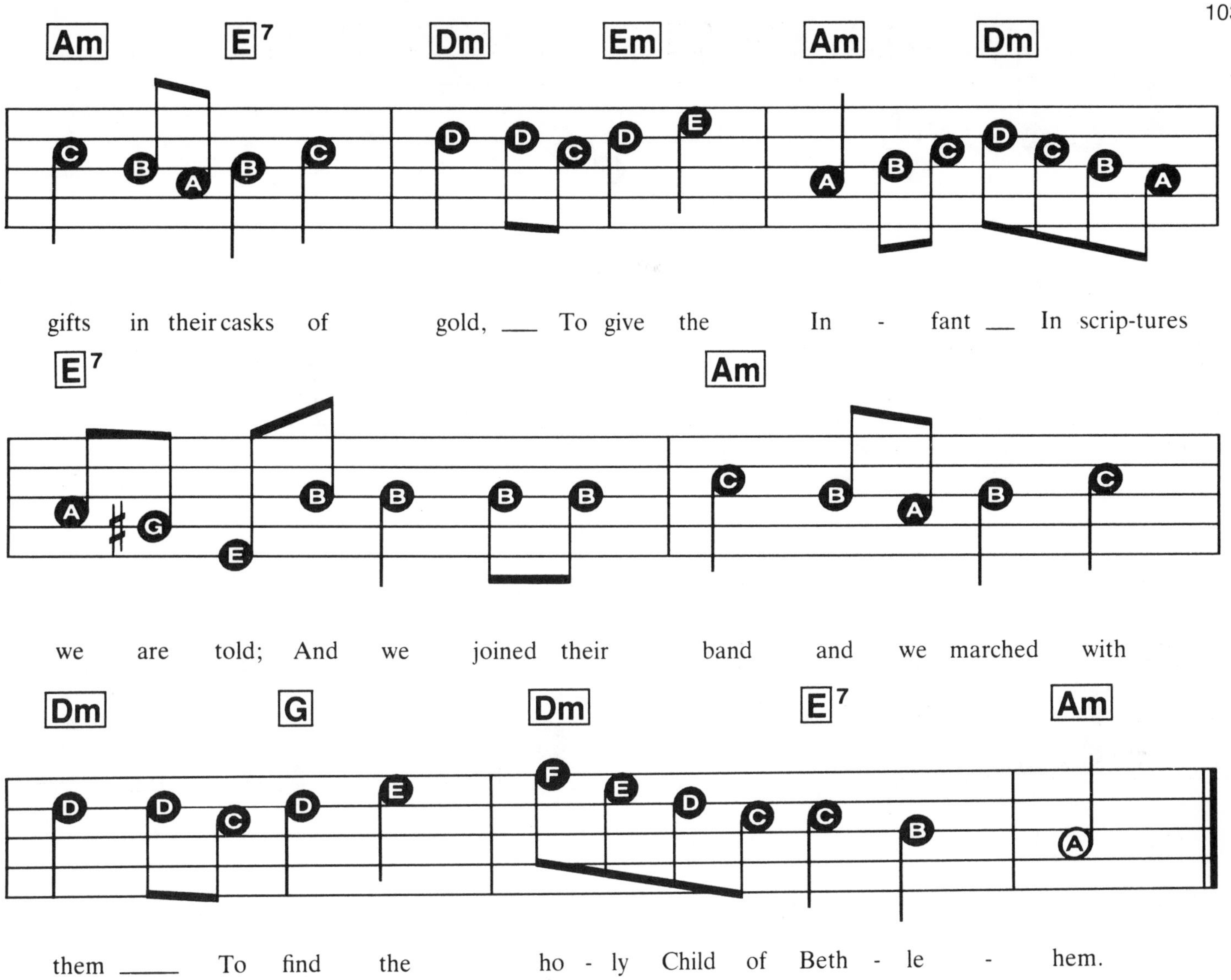

Am E7 Dm Em Am Dm
gifts in their casks of gold, ___ To give the In - fant ___ In scrip-tures
E7 Am
we are told; And we joined their band and we marched with
Dm G Dm E7 Am
them ___ To find the ho - ly Child of Beth - le - hem.

MARCH OF THE TOYS

TRUMPET
BRIGHT 'N' BRASSY
Medium MARCH

N.C.

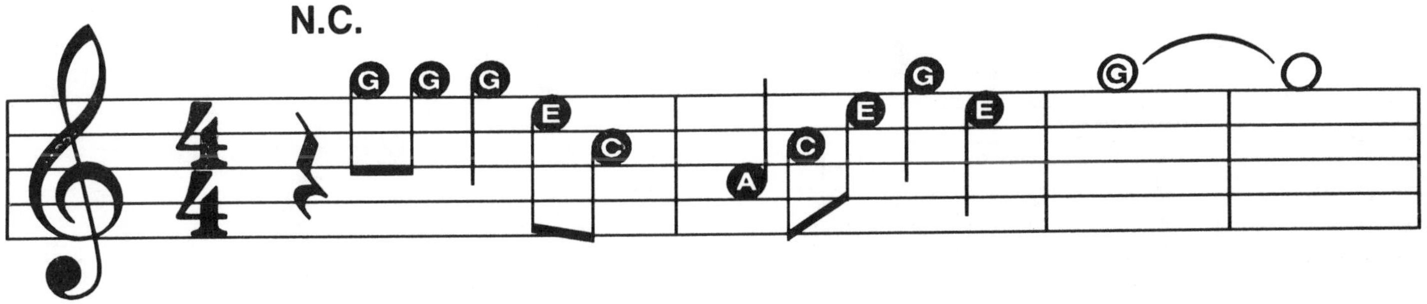

Am
E7
Am
E7
Am
E7
Am
E7
Am
E7
Am
E7

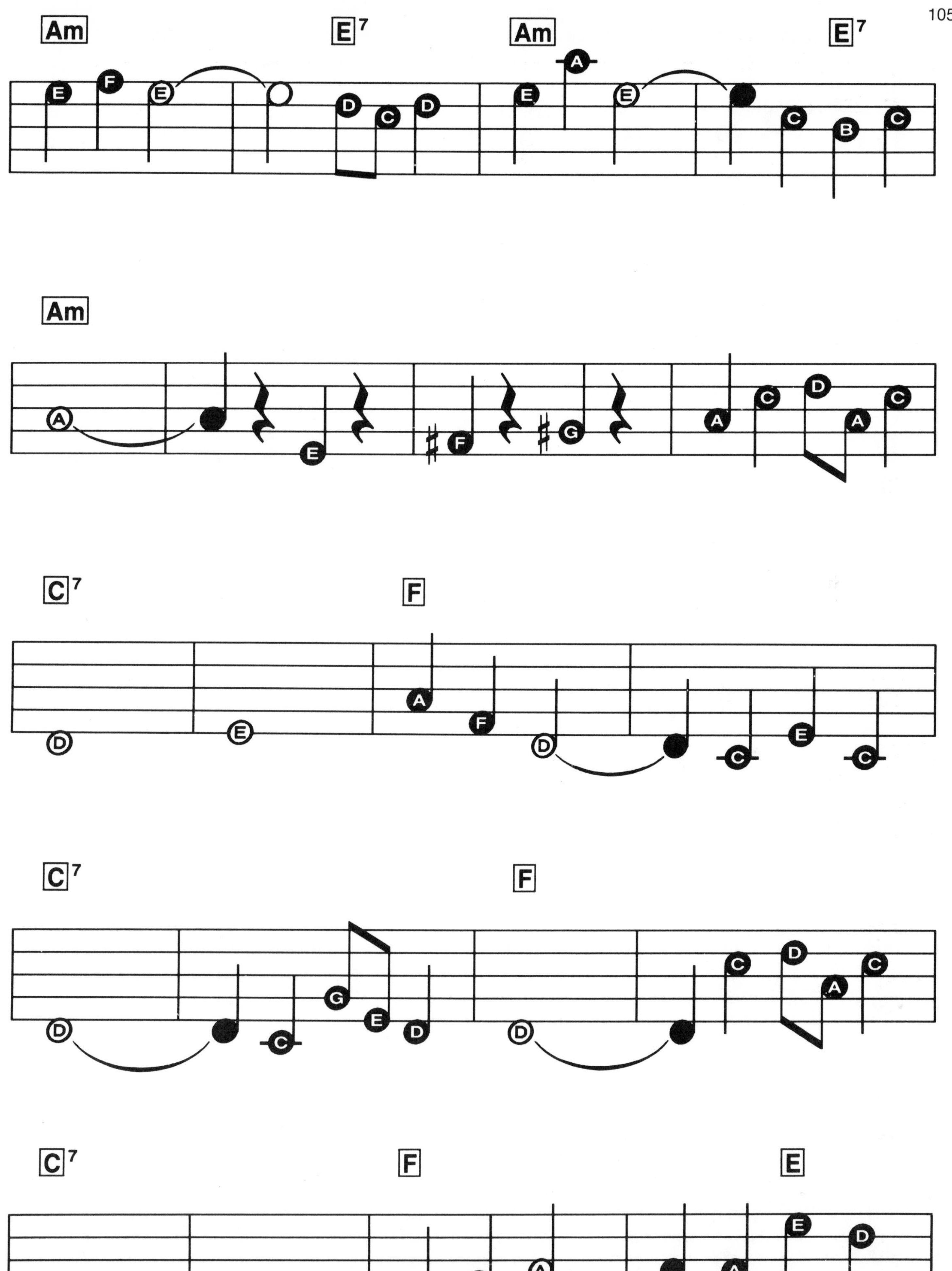
Am
E7
Am
E7
Am
C7
F
C7
F
C7
F
E

A E A E7 A N.C.
Gm C7 F
Gm C7 F
Gm A Dm G7 F
Gm C7 F

THE NIGHT BEFORE CHRISTMAS SONG

PIANO
FULL 'N' MELLOW
Medium WALTZ

Words by CLEMENT MOORE
Music by JOHNNY MARKS

G7 C7 F
soon would be there. Then what to my won - der - ing
bel - ly was round, He spoke not a word but went
C G7
eyes would ap - pear, A min - ia - ture sleigh and eight
straight to his work And filled all the stock - ings, then
C C7 F
ti - ny rein - deer. A lit - tle old driv - er so
turned with a jerk, And lay - ing a fin - ger a -
C D7
live - ly and quick I knew in a mo - ment it
side of his nose Then giv - ing a nod up the
G7 C
must be St. Nick, And more rap - id than ea - gles his
chim - ney he rose; But I heard him ex - claim as he

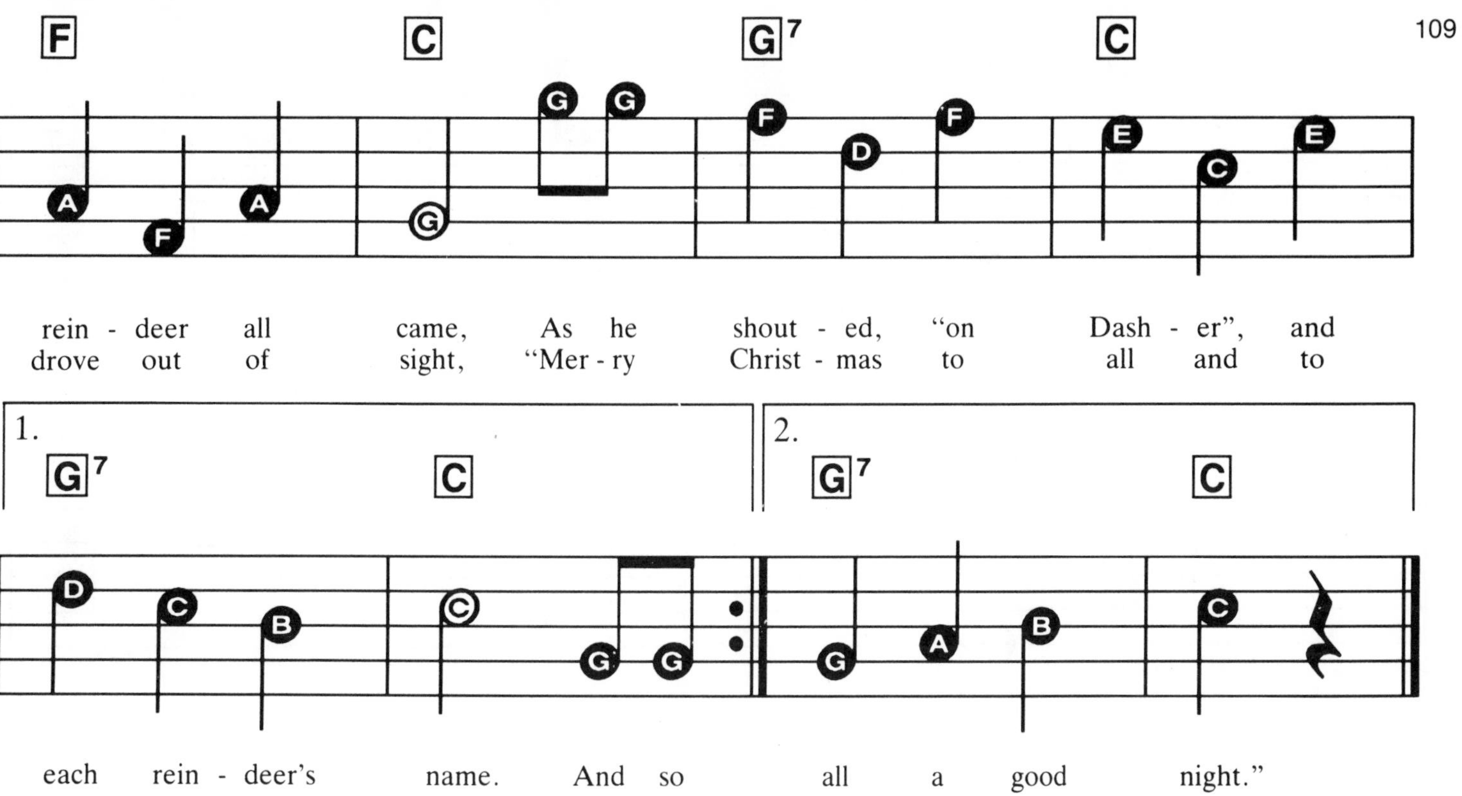
F C G7 C
rein - deer all came, As he shout - ed, "on Dash - er", and
drove out of sight, "Mer - ry Christ - mas to all and to
1. G7 C
2. G7 C
each rein - deer's name. And so all a good night."

From the Videocraft TV Musical Spectacular "RUDOLPH THE RED-NOSED REINDEER"
(Joyeux Noel, Bon Natale, Feliz Navidad)

A MERRY, MERRY CHRISTMAS TO YOU

SAXOPHONE
FULL 'N' MELLOW
Medium WALTZ

Words and Music by
JOHNNY MARKS

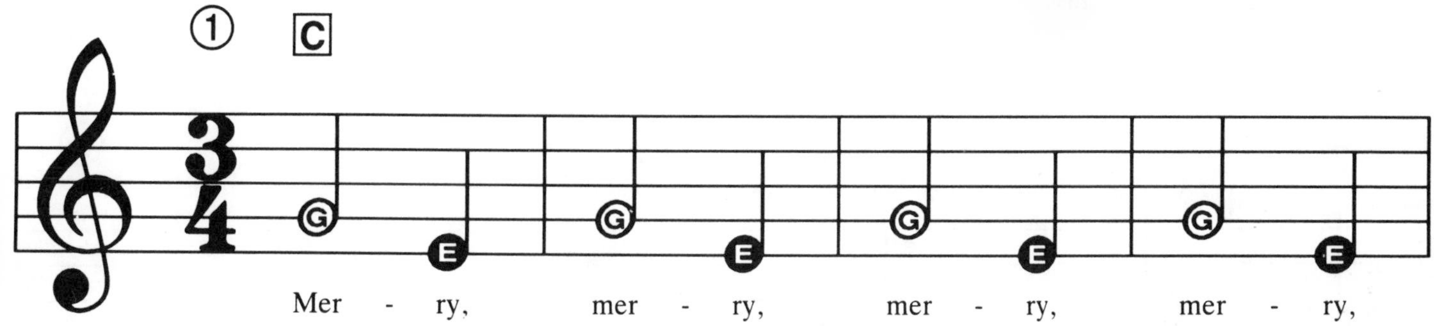

① C

Mer - ry, mer - ry, mer - ry, mer - ry,

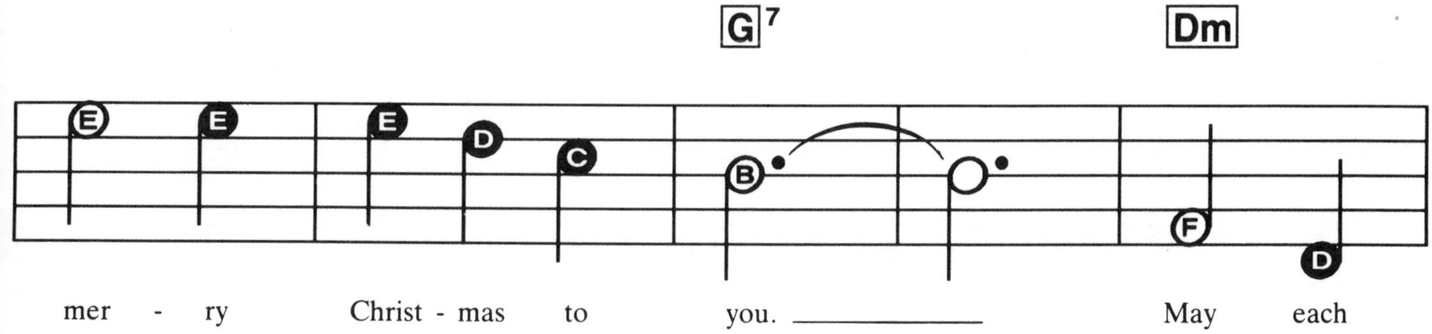

G7 Dm

mer - ry Christ - mas to you. ____________ May each

G7

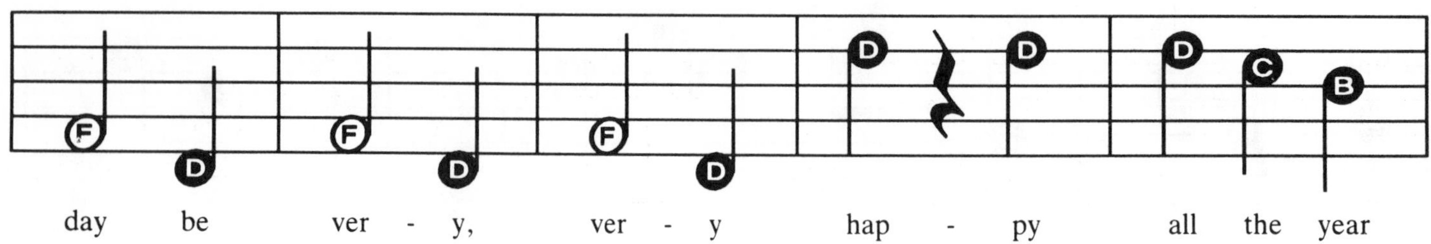
day be ver - y, ver - y hap - py all the year

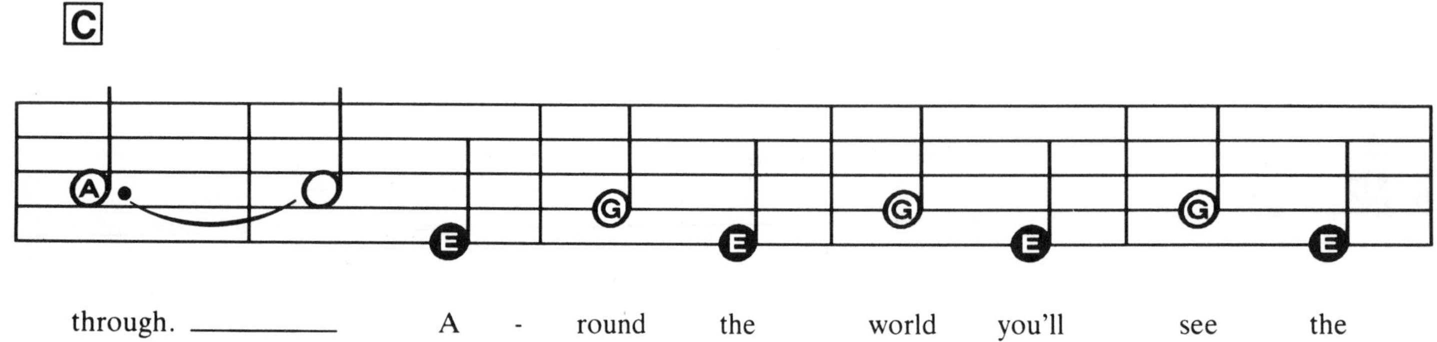
C
through. ______ A - round the world you'll see the

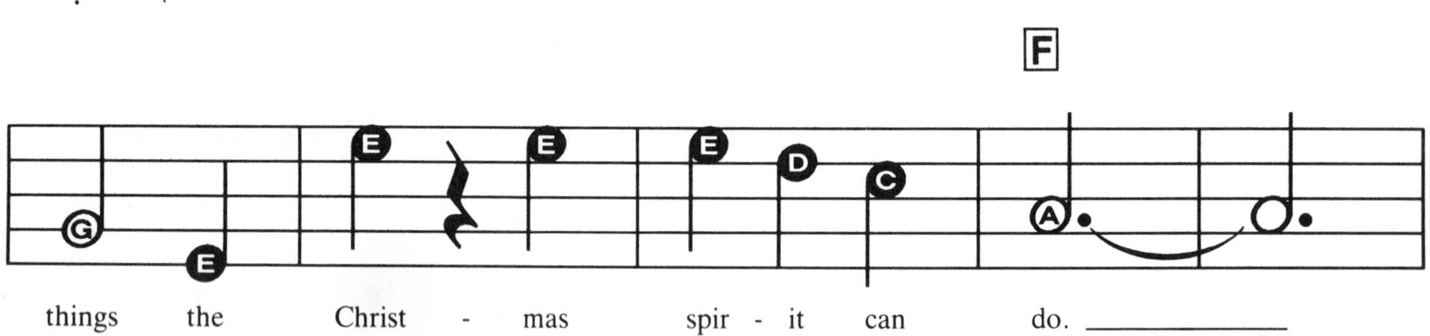
F
things the Christ - mas spir - it can do. ______

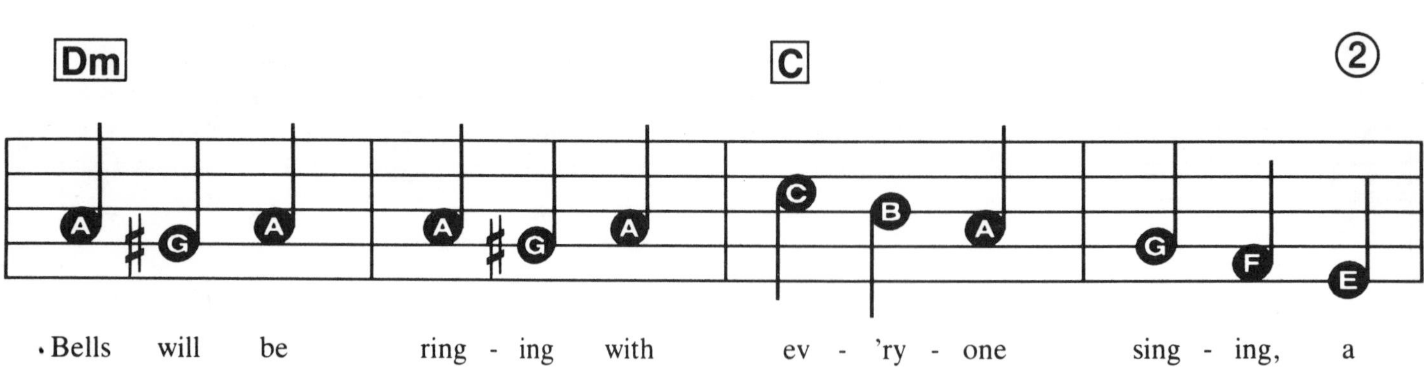
Dm
C
②
Bells will be ring - ing with ev - 'ry - one sing - ing, a

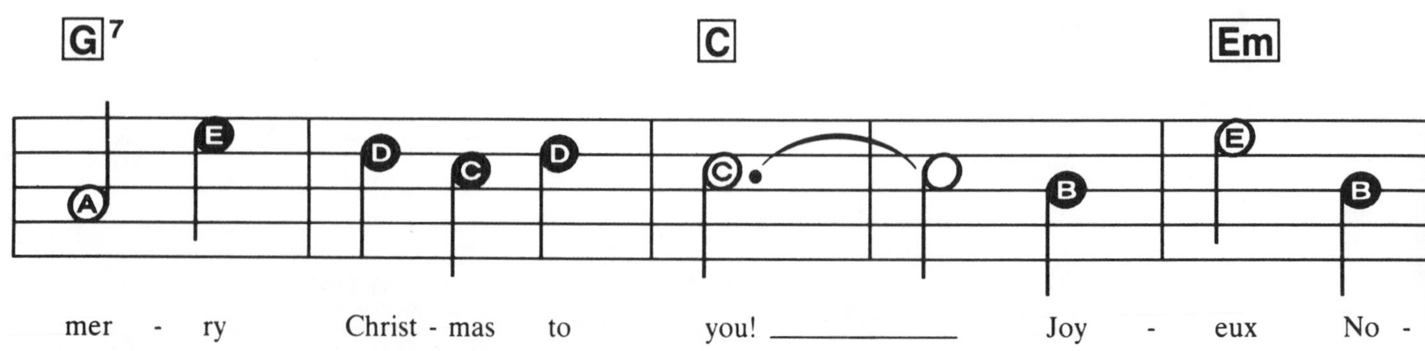
G7
C
Em
mer - ry Christ - mas to you! ______ Joy - eux No -

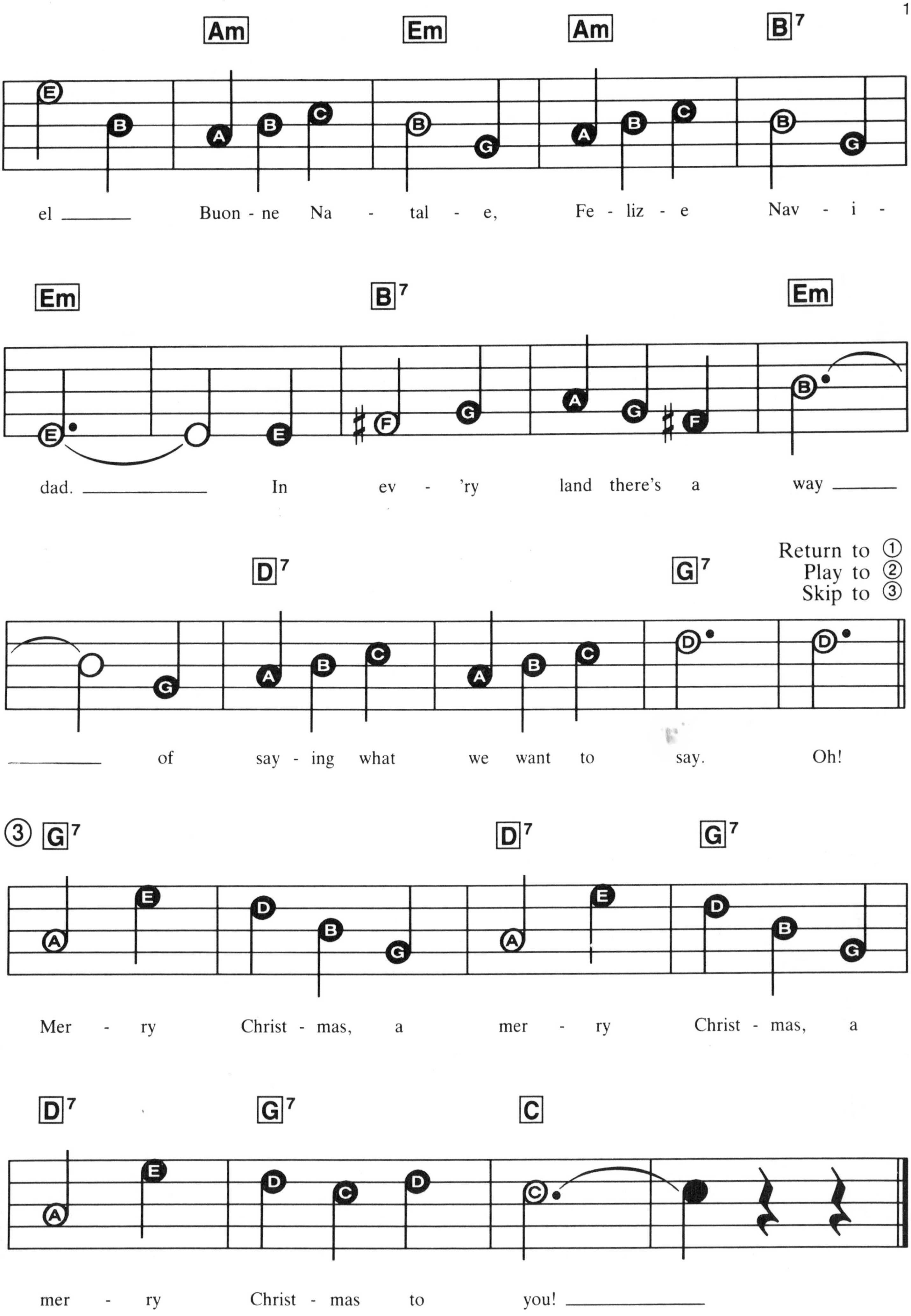

Am Em Am B7

el ___ Buon - ne Na - tal - e, Fe - liz - e Nav - i -

Em B7 Em

dad. ___ In ev - 'ry land there's a way ___

D7 G7

Return to ①
Play to ②
Skip to ③

___ of say - ing what we want to say. Oh!

③ G7 D7 G7

Mer - ry Christ - mas, a mer - ry Christ - mas, a

D7 G7 C

mer - ry Christ - mas to you! ___

MERRY CHRISTMAS, DARLING

CLARINET
SOFT SOLO
Medium SWING

Lyric by FRANK POOLER
Music by RICHARD CARPENTER

G7 F Gm
you. The __ lights on my tree, I wish you could see
Cm B♭ Gm
I wish it ev - 'ry day. The logs on the fire
G7
fill me with de - sire, To see you and to __ say; That I
C F C F
wish you Mer - ry Christ - mas, Hap - py New Year too; I've
C G7 C
just one wish on this Christ - mas Eve; I wish I were with you.

From the Videocraft TV Musical Spectacular "RUDOLPH THE RED-NOSED REINDEER"

THE MOST WONDERFUL DAY OF THE YEAR

WOODWINDS
FULL 'N' MELLOW
Medium WALTZ

Words and Music by
JOHNNY MARKS

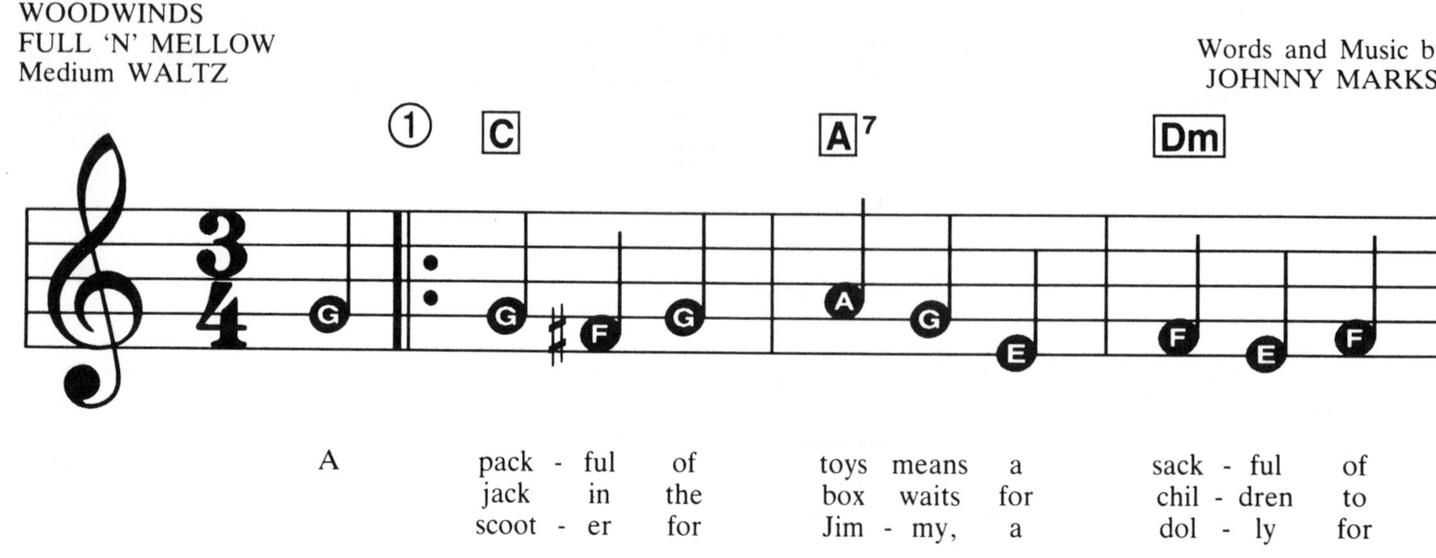

1
C
A7
Dm
G
G F G
A G E
F E F
A pack - ful of toys means a sack - ful of
jack in the box waits for chil - dren to
scoot - er for Jim - my, a dol - ly for

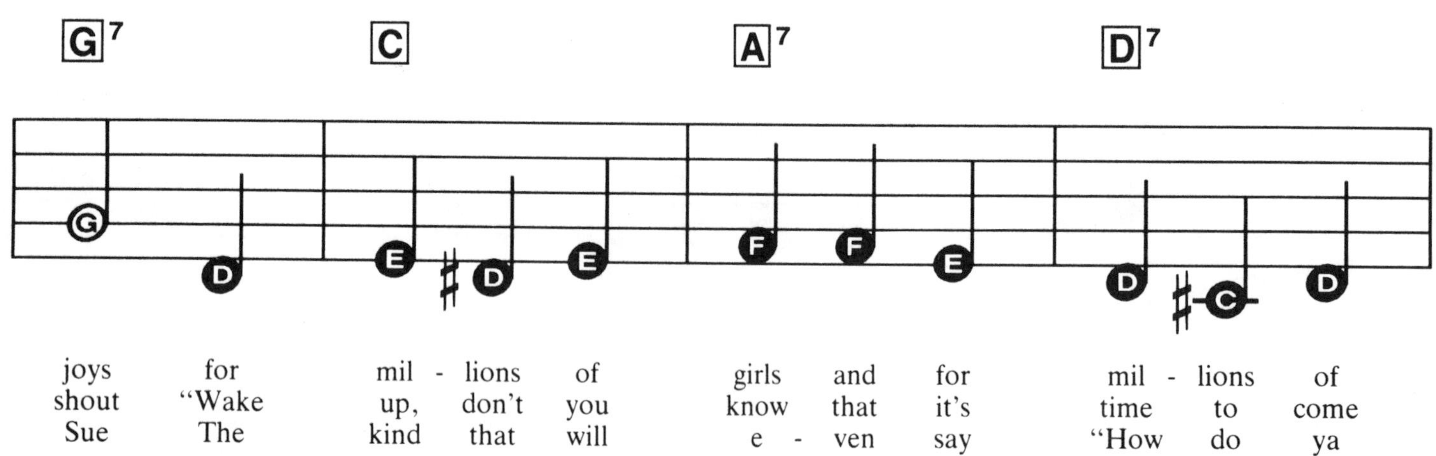

G7
C
A7
D7
G D
E D E
F F E
D C D
joys for mil - lions of girls and for mil - lions of
shout "Wake up, don't you know that it's time to come
Sue The kind that will e - ven say "How do ya

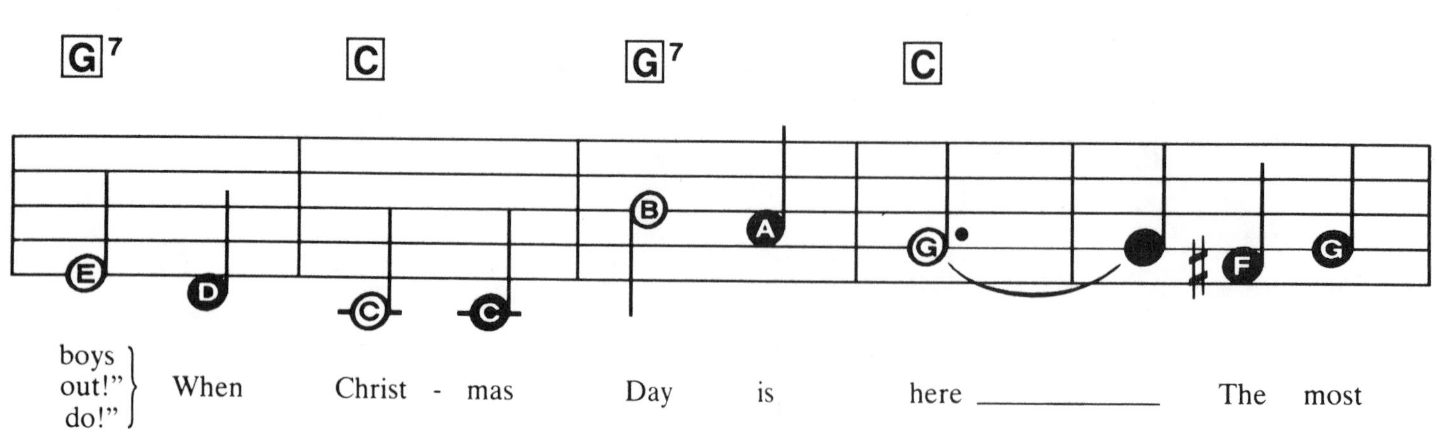

G7
C
G7
C
E D
C C
B A
G F G
boys out!" do!" When Christ - mas Day is here The most

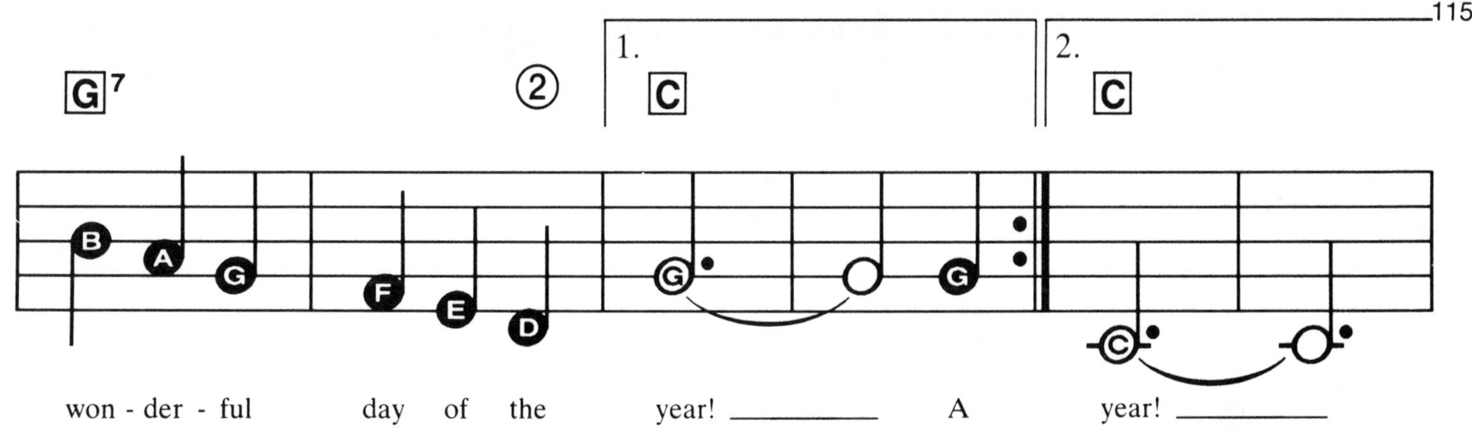
G7
②
1.
C
2.
C
B A G F E D G G C C
won - der - ful day of the year! A year!

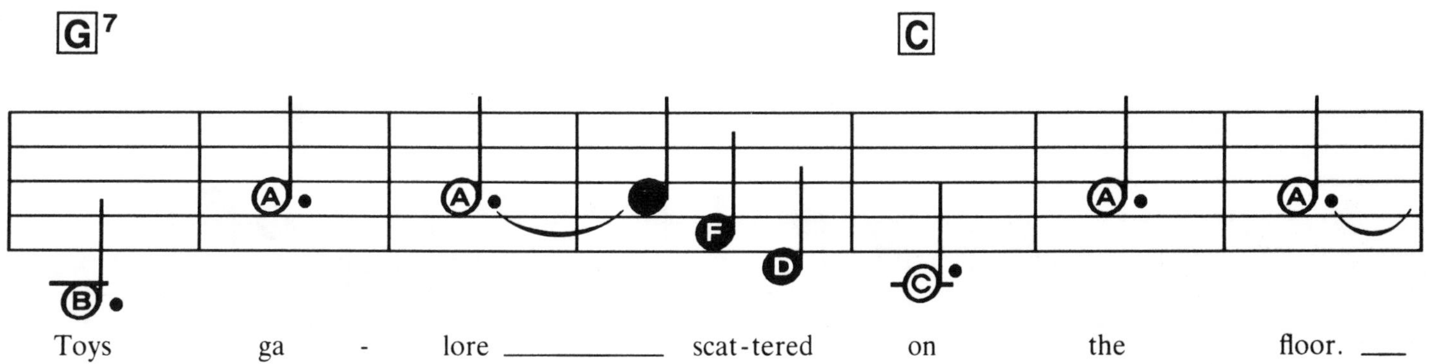
G7
C
B A A F D C A A
Toys ga - lore scat-tered on the floor.

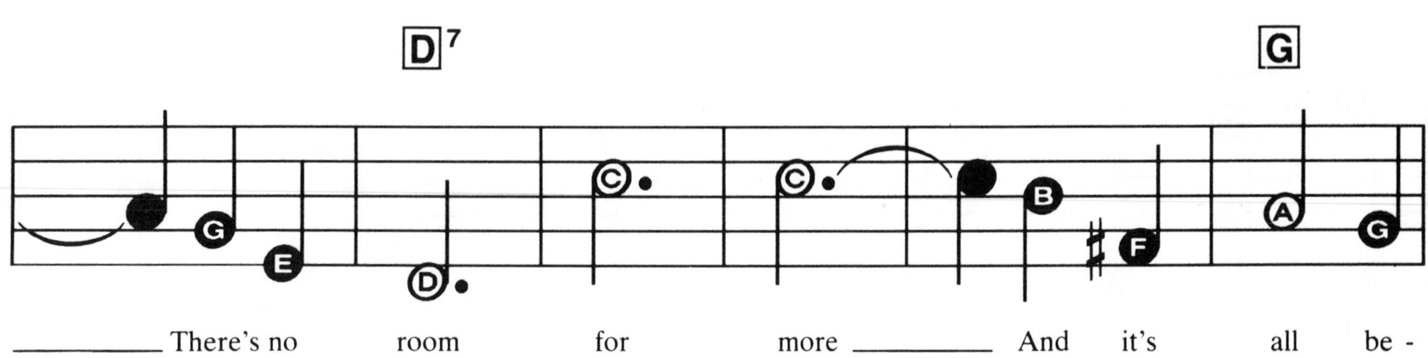
D7
G
G E D C C B F A G
There's no room for more And it's all be -

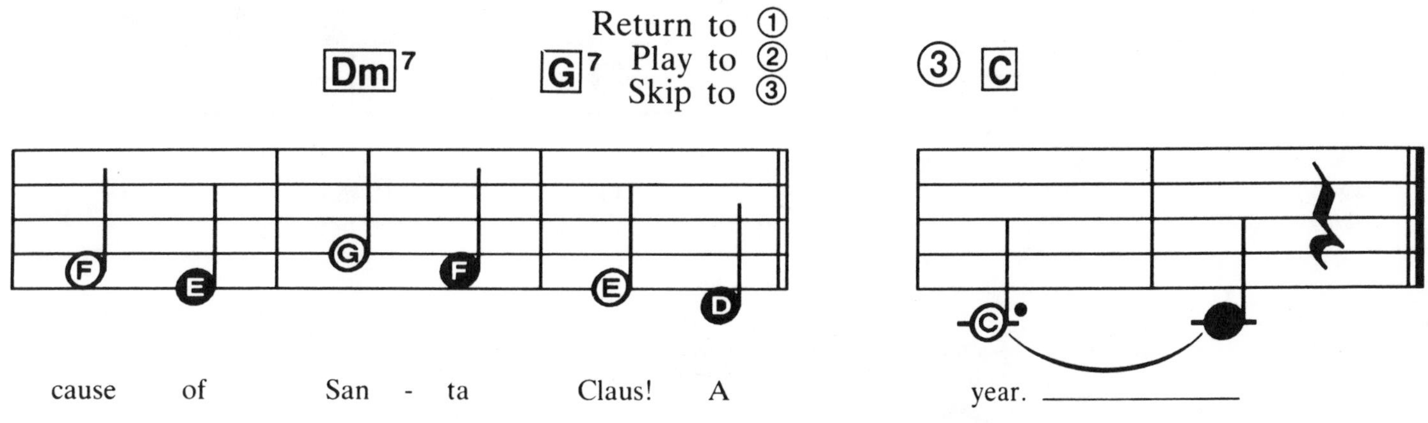
Dm7
G7
Return to ①
Play to ②
Skip to ③
③ C
F E G F E D C
cause of San - ta Claus! A
year.

O CHRISTMAS TREE
(O Tannenbaum)

HARPSICHORD
SOFT SOLO
Medium WALTZ

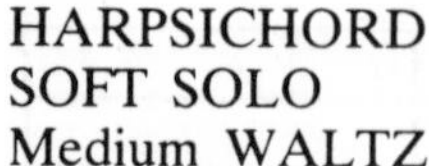

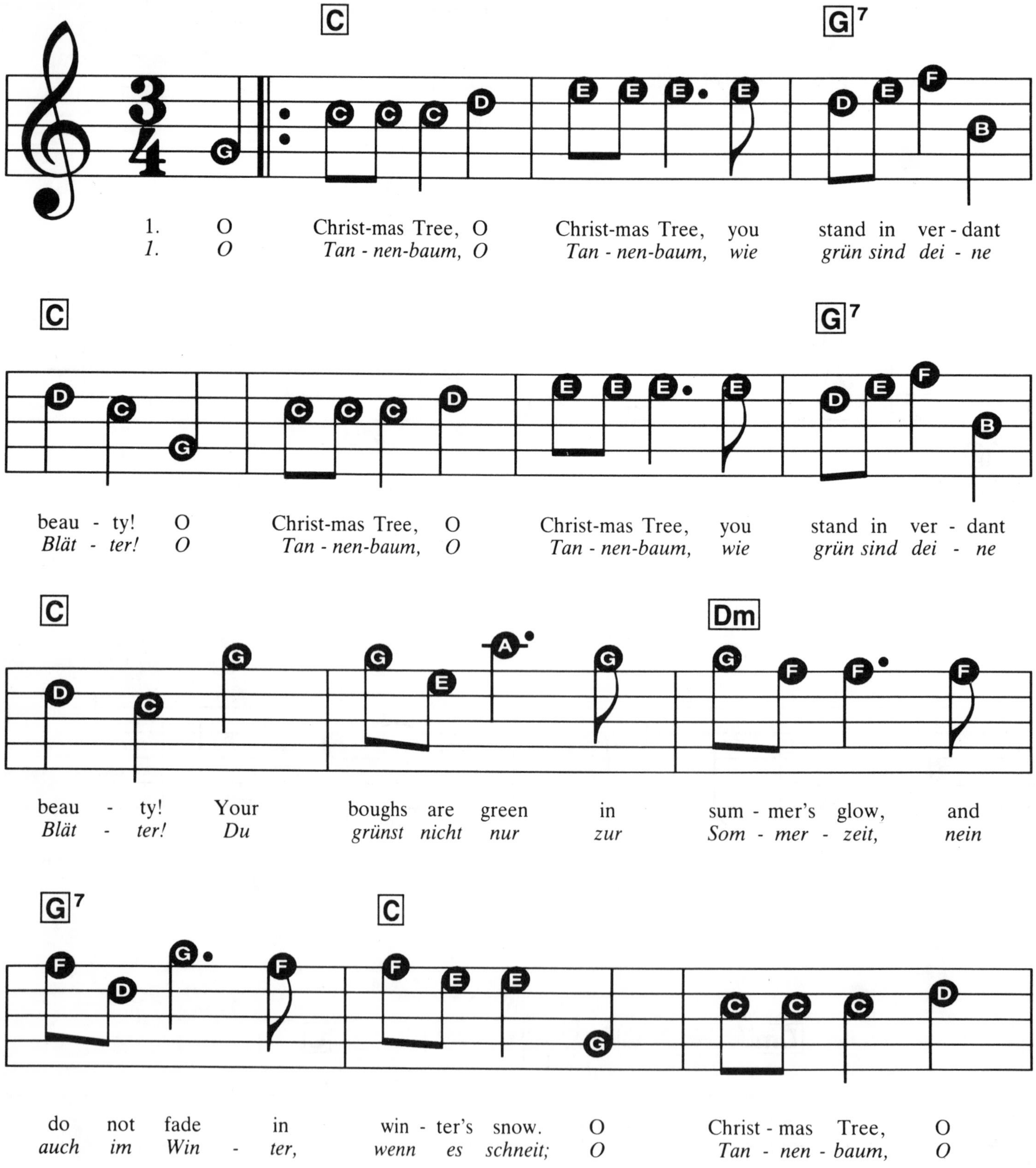

C
G7
1. O Christ-mas Tree, O Christ-mas Tree, you stand in ver - dant
1. O Tan - nen-baum, O Tan - nen-baum, wie grün sind dei - ne
C
G7
beau - ty! O Christ-mas Tree, O Christ-mas Tree, you stand in ver - dant
Blät - ter! O Tan - nen-baum, O Tan - nen-baum, wie grün sind dei - ne
C
Dm
beau - ty! Your boughs are green in sum - mer's glow, and
Blät - ter! Du grünst nicht nur zur Som - mer - zeit, nein
G7
C
do not fade in win - ter's snow. O Christ - mas Tree, O
auch im Win - ter, wenn es schneit; O Tan - nen - baum, O

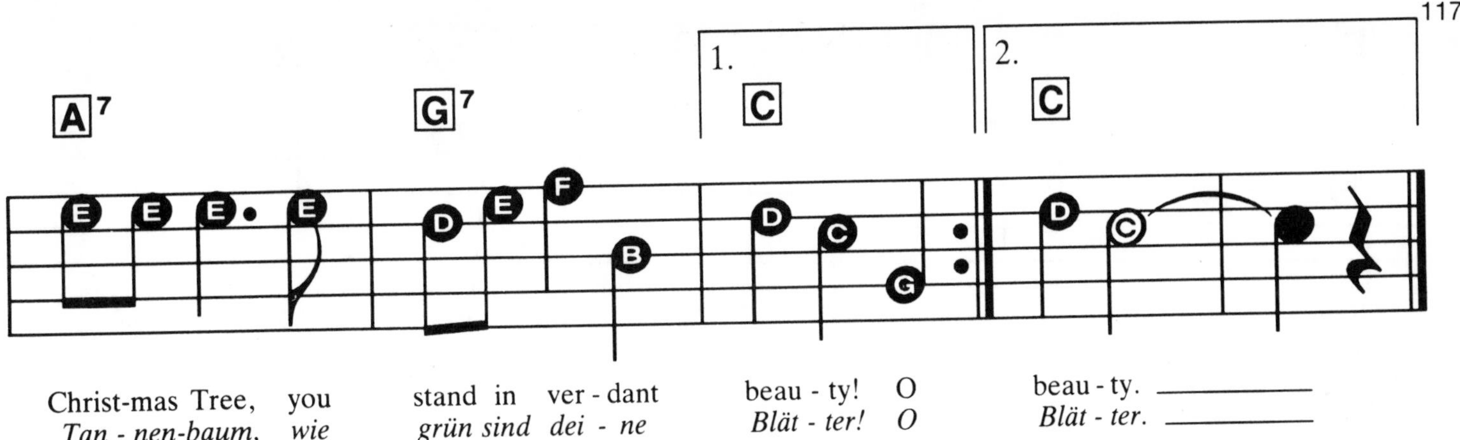
A7
G7
1.
C
2.
C
E E E E D E F B D C G D C
Christ-mas Tree, you stand in ver - dant beau - ty! O beau - ty.
Tan - nen-baum, wie grün sind dei - ne Blät - ter! O Blät - ter.

2. *O Tannenbaum, o Tannenbaum,*
du kannst mir sehr gefallen!
Wie oft hat mich zur Weinachtszeit
ein Baum von dir mich hocherfreut!
O Tannenbaum, o Tannenbaum,
du kannst mir sehr gefallen!

3. *O Tannenbaum, o Tannenbaum!*
Dein Kleid will mich was lehren:
die Hoffnung und Beständigkeit,
gibt Trost und Kraft zu jeder Zeit!
O Tannenbaum, o Tannenbaum,
dein Kleid will mich was lehren.

O COME, ALL YE FAITHFUL

(Adeste Fideles)

ORGAN
CLASSICAL
Medium SWING

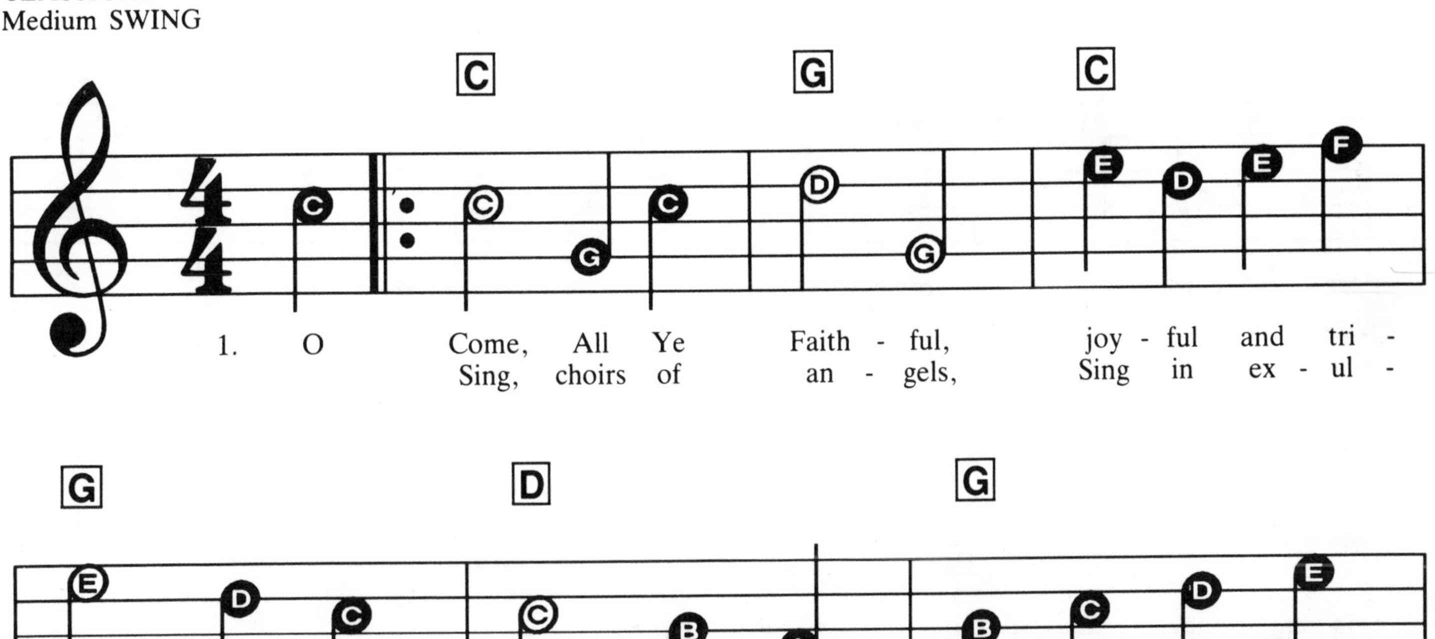
C
G
C
C C G C D G E D E F
1. O Come, All Ye Faith - ful, joy - ful and tri -
Sing, choirs of an - gels, Sing in ex - ul -
G
D
G
E D C C B A B C D E

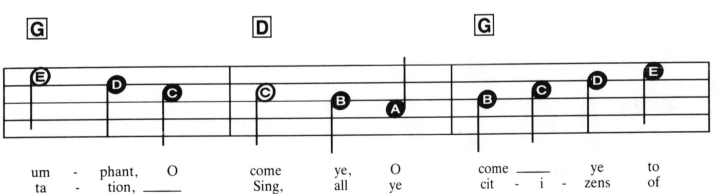

um - phant, O come ye, O come ___ ye to
ta - tion, ___ Sing, all ye cit - i - zens of

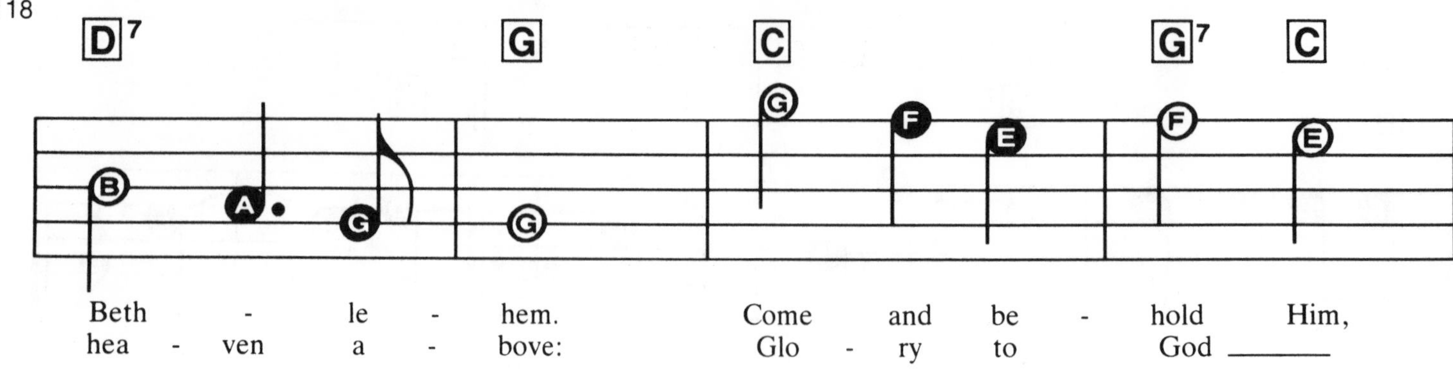
D7
G
C
G7
C
B A G G G F E F E
Beth - le - hem. Come and be - hold Him,
hea - ven a - bove: Glo - ry to God

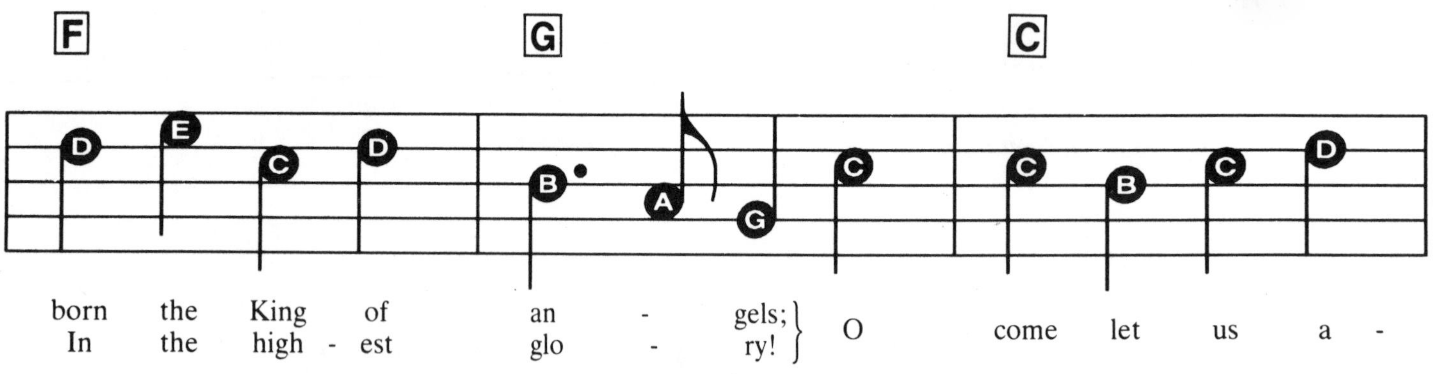
F
G
C
D E C D B A G C C B C D
born the King of an - gels;
In the high - est glo - ry!
O come let us a -

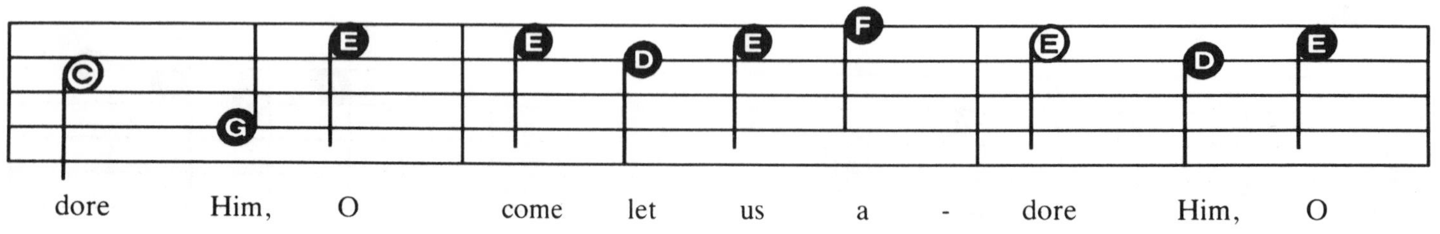
C G E E D E F E D E
dore Him, O come let us a - dore Him, O

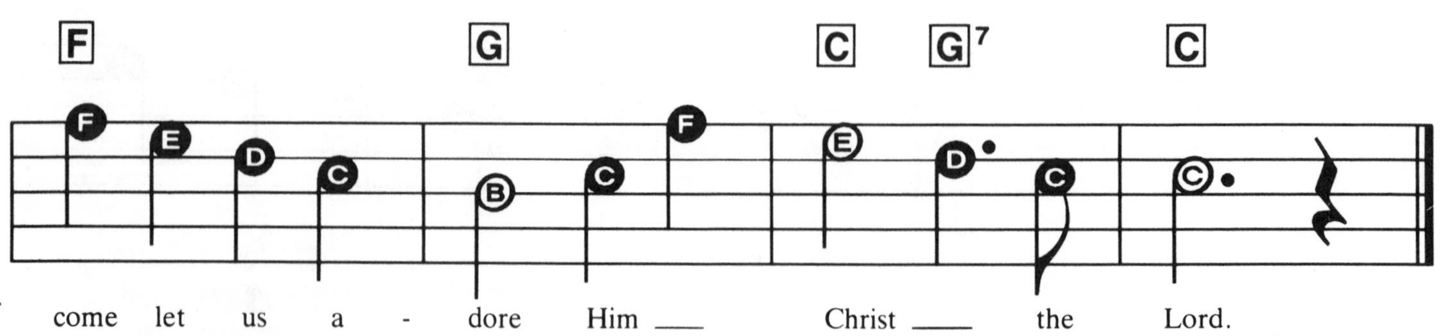
F
G
C
G7
C
F E D C B C F E D C C
come let us a - dore Him Christ the Lord.

O SANCTISSIMA

ORGAN
FULL 'N' BRILLIANT
No Rhythm

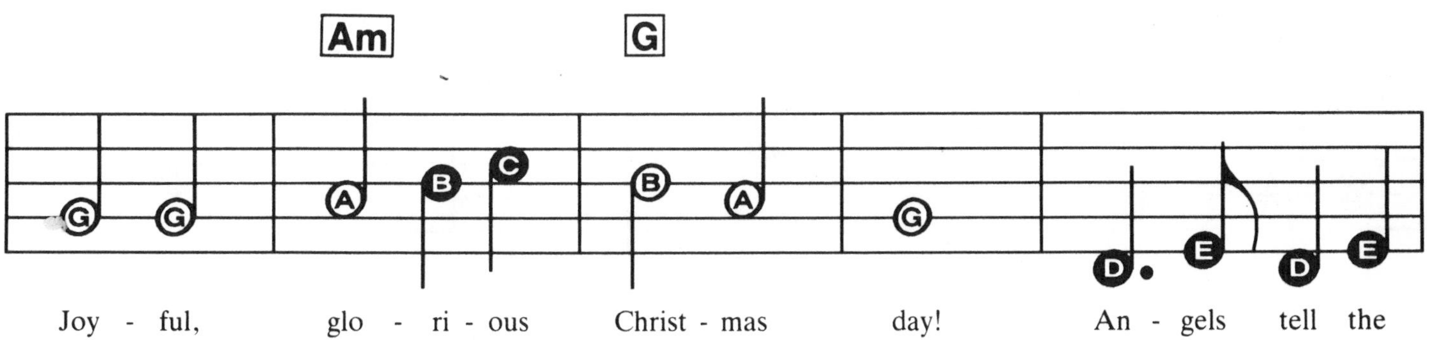

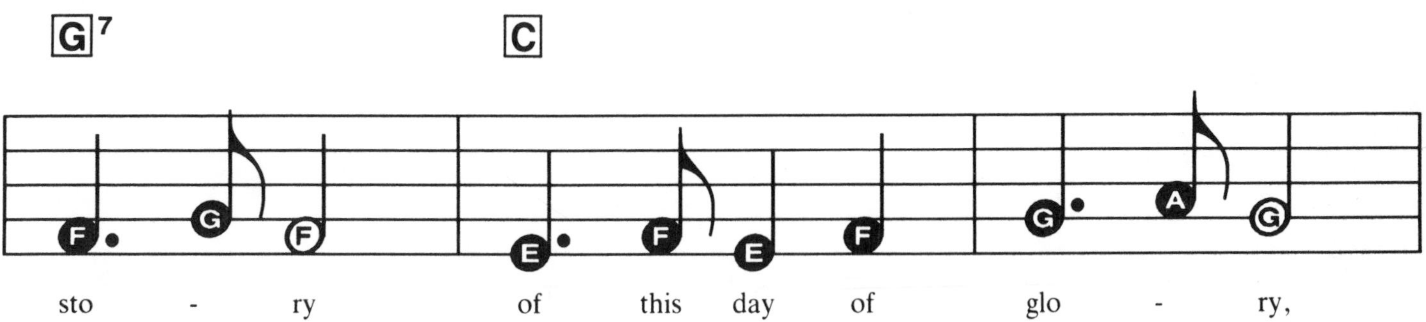

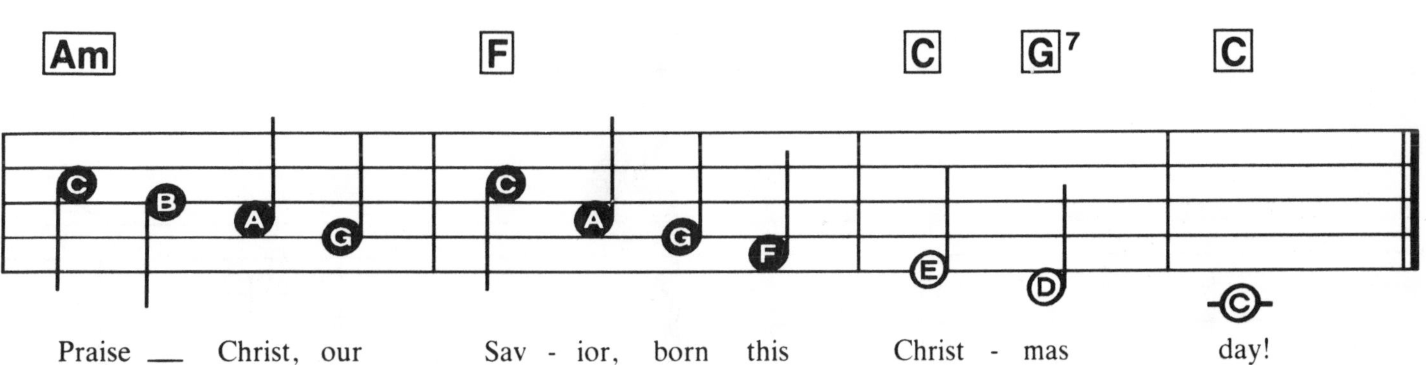

OVER THE RIVER AND THROUGH THE WOODS

TRUMPET
BRILLIANT SOLO
Bright WALTZ

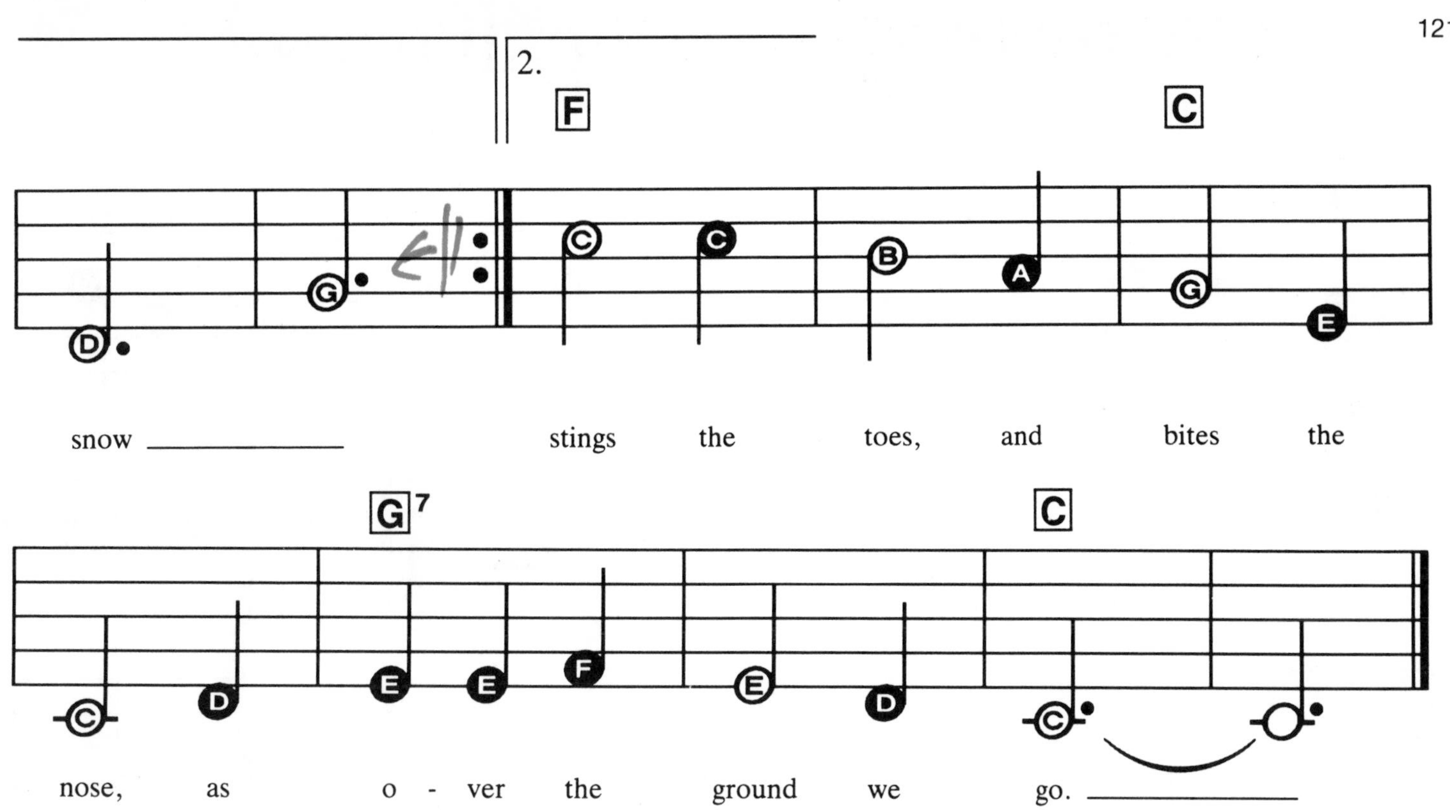
2.
F
C
snow stings the toes, and bites the
G7
C
nose, as o - ver the ground we go.

NOW SING WE ALL MERRILY

PIANO
FULL 'N' MELLOW
Fast WALTZ

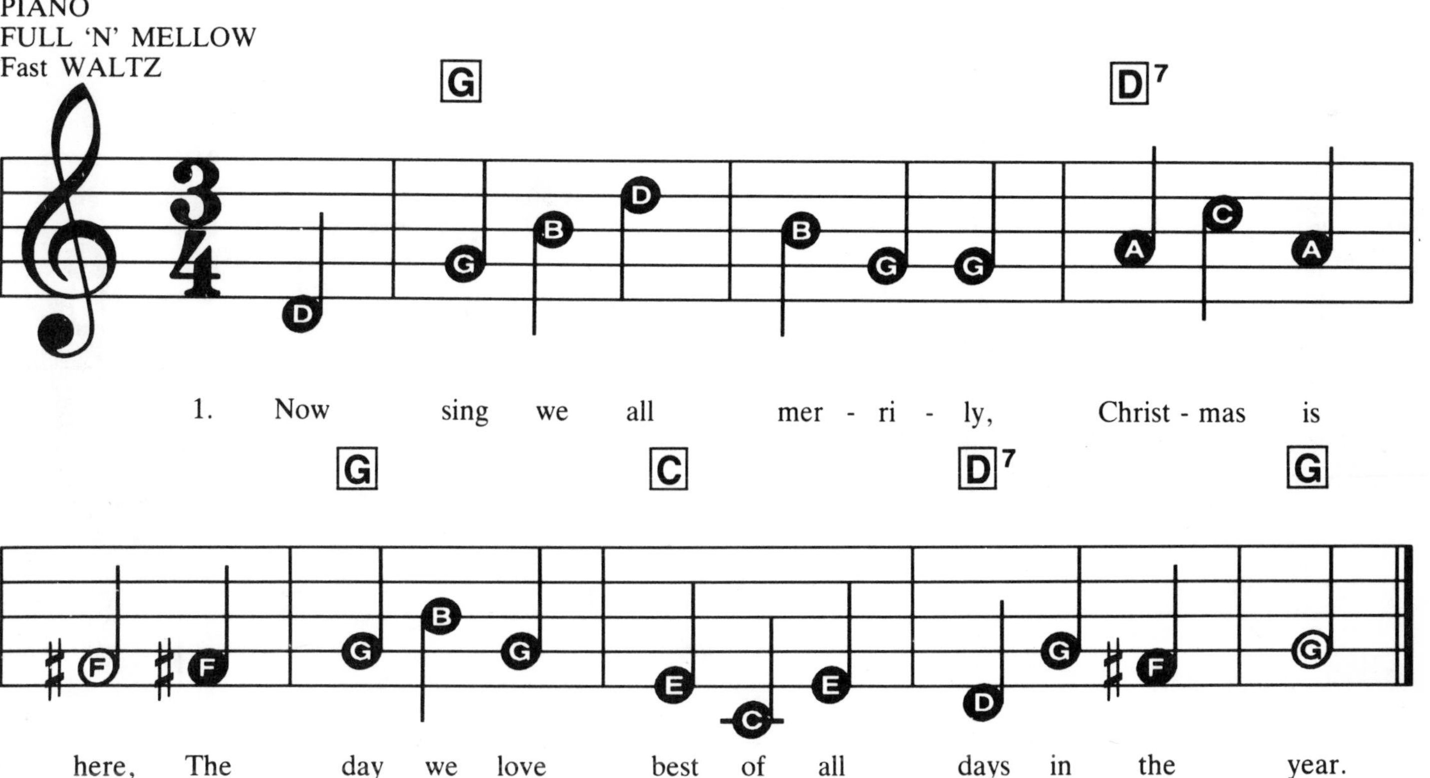
G
D7
1. Now sing we all mer - ri - ly, Christ - mas is
G
C
D7
G
here, The day we love best of all days in the year.

2. Bring out the green holly, the fir and the bay,
And deck every cottage for glad Christmas Day.

3. The children are happy, with presents in hand,
From Santa to children all over the land.

ORGAN
CLASSICAL
Medium MARCH

O COME, LITTLE CHILDREN

F C F
1. O come, lit - tle chil - dren, O come one and all, To
born in a sta - ble for you and for me, Draw
Ma - ry and Jo - seph with love beam-ing eyes Are
C F
Beth - le - hem haste, to the man - ger so small, God's
near by the bright gleam - ing Star - light to see, In
gaz - ing up - on the rude bed where he lies, The
C C7 F B♭
Son for a gift has been sent you this night To
swad - dling clothes ly - ing so meek and so mild, And
shep - herds are kneel - ing, with hearts full of love, While
C7 F C7
1.2.
F
3.
F
be your re - deem - er, your joy and de - light. 2. He's
pur - er than an - gels the heav - en - ly child. 3. See
an - gels sing loud hal - le - lu - jahs a - bove.

O COME, O COME IMMANUEL

HARPSICHORD
CLASSICAL
No Rhythm

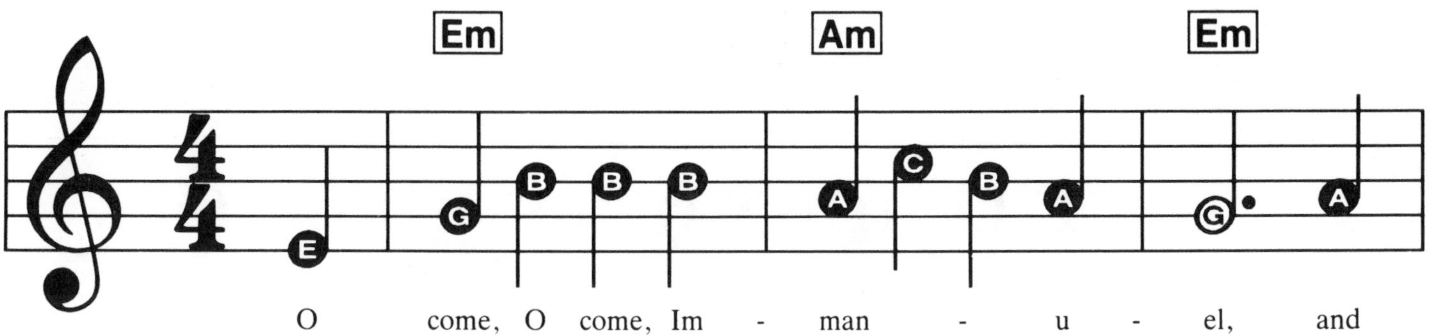

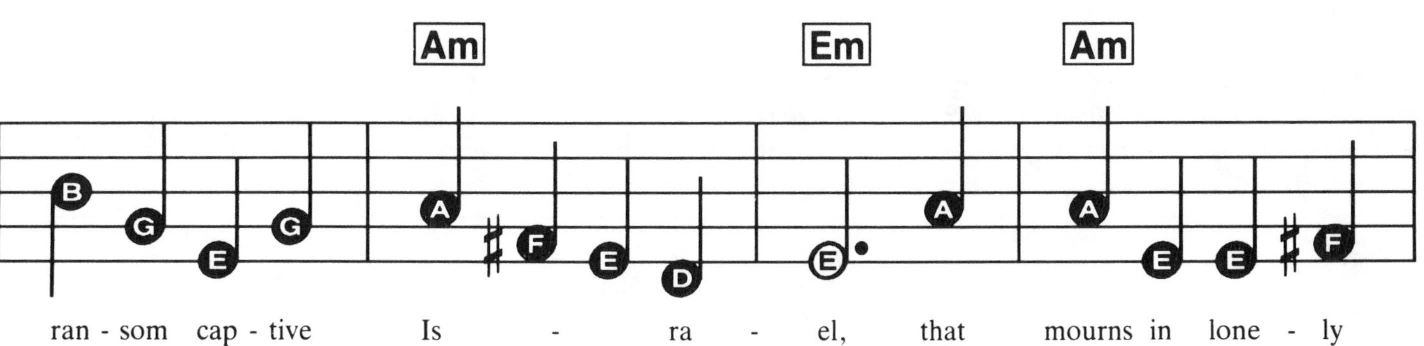

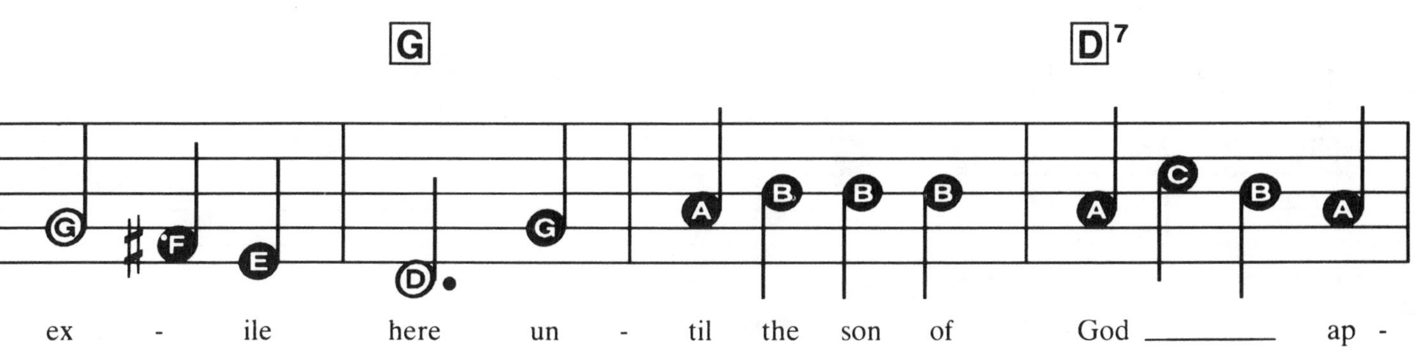

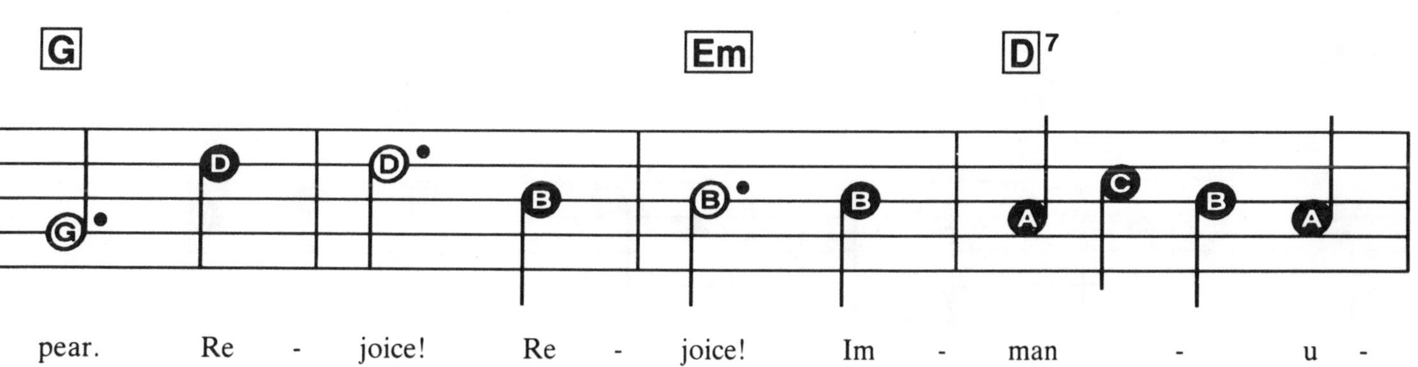

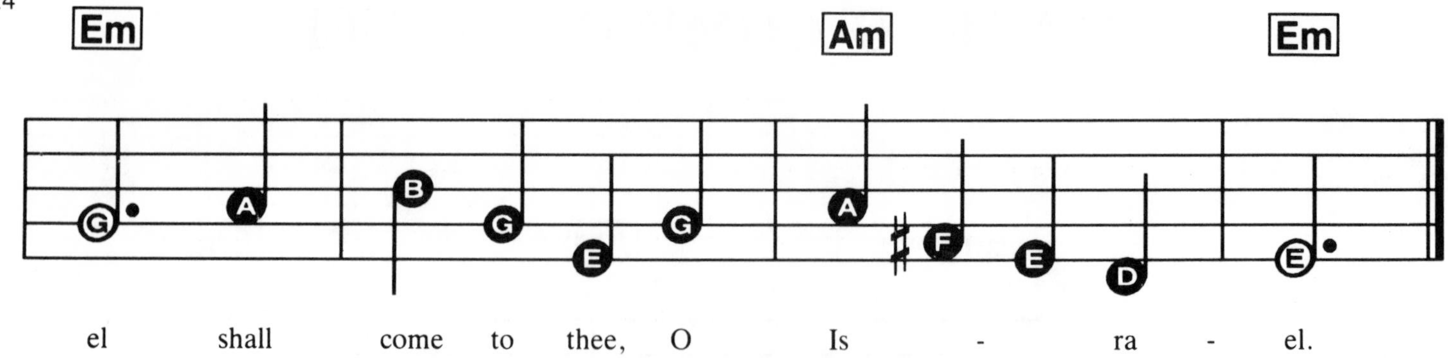
Em
Am
Em
el shall come to thee, O Is - ra - el.

O LITTLE TOWN OF BETHLEHEM

VIOLIN or FLUTE
SOFT SOLO
Slow SWING

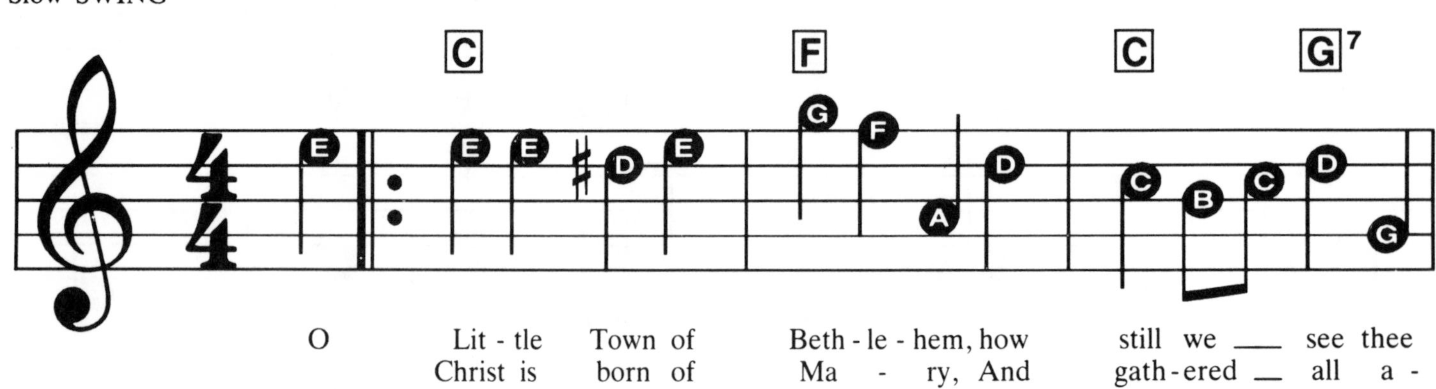
C
F
C
G7
O Lit - tle Town of Beth - le - hem, how still we ___ see thee
Christ is born of Ma - ry, And gath - ered ___ all a -

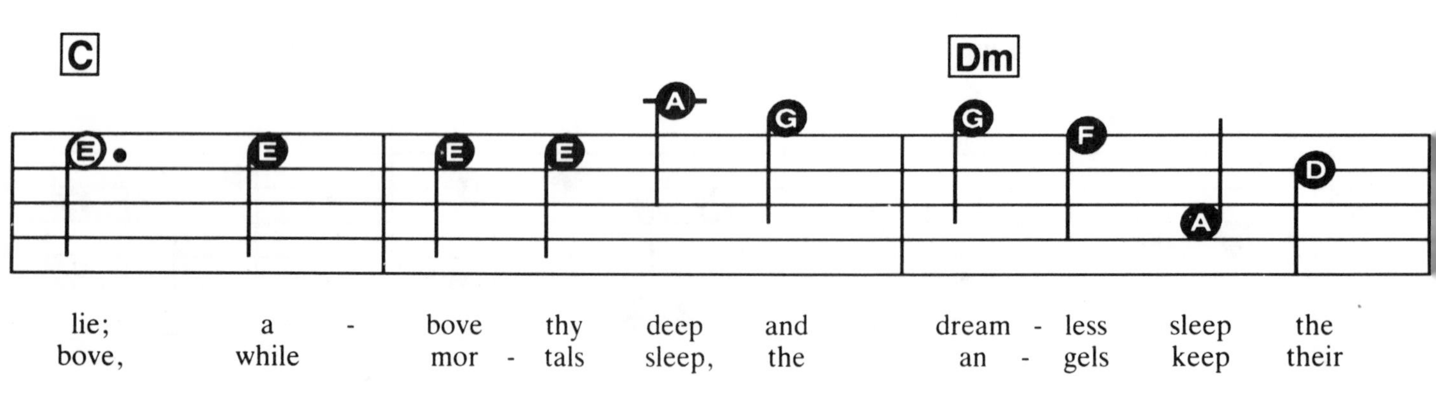
C
Dm
lie; a - bove thy deep and dream - less sleep the
bove, while mor - tals sleep, the an - gels keep their

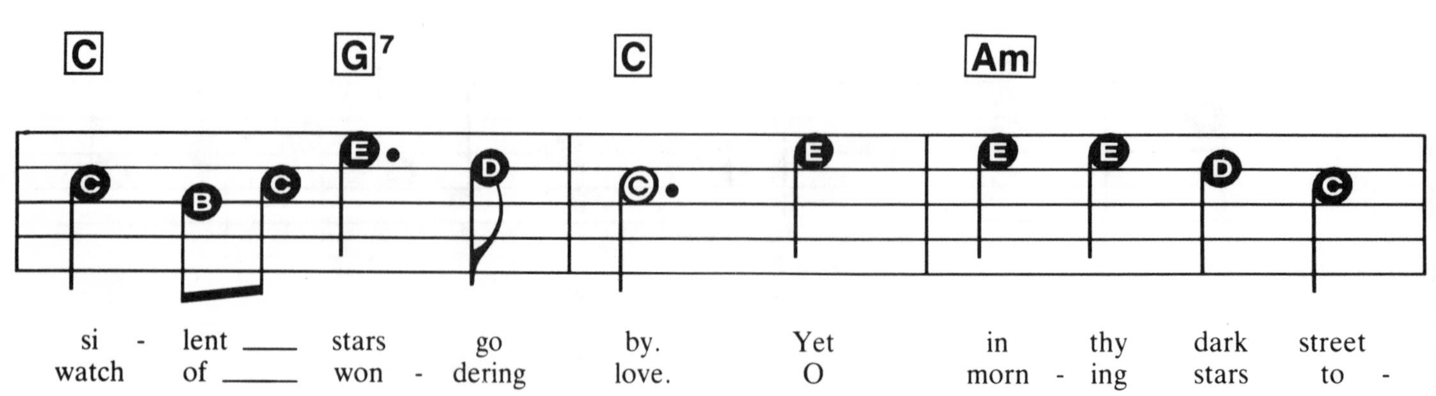
C
G7
C
Am
si - lent ___ stars go by. Yet in thy dark street
watch of ___ won - dering love. O morn - ing stars to -

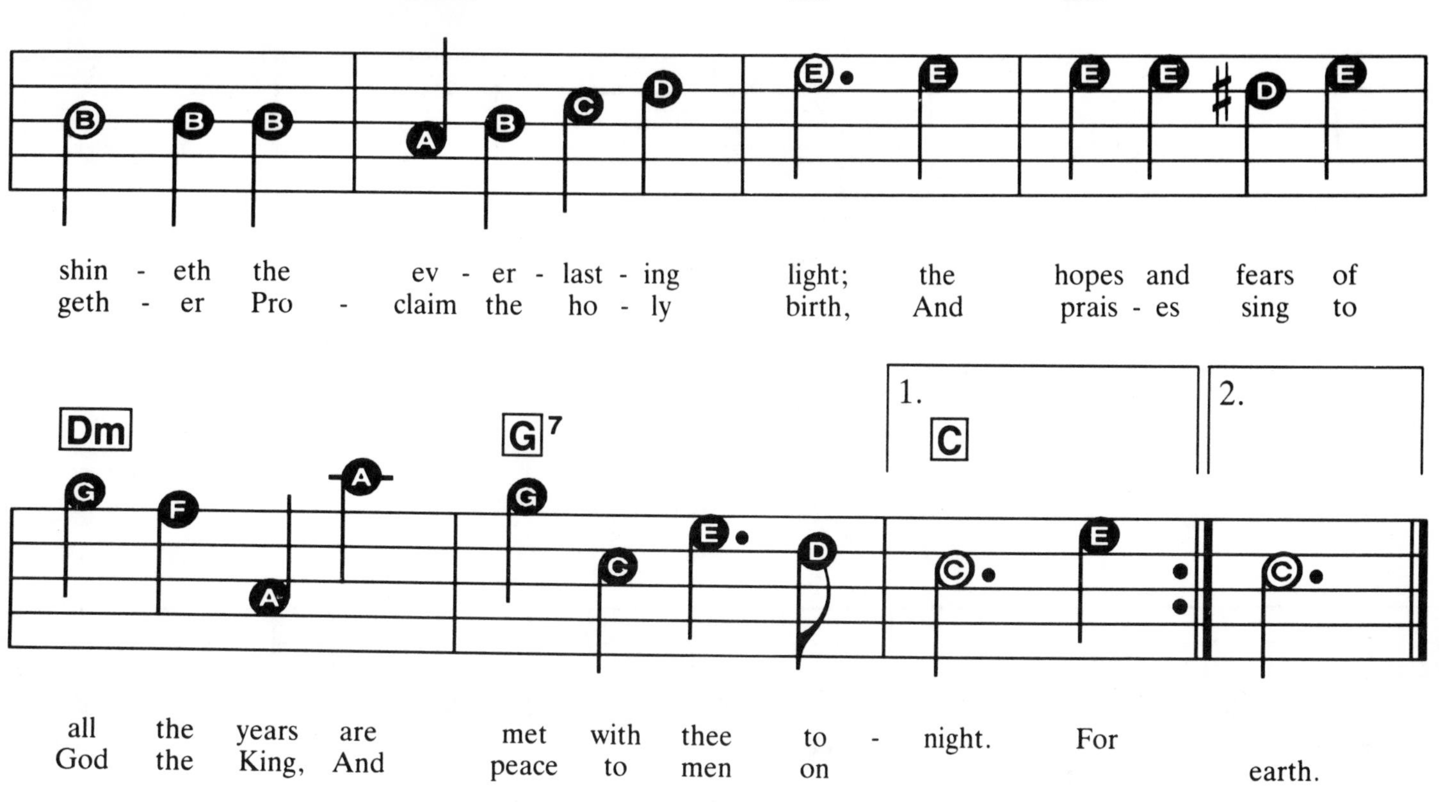
E Am E C
shin - eth the ev - er - last - ing light; the hopes and fears of
geth - er Pro - claim the ho - ly birth, And prais - es sing to
Dm G7 1. C 2.
all the years are met with thee to - night. For
God the King, And peace to men on earth.

O HOLY NIGHT

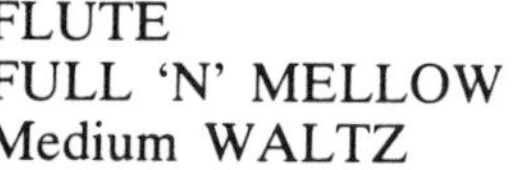
FLUTE
FULL 'N' MELLOW
Medium WALTZ

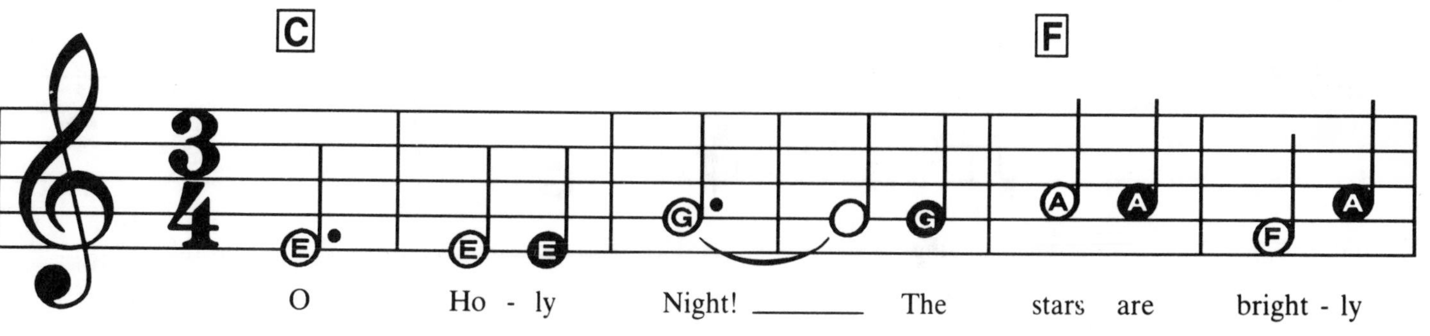
C F
O Ho - ly Night! The stars are bright - ly

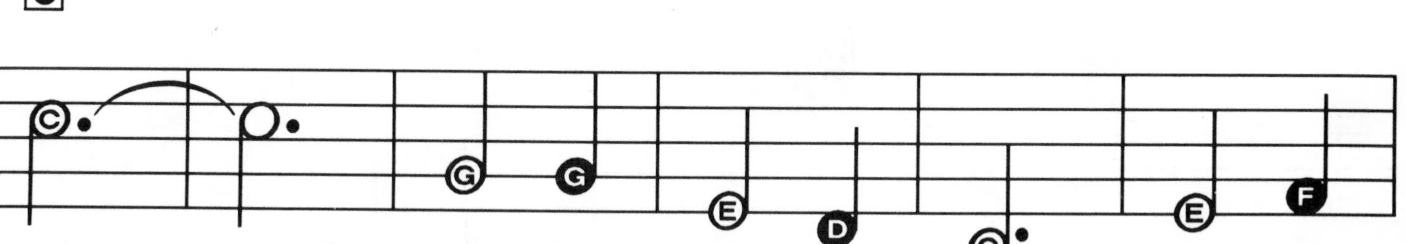
C
shin - ing, it is the night of the

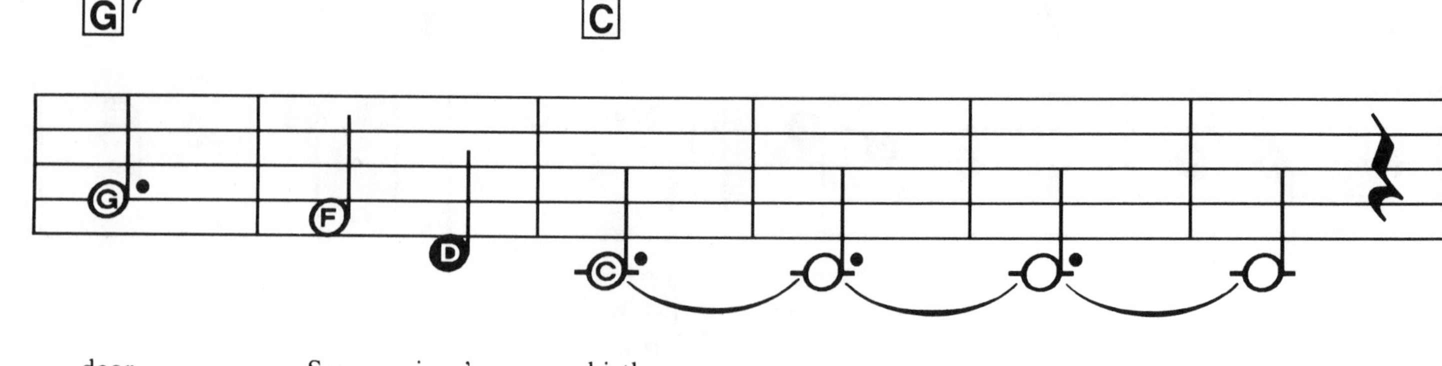
G7
C
dear Sav - iour's birth.

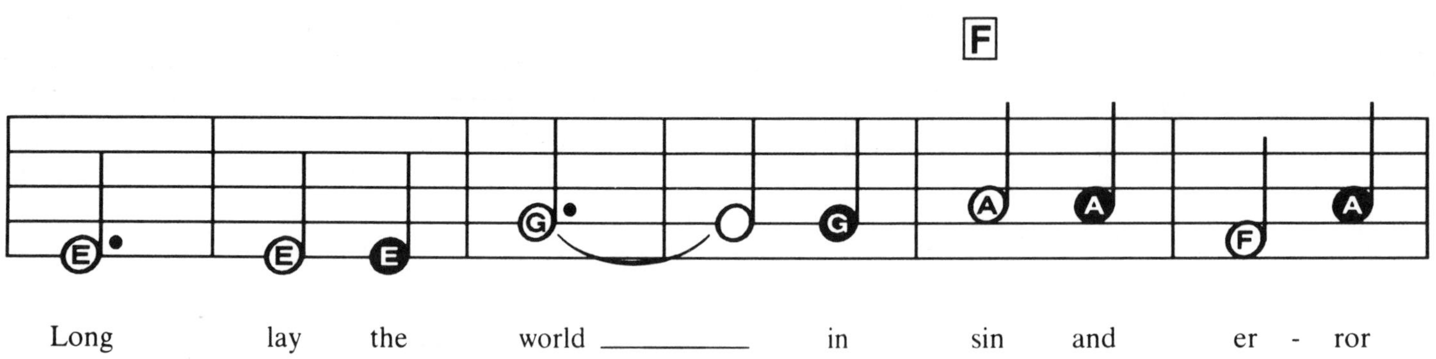
F
Long lay the world in sin and er - ror

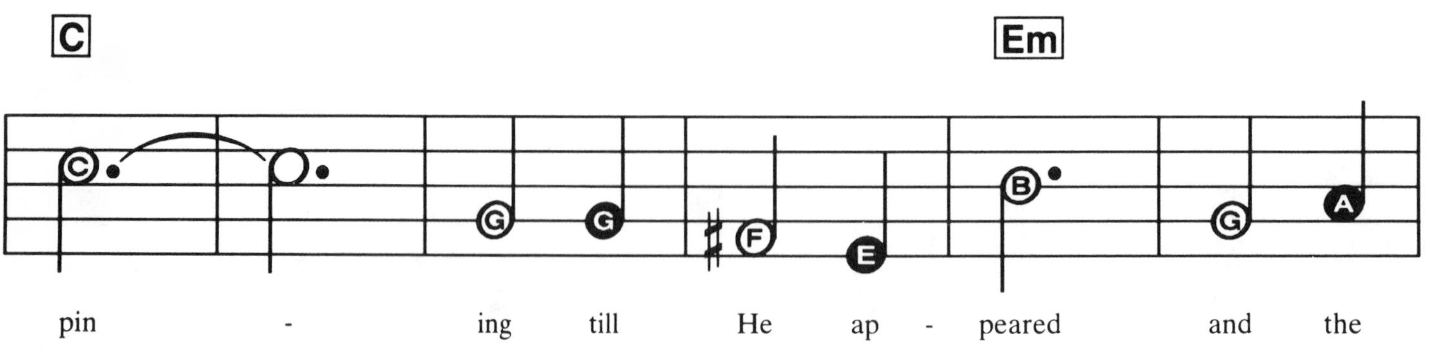
C
Em
pin - ing till He ap - peared and the

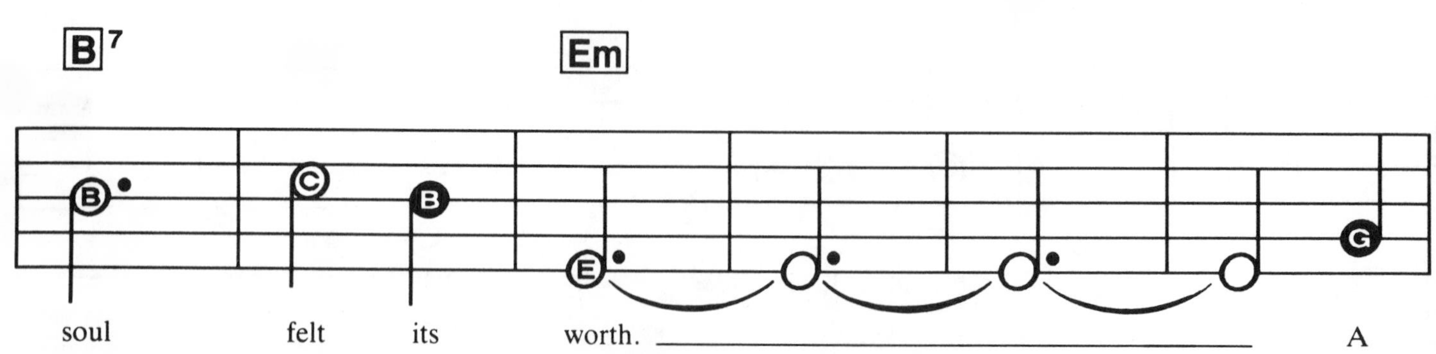
B7
Em
soul felt its worth. A

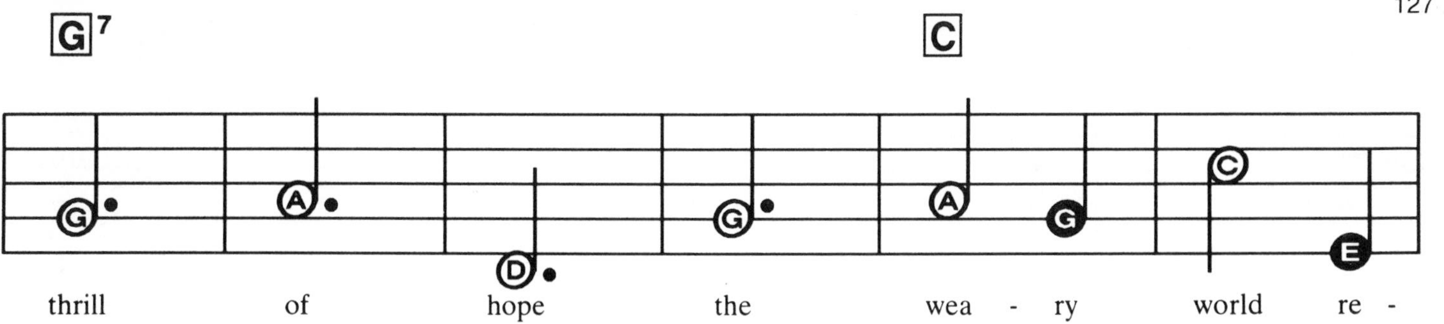
G7
C
G
A
D
G
A
G
C
E
thrill of hope the wea - ry world re -

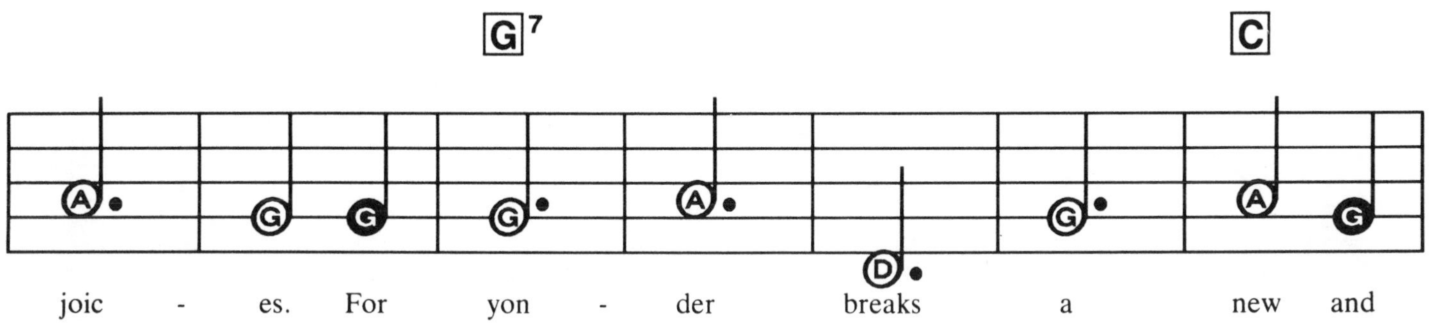
G7
C
A
G
G
G
A
D
G
A
G
joic - es. For yon - der breaks a new and

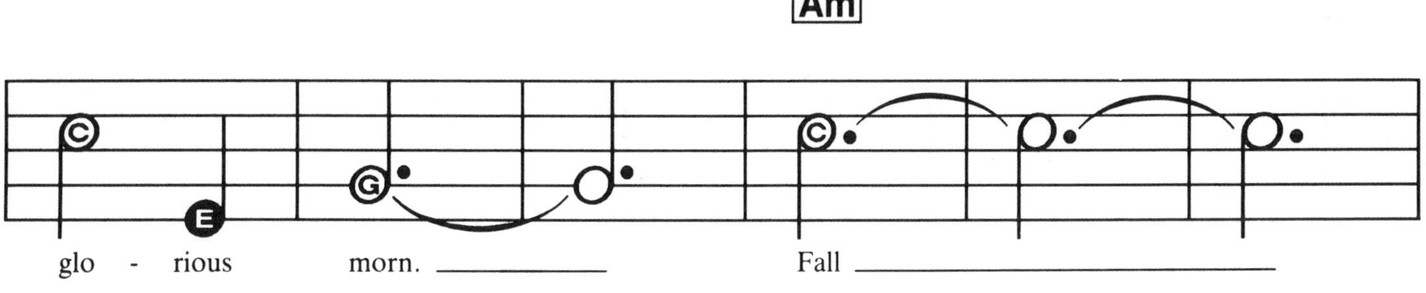
Am
C
E
G
C
glo - rious morn.
Fall

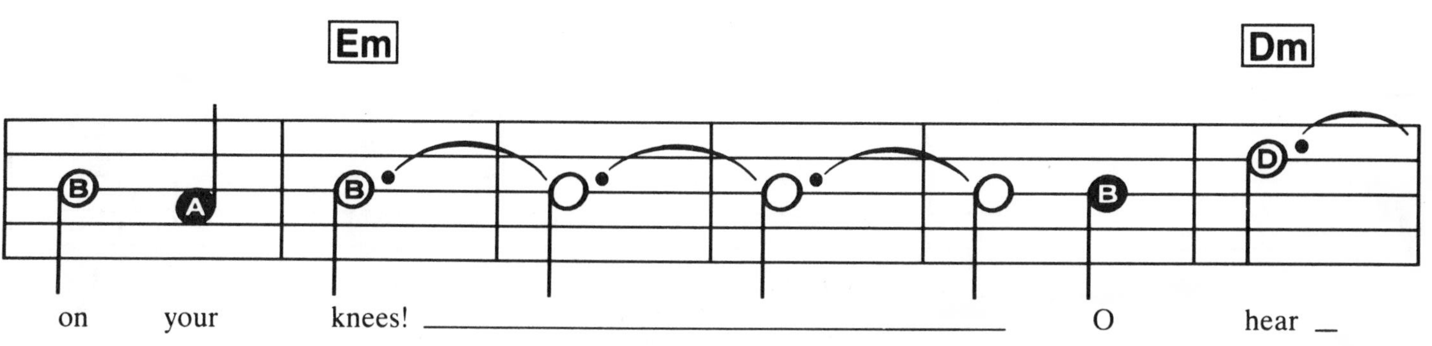
Em
Dm
B
A
B
B
D
on your knees!
O hear

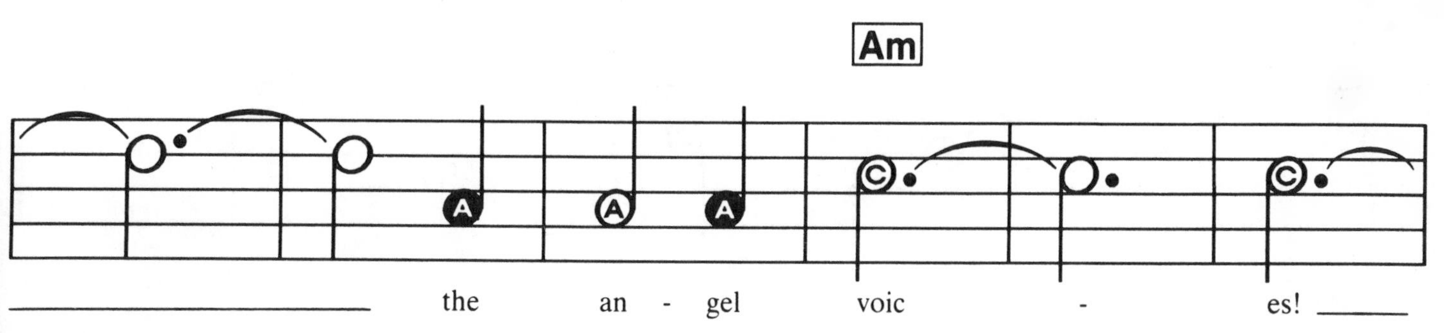
Am
A
A
A
C
C
the an - gel voic - es!

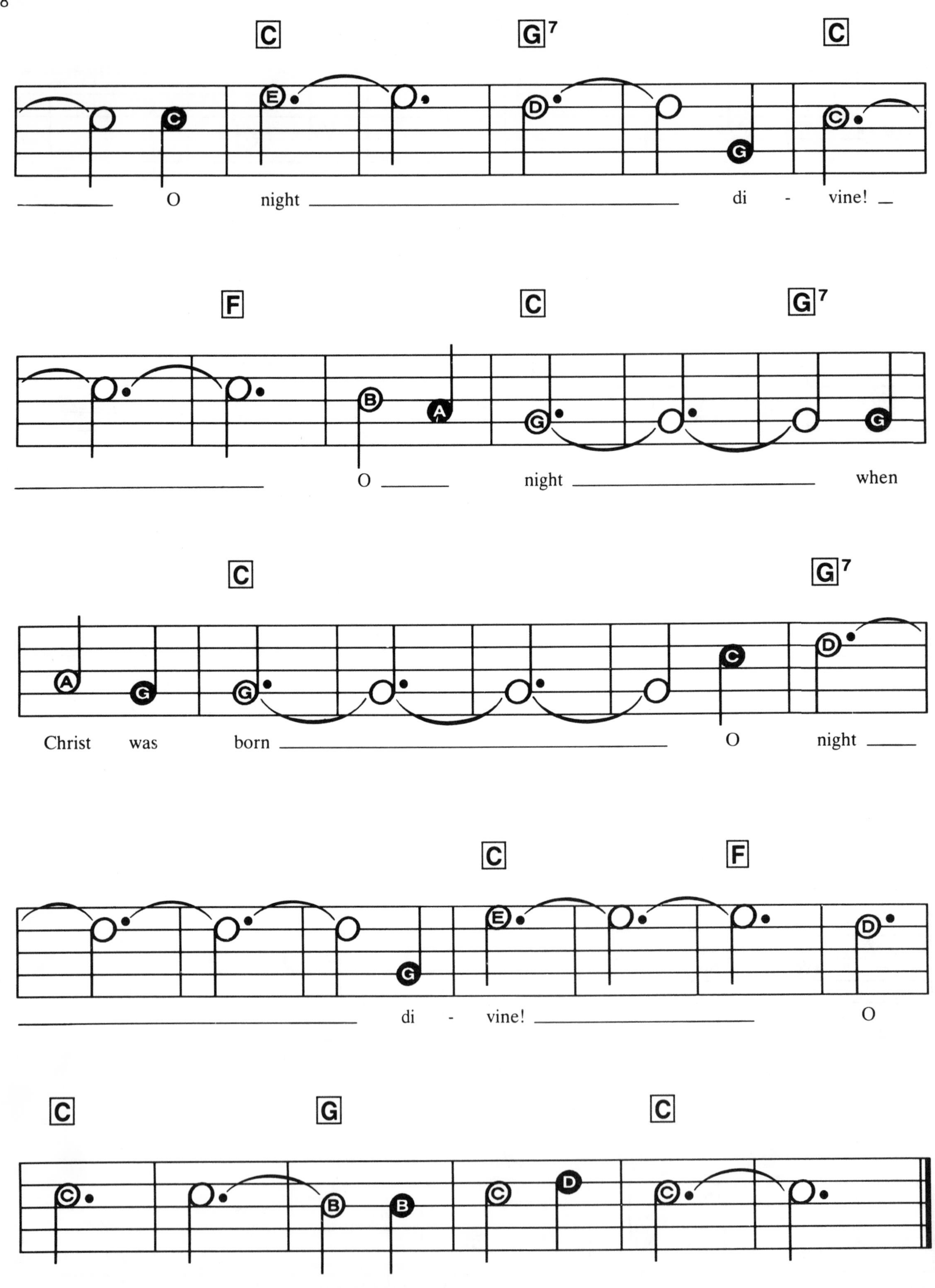
C G7 C
O night di - vine!
F C G7
O night when
C G7
Christ was born O night
C F
di - vine! O
C G C
night O night di - vine.

O THOU JOYFUL DAY

TROMBONE
FULL 'N' MELLOW
Moderate MARCH

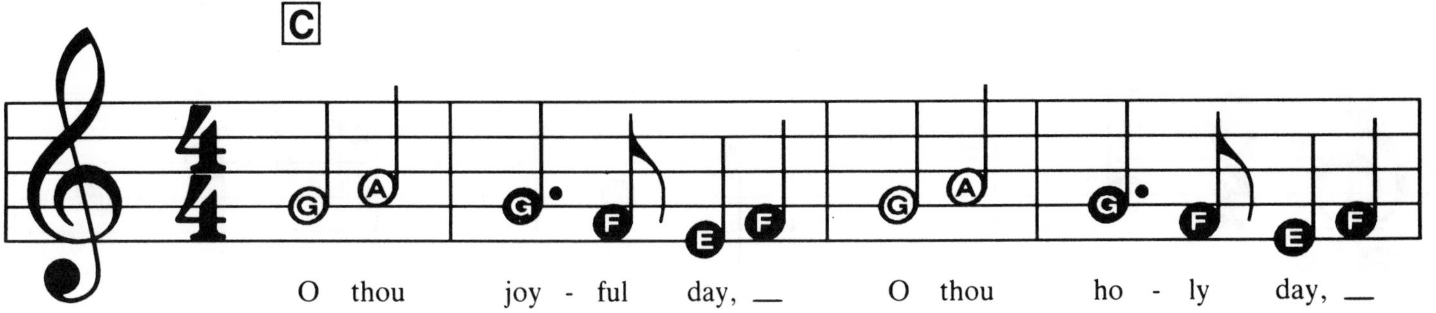
C
G A G F E F G A G F E F
O thou joy - ful day, O thou ho - ly day,

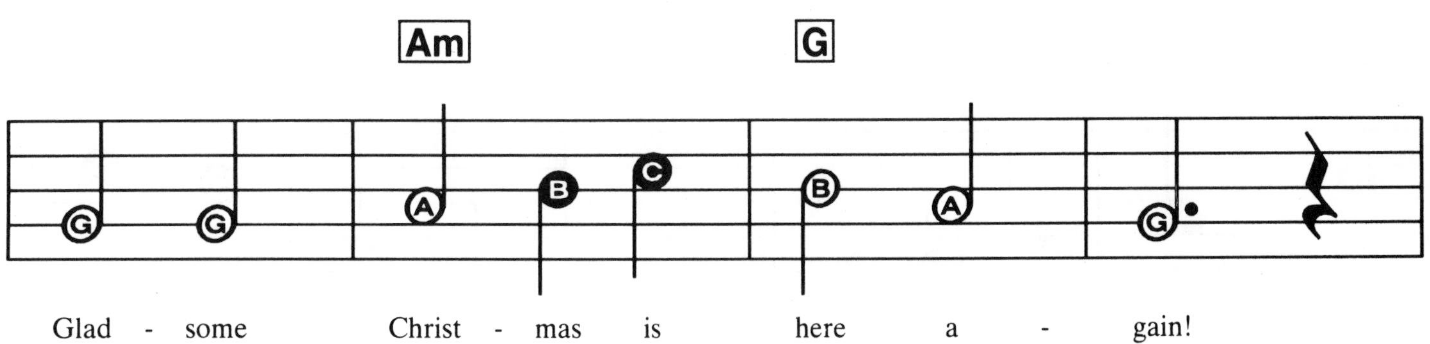
Am G
G G A B C B A G
Glad - some Christ - mas is here a - gain!

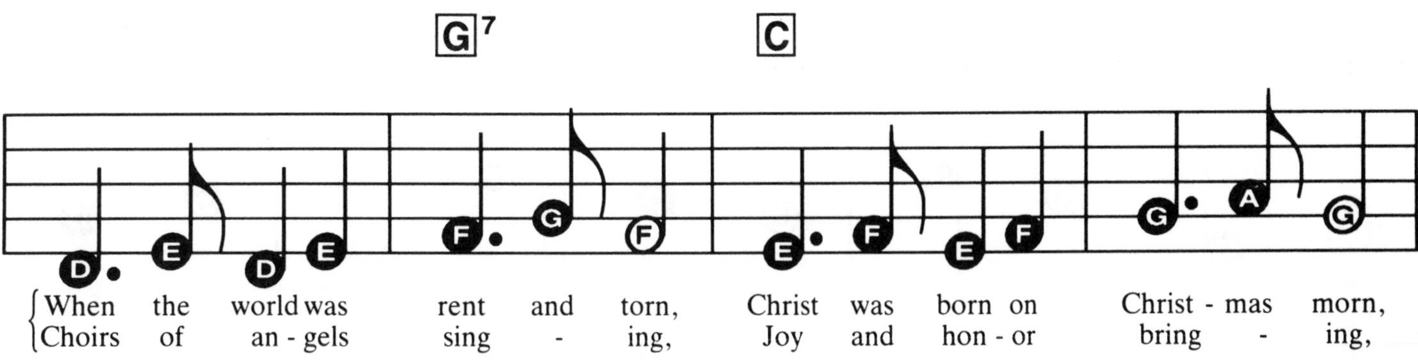
G7 C
D E D E F G F E F E F G A G
When the world was rent and torn, Christ was born on Christ - mas morn,
Choirs of an - gels sing - ing, Joy and hon - or bring - ing,

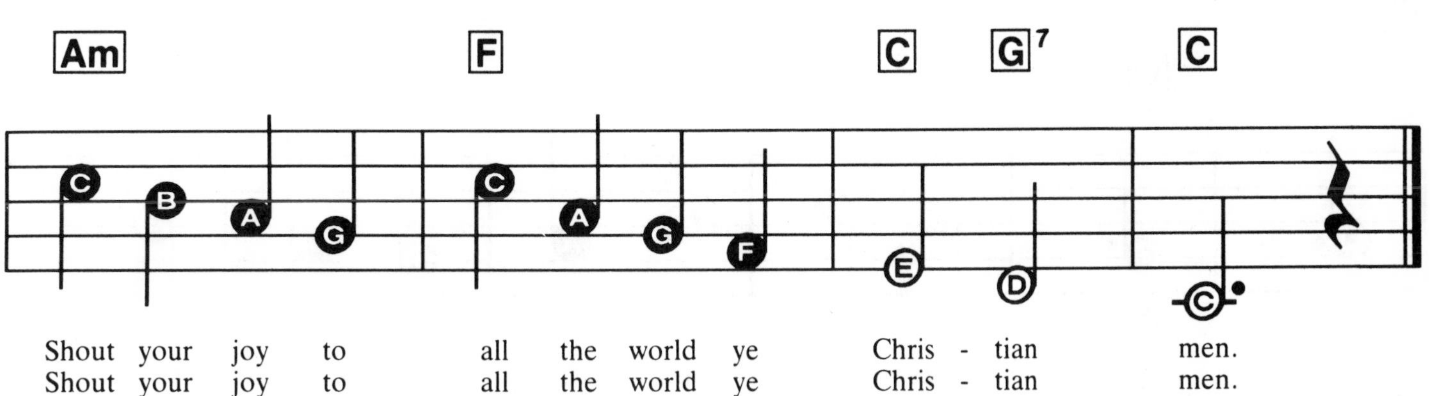
Am F C G7 C
C B A G C A G F E D C
Shout your joy to all the world ye Chris - tian men.
Shout your joy to all the world ye Chris - tian men.

RING OUT, YE WILD AND MERRY BELLS

WOODWINDS
FULL 'N' MELLOW
Medium WALTZ

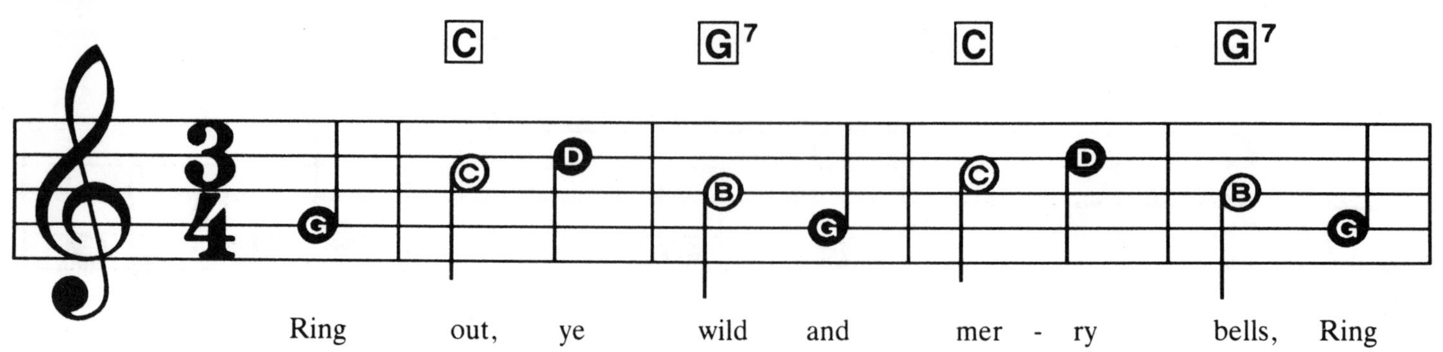

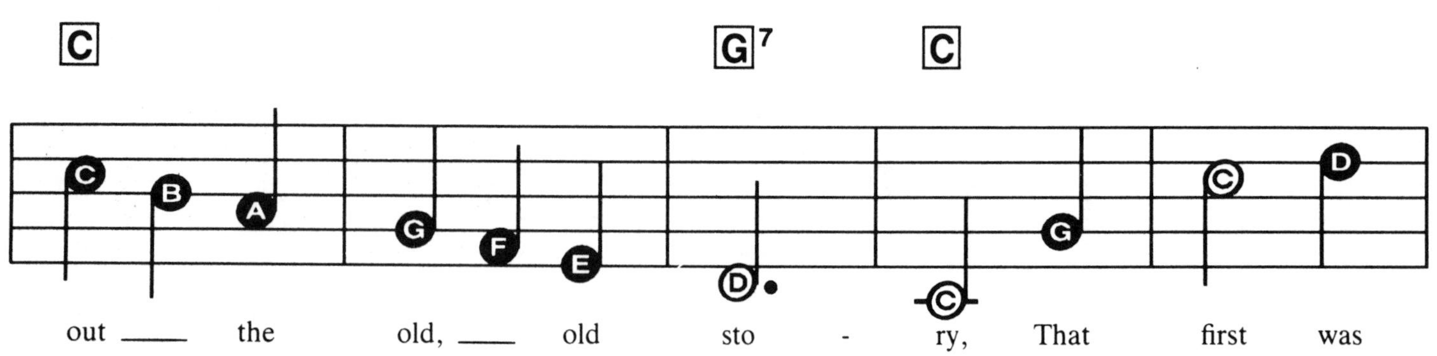

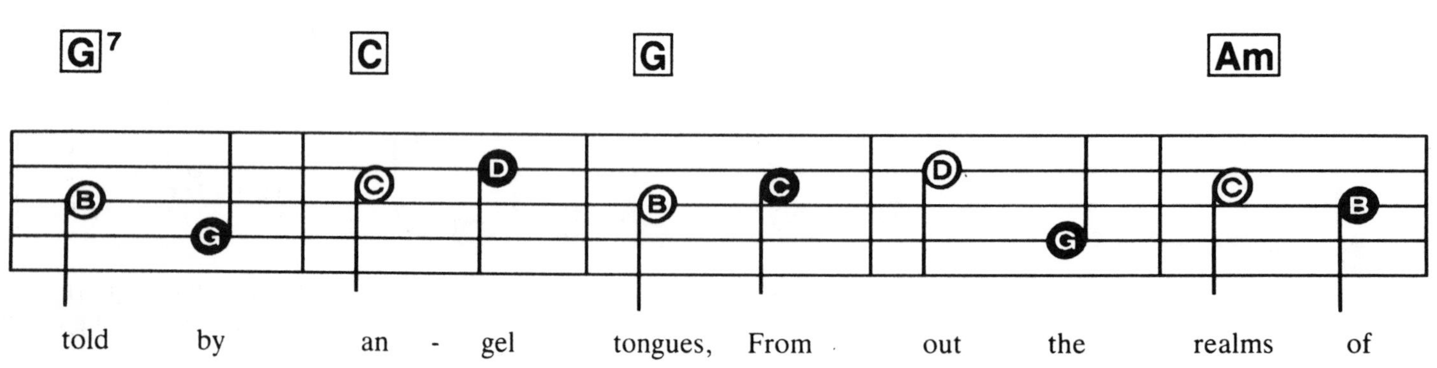

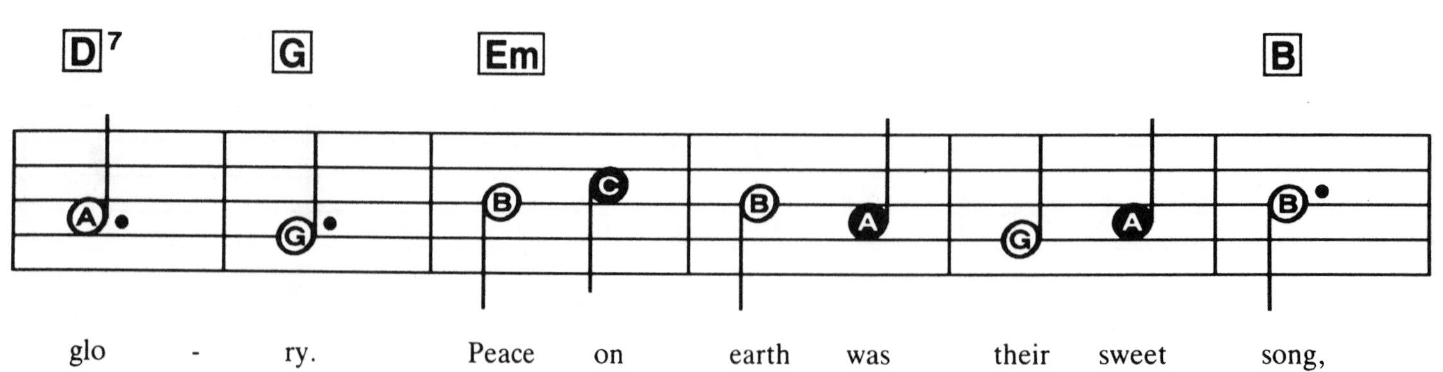

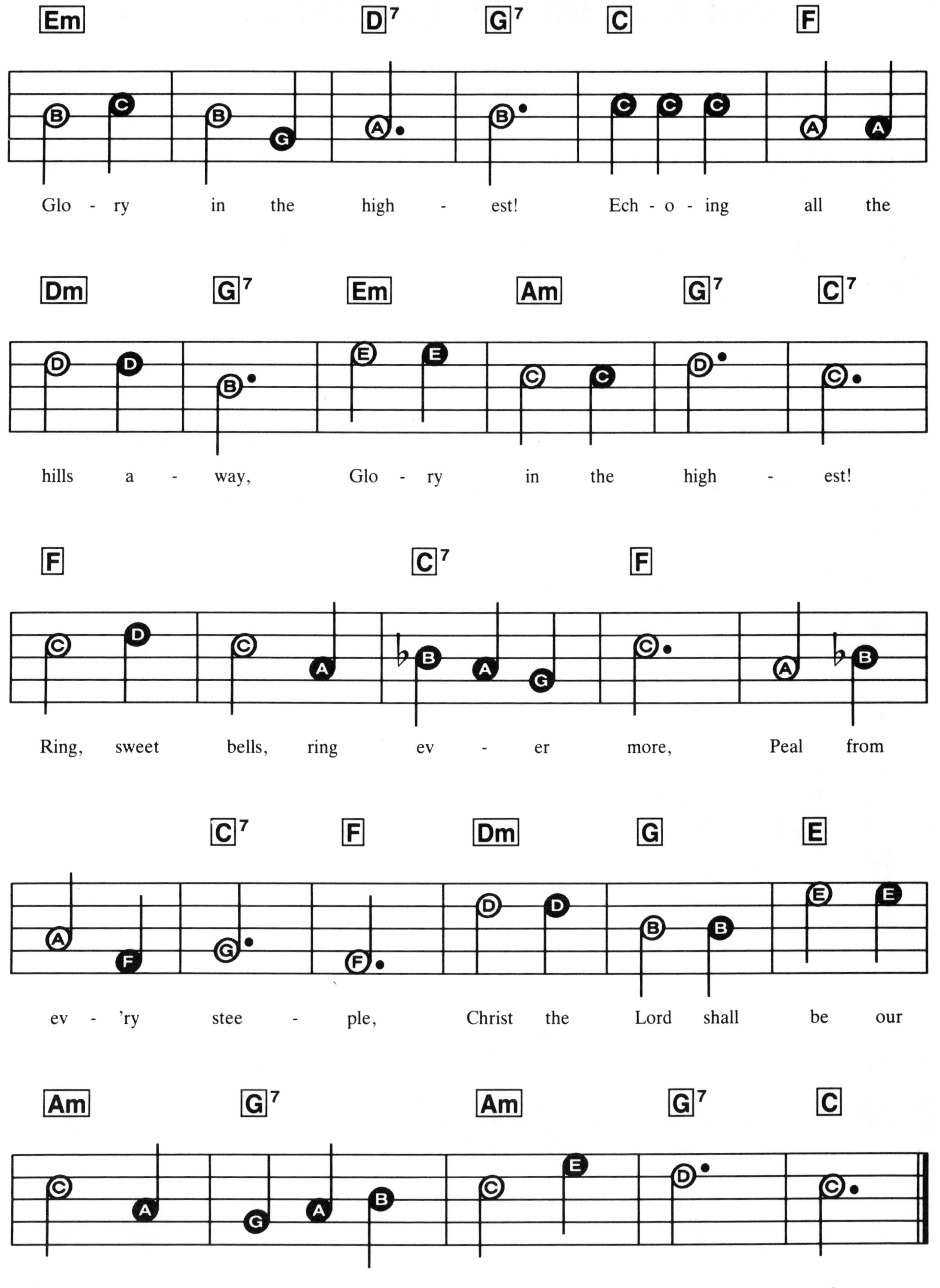
Em D7 G7 C F
B C B G A B C C C A A
Glo - ry in the high - est! Ech - o - ing all the
Dm G7 Em Am G7 C7
D D B E E C C D C
hills a - way, Glo - ry in the high - est!
F C7 F
C D C A B A G C A B
Ring, sweet bells, ring ev - er more, Peal from
C7 F Dm G E
A F G F D D B B E E
ev - 'ry stee - ple, Christ the Lord shall be our
Am G7 Am G7 C
C A G A B C E D C
God, And we shall be his peo - ple.

ONCE IN ROYAL DAVID'S CITY

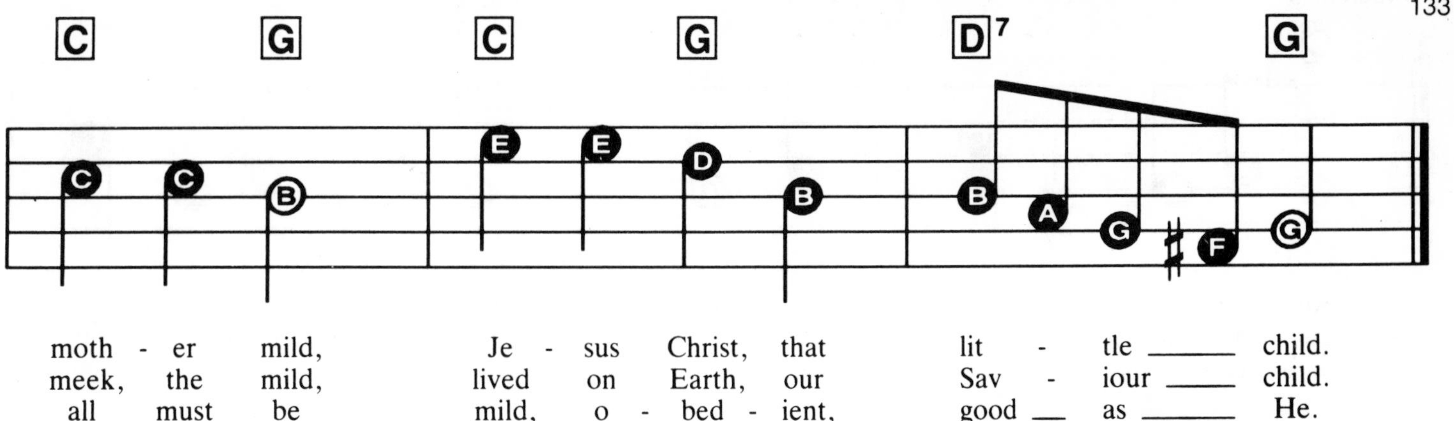
C G C G D7 G
moth - er mild, Je - sus Christ, that lit - tle child.
meek, the mild, lived on Earth, our Sav - iour child.
all must be mild, o - bed - ient, good as He.

RUDOLPH, THE RED-NOSED REINDEER

SAXOPHONE
BRIGHT 'N' BRASSY
SLOW No Rhythm

Words and Music by
JOHNNY MARKS

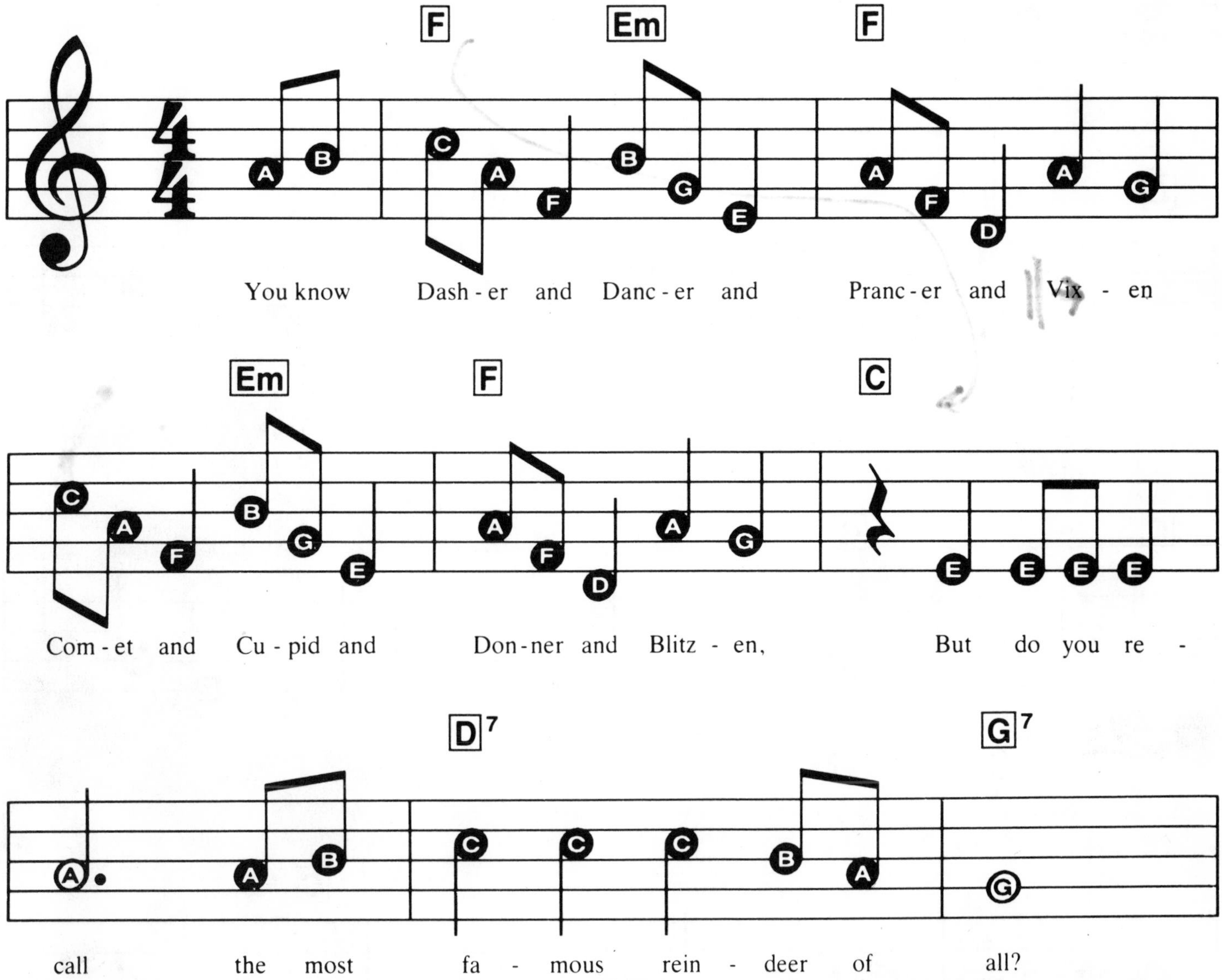

F Em F

You know Dash - er and Danc - er and Pranc - er and Vix - en

Em F C

Com - et and Cu - pid and Don - ner and Blitz - en, But do you re -

D7 G7

call the most fa - mous rein - deer of all?

Medium SWING

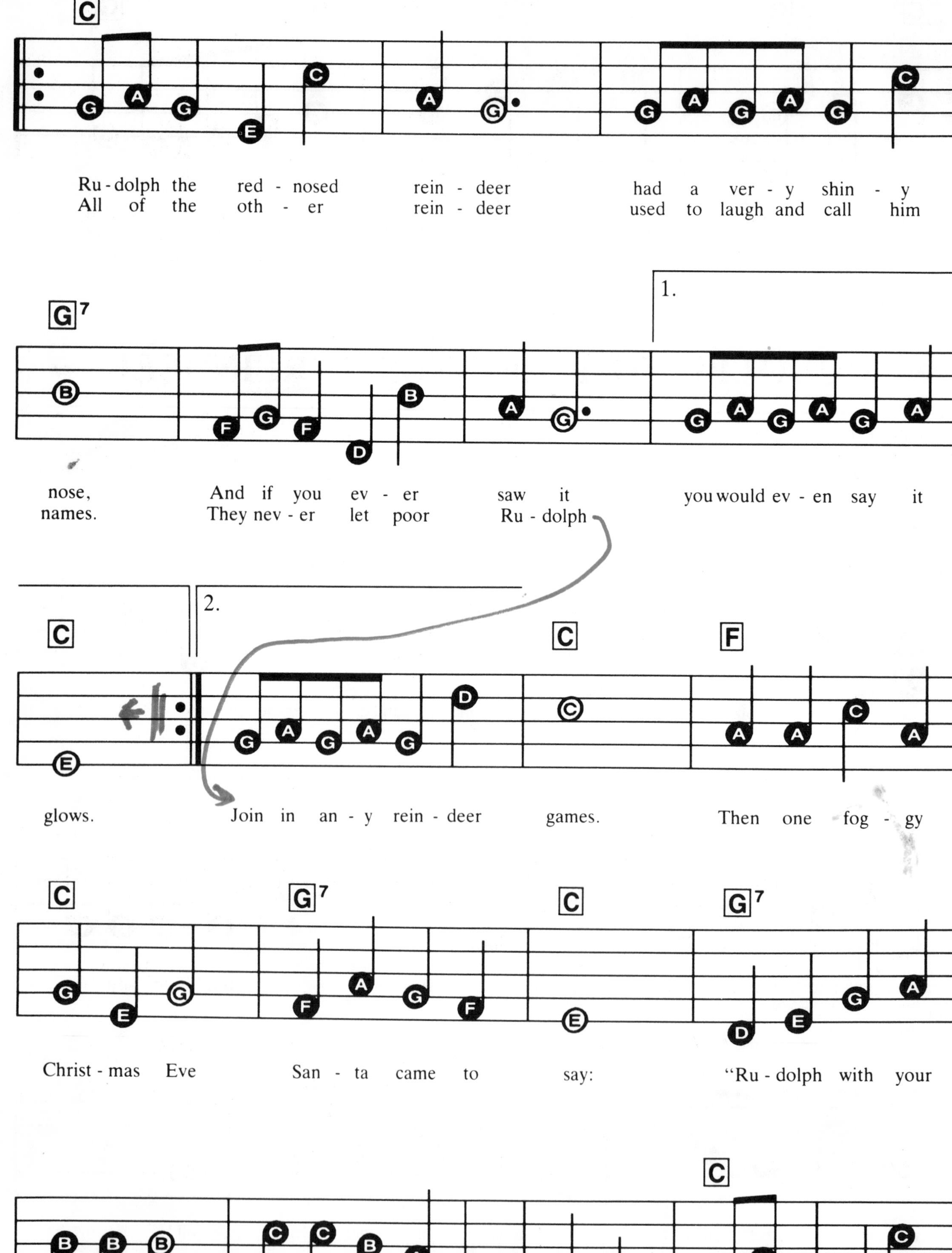

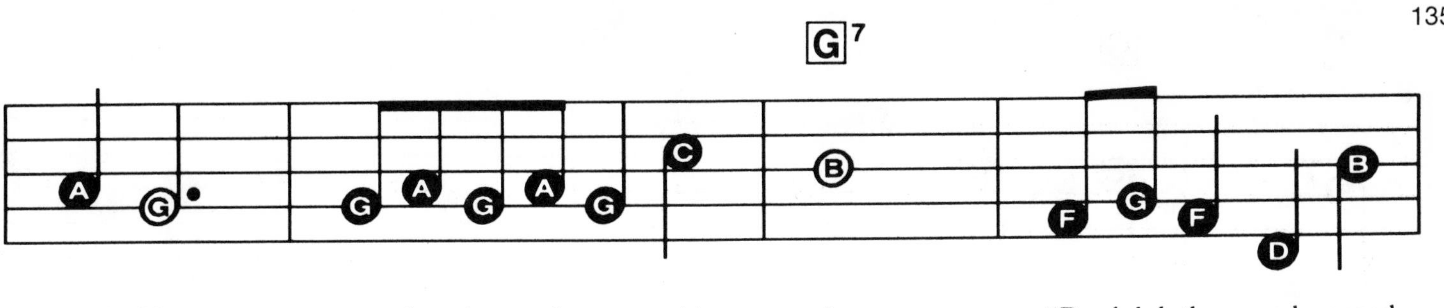
G7
A
G
G
A
G
A
G
C
B
F
G
F
D
B
loved him, as they shout-ed out with glee: "Ru-dolph the red - nosed

C
A
G
G
A
G
A
G
D
C
rein - deer, you'll go down in his - to - ry."

SILENT NIGHT

VIOLIN
SOFT SOLO
Slow WALTZ

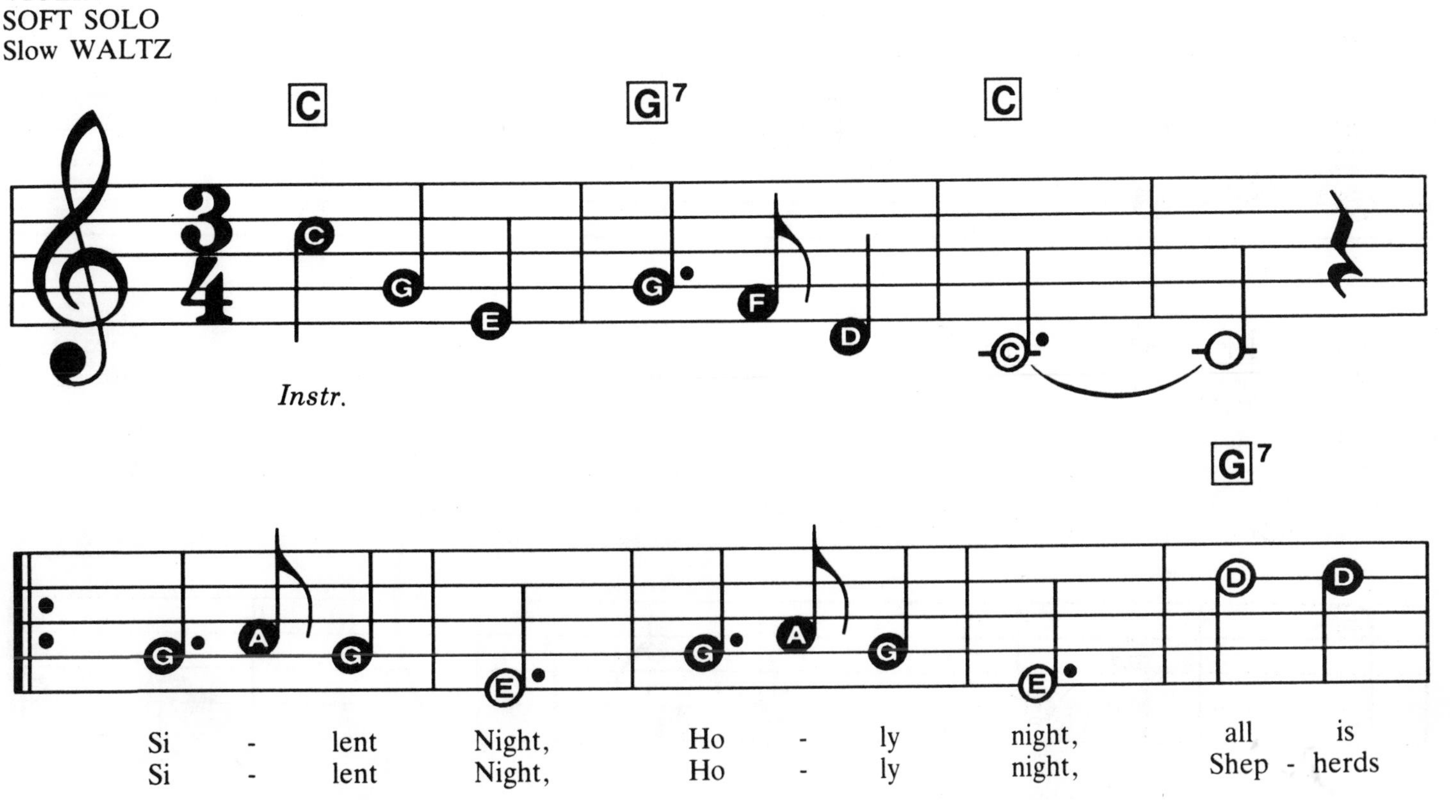
C
G7
C
C
G
E
G
F
D
C
Instr.
G7
G
A
G
E
G
A
G
E
D
D
Si - lent Night, Ho - ly night, all is
Si - lent Night, Ho - ly night, Shep - herds

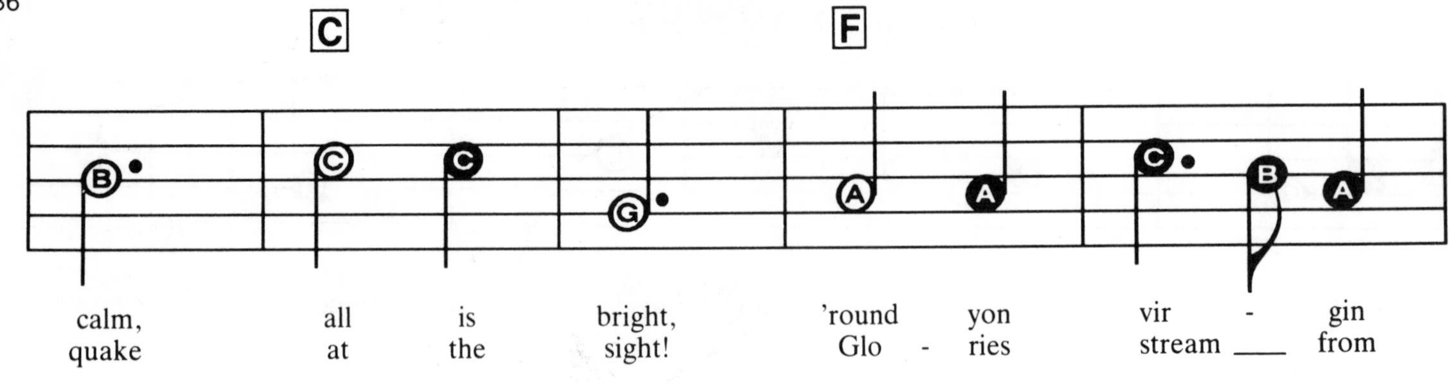
C
F
B C C G A A C B A
calm, all is bright, 'round yon vir - gin
quake at the sight! Glo - ries stream from

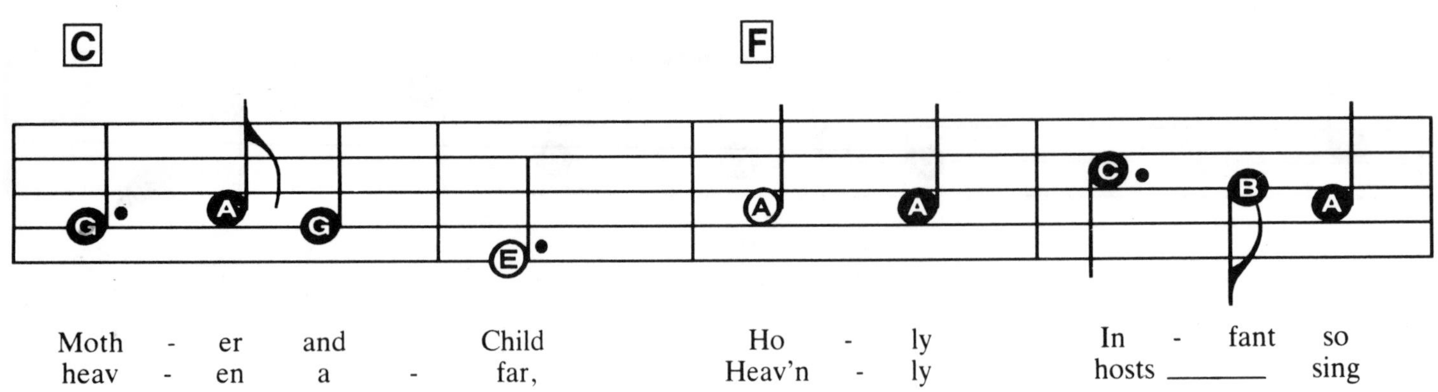
C
F
G A G E A A C B A
Moth - er and Child Ho - ly In - fant so
heav - en a - far, Heav'n - ly hosts sing

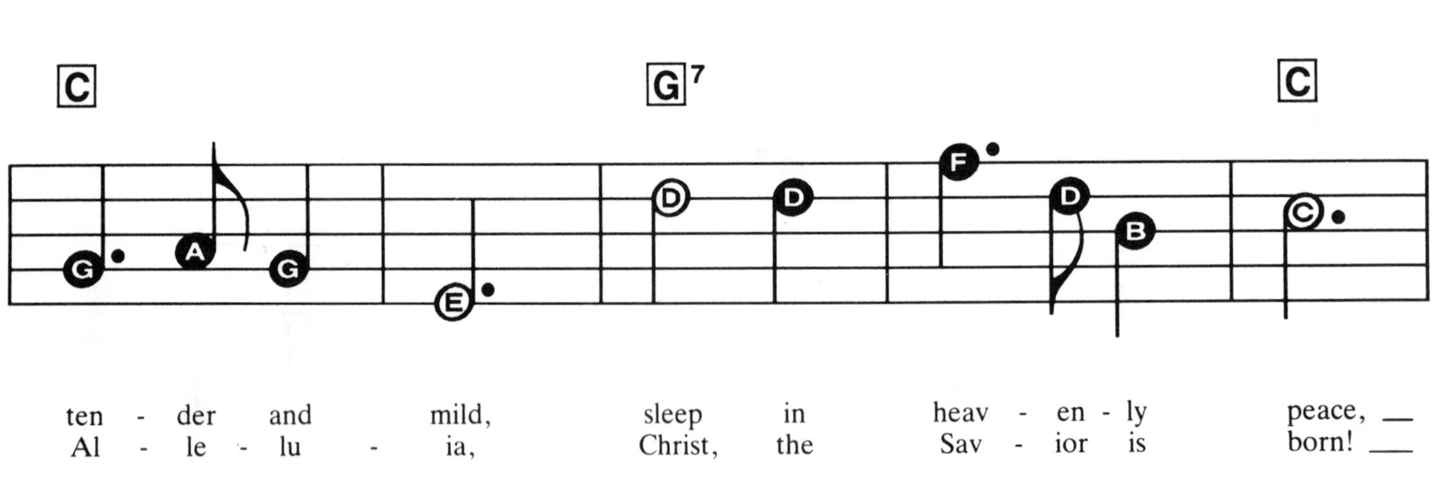
C
G7
C
G A G E D D F D B C
ten - der and mild, sleep in heav - en - ly peace,
Al - le - lu - ia, Christ, the Sav - ior is born!

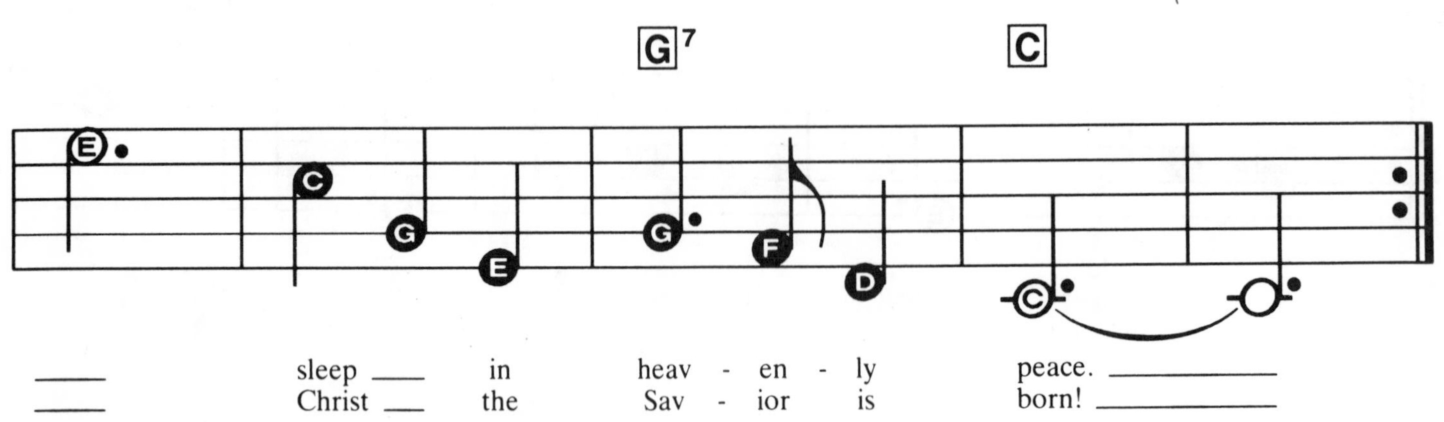
G7
C
E C G E G F D C
sleep in heav - en - ly peace.
Christ the Sav - ior is born!

REJOICE AND BE MERRY

ORGAN
CLASSICAL
Medium WALTZ

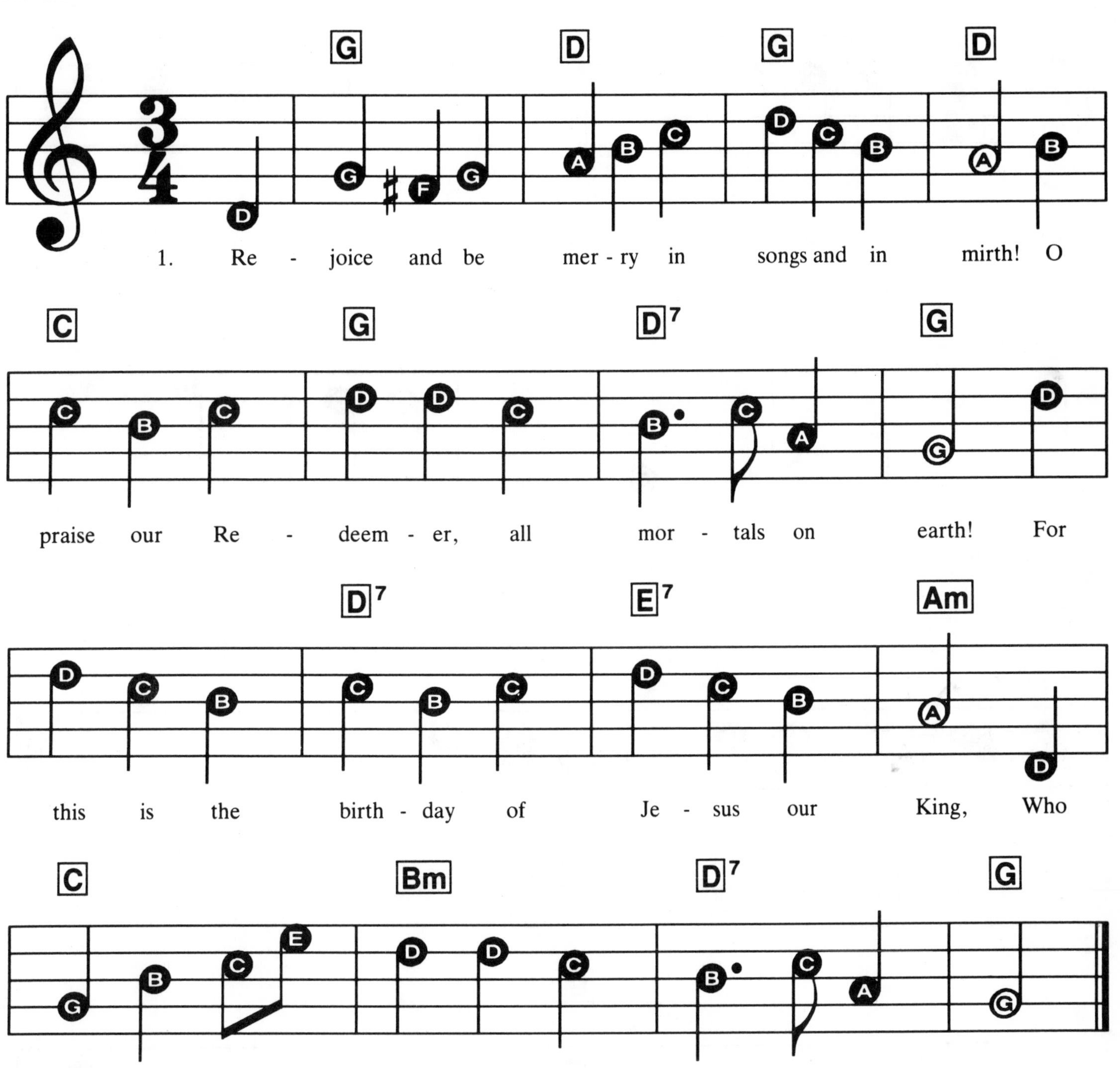

2. A heavenly vision appeared in the sky;
Vast numbers of angels the shepherds did spy,
Proclaiming the birthday of Jesus our King,
Who brought us salvation His praises we'll sing!

3. Likewise a bright star in the sky did appear,
Which led the Wise Men from the east to draw near;
They found the Messiah, sweet Jesus our King,
Who brought us salvation His praises we'll sing!

ROCKIN' AROUND THE CHRISTMAS TREE

TRUMPET
BRIGHT 'N' BRASSY
Medium SWING
Words and Music by
JOHNNY MARKS
F
Rock - in' a - round the Christ - mas tree { at the / let the
C7
Christ - mas par - ty hop. Mis - tle - toe hung where
Christ - mas spir - it ring. Lat - er we'll have some
1.
F
you can see ev - 'ry cou - ple tries to stop.
pump - kin pie and we'll
2.
F
B♭
do some car - ol - ing. You will get a sen - ti - men - tal

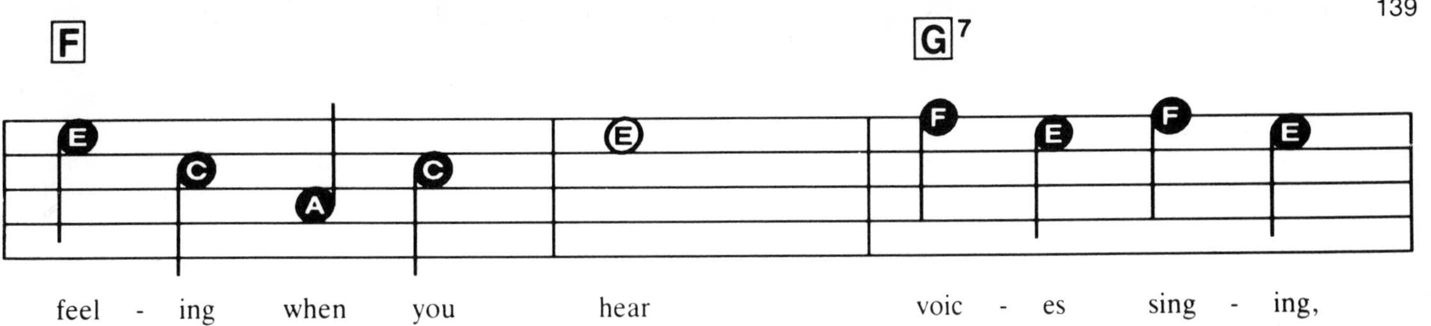
F
G7
E
C
A
C
E
F
E
F
E
feel - ing when you hear voic - es sing - ing,

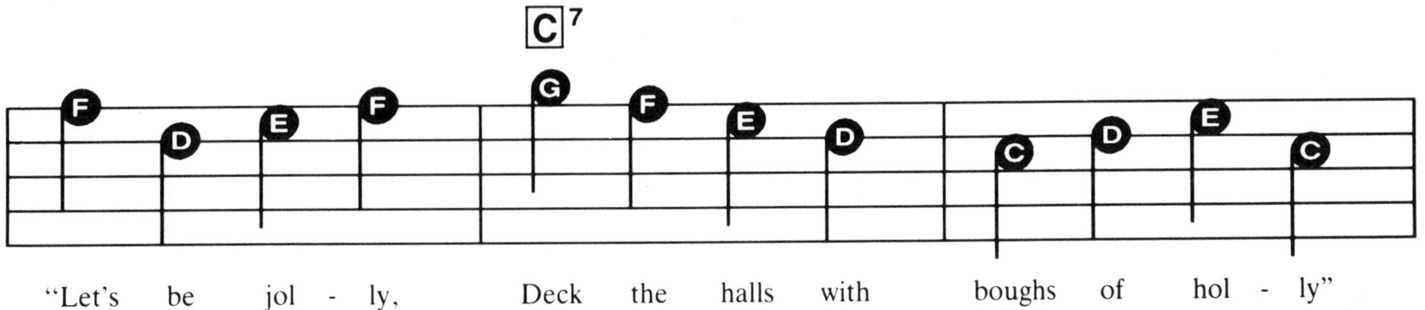
C7
F
D
E
F
G
F
E
D
C
D
E
C
"Let's be jol - ly, Deck the halls with boughs of hol - ly"

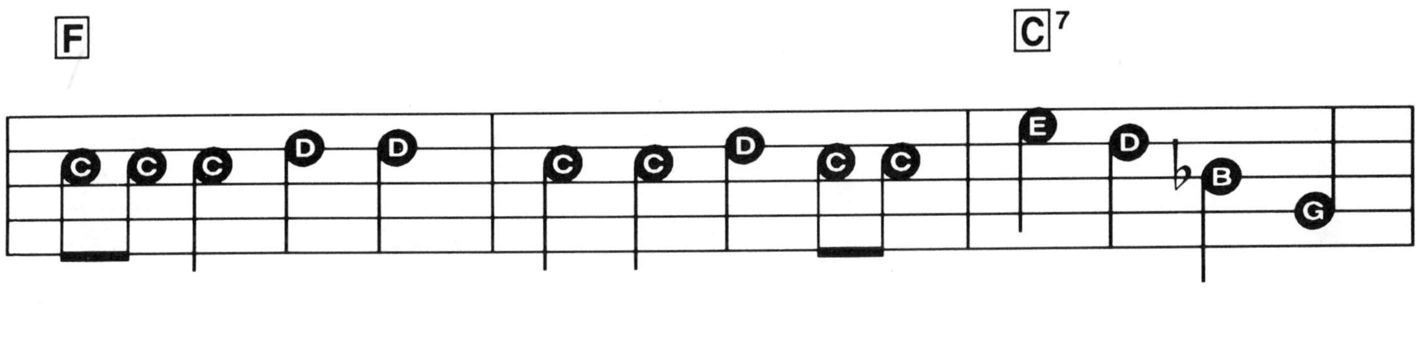
F
C7
C
C
C
D
D
C
C
D
C
C
E
D
B
G
Rock - in' a - round the Christ - mas tree have a hap - py hol - i -

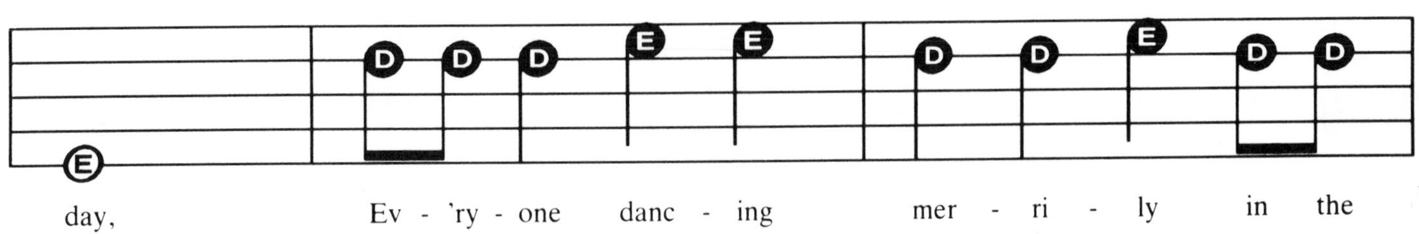
E
D
D
D
E
E
D
D
E
D
D
day, Ev - 'ry - one danc - ing mer - ri - ly in the

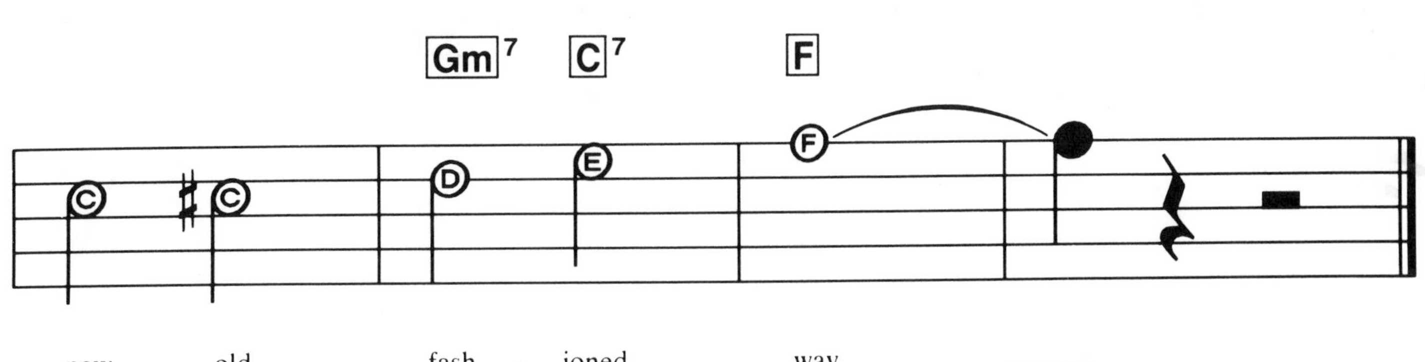
Gm7
C7
F
C
C
D
E
F
new old fash - ioned way.

SANTA CLAUS IS COMIN' TO TOWN

TRUMPET
BRIGHT 'N' BRASSY
Fast SWING

Words by HAVEN GILLESPIE
Music by J. FRED COOTS

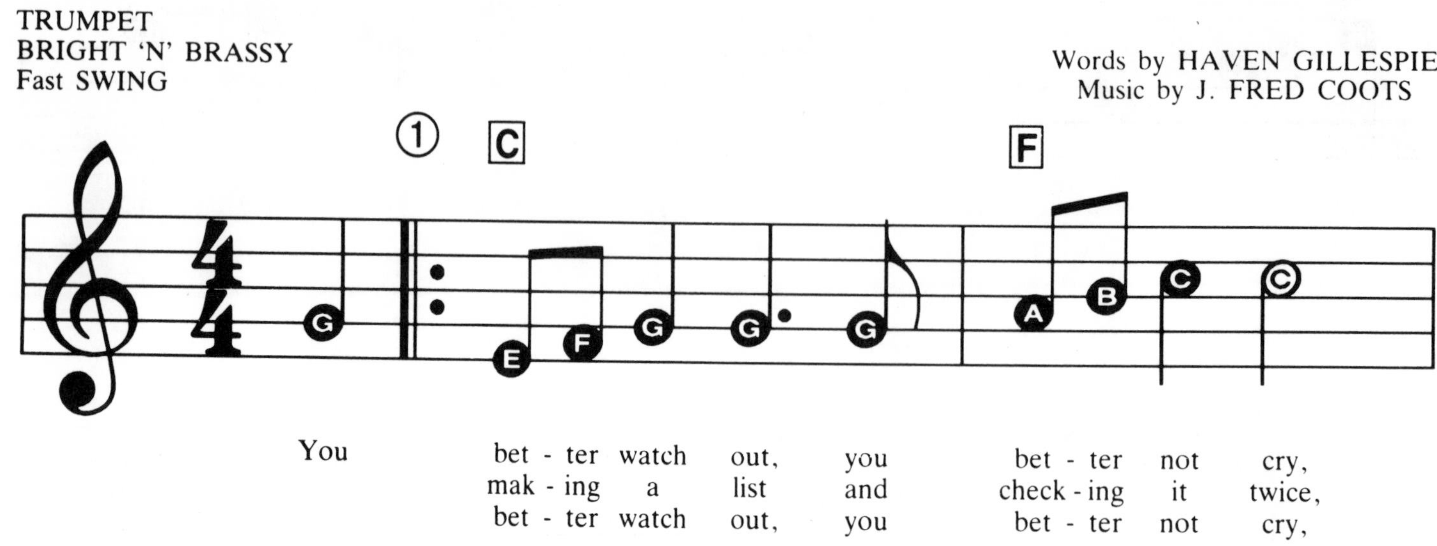

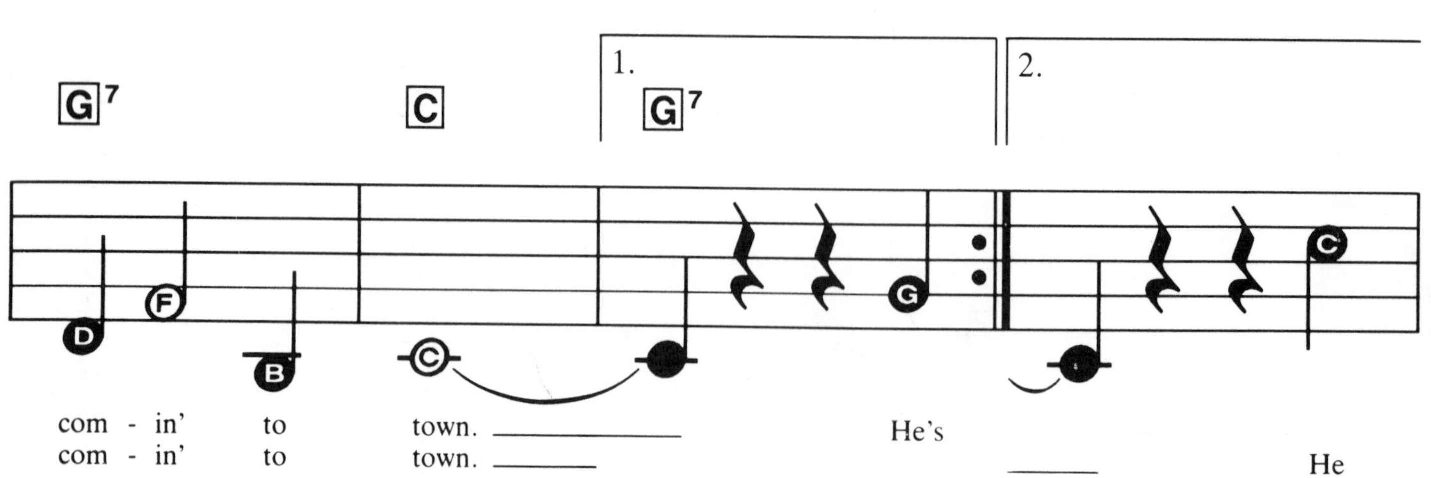

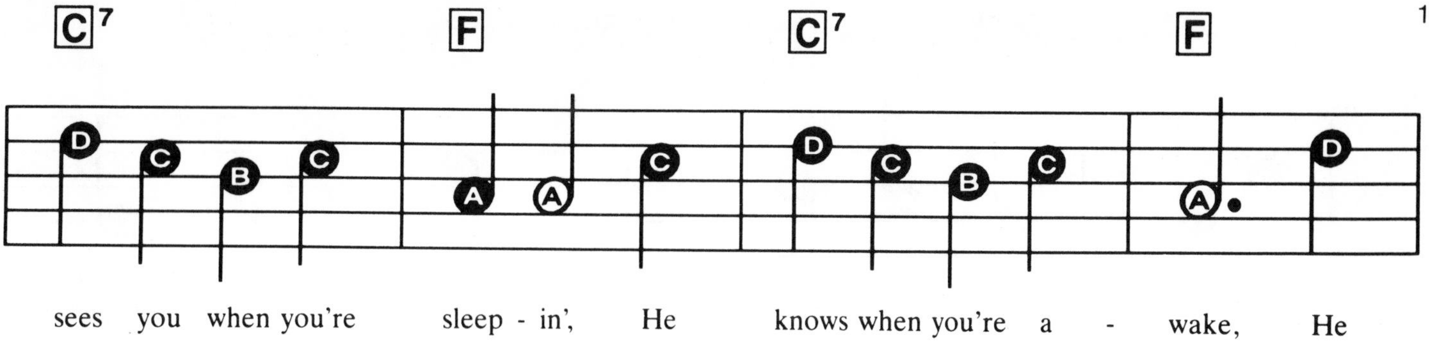

C7 F C7 F

sees you when you're sleep - in', He knows when you're a - wake, He

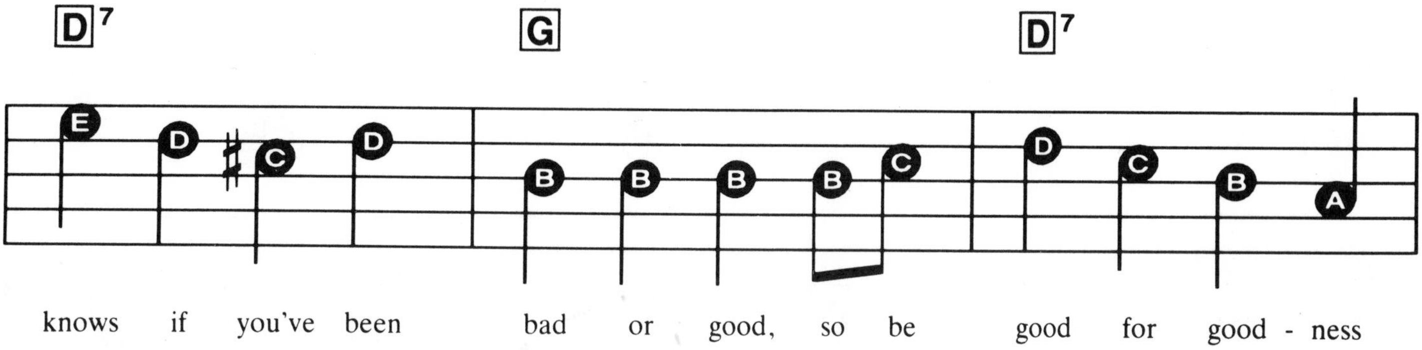

D7 G D7

knows if you've been bad or good, so be good for good - ness

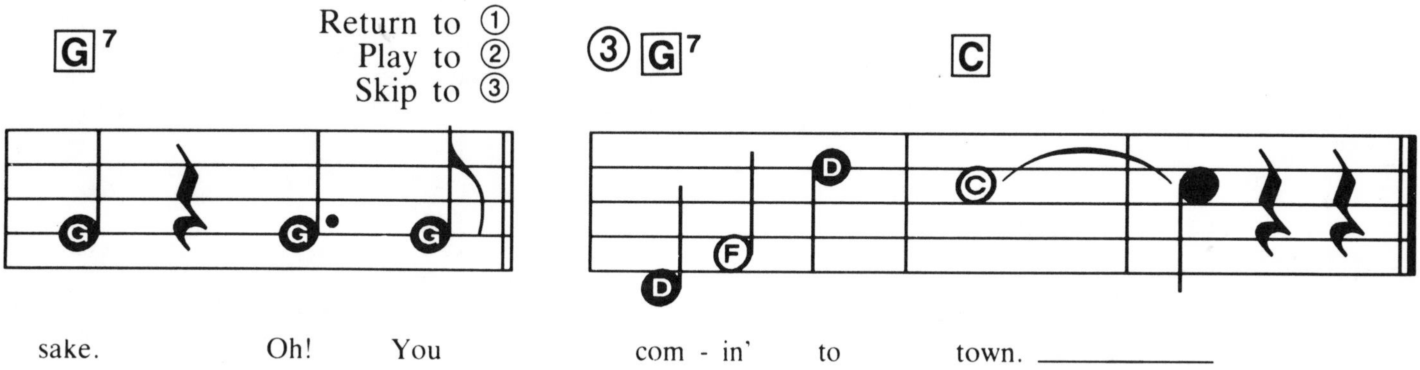

G7 Return to ① Play to ② Skip to ③ ③ G7 C

sake. Oh! You com - in' to town.

THE SON OF GOD IS BORN FOR ALL

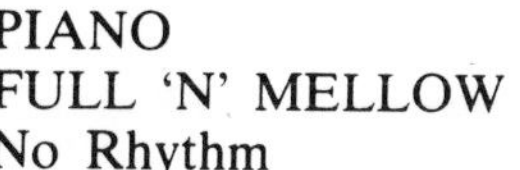
PIANO
FULL 'N' MELLOW
No Rhythm

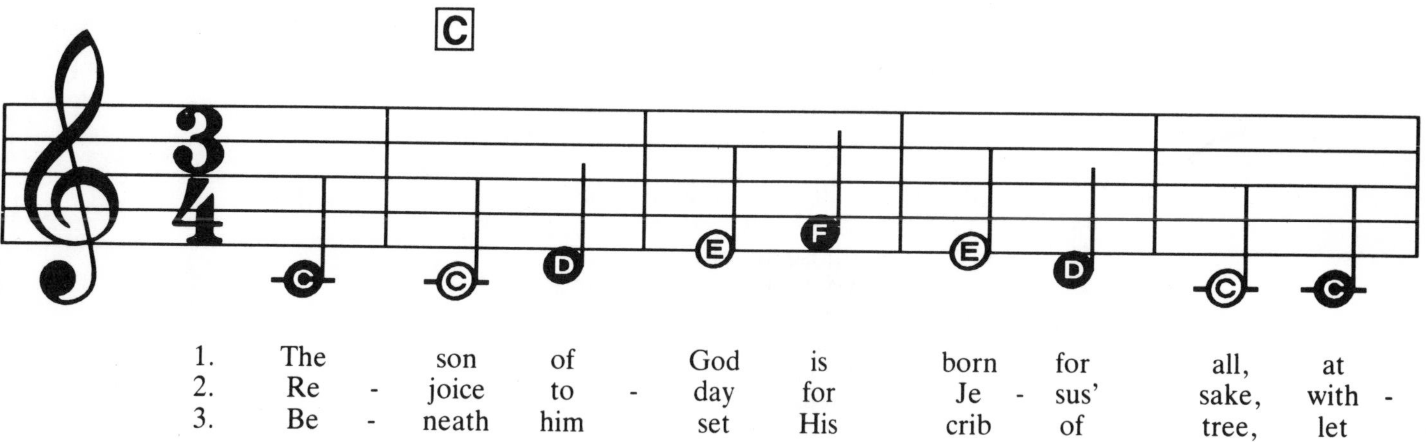
C
1. The son of God is born for all, at
2. Re - joice to - day for Je - sus' sake, with -
3. Be - neath him set His crib of tree, let

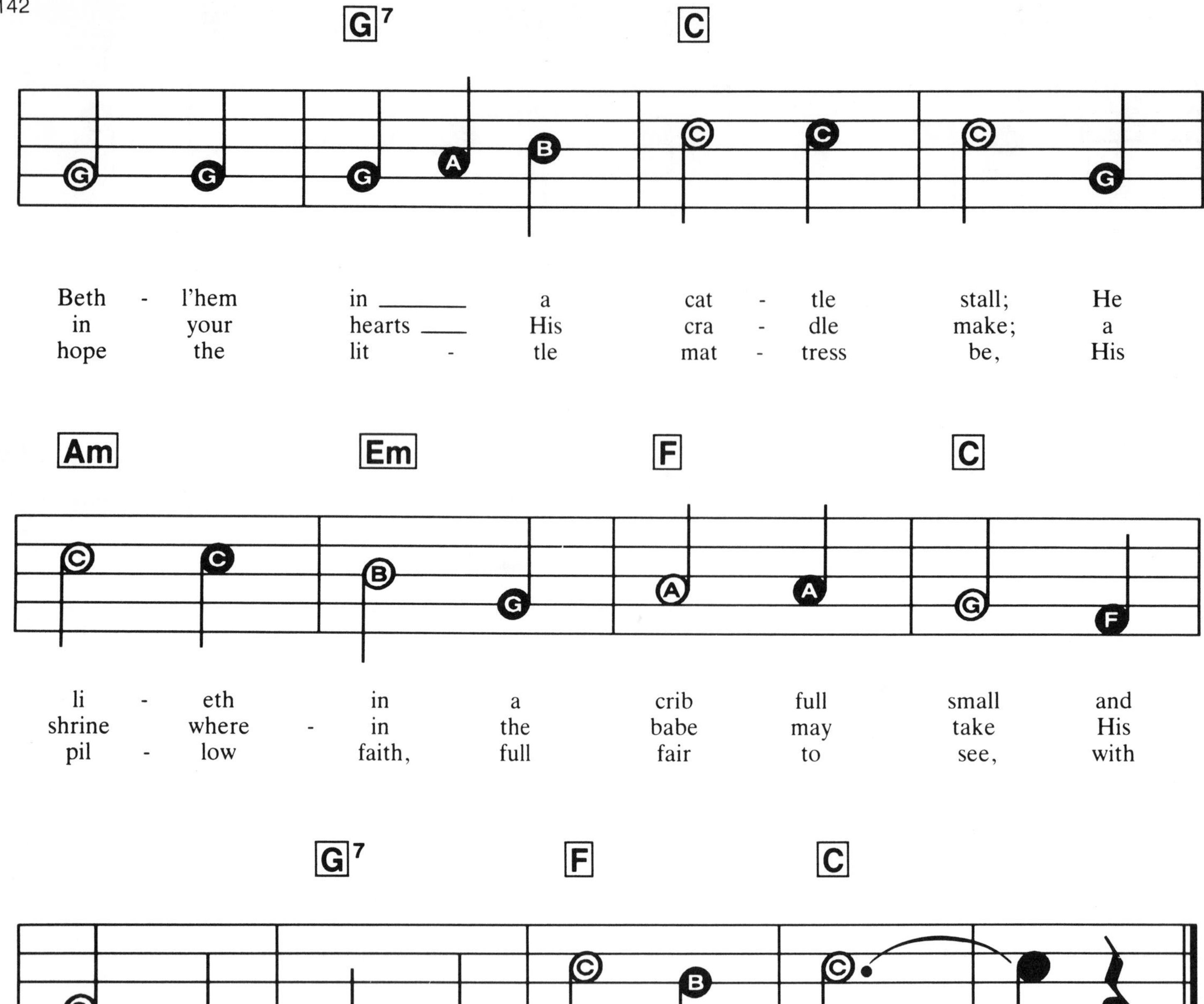
G7 C
G G G A B C C C G
Beth - l'hem in a cat - tle stall; He
in your hearts His cra - dle make; a
hope the lit - tle mat - tress be, His
Am Em F C
C C B G A A G F
li - eth in a crib full small and
shrine where - in the babe may take His
pil - low faith, full fair to see, with
G7 F C
G E D E C B C
wrapt in swad - dling clothes with - al.
rest in slum - ber or a - wake.
cov - er - let of char - i - ty.

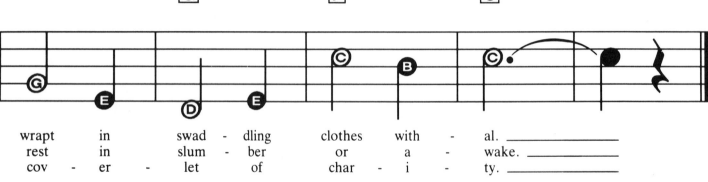

4. In bodies pure and undefiled
Prepare a chamber for the Child.
To Him give incense, myrrh and gold,
Nor raiment, meat and drink withhold.

5. Draw nigh, the son of God to kiss;
Greet Mary's Child, the Lord He is;
Upon those lovely lips of His;
Jesus your hearts; desire and bliss.

6. Come rock His cradle cheerily,
As doth His mother, so do ye,
Who nursed Him sweetly on her knee,
As told it was by prophecy.

7. "By, by, lullay", before Him sing;
Go wind the horn and pluck the string
Till all the place with music ring
And bid one pray'r to Christ the King.

SING, O SING, THIS BLESSED MORN

ORGAN
CLASSICAL
No Rhythm

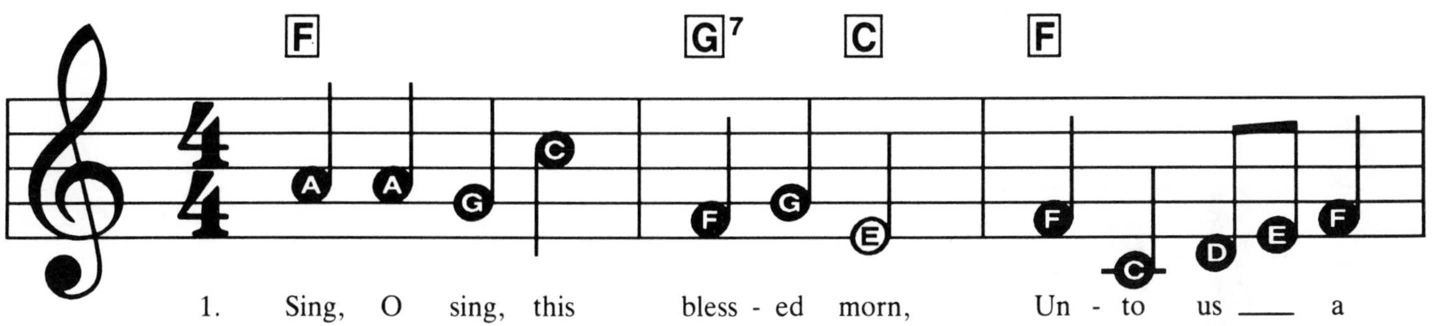
F
G7
C
F
A A G C F G E F C D E F
1. Sing, O sing, this bless - ed morn, Un - to us ___ a

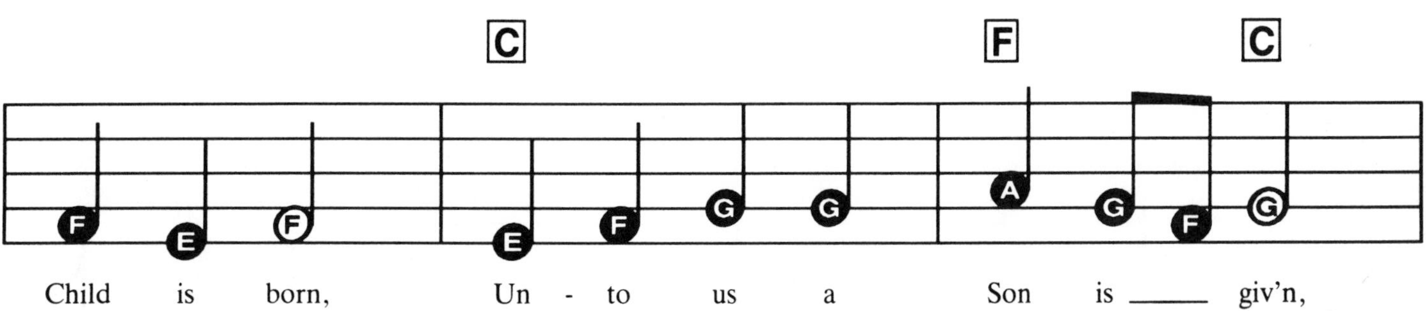
C
F
C
F E F E F G G A G F G
Child is born, Un - to us a Son is ___ giv'n,

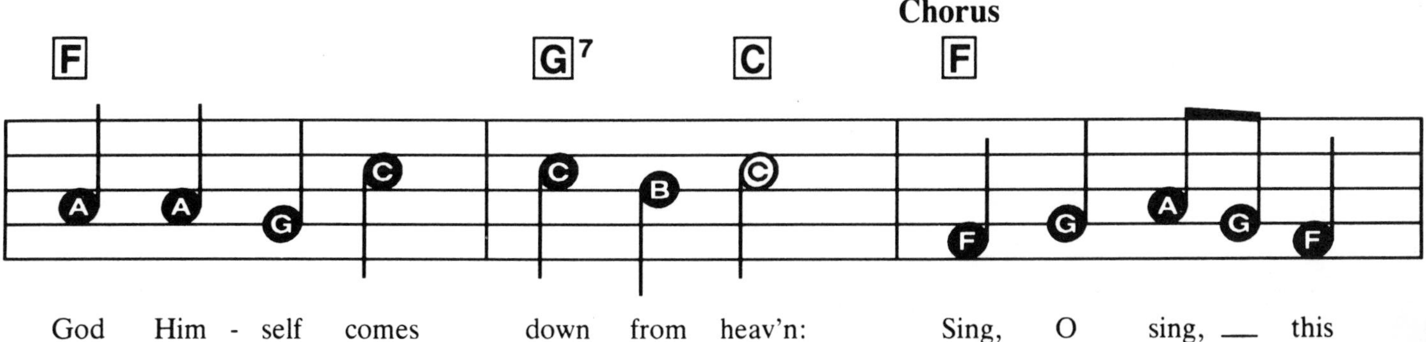
Chorus
F
G7
C
F
A A G C C B C F G A G F
God Him - self comes down from heav'n: Sing, O sing, ___ this

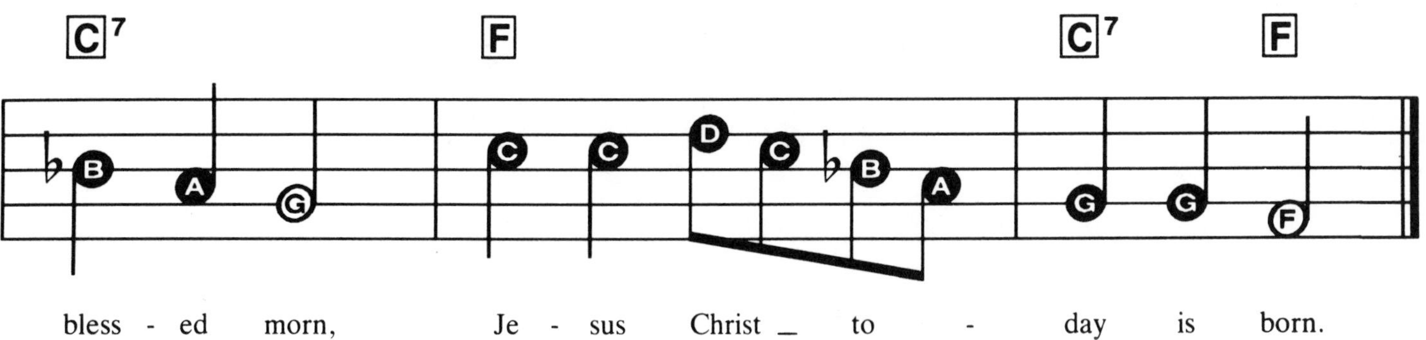
C7
F
C7
F
B A G C C D C B A G G F
bless - ed morn, Je - sus Christ _ to - day is born.

God with us, Immanuel,
Deigns for ever now to dwell,
And on Adam's fallen race
Sheds the fullness of His grace:
Chorus

3. God comes down that man may rise,
Lifted by Him to the skies;
Christ is Son of Man that we
Sons of God in Him may be:
Chorus

4. O renew us, Lord, we pray,
With Thy spirit day by day;
That we ever one may be
With the Father and with Thee:
Chorus

From the Paramount Picture "THE LEMON DROP KID"

SILVER BELLS

CELESTE
FULL 'N' MELLOW
Slow WALTZ

By JAY LIVINGSTON
and RAY EVANS

C

Cit - y side - walks, bus - y side - walks dressed in
street lights, ev - en stop lights blink a

F G7

hol - i - day style. In the air there's a feel - ing of
bright red and green, As the shop - pers rush home with their

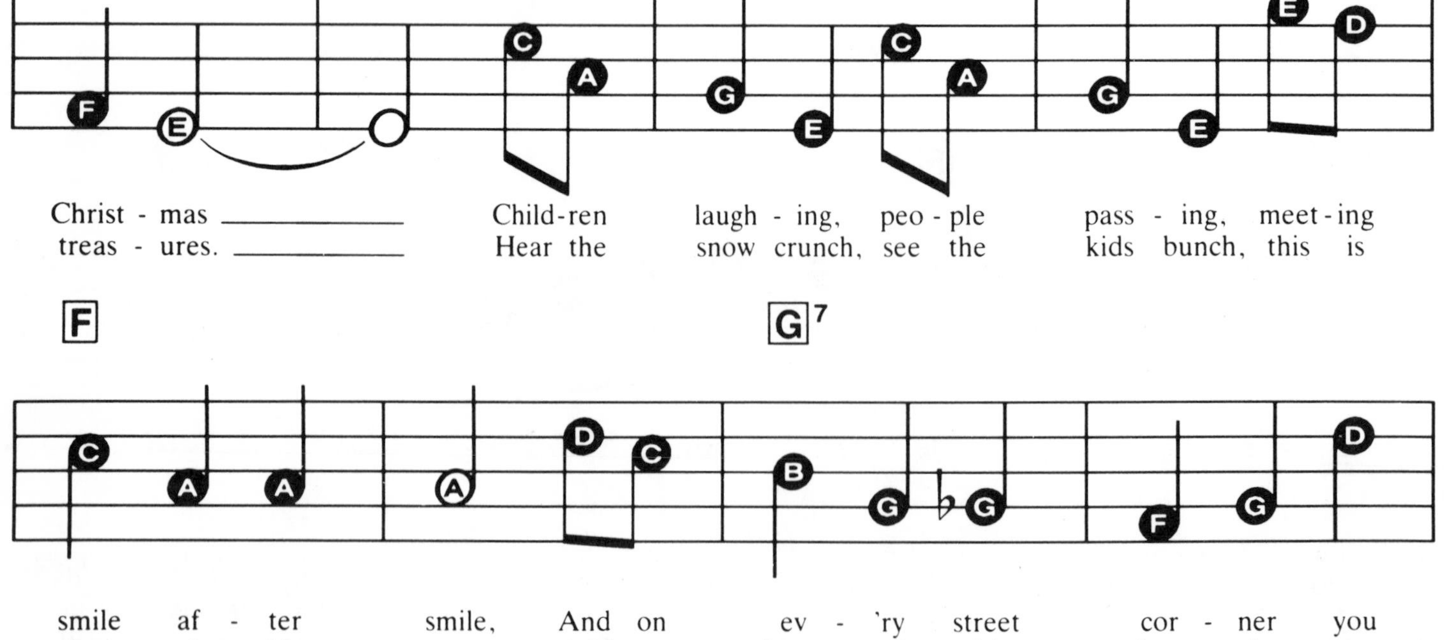
C
Christ - mas ___ Child-ren laugh - ing, peo - ple pass - ing, meet - ing
treas - ures. ___ Hear the snow crunch, see the kids bunch, this is
F
G7
smile af - ter smile, And on ev - 'ry street cor - ner you
San - ta's big scene, And a - bove all this bus - tle you

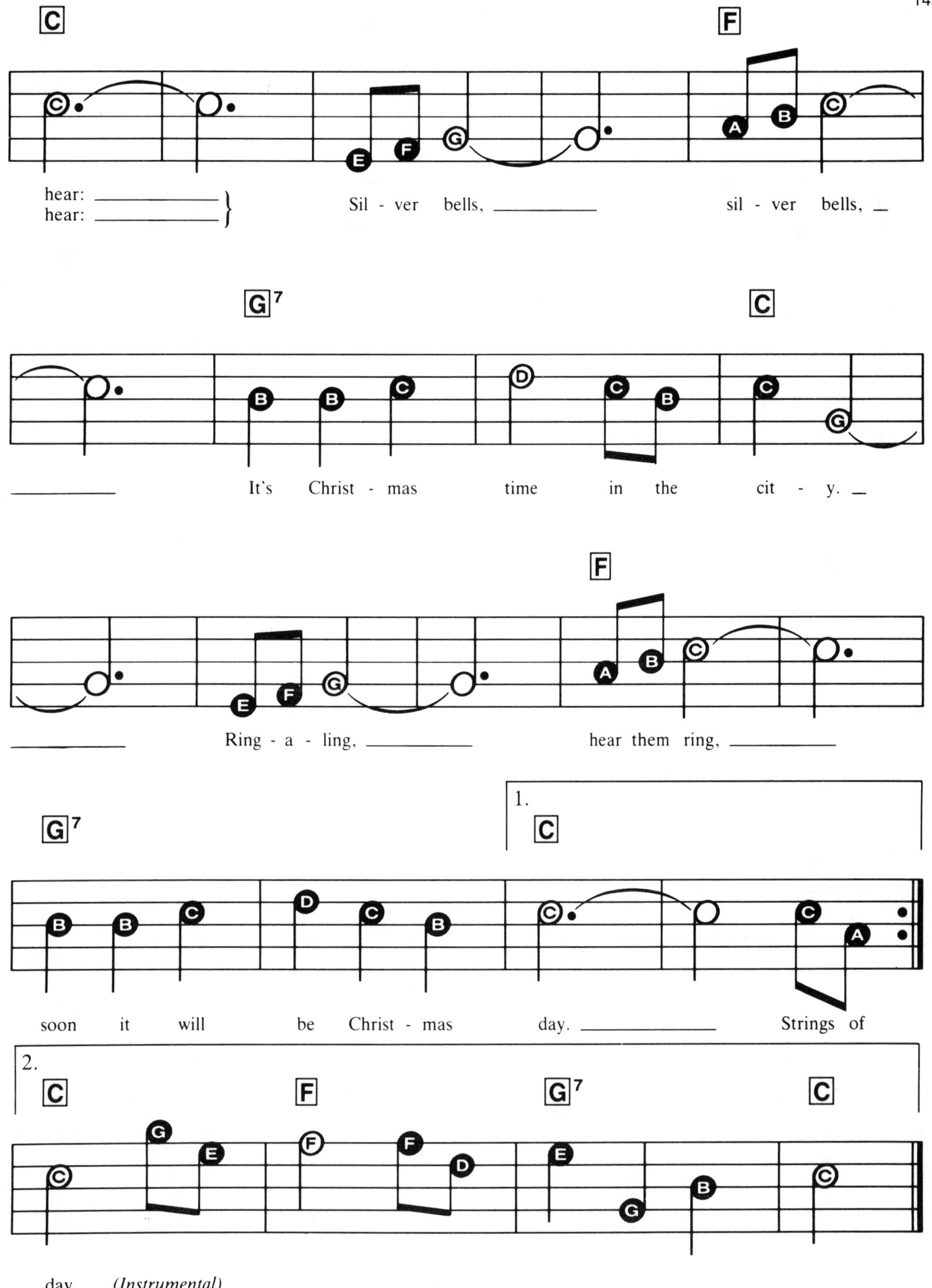
C
F
hear:
hear:
Sil - ver bells,
sil - ver bells,
G7
C
It's Christ - mas time in the cit - y.
F
Ring - a - ling,
hear them ring,
G7
1.
C
soon it will be Christ - mas day.
Strings of
2.
C
F
G7
C
day. (Instrumental)

SLEIGH RIDE

CLARINET
BRIGHT 'N' BRASSY
Fast SWING
Words by MITCHELL PARISH
Music by
LEROY ANDERSON
Just hear those sleigh bells jin - gle - ing, ring - ting - tin - gle - ing, too, ___
snow is fall - ing and friends are call - ing "yoo hoo," ___
Come on, it's love - ly weath - er for a sleigh ride to - geth - er with you, ___ Out - side the
1.
2.
Gid - dy - yap, gid - dy - yap, gid - dy - yap, let's go,

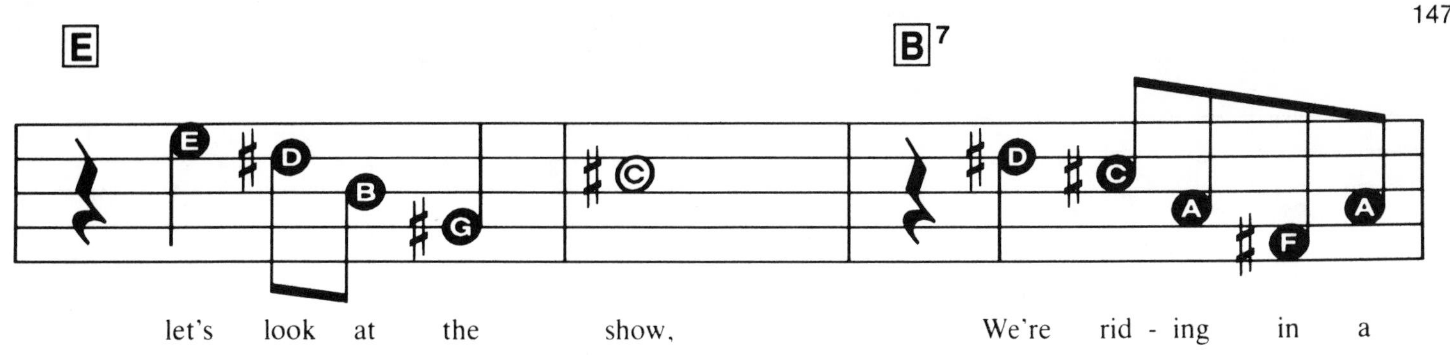
E
B7
E
D
B
G
C
D
C
A
F
A
let's look at the show, We're rid - ing in a

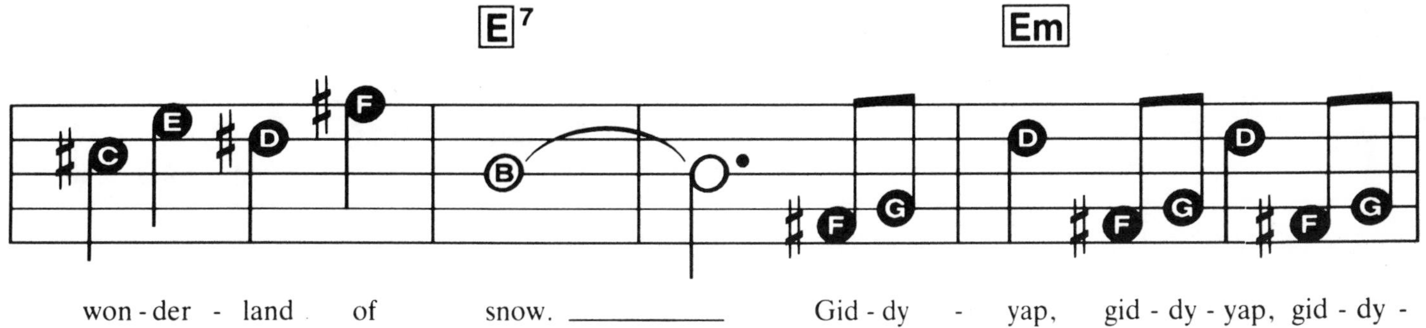
E7
Em
C
E
D
F
B
F
G
D
F
G
D
F
G
won - der - land of snow.
Gid - dy - yap, gid - dy - yap, gid - dy -

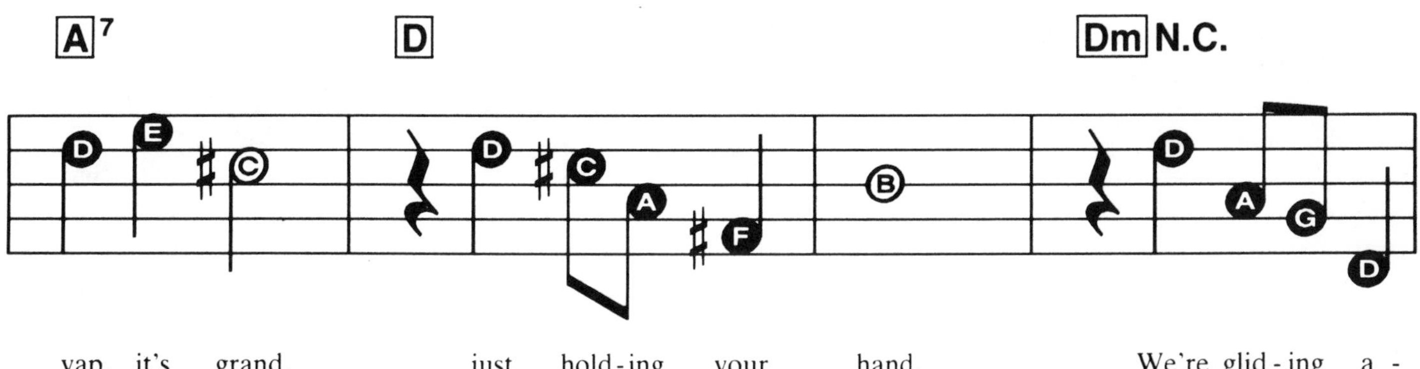
A7
D
Dm N.C.
D
E
C
D
C
A
F
B
D
A
G
D
yap, it's grand, just hold - ing your hand, We're glid - ing a -

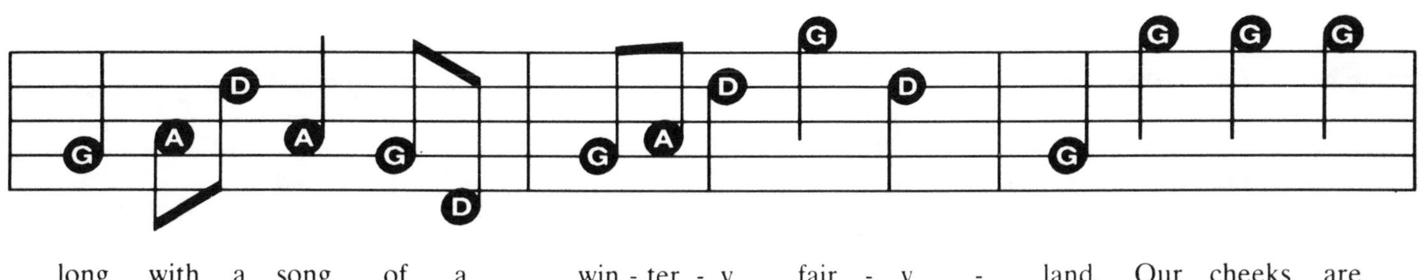
G
A
D
A
G
D
G
A
D
G
D
G
G
G
G
long with a song of a win - ter - y fair - y - land. Our cheeks are

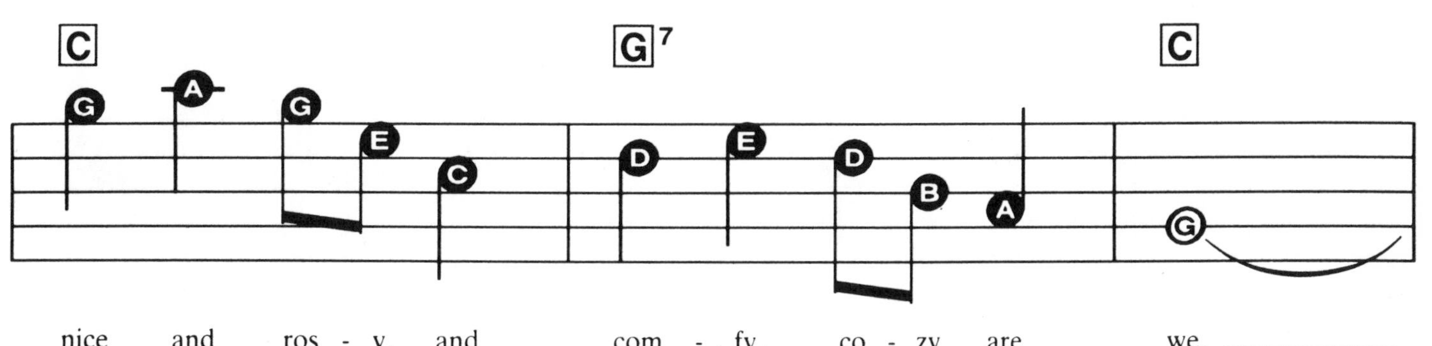
C
G7
C
G
A
G
E
C
D
E
D
B
A
G
nice and ros - y, and com - fy co - zy are we,

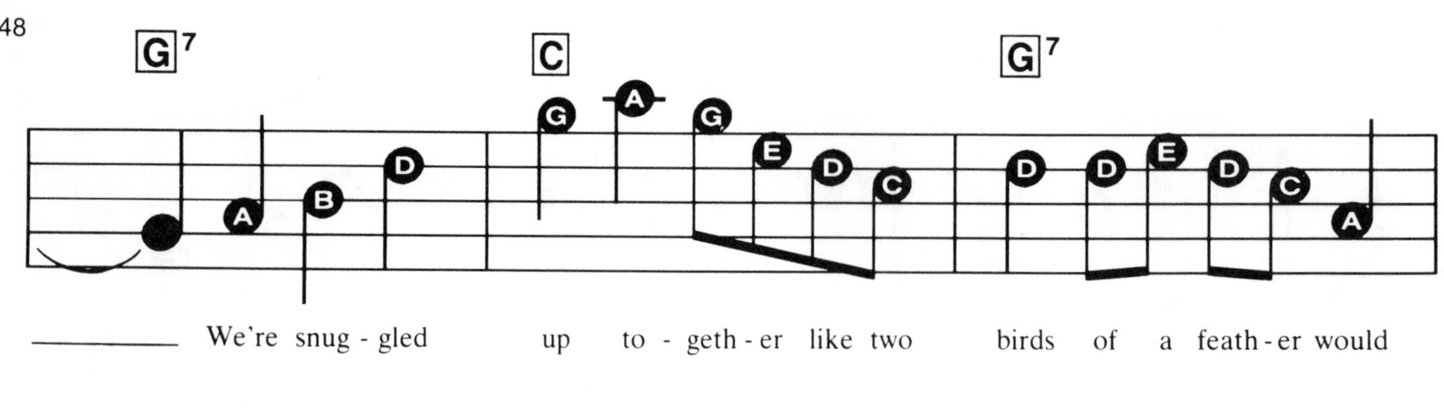
G7
C
G7
G
A
G
E
D
C
A
B
D
D
D
E
D
C
A
We're snug - gled up to - geth - er like two birds of a feath - er would

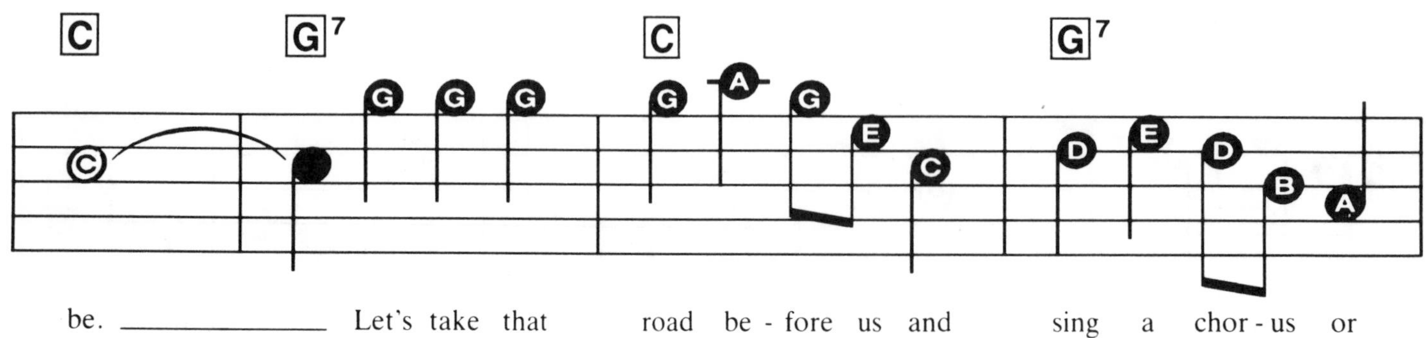
C
G7
C
G7
G
G
G
G
A
G
E
C
D
E
D
B
A
be. Let's take that road be - fore us and sing a chor - us or

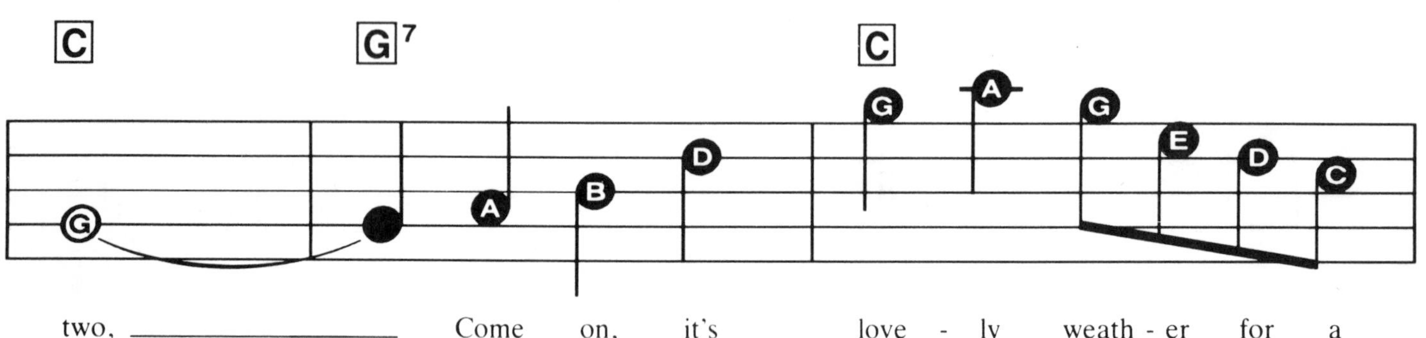
C
G7
C
G
A
B
D
G
A
G
E
D
C
two, Come on, it's love - ly weath - er for a

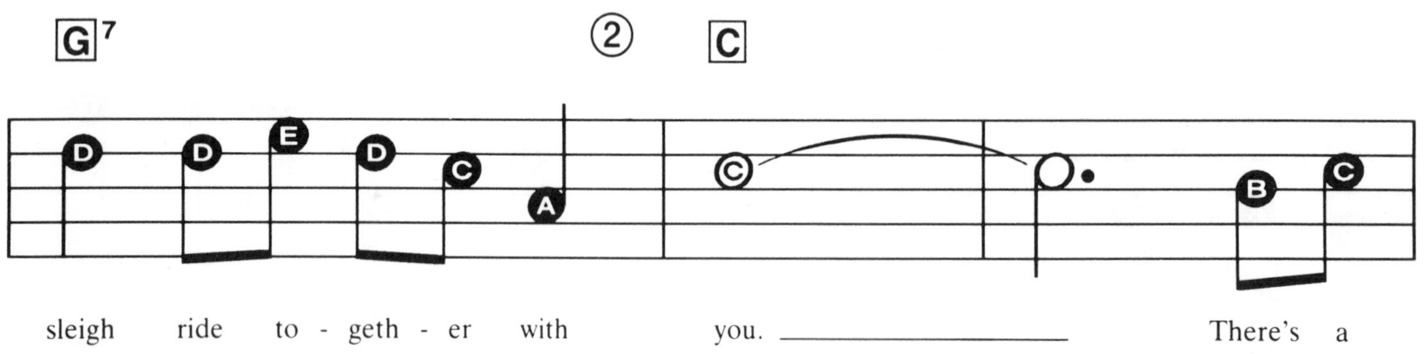
G7
②
C
D
D
E
D
C
A
C
B
C
sleigh ride to - geth - er with you. There's a

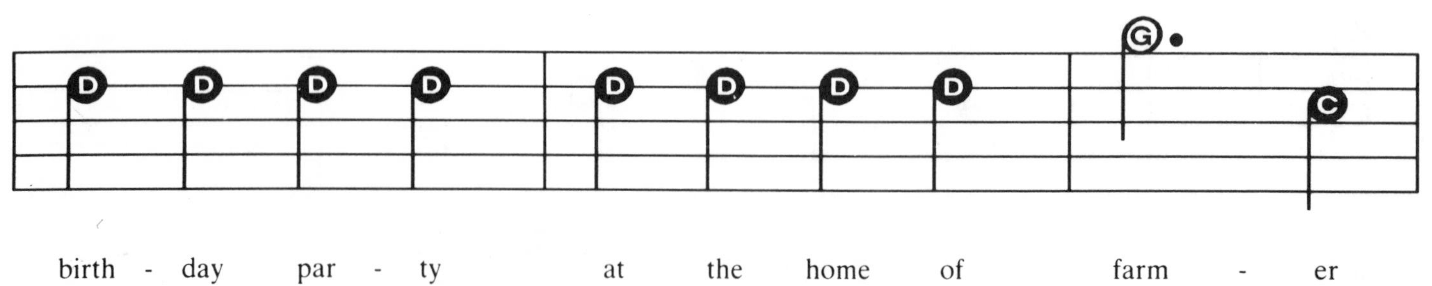
D
D
D
D
D
D
D
D
G
C
birth - day par - ty at the home of farm - er

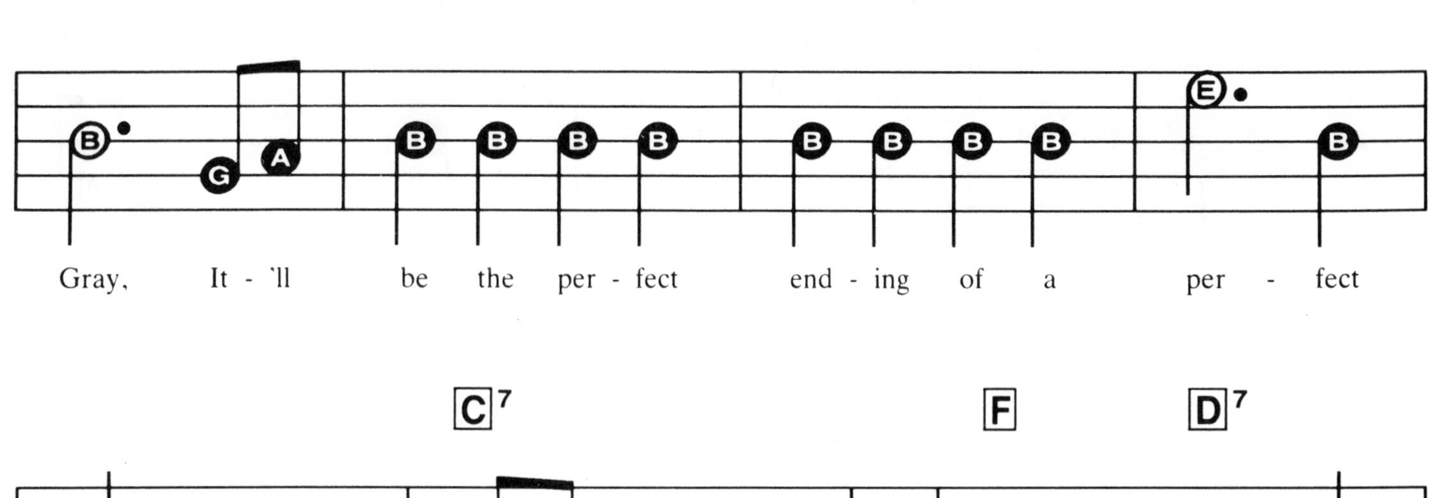
Gray, It - 'll be the per - fect end - ing of a per - fect

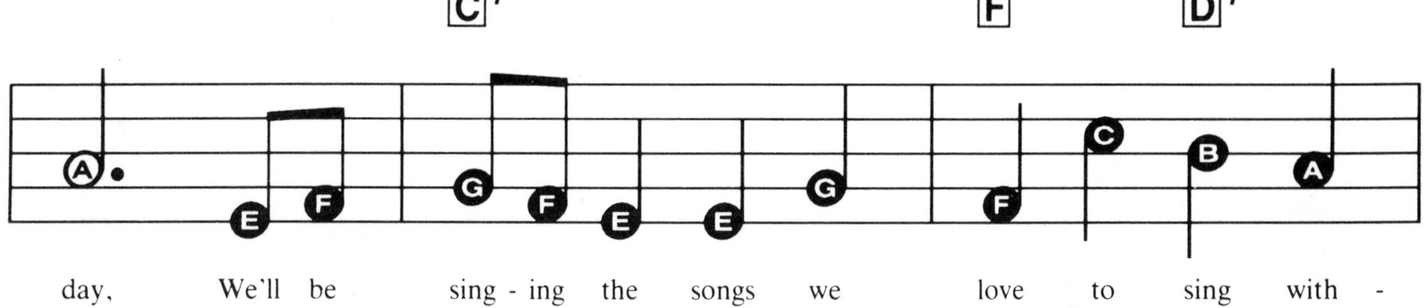
C7 F D7
day, We'll be sing - ing the songs we love to sing with -

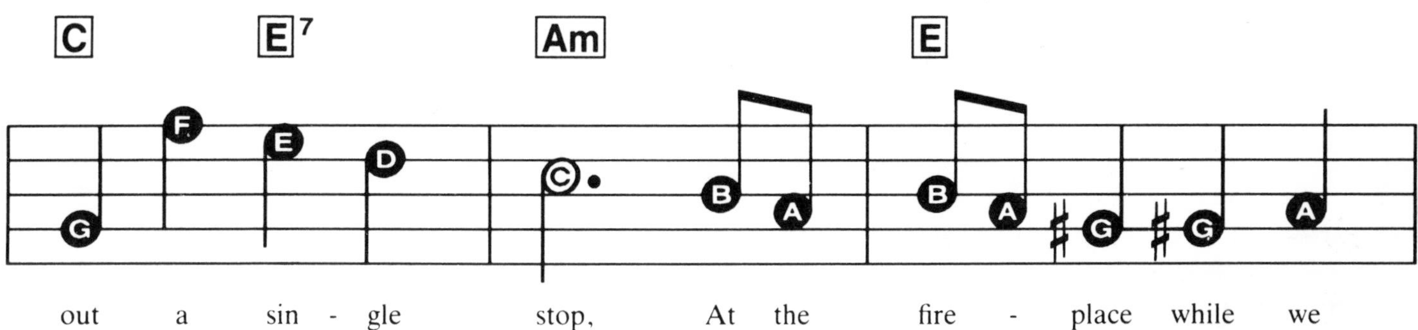
C E7 Am E
out a sin - gle stop, At the fire - place while we

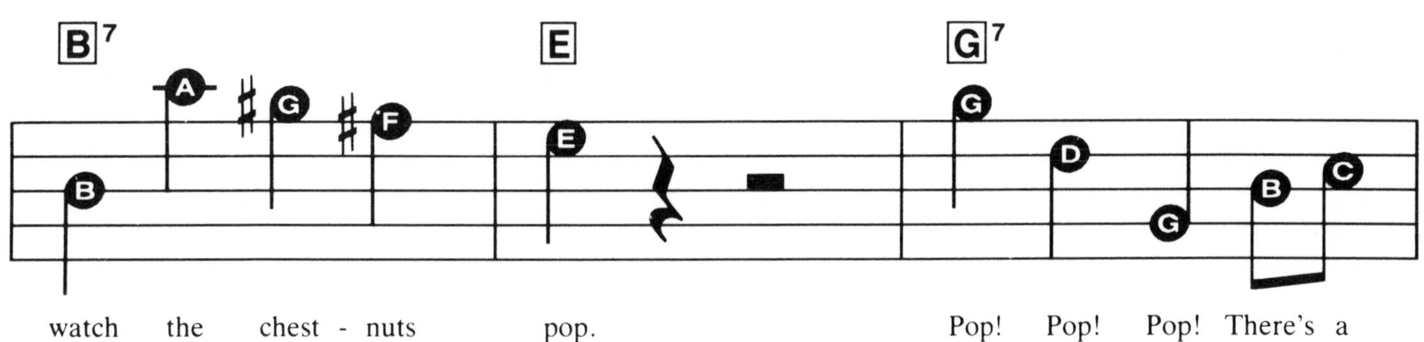
B7 E G7
watch the chest - nuts pop. Pop! Pop! Pop! There's a

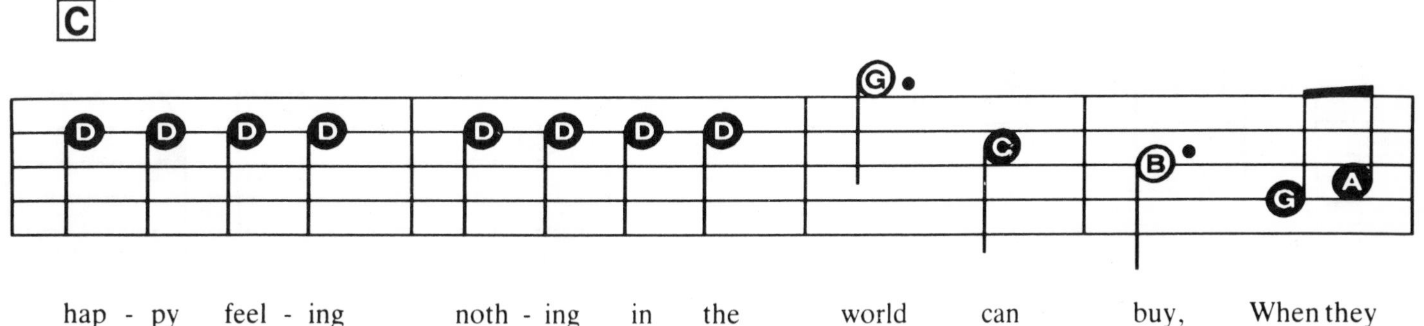
C
hap - py feel - ing noth - ing in the world can buy, When they

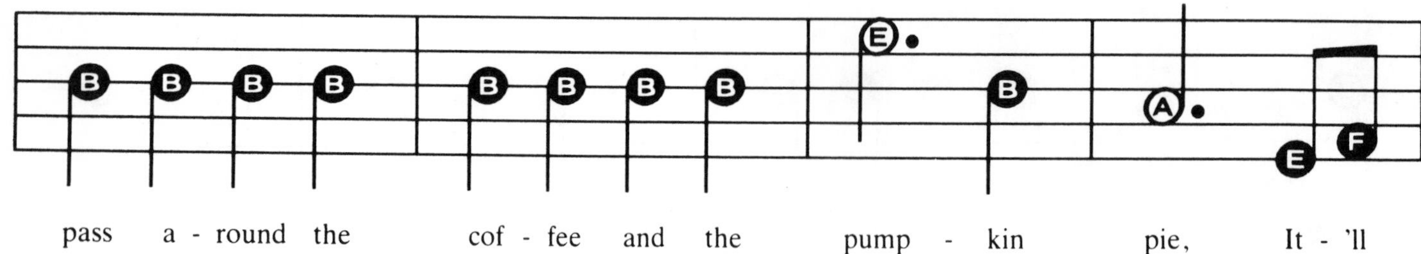
B B B B B B B B E B A E F
pass a - round the cof - fee and the pump - kin pie, It - 'll

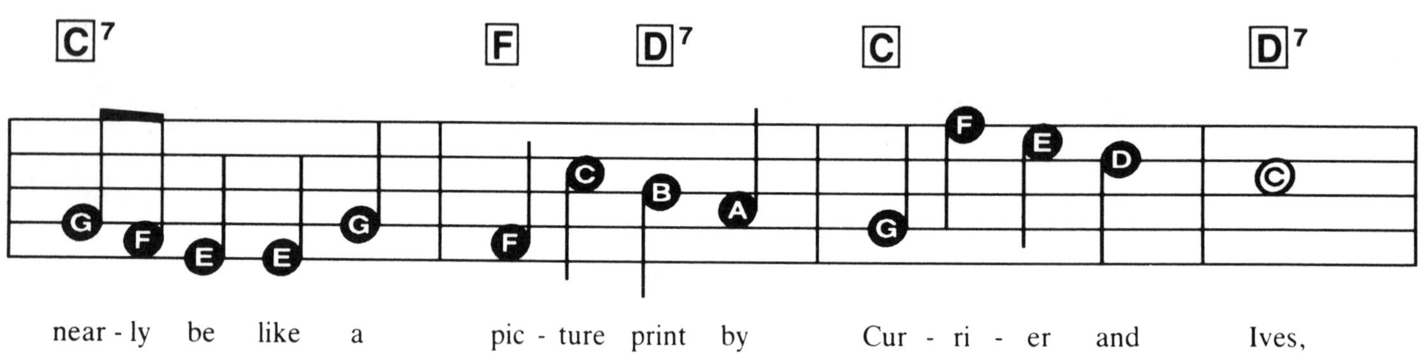
C7 F D7 C D7
G F E E G F C B A G F E D C
near - ly be like a pic - ture print by Cur - ri - er and Ives,

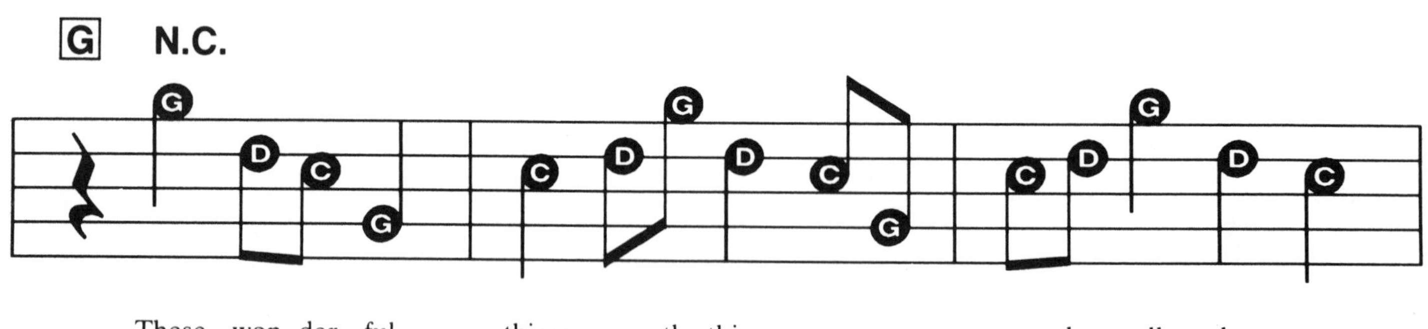
G N.C.
G D C G C D G D C G C D G D C
These won - der - ful things are the things we re - mem - ber all thru our

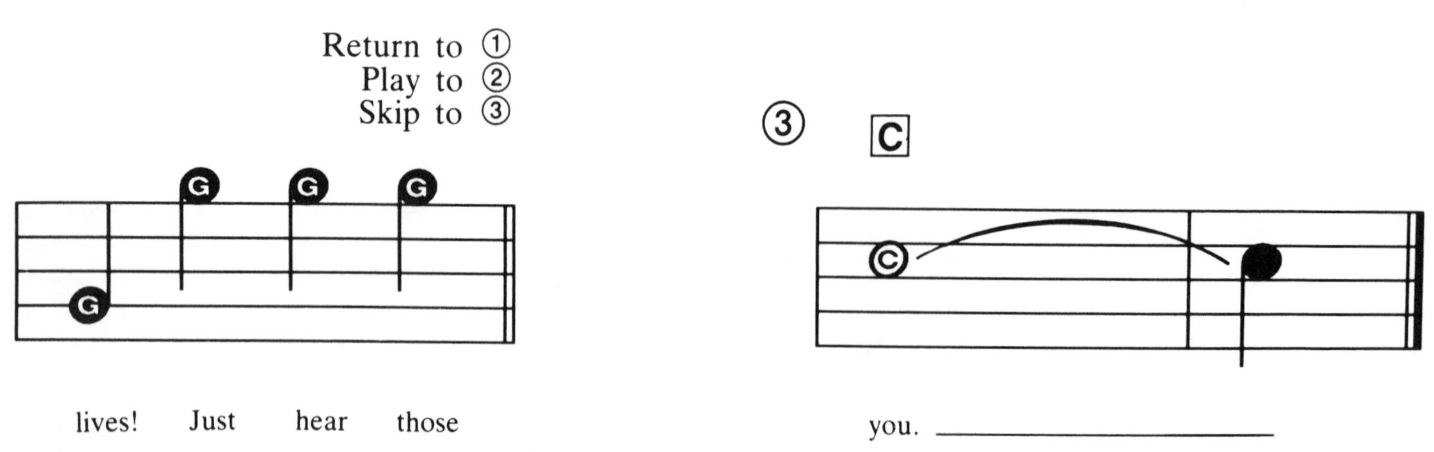
Return to ①
Play to ②
Skip to ③
G G G G
lives! Just hear those
③ C
C
you.

SONGS OF PRAISE THE ANGELS SANG

ORGAN
FULL 'N' BRILLIANT
Slow MARCH

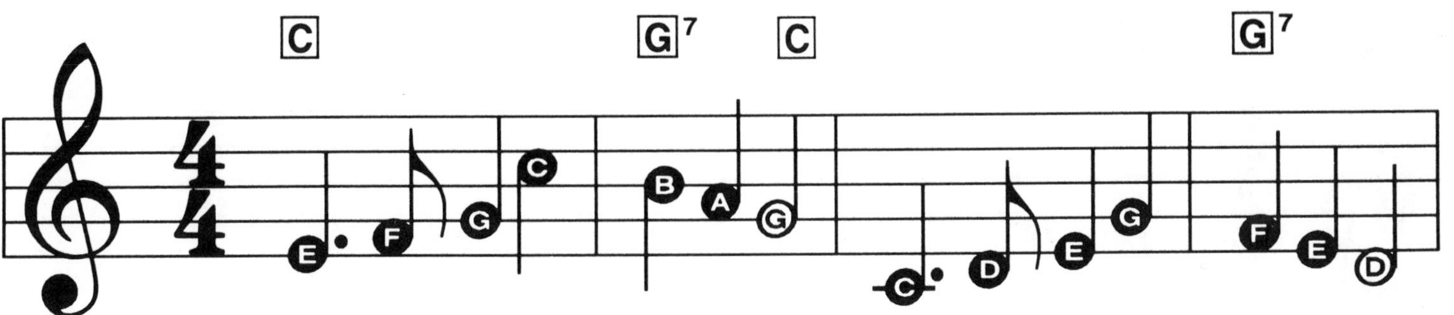
C
G7
C
G7
E F G C
B A G
C D E G
F E D
1. Songs of praise the an - gels sang, heav'n with al - le - lu - ias rang,

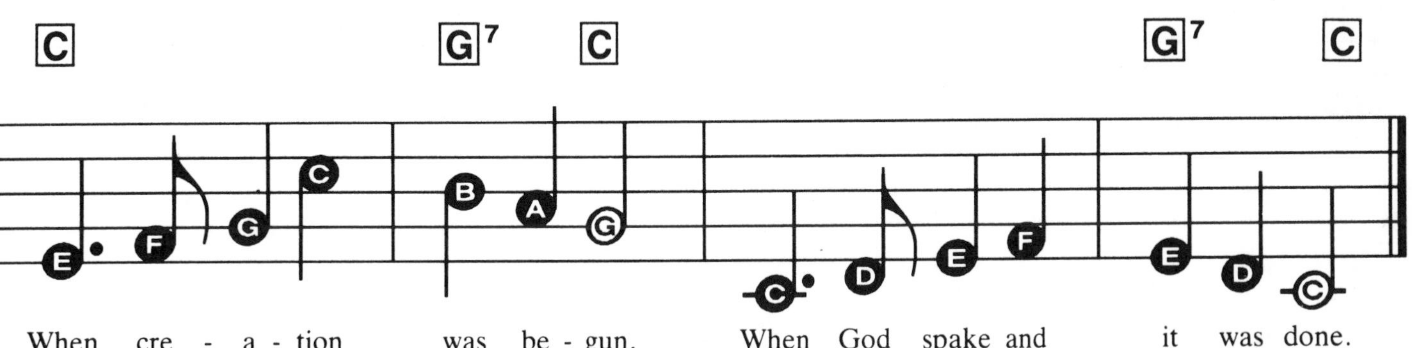
C
G7
C
G7
C
E F G C
B A G
C D E F
E D C
When cre - a - tion was be - gun, When God spake and it was done.

2. Songs of praise awoke the morn
When the Prince of Peace was born;
Songs of praise arose when He
Captive led captivity.

3. Heav'n and earth must pass away;
Songs of praise shall crown that day.
God will make new heav'ns and earth;
Songs of praise shall hail their birth.

4. Saints below, with heart and voice,
Still in songs of praise rejoice;
Learning here, by faith and love,
Songs of praise to sing above.

5. Borne upon their latest breath,
Songs of praise shall conquer death;
Then, amidst eternal joy,
Songs of praise their powers employ.

From the Videocraft TV Musical Spectacular "RUDOLPH THE RED-NOSED REINDEER"

SILVER AND GOLD

FLUTE
SOFT SOLO
Medium Slow WALTZ

Words and Music by
JOHNNY MARKS

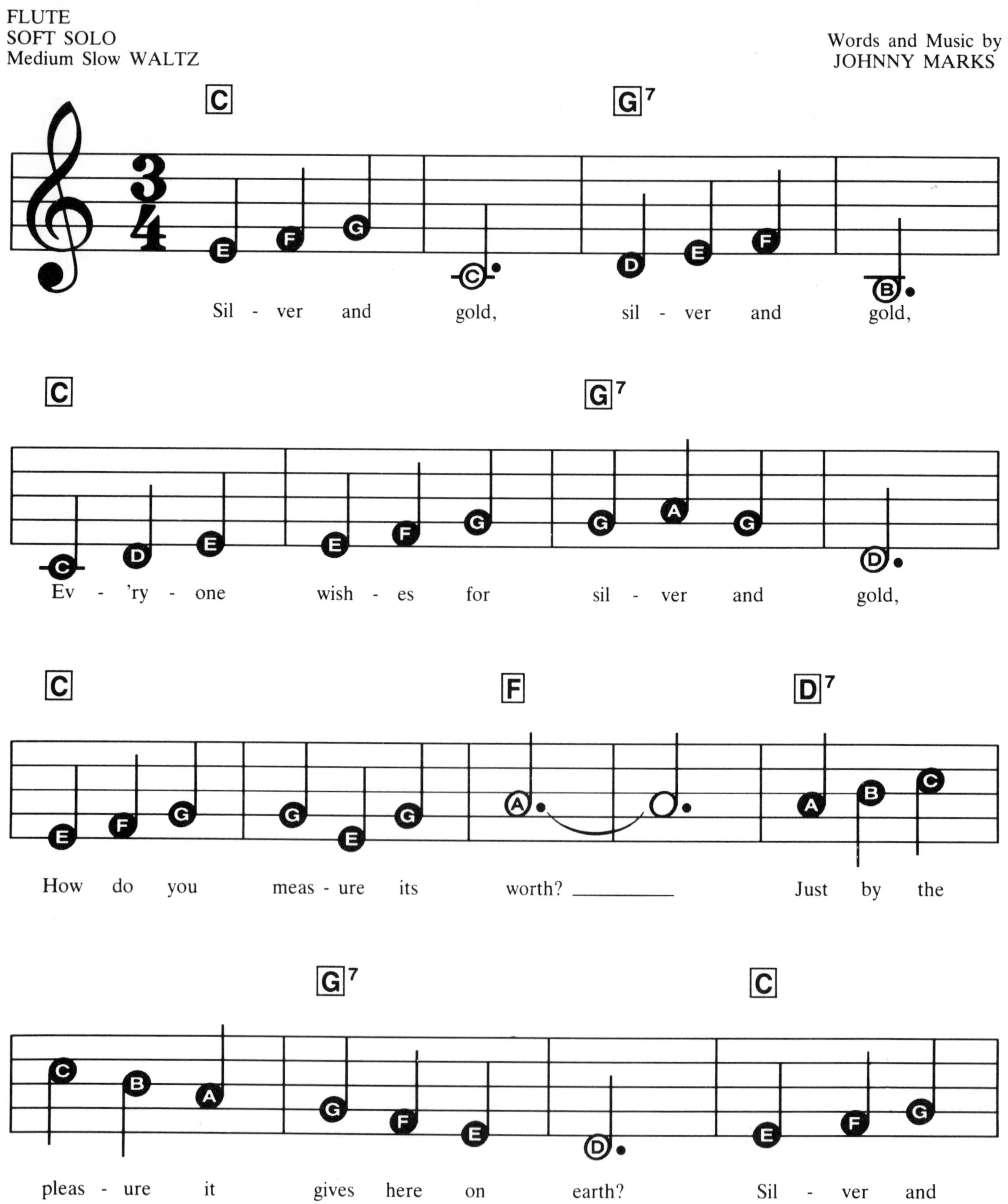

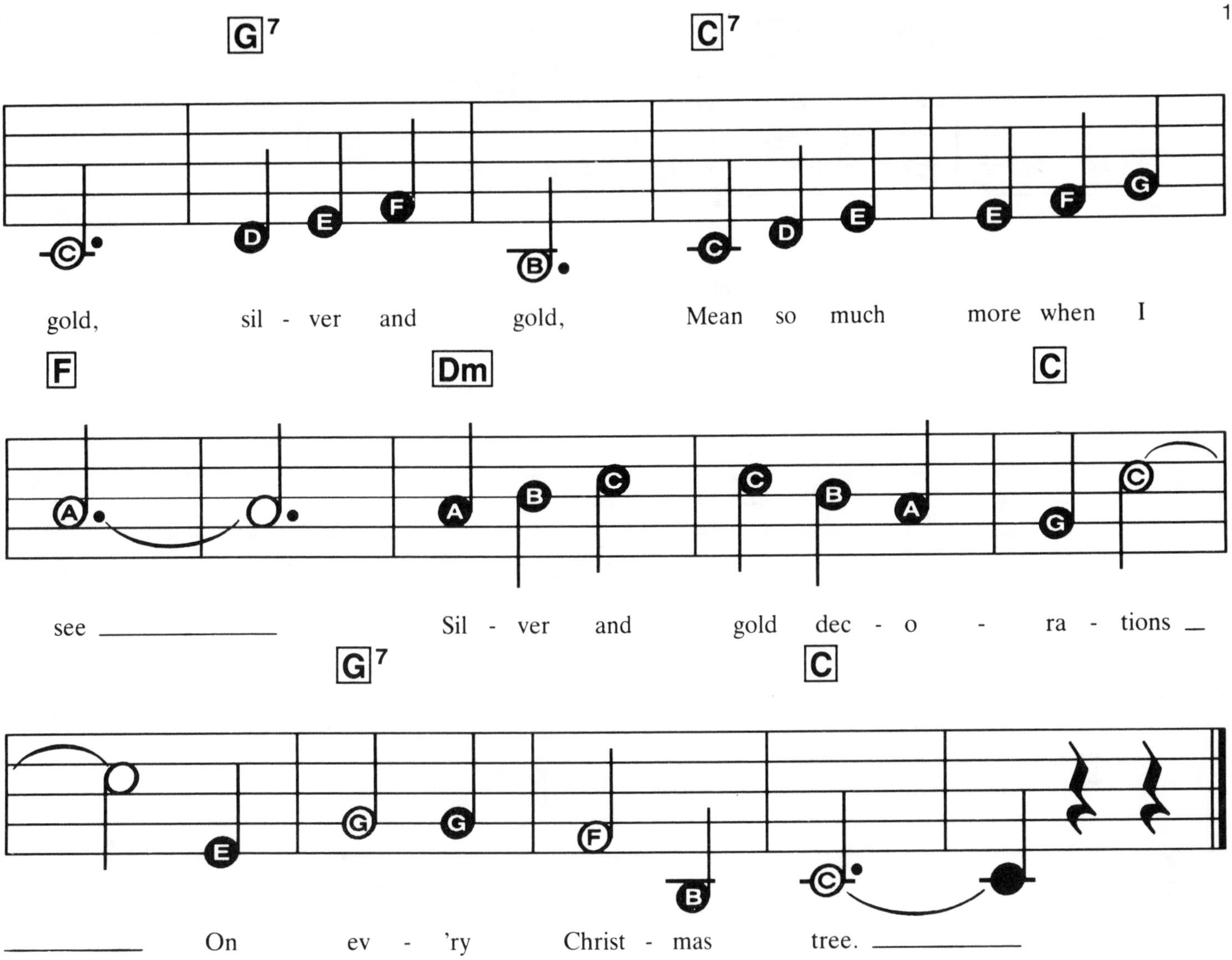

G7 C7

gold, sil - ver and gold, Mean so much more when I

F Dm C

see ______ Sil - ver and gold dec - o - ra - tions __

G7 C

______ On ev - 'ry Christ - mas tree. ______

THE TWELVE DAYS OF CHRISTMAS

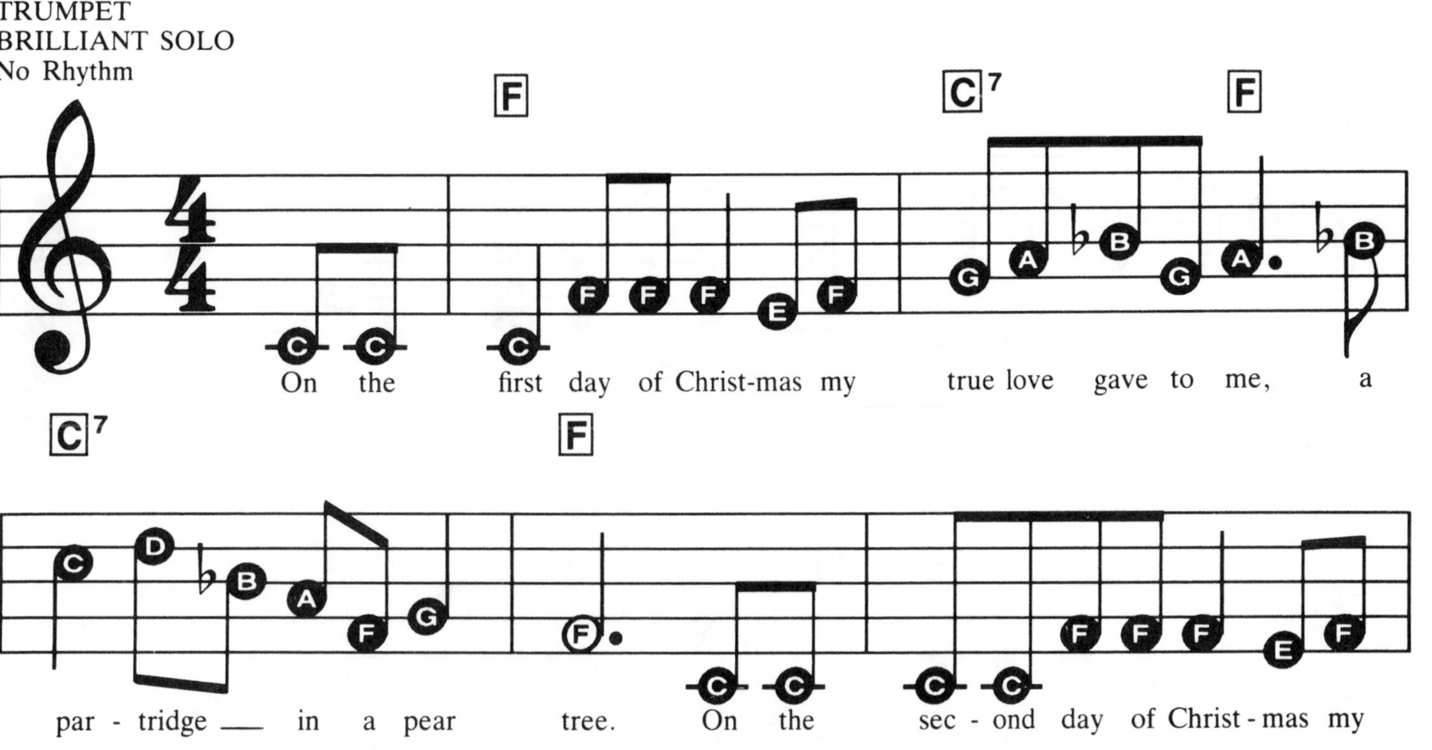
TRUMPET
BRILLIANT SOLO
No Rhythm
F C7 F
On the first day of Christ-mas my true love gave to me, a
C7 F
par - tridge __ in a pear tree. On the sec - ond day of Christ - mas my

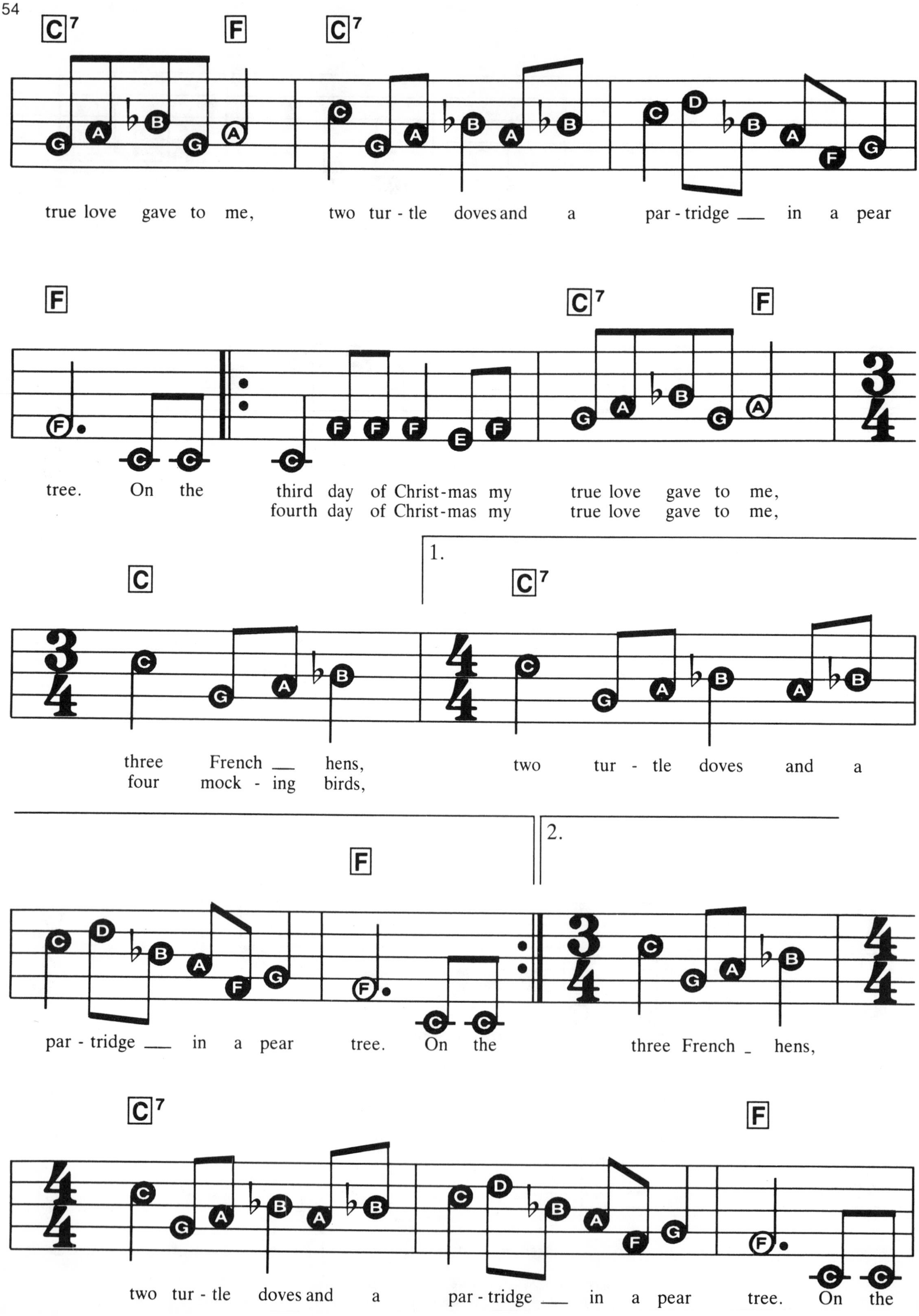

true love gave to me, two tur - tle doves and a par - tridge ___ in a pear

F C7 F

tree. On the third day of Christ-mas my true love gave to me,

fourth day of Christ-mas my true love gave to me,

C 1. C7

three French ___ hens, two tur - tle doves and a

four mock - ing birds,

F 2.

par - tridge ___ in a pear tree. On the three French _ hens,

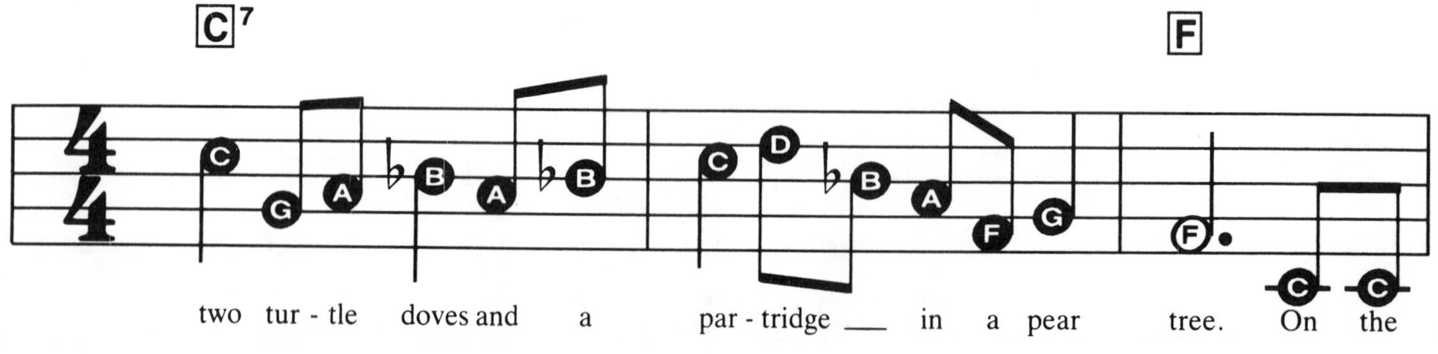

C7
F
G7
fifth day of Christ - mas my
true love gave to me,
five gold - en
C7
F
B♭
rings;
four mock - ing birds,
three French hens,
C7
two tur - tle doves and a
par - tridge in a pear
F
C7
F
tree. On the
sixth day of Christ - mas my
true love gave to me,
C
F
G7
C7
six geese a - lay - ing
five gold - en
rings;

F B♭

four ___ mock - ing birds, three French hens,

C7

two ___ tur - tle doves and a par - tridge ___ in a pear

F C7 F

tree. On the sev - enth day of Christ-mas my true love gave to me,

C

sev - en swans a swim - ming, six geese a - lay - ing,

F G7 C7 F B♭

five gold - en rings; four ___ mock-ing birds, three French hens,

C7 F

two ___ tur - tle doves and a par - tridge ___ in a pear tree. On the

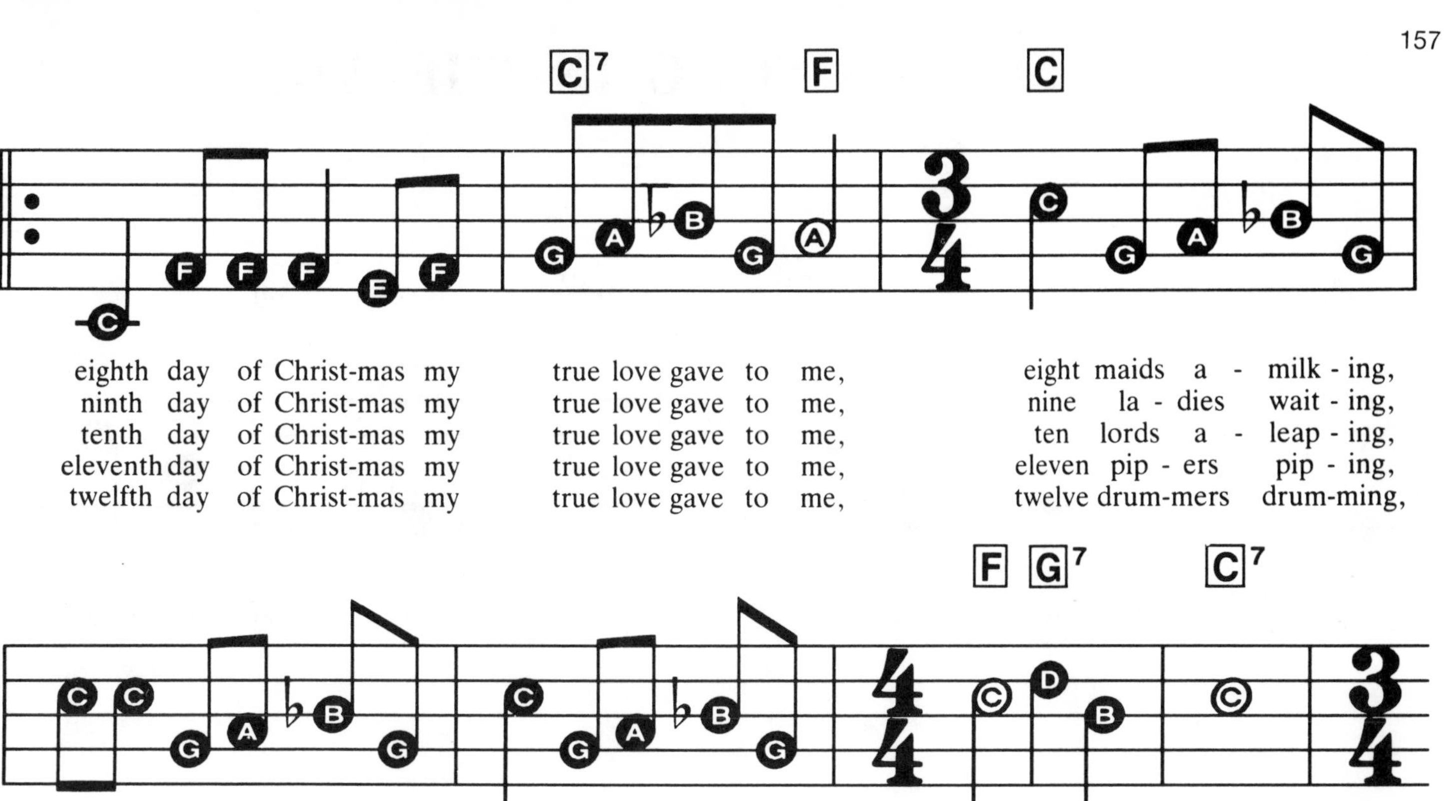
C7
F
C
eighth day of Christ-mas my true love gave to me, eight maids a - milk - ing,
ninth day of Christ-mas my true love gave to me, nine la - dies wait - ing,
tenth day of Christ-mas my true love gave to me, ten lords a - leap - ing,
eleventh day of Christ-mas my true love gave to me, eleven pip - ers pip - ing,
twelfth day of Christ-mas my true love gave to me, twelve drum-mers drum-ming,
F G7 C7
sev - en swans a - swim-ming six geese a - lay - ing, five gold - en rings;

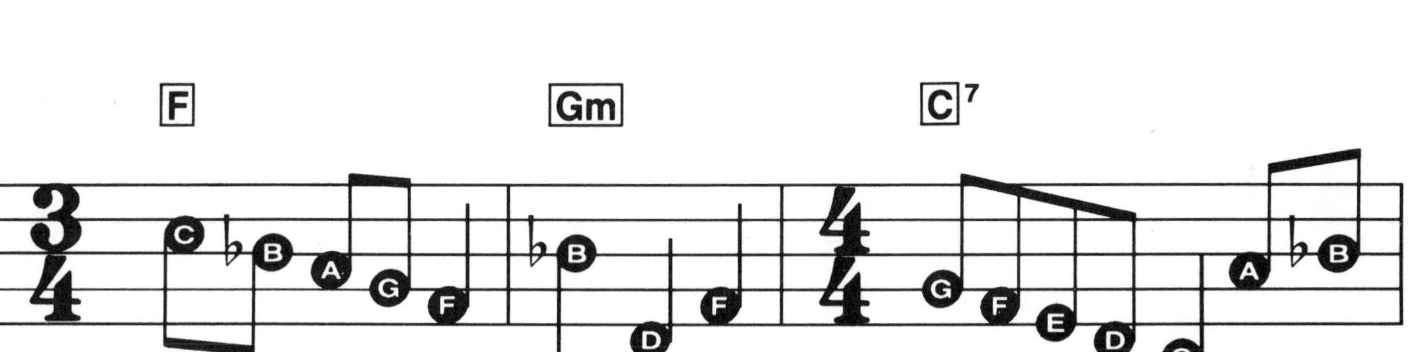
F
Gm
C7
four ___ mock-ing birds, three French hens, two __ tur - tle doves and a

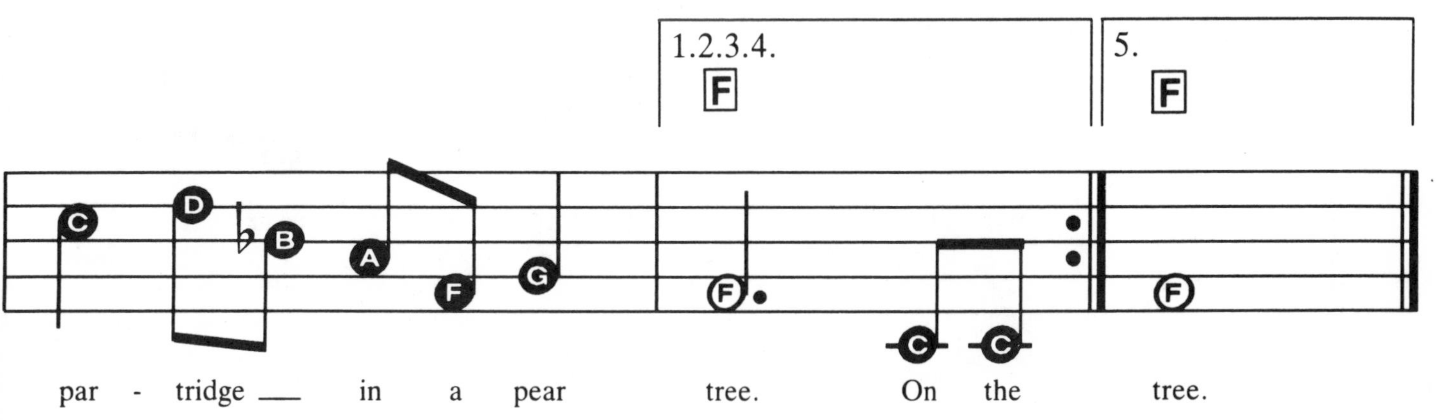
1.2.3.4.
F
5.
F
par - tridge ___ in a pear tree. On the tree.

THERE'S A SONG IN THE AIR

TRUMPET
FULL 'N' MELLOW
Medium WALTZ

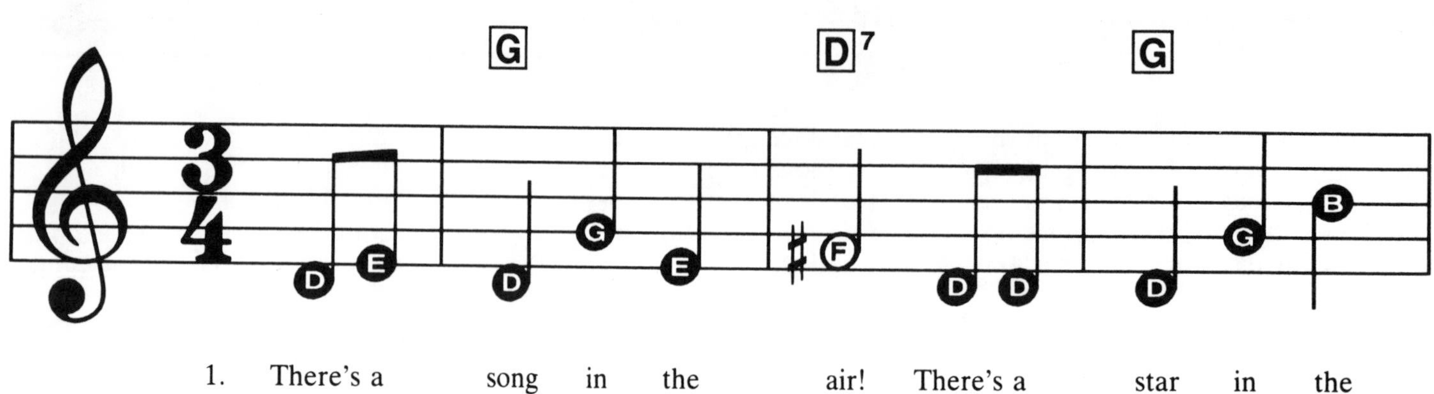
G
D7
G
D E D G E F D D D G B
1. There's a song in the air! There's a star in the

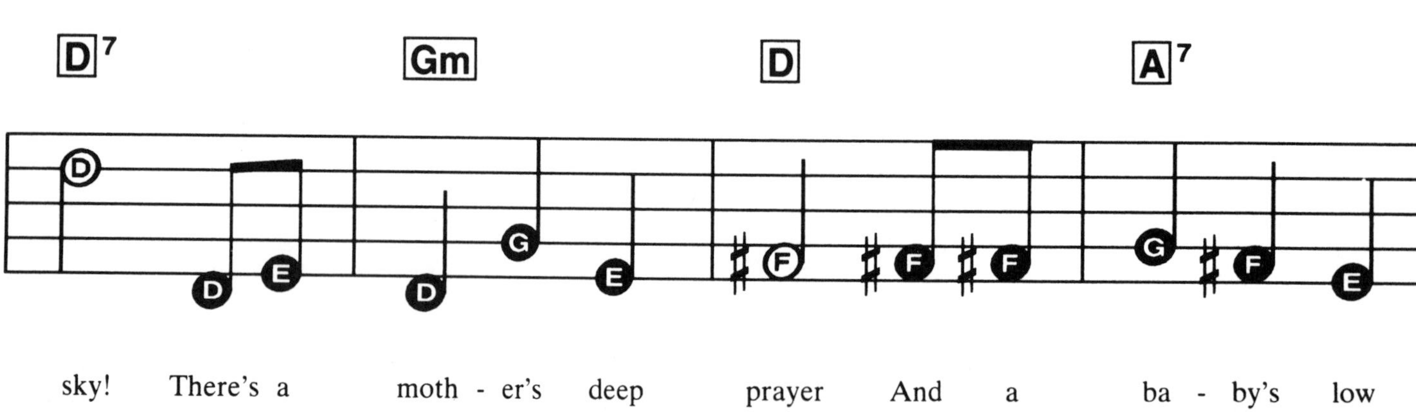
D7
Gm
D
A7
D D E D G E F F F G F E
sky! There's a moth - er's deep prayer And a ba - by's low

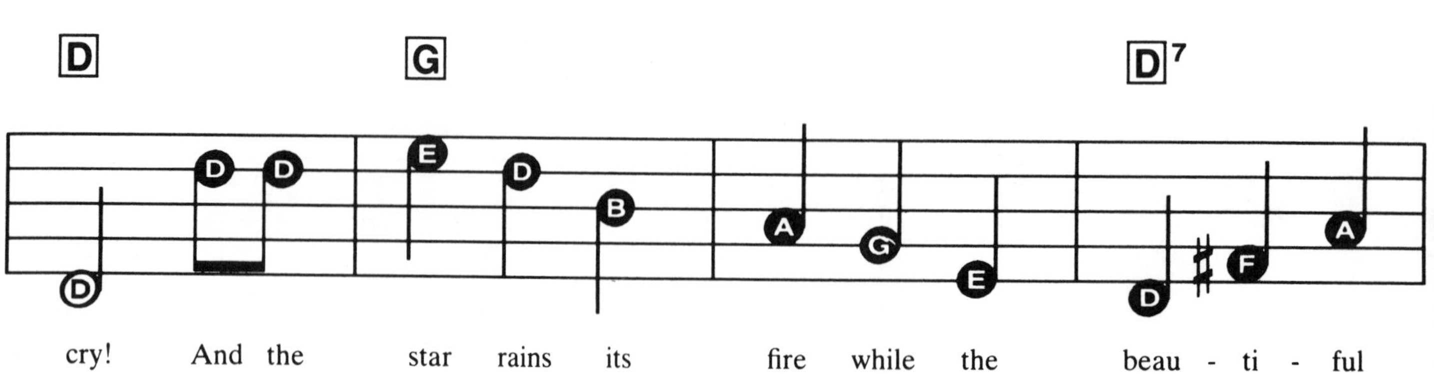
D
G
D7
D D D E D B A G E D F A
cry! And the star rains its fire while the beau - ti - ful

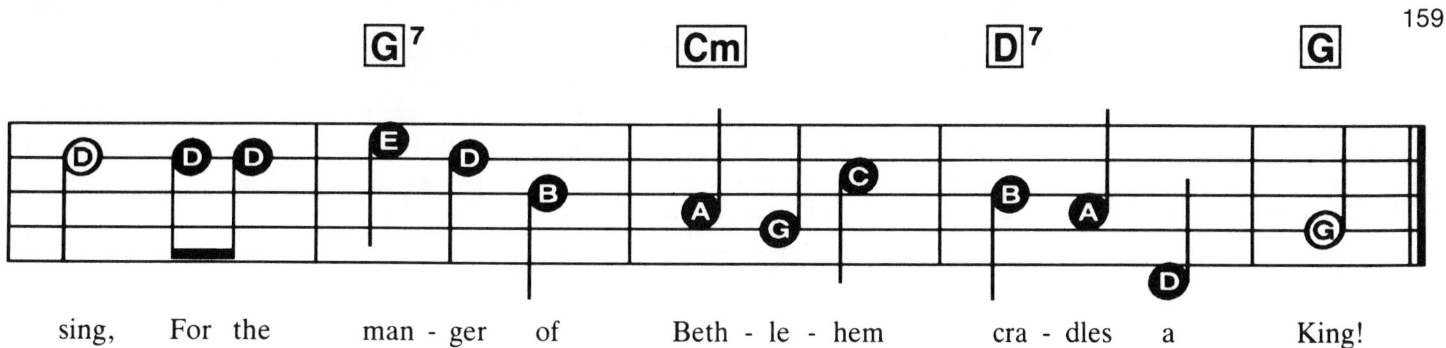
G7
Cm
D7
G
D D D E D B A G C B A D G
sing, For the man - ger of Beth - le - hem cra - dles a King!

2. There's tumult of joy
   O'er the wonderful birth
   For the Virgin's sweet boy
   Is the Lord of the earth.
   Ay! the star rains its fire
      while the beautiful sing,
   for the manger of Bethlehem
      cradles the King!

3. We rejoice in the light,
   And we echo the song
   That comes down through the night
   From the heavenly throng.
   Ay! we shout to the lovely
      evangel they bring,
   And we greet in His cradle
      our Saviour and King!

'TWAS THE NIGHT BEFORE CHRISTMAS

TROMBONE
FULL 'N' MELLOW
Slow SWING

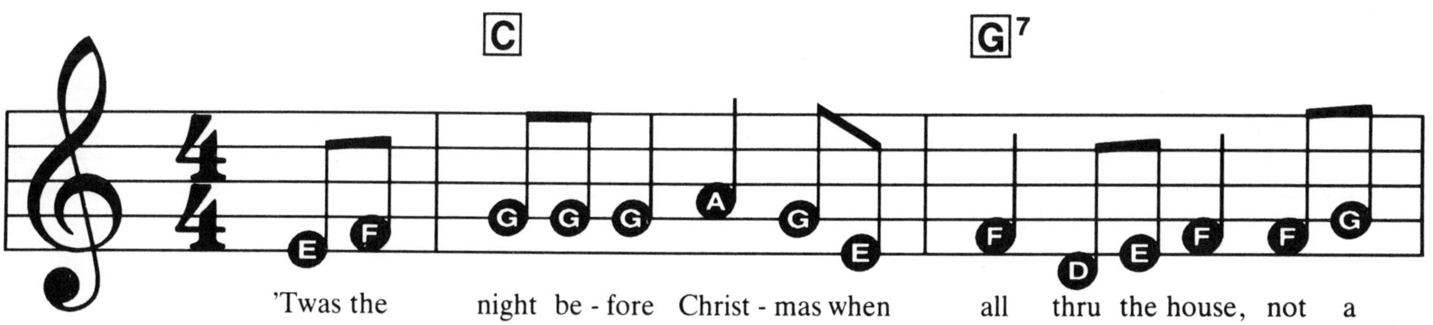
C
G7
E F G G G A G E F D E F F G
'Twas the night be - fore Christ - mas when all thru the house, not a

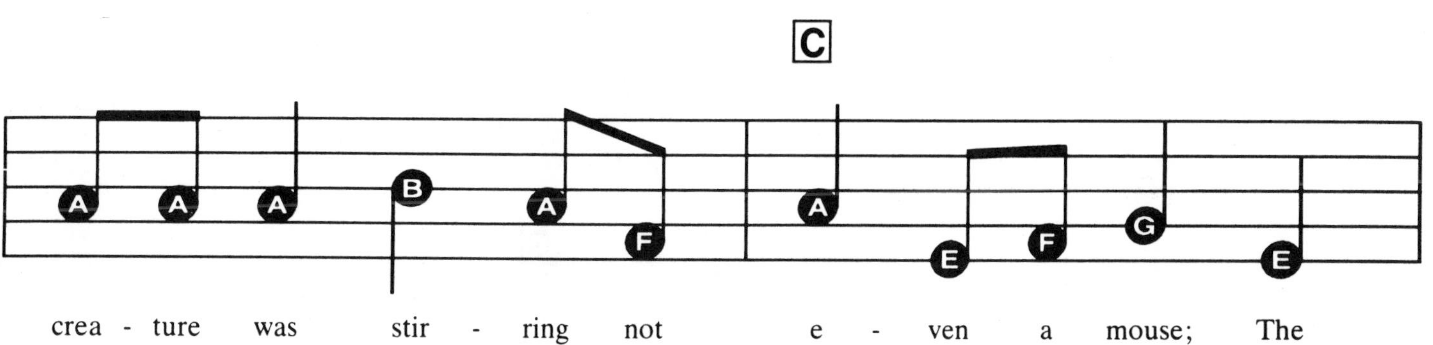
C
A A A B A F A E F G E
crea - ture was stir - ring not e - ven a mouse; The

G
G G G A G E G G A B B
stock - ings were hung by the chim - ney with care, in
D7 G7
C A B C B A B B C D E
hopes that St. Nich - o - las soon would be there; The
C G7
G G G A G E G D E F F
chil - dren were nes - tled, all snug in their beds, while
C
A A A B B B C G A B B
vis - ions of su - gar plums danced thru their heads; And
F C
A A F A C A A G E G A A B
Ma - ma in her 'ker - chief and I in my cap, had just
D7 G7 C
C C A C B C D A B C
set - tled our brains for a long win - ter's nap.

When out on the lawn there arose such a clatter,
I sprang from my bed to see what was the matter.
Away to the window I flew like a flash,
Tore open the shutters and threw up the sash.
The moon, on the breast of the new-fallen snow,
Gave a lustre of midday to objects below;
When what to my wondering eyes should appear
But a miniature sleigh and eight tiny Reindeer.

With a little old driver, so lively and quick,
I knew in a moment it must be St. Nick.
More rapid than eagles his coursers they came,
And he whistled and shouted, and called them by name:
"Now, Dasher! Now, Dancer! Now, Prancer! now, Vixen,
On, Comet! On, Cupid! On, Donner and Blitzen!
To the top of the porch, to the top of the wall!
Now dash away, dash away, dash away all."

As dry leaves that before the wild hurricane fly,
When they meet with an obstacle, mount to the sky,
So up to the house-top the coursers they flew,
With the sleigh full of toys, and St. Nicholas, too.
And then in a twinkling I heard on the roof
The prancing and pawing of each little hoof.
As I drew in my head, and was turning around,
Down the chimney St. Nicholas came with a bound.

He was dressed all in fur from his head to his foot,
And his clothes were all tarnished with ashes and soot;
A bundle of toys he had flung on his back,
And he looked like a peddler just opening his pack.
His eyes how they twinkled! His dimples how merry!
His cheeks were like roses, his nose like cherry,
His droll little mouth was drawn up like a bow,
And the beard of his chin was as white as the snow.

The stump of a pipe he held tight in his teeth,
And the smoke, it encircled his head like a wreath.
He had a broad face, and a round little belly
That shook, when he laughed, like a bowl full of jelly.
He was chubby and plump - a right jolly old elf -
And I laughed when I saw him, in spite of myself.
A wink of his eye, and a twist of his head,
Soon gave me to know I had nothing to dread.

He spake not a word, but went straight to his work,
And filled all the stockings; Then turned with a jerk,
And laying his finger aside of his nose,
And giving a nod up the chimney he rose.
He sprang to his sleigh, to his team gave a whistle,
And away they all fled like the down of a thistle;
But I heard him exclaim, ere he drove out of sight -
"Happy Christmas to all, And to all a good-night!"

From the Videocraft T.V. Musical Spectacular "RUDOLPH THE RED-NOSED REINDEER"

THERE'S ALWAYS TOMORROW

TRUMPET
SOFT SOLO
Slow WALTZ

Words and Music by
JOHNNY MARKS

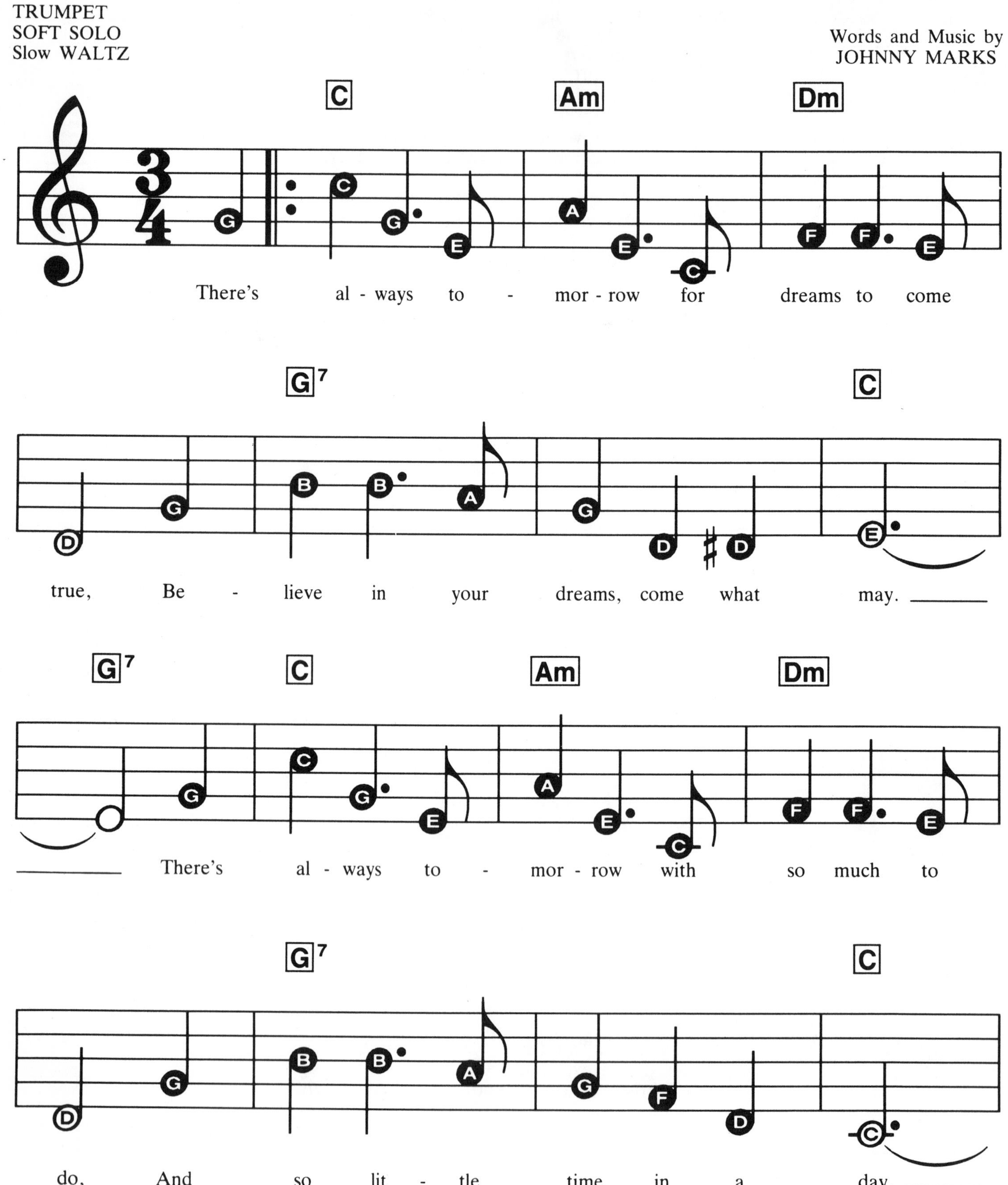

F
Em
A
F
C
A
B
A
G
A
C
We all pre - tend the rain - bow has an
B7
Em
B
G
A
G
F
G
A
F
B
end And you'll be there, my friend some - day.
G7
C
Am
Dm
G
C
G
E
A
E
C
F
F
E
D
G
There's al - ways to - mor-row for dreams to come true To -
1.
G7
C
G7
B
B
A
G
F
D
C
G
mor - row is not far a - way. There's
2.
G7
C
B
B
A
G
F
D
C
mor - row is not far a - way.

WATCHMAN, TELL US OF THE NIGHT

SAXOPHONE
FULL 'N' MELLOW
No Rhythm

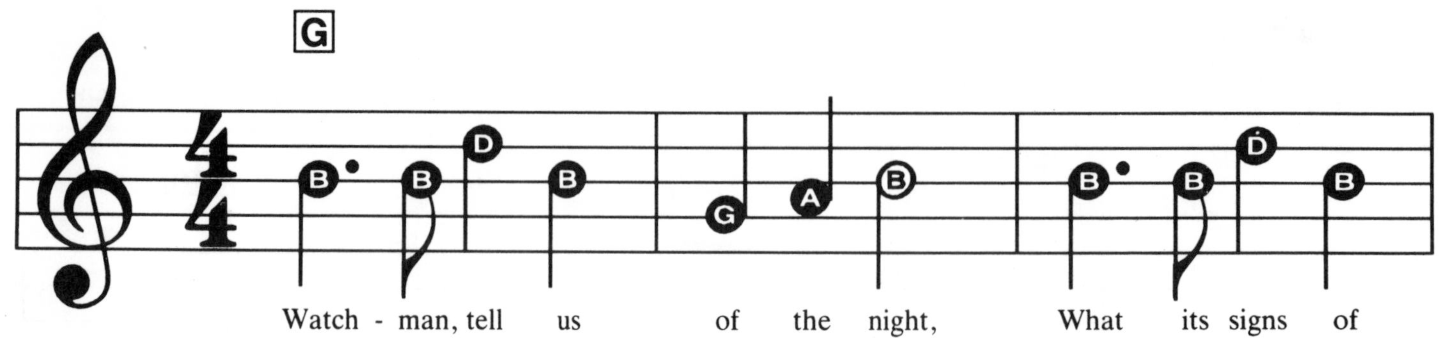
G
B B D B G A B B B D B
Watch - man, tell us of the night, What its signs of

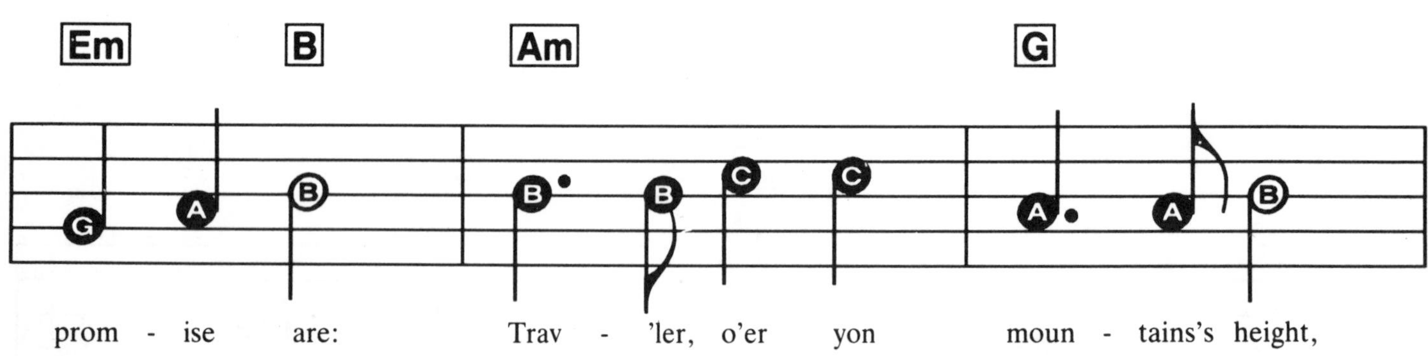
Em B Am G
G A B B B C C A A B
prom - ise are: Trav - 'ler, o'er yon moun - tains's height,

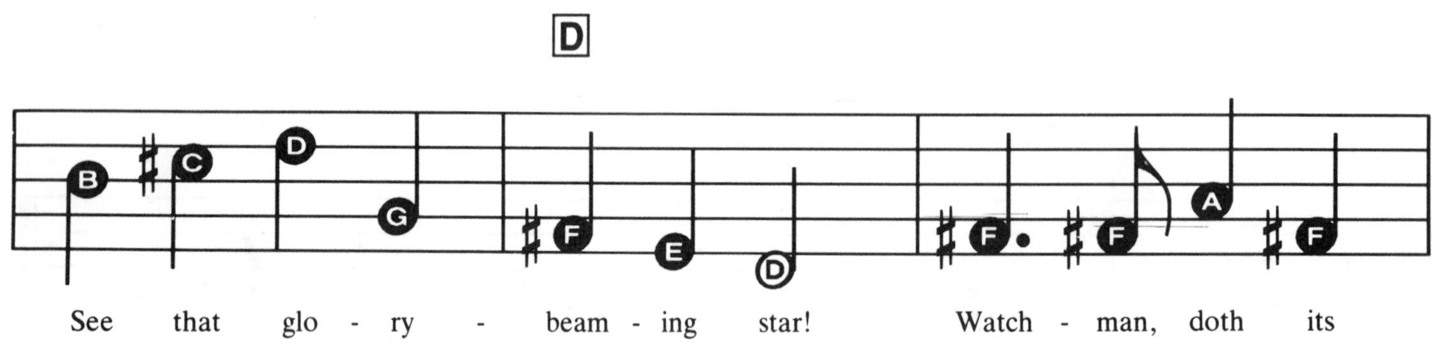
D
B C D G F E D F F A F
See that glo - ry - beam - ing star! Watch - man, doth its

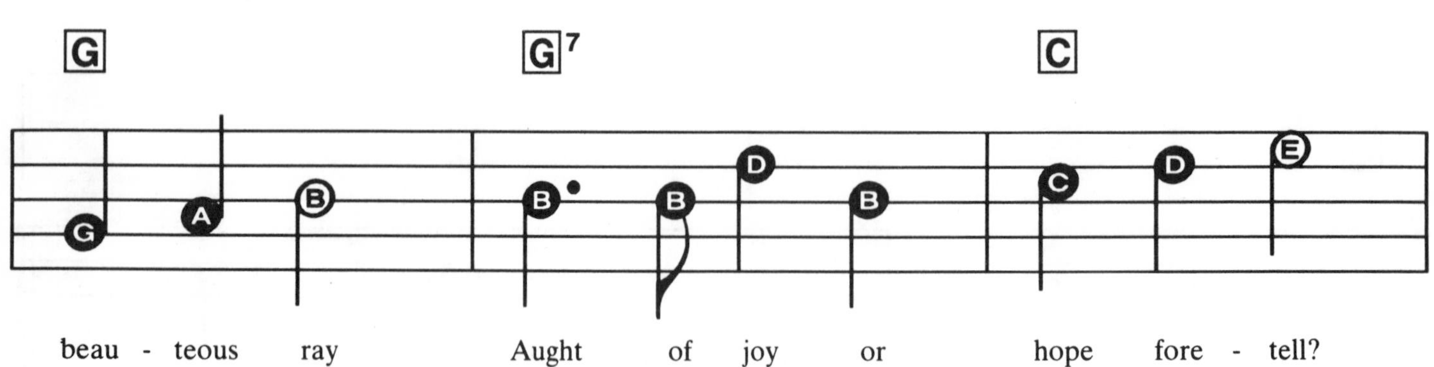
G G7 C
G A B B B D B C D E
beau - teous ray Aught of joy or hope fore - tell?

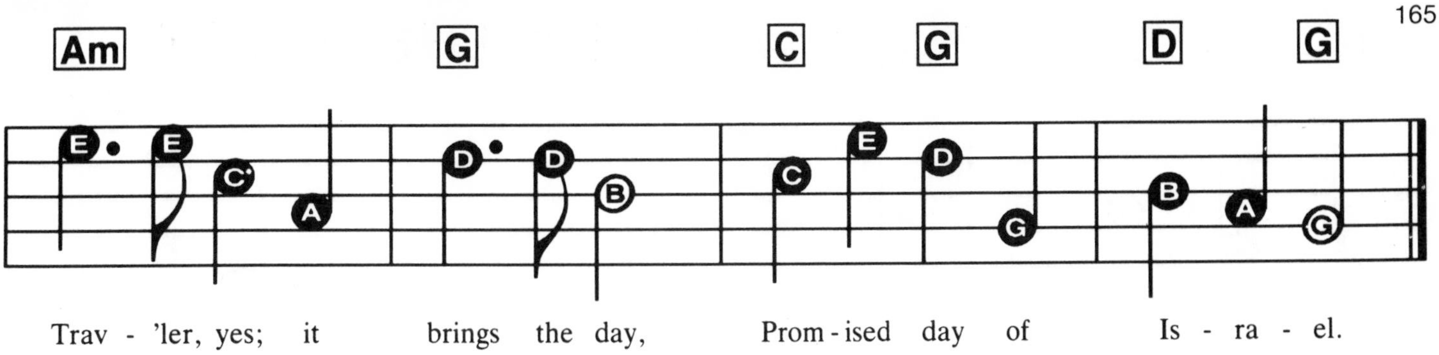

Am G C G D G
E E C A D D B C E D G B A G
Trav - 'ler, yes; it brings the day, Prom - ised day of Is - ra - el.

2. Watchman, tell us of the night, higher yet that star ascends:
Traveler, blessedness and light, peace and truth, its course portends.
Watchman, will its beams alone gild the spot that gave them birth?
Traveler, ages are its own, and it bursts o'er all the earth!

3. Watchman, tell us of the night, for the morning seems to dawn:
Traveler, darkness takes its flight; Doubt and terror are with-drawn.
Watchman, let thy wanderings cease; hie thee to thy quiet home.
Traveler, lo, the Prince of Peace, lo, the Son of God, is come!

UP ON THE HOUSE TOP

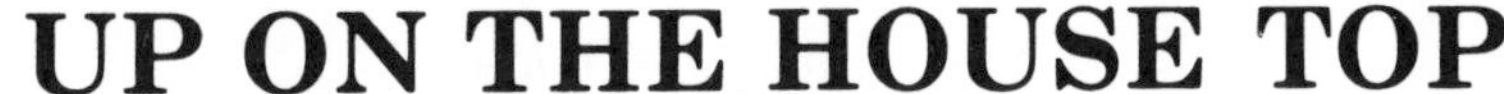

PIANO
BRIGHT 'N' BRASSY
Medium Fast SWING

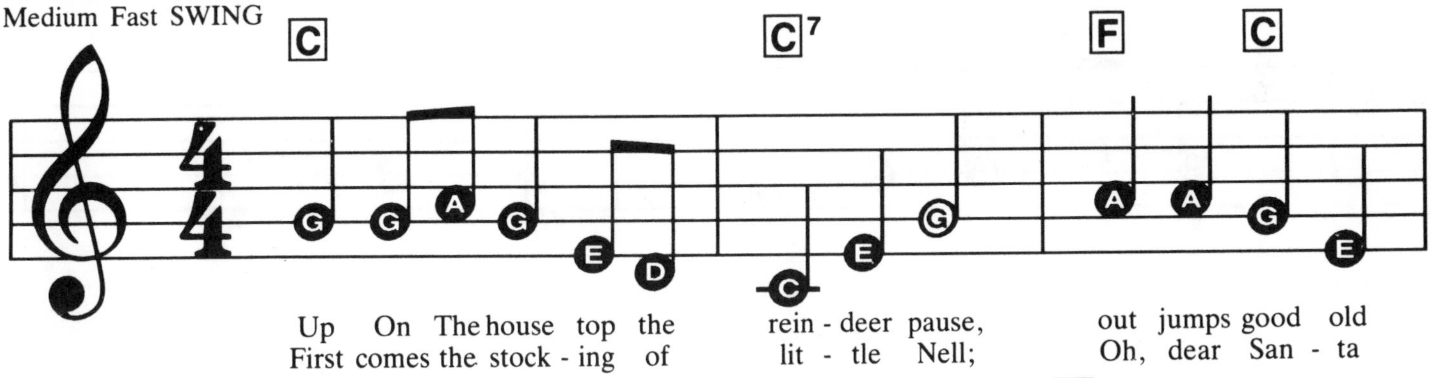

C C7 F C
G G A G E D C E G A A G E
Up On The house top the rein - deer pause, out jumps good old
First comes the stock - ing of lit - tle Nell; Oh, dear San - ta

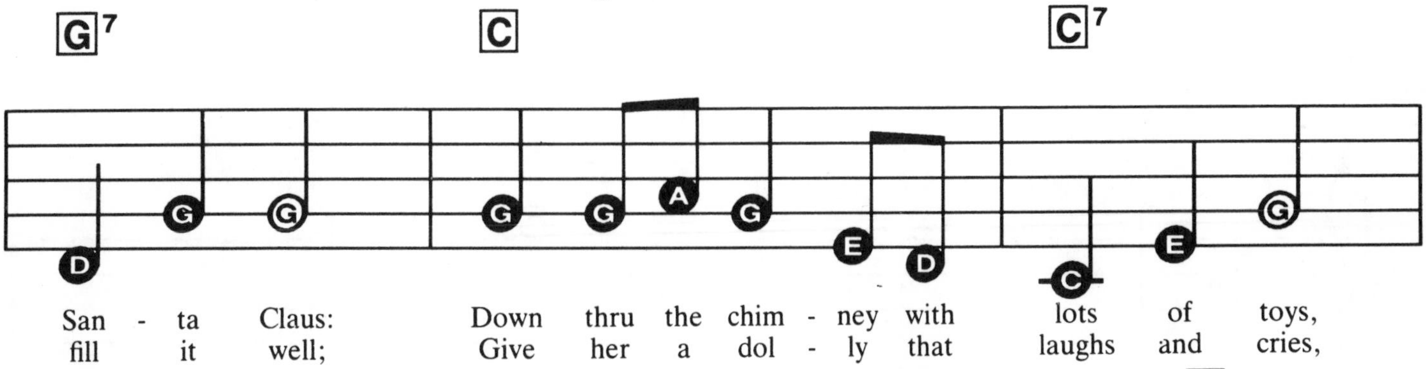

G7 C C7
D G G G G A G E D C E G
San - ta Claus: Down thru the chim - ney with lots of toys,
fill it well; Give her a dol - ly that laughs and cries,

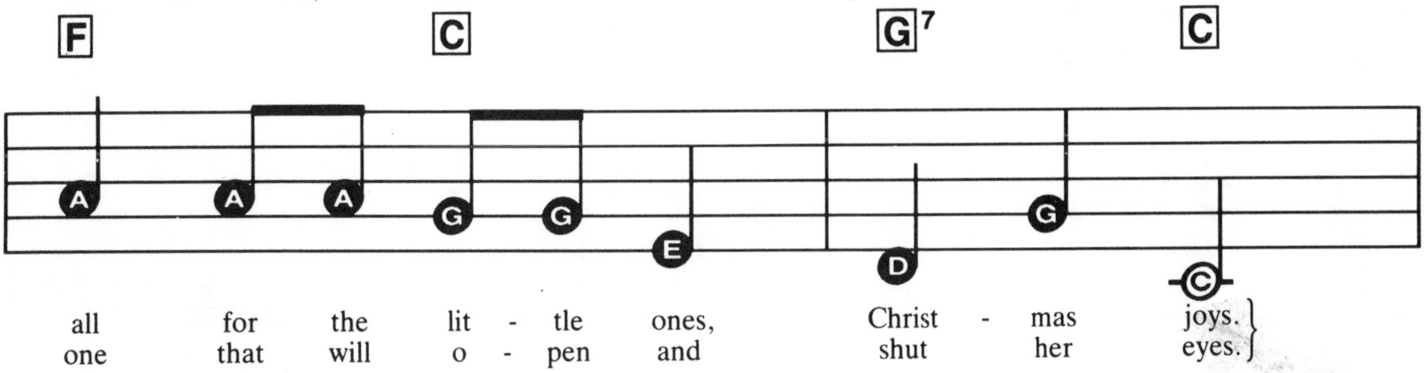

F C G7 C
A A A G G E D G C
all for the lit - tle ones, Christ - mas joys.
one that will o - pen and shut her eyes.

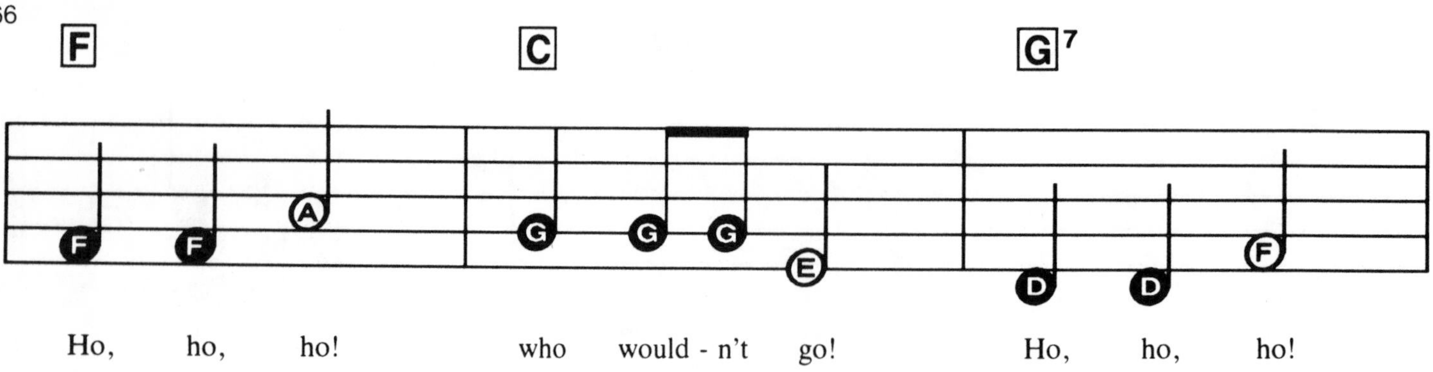

F C G7

Ho, ho, ho! who would - n't go! Ho, ho, ho!

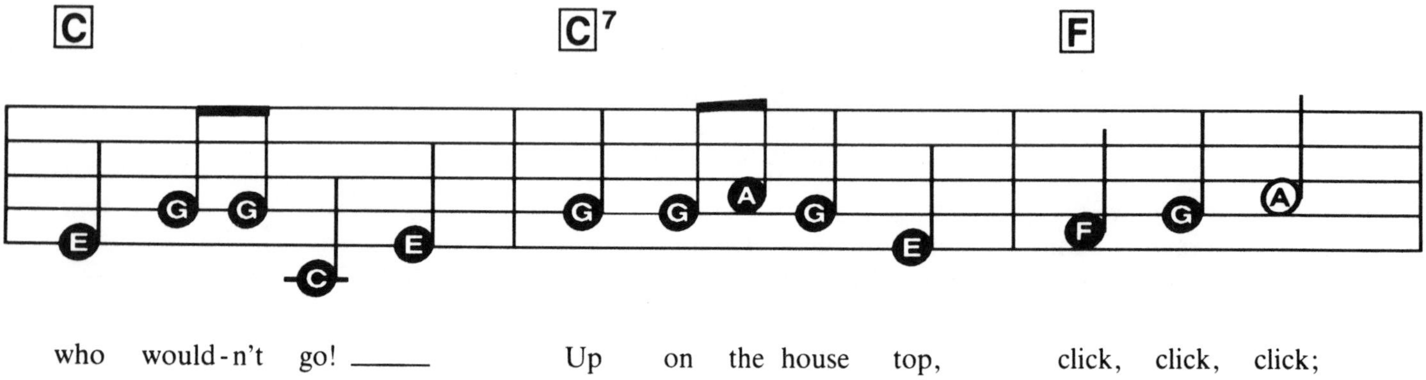

C C7 F

who would-n't go! ___ Up on the house top, click, click, click;

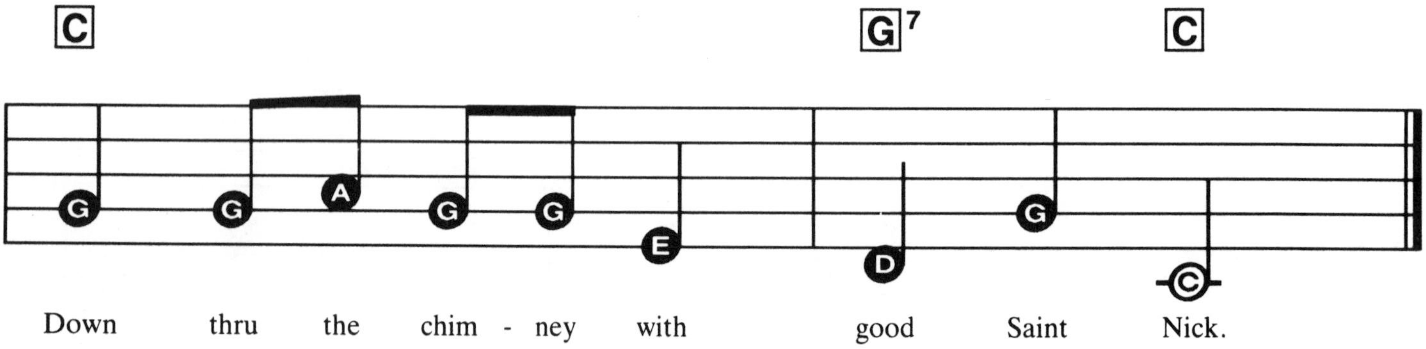

C G7 C

Down thru the chim - ney with good Saint Nick.

TOYLAND

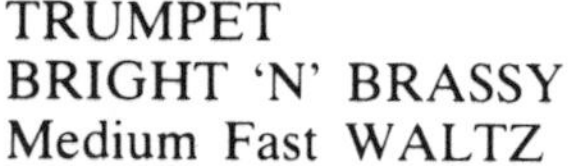
TRUMPET
BRIGHT 'N' BRASSY
Medium Fast WALTZ

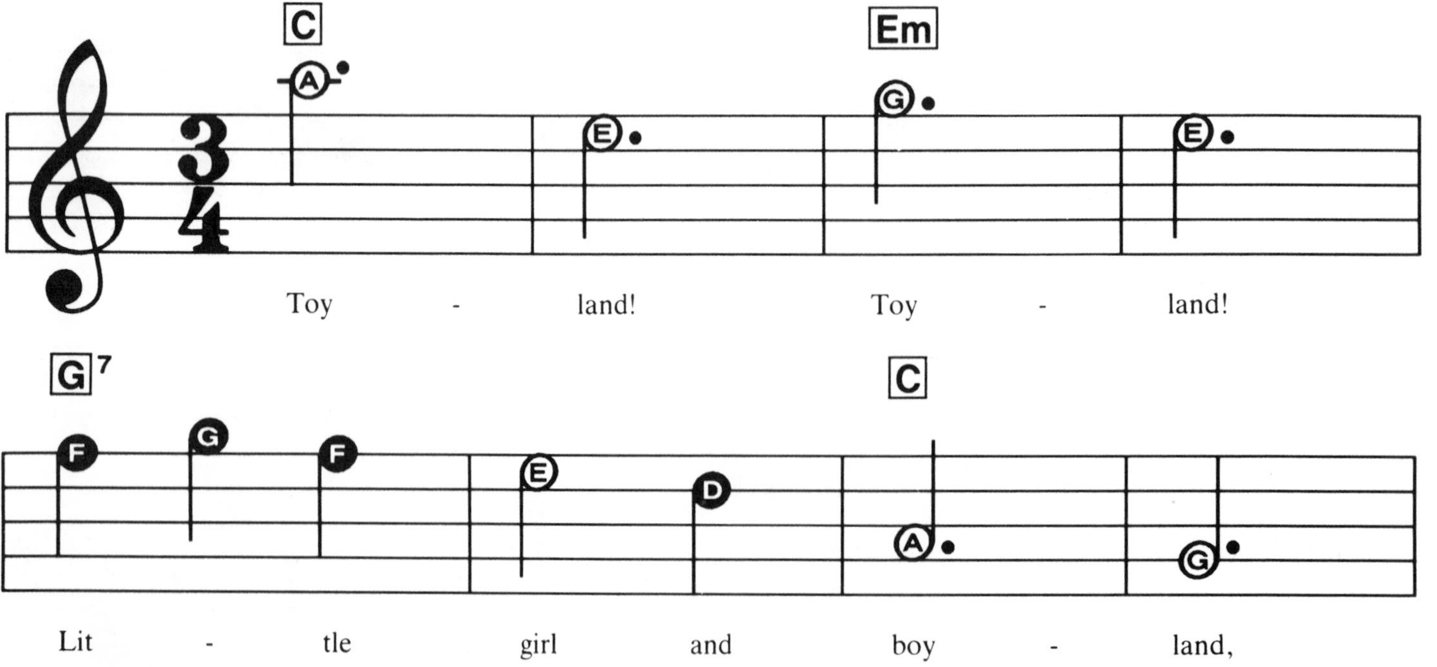
C
Em
Toy - land! Toy - land!
G7
C
Lit - tle girl and boy - land,

F Fm C A7

While you dwell with - in it ______ You are

D7 G7 C

ev - er hap - py then ______ Child -

Em G G7

hood's Joy - land, Mys - tic mer - ry

C F Fm C

Toy - land! Once you pass it's bor - ders

A7 G7 C

You can ne'er ___ re - turn a - gain. ______

WHAT CHILD IS THIS?

OBOE
FULL 'N' BRILLIANT
Slow WALTZ

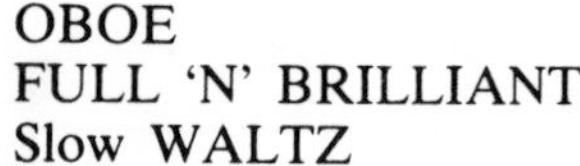

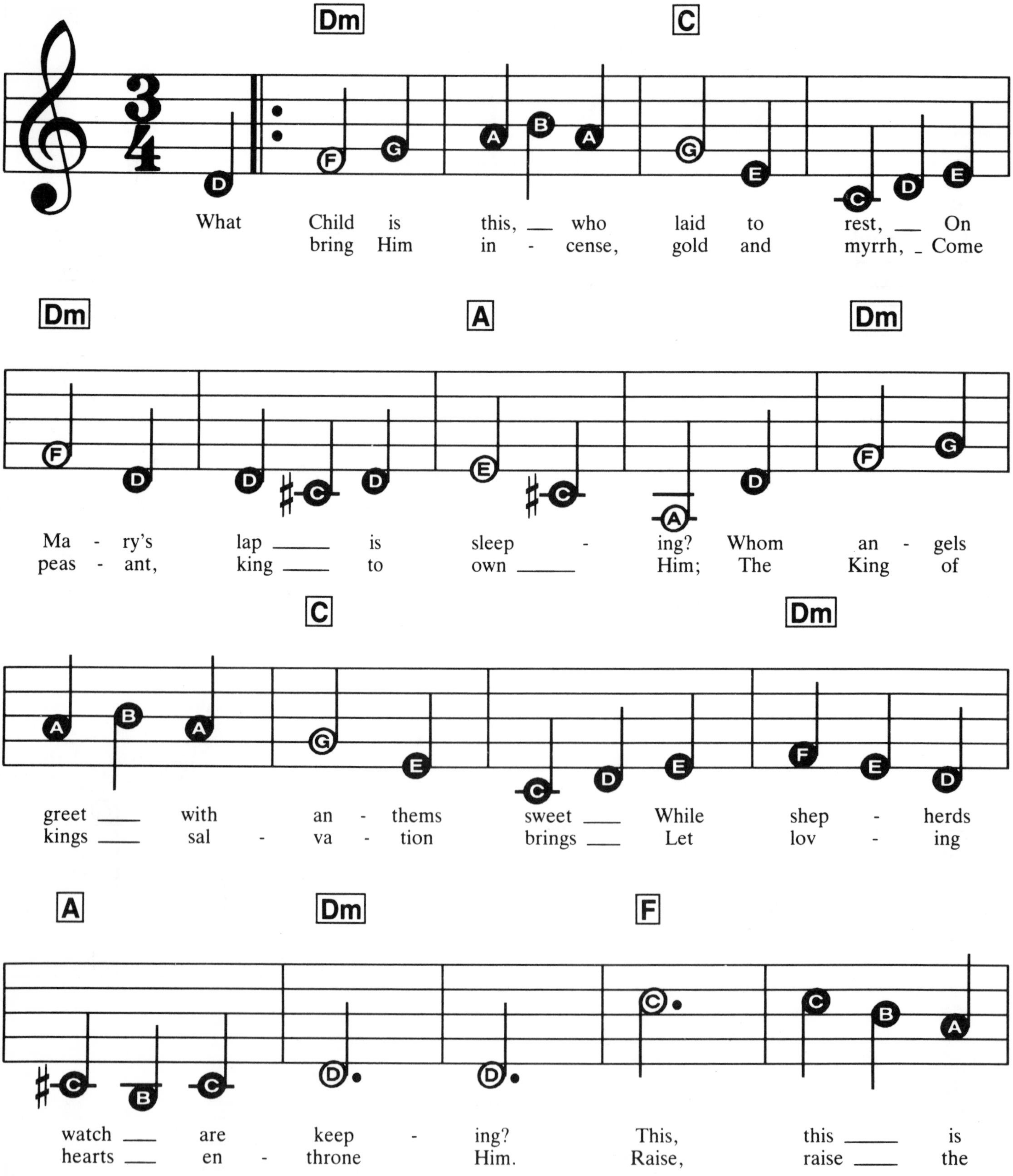

Dm C
What Child is this, who laid to rest, On
bring Him in - cense, gold and myrrh, Come
Dm A Dm
Ma - ry's lap is sleep - ing? Whom an - gels
peas - ant, king to own Him; The King of
C Dm
greet with an - thems sweet While shep - herds
kings sal - va - tion brings Let lov - ing
A Dm F
watch are keep - ing? This, this is
hearts en - throne Him. Raise, raise the

C Dm A
Christ the King; — Whom shep - herds guard — and an - gels
song on high, — The Vir - gin sings — her lul - la -
F C
sing; Haste, haste, — to bring Him laud, — The
by: Joy, joy, — for Christ is born, — The
Dm A Dm 1. 2.
Babe — the Son — of Ma - ry. So
Babe — the Son — of Ma - ry.
From the Videocraft T.V. Musical Spectacular "RUDOLPH THE RED-NOSED REINDEER"
TRUMPET
BRIGHT 'N' BRASSY
Medium Fast MARCH
WE ARE SANTA'S ELVES
Words and Music by
JOHNNY MARKS
B♭ Am C7 F
Ho! Ho! Ho! Ho! Ho! Ho! We are San - ta's elves!
C7
We are San - ta's elves fill - ing San - ta's shelves
We work hard all day, but our work is play.

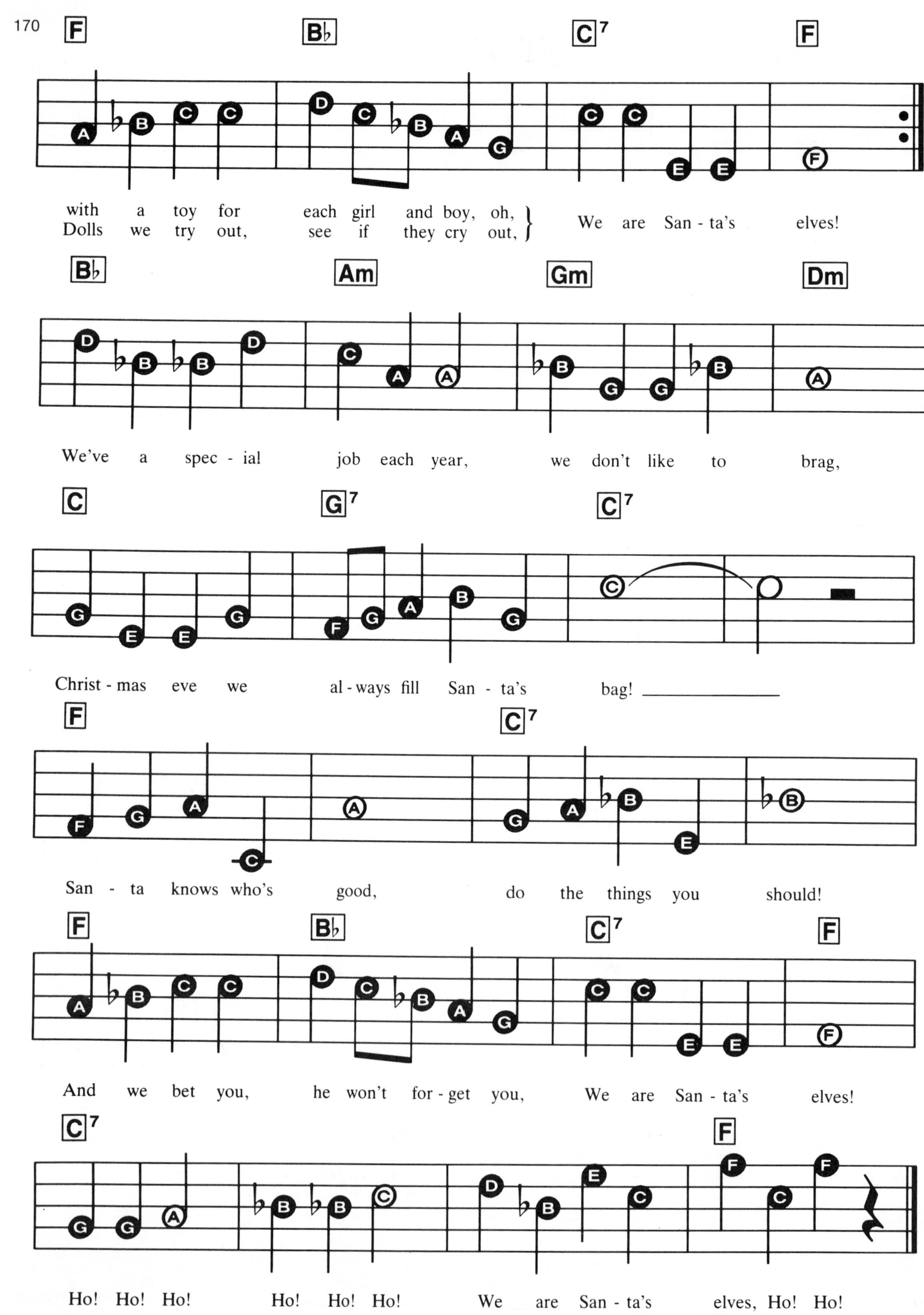
F
B♭
C7
F
with a toy for each girl and boy, oh,
Dolls we try out, see if they cry out,
We are San - ta's elves!
B♭
Am
Gm
Dm
We've a spec - ial job each year, we don't like to brag,
C
G7
C7
Christ - mas eve we al - ways fill San - ta's bag!
F
C7
San - ta knows who's good, do the things you should!
F
B♭
C7
F
And we bet you, he won't for - get you, We are San - ta's elves!
C7
F
Ho! Ho! Ho! Ho! Ho! Ho! We are San - ta's elves, Ho! Ho!

WE HAIL THEE WITH REJOICING HEART

PIANO
CLASSICAL
Medium WALTZ

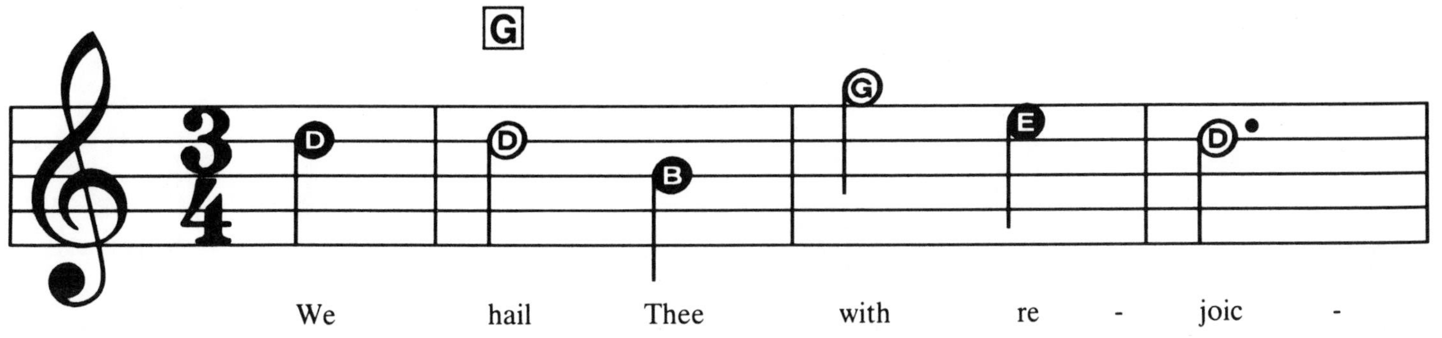
G
D
D
B
G
E
D
We
hail
Thee
with
re - joic -

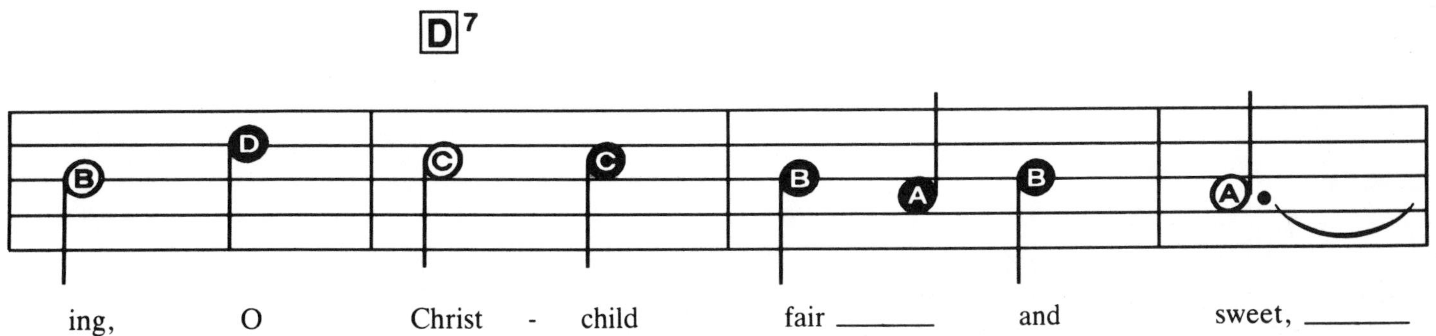
D7
B
D
C
C
B
A
B
A
ing,
O
Christ - child
fair
and
sweet,

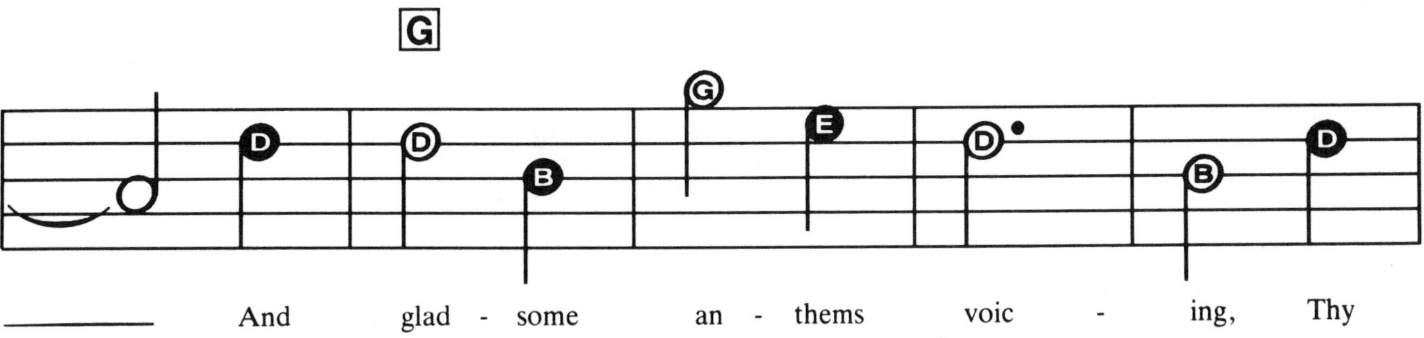
G
D
D
B
G
E
D
B
D
And
glad - some
an - thems
voic - ing,
Thy

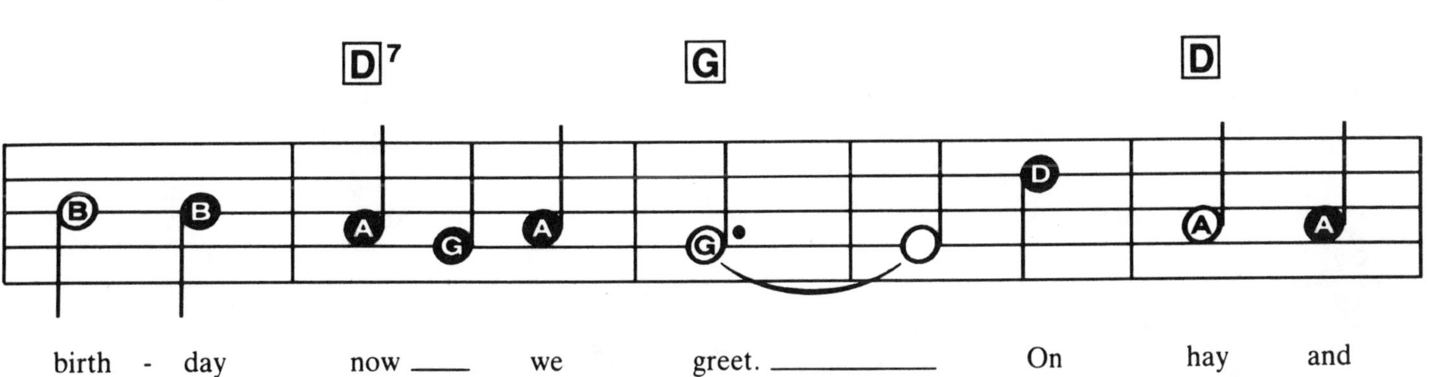
D7
G
D
B
B
A
G
A
G
D
A
A
birth - day
now
we
greet.
On
hay
and

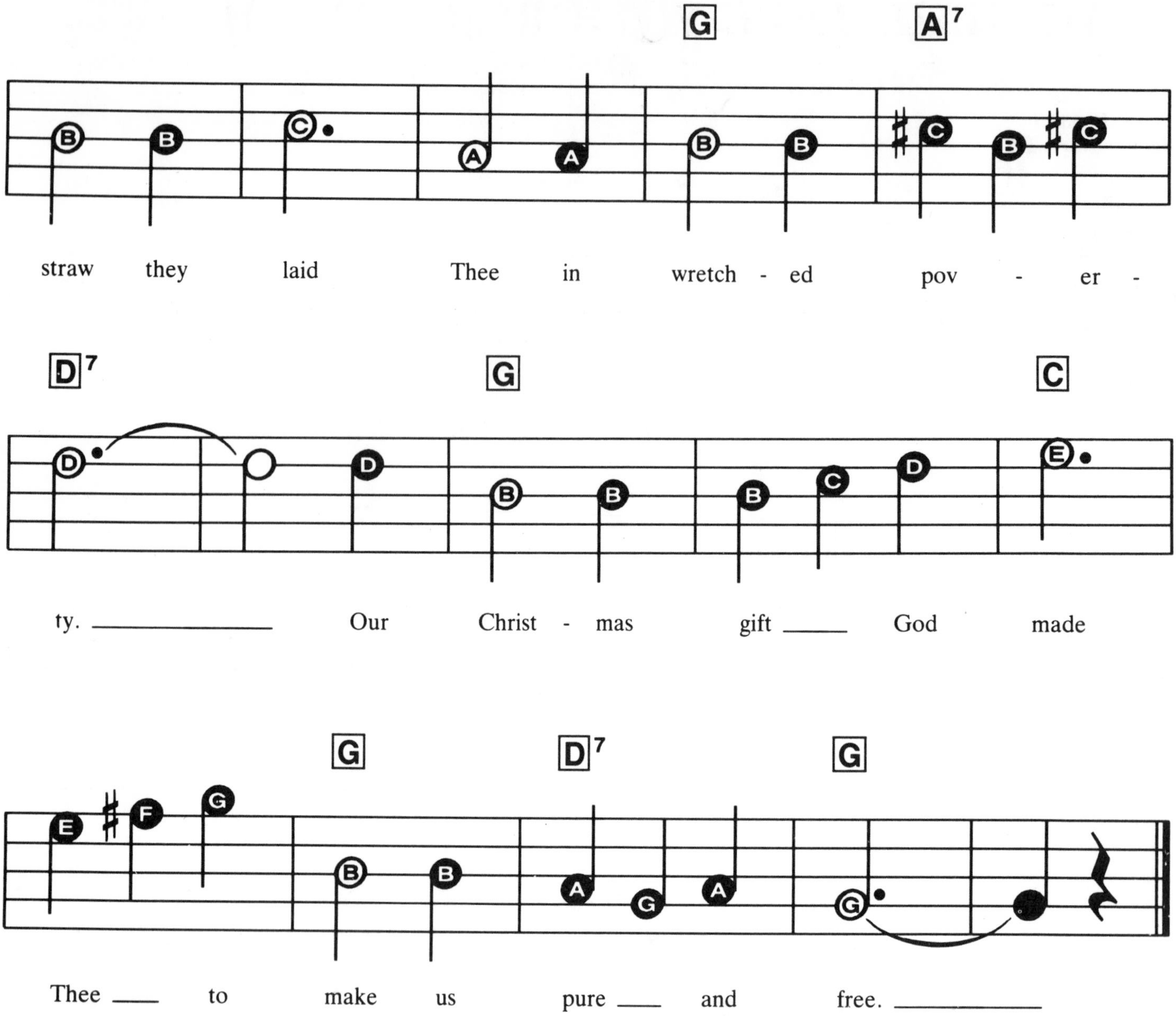

G A7

B B C A A B B C B C

straw they laid Thee in wretch - ed pov - er -

D7 G C

D D B B B C D E

ty. ___ Our Christ - mas gift ___ God made

G D7 G

E F G B B A G A G

Thee ___ to make us pure ___ and free. ___

WE THREE KINGS OF ORIENT ARE

TRUMPET or OBOE
CLASSICAL
Medium WALTZ

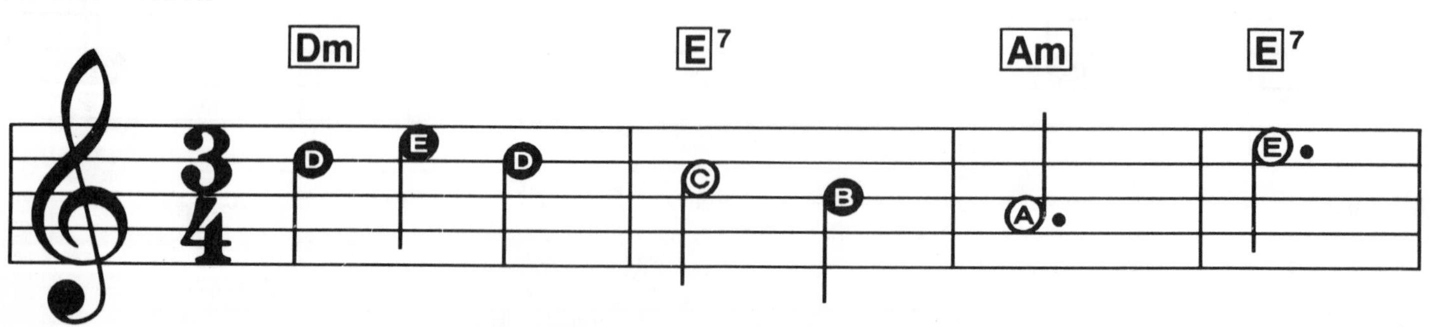

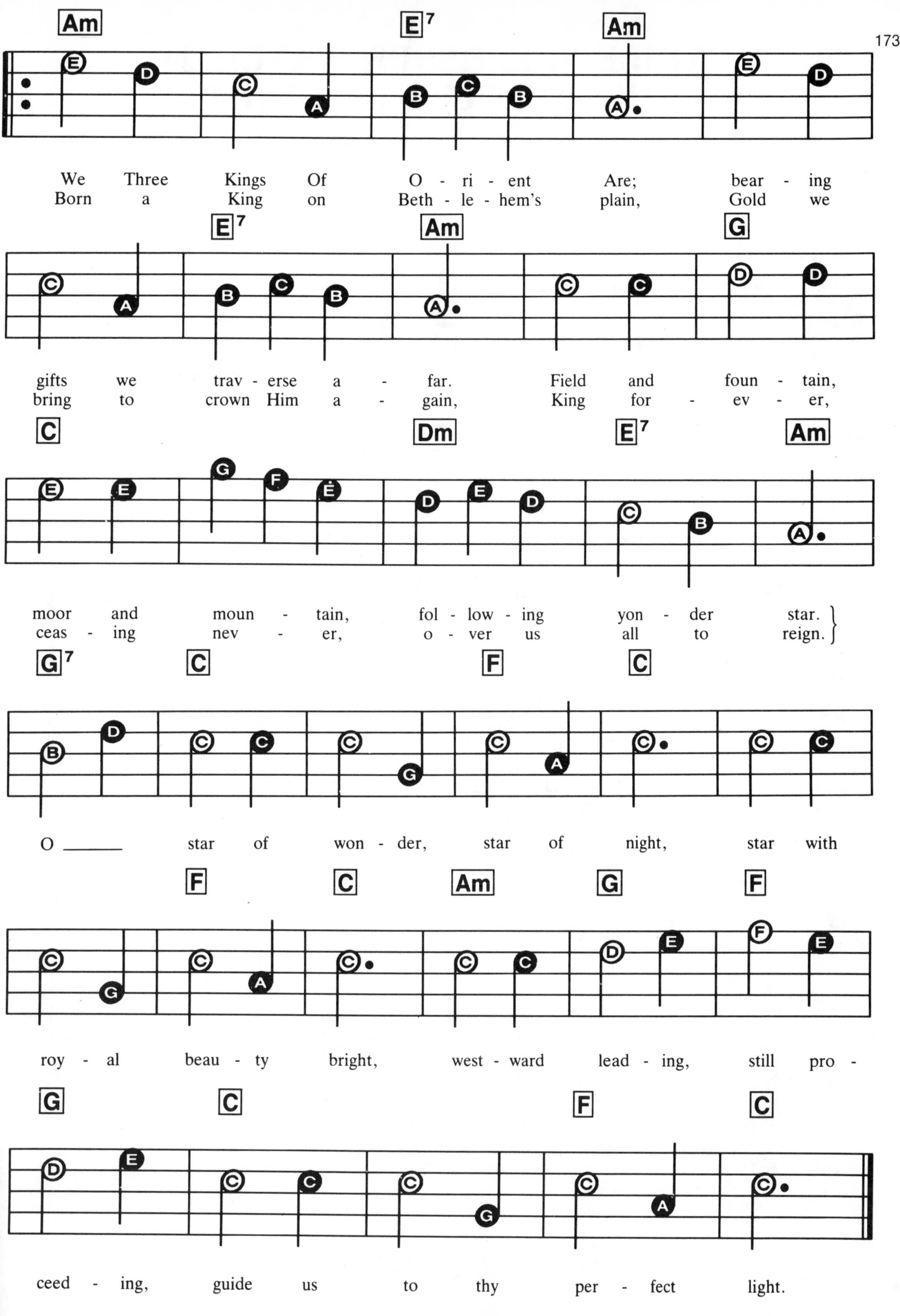

Am E7 Am
We Three Kings Of O - ri - ent Are; bear - ing
Born a King on Beth - le - hem's plain, Gold we
E7 Am G
gifts we trav - erse a - far. Field and foun - tain,
bring to crown Him a - gain, King for - ev - er,
C Dm E7 Am
moor and moun - tain, fol - low - ing yon - der star.
ceas - ing nev - er, o - ver us all to reign.
G7 C F C
O ___ star of won - der, star of night, star with
F C Am G F
roy - al beau - ty bright, west - ward lead - ing, still pro -
G C F C
ceed - ing, guide us to thy per - fect light.

WHILE SHEPHERDS WATCHED THEIR FLOCKS BY NIGHT

FLUTE
FULL 'N' MELLOW
Medium SWING

C

While _ shep - herds watch'd their flocks by ___ night; All ___
not"! said he; for might - y ___ dread Had ___

G7

seat - ed on the ___ ground, _ The ___ an - gel of the
seized their troub - led ___ mind, ___ Glad _ ti - dings of great

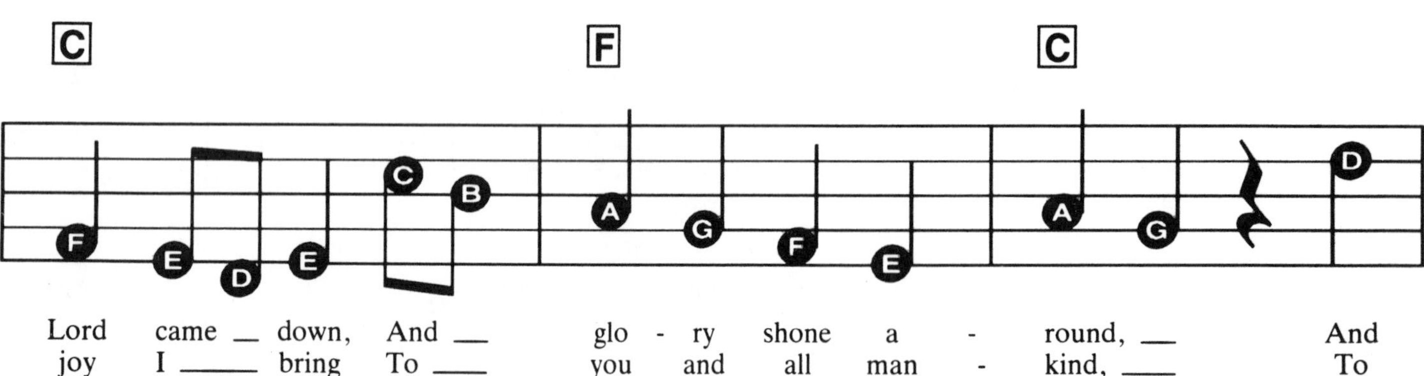

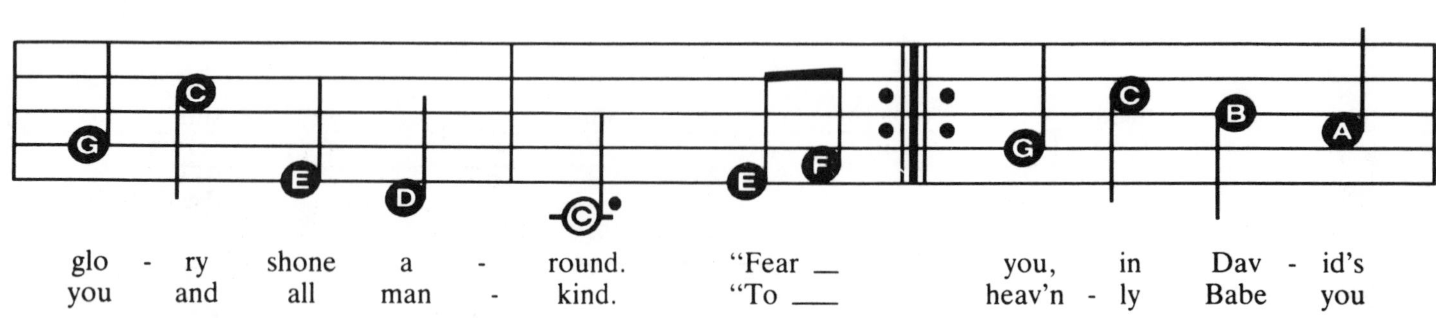

town, this ___ day Is ___ born of Da - vid's ___
there shall ___ find To ___ hu - man view dis -

G7

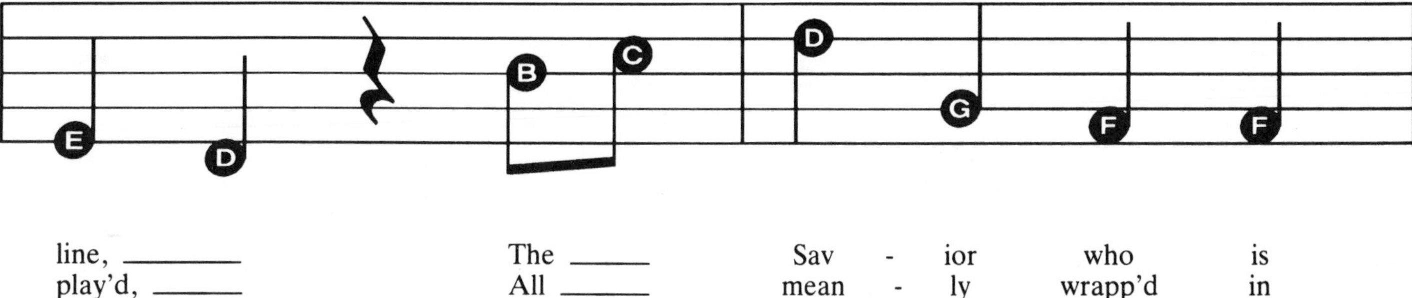
line, ___ The ___ Sav - ior who is
play'd, ___ All ___ mean - ly wrapp'd in

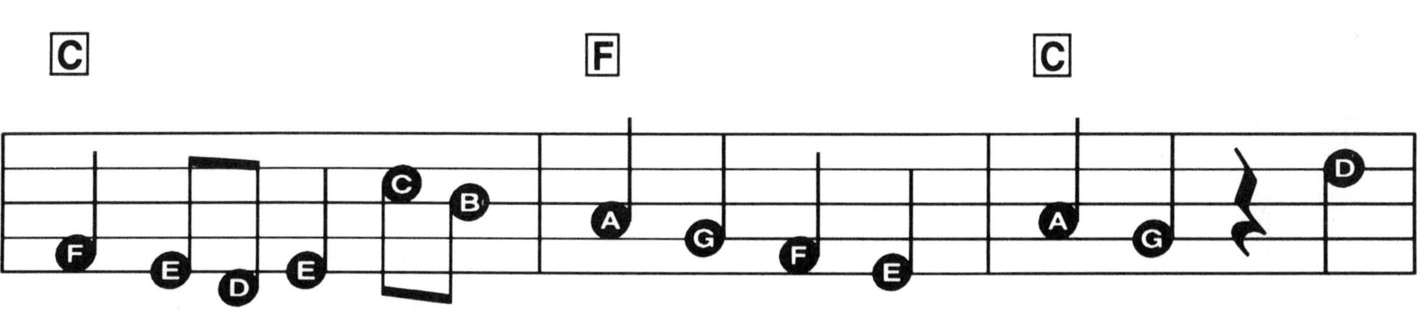
C
F
C

Christ the ___ Lord; And ___ this shall be the sign, ___ And
swath - ing ___ bands, And ___ in a man - ger laid, ___ And

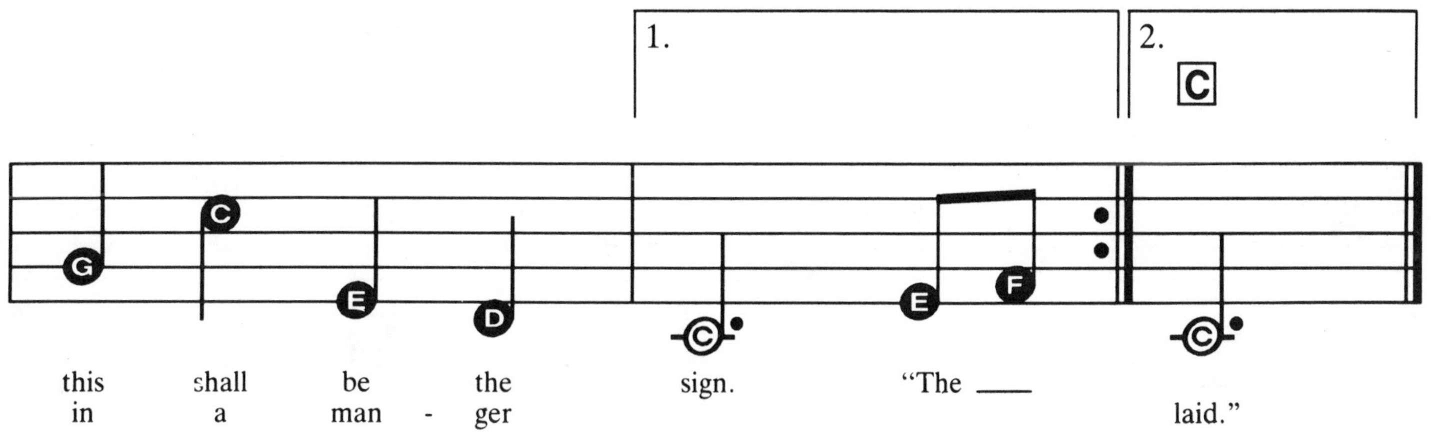
1.
2.
C
this shall be the sign. "The ___
in a man - ger laid."

WE WISH YOU A MERRY CHRISTMAS